Writing Systems

Writing Systems

Second Edition

Geoffrey Sampson

SHEFFIELD UK BRISTOL CT

Published by Equinox Publishing Ltd.

UK: Office 415, The Workstation, 15 Paternoster Row, Sheffield, South Yorkshire S1 2BX
USA: ISD, 70 Enterprise Drive, Bristol, CT 06010

www.equinoxpub.com

The first edition was published by Hutchinson, London, and Stanford University Press, California, in 1985. A revised paperback version was published by Hutchinson in 1987. This second edition first published in 2015.

ISBN 978-1-78179-103-5 (hardback)
978-1-78179-104-2 (paperback)

British Library Cataloguing-in-Publication Data

A catalogue record for this book is available from the British Library.

Library of Congress Cataloging-in-Publication Data

Sampson, Geoffrey.
Writing systems / Geoffrey Sampson.
pages cm. -- (Second edition)
Includes bibliographical references and index.
ISBN 978-1-78179-103-5 (hb) -- ISBN 978-1-78179-104-2 (pb)
1. Writing--History. 2. Typology (Linguistics) I. Title.
P211.S36 2015
411.09--dc23

2014039977

Typeset by CA Typesetting Ltd, Sheffield, www.sheffieldtypesetting.com
Printed and bound in Great Britain by Lightning Source UK Ltd., Milton Keynes and Lightning Source Inc., La Vergne, TN

Sophie's book

The dedication above, which reads *gadub* ^{geme}*nam-igi-gál*, literally "tablet-collection of Lady Wisdom", is written in 5000-year-old Archaic Sumerian script, the earliest form of writing known.

Contents

Acknowledgements

I could not have written the original edition of this book without the encouragement and advice, often given at considerable cost in time, of numerous experts on areas where my knowledge was limited. And for this new edition, again, many fellow scholars have been generous in sharing their time and expertise with me. I should like to express my warmest thanks to those who helped with either or both editions:

> Ruth Bowler, Walters Art Museum, Baltimore; Jerry Cinamon; Guy Deutscher, University of Manchester; Andrew Ellis, University of Lancaster; Gideon Goldenberg, Hebrew University of Jerusalem; Soo-nai Ham, University of Lancaster; James Hartley, University of Keele; William Labov, University of Pennsylvania; W.G. Lambert, University of Birmingham; Lee Ki-moon, Seoul National University; David Lewin; Mats Lundälv, Queen Silvia Children's Hospital, Gothenburg; James McCawley, University of Chicago; Anna Morpurgo Davies, Oxford University; James Mosley, University of Reading; Edwin Pulleyblank, University of British Columbia; Michael Pye, University of Leeds; John Randall, University of Lancaster; Vera Sampson; John Sawyer, University of Newcastle upon Tyne; D.G. Scragg, University of Manchester; W.E. Skillend, School of Oriental and African Studies, London; David Smith, University of Lancaster; Michael Twyman, University of Reading; John Younger, University of Kansas; Valerie Yule, University of Aberdeen.

In interpreting their various expertises to the layman I have striven not to distort them, but I feel sure there must be places where I have failed in this endeavour. If so, the faults are mine, not theirs. Mine, too, is responsibility for conclusions I have drawn about issues which are open to debate.

I am grateful to the following for permission to reproduce graphics:

> The Walters Art Museum, Baltimore, for Figure 9; Gerald Cinamon for permission to reproduce Figure 25 from his private collection; George Douros for his Aegean font used at various points. The extract from the 23rd Psalm shown in Figure 18 is from the

Hebrew (Snaith) Old Testament Edition © British and Foreign Bible Society, whom I thank for permission to reproduce it.

Every effort has been made to trace all rights holders and obtain permissions. The author and publishers sincerely apologize for any inadvertent errors or omissions and will be happy to correct them in any future editions.

1 Introduction

This book is based on the premiss that the study of writing systems should be treated as a standard branch of linguistics, alongside established branches such as syntax, phonology, and so on.

That might seem too obvious to be worth saying. Surprisingly, within linguistics it is a rather recent idea. Ferdinand de Saussure, the Swiss who founded modern linguistics with his lectures at the University of Geneva in the years before the First World War, said that the object of linguistic study "is not both the written and the spoken forms of words; the spoken forms alone constitute the object" (Saussure [1915] 1966: 23–4). This was perhaps an understandable exaggeration of the centrality of speech; linguists then were struggling to establish that spoken language was a valid topic of study at all, and that unwritten Third World languages contained systematic structure fully as much as the languages of long-established high civilizations, which were all that traditional philological scholarship cared about. Understandable or not, though, Saussure's pronouncement had no logical basis. If a language has a written form, why would that not merit study alongside its spoken form?

Nevertheless, for many decades Saussure's sidelining of written language shaped the development of the discipline. Fred Householder (1969: 886) rightly characterized the American tradition of linguistics as holding that "Language is basically speech, and writing is of no theoretical interest." Jacques Derrida called writing "the wandering outcast of linguistics" (Derrida 1976: 44). When the first edition of the present book appeared in the 1980s, it was seen by reviewers as an unprecedented attempt to apply the insights of modern linguistics to written language.

Many key principles of Saussurean linguistics were overthrown by the "Chomskyan revolution" which began in the 1960s. But the new ideas about language advocated by the American Noam Chomsky, and popularized by the Canadian Steven Pinker in his bestselling *The Language Instinct* (Pinker 1995), only reinforced the exclusion of written language from serious consideration. The central idea of this "revolution" was that the essence of language structure is not a component of culture but of biology: infants succeed in mastering their parents' language (so it was claimed) thanks to the fact that most of its structure is built into their minds genetically, as the detailed structure of their body is laid down in their genes. If that were true, writing would indeed be a side-issue: it is quite clearly a cultural acquisition, with the earliest scripts being only a few thousand years old and some societies not yet having writing of their own, whereas spoken language is universal among mankind and originated long before the beginnings of history.

Happily, in the last twenty years or so, all this has changed, and writing is now commonly accorded its rightful place within the discipline of linguistics. Many new books have appeared, including encyclopaedic treatments (e.g. Daniels and Bright 1996) of a kind that simply did not exist before the 1990s. New journals have been founded. Keren Rice and Michael Cahill (2014: 2) list a long series of indicators that the linguistics of writing systems is now an accepted branch of the subject.

The suggestion that written language is "only" culture rather than biology has lost its force, now that the Chomskyan star has faded and fewer linguists believe in the innateness of language structure.[1] And if language as a whole is a cultural development, what reason is there to ignore an aspect of that development which first emerged a few thousand rather than tens of thousands of years ago? Now that writing has emerged, it has become an extremely significant element of culture. People have often made remarkably large claims for the crucial role of literacy in individual intellectual activity and in the life of complex societies. J.H. Breasted believed that the invention of writing "had a greater influence in uplifting the human race than any other intellectual achievement ... It was more important than all the battles ever fought and all the constitutions ever devised" (1926: 53–4).

True, some would say that this exaggerated the significance of writing. Elizabeth Eisenstein (1979) argued that many phenomena commonly associated with the invention of writing in fact only appeared with the much more recent invention of printing. Sylvia Scribner and Michael Cole (1981) suspected that intellectual habits often attributed to literacy might rather be caused by the disciplines of schooling; they investigated a script (that of the Vai of the Liberia/Sierra Leone border) which is learned exclusively in informal, non-school settings, and concluded that the intellectual implications of literacy as such may be fairly limited. Arguably, the reasons why states promote literacy have to do less with benefits to the individual than with the fact that literacy enables people to fulfil their duties as citizens or serve as useful employees (cf. Pitt 2000; Stubbs 1980: 14).

But even if writing is possibly not quite so all-important as implied by Breasted's remark, it is certainly far more than an inessential frill on the margin of linguistic behaviour. From now on I shall take it for granted that written language falls squarely within the subject domain of linguistics.

* * *

Like a textbook on any other branch of linguistics, this one sets out to examine various general principles which apply to its subject, using particular languages (and in this case particular scripts) as illustrations.

My book does not aim to be a comprehensive survey of every script that exists or has existed in the world. Nowadays there are excellent books which do that; but they are far bulkier than the present book. A general survey on the scale of the present volume could only be a superficial ramble through one set of graphic shapes after another, with no space to delve into the structural issues that arise behind the outward forms.

Rather than that, most of this book is organized round a series of case studies of seven individual scripts, selected to exemplify the different types of writing system that exist, and each discussed at chapter length, with enough detail to give the reader a sense of the diverse kinds of problem a script has to solve in practice, and the kinds of solution that have been adopted. Probably every leading script gets a look-in at some point in the book, but where a script is essentially similar in type to one of our case studies, it may be mentioned only quite briefly in connexion with some specialized issue.

From a linguistic point of view, the structural aspects of writing systems can be grouped under three headings: *typology*, *history*, and *psychology*. We should like to know what different types of script are (or have been) used, and our case studies are chosen to illustrate that. Also, we would like to know what kind of structural changes can apply to a script over time, and what external influences are relevant to such changes; and we shall be interested in knowing how scripts function for the reader and for the writer, in terms of the mental processing they require. These latter aspects of the subject are covered largely in the course of the chapters on the various case studies, though for instance Chapter 3, on Sumerian writing, is included mainly for its historical interest (Sumerian is the oldest known writing system, and beginnings are always interesting), and Chapter 7 discusses social and other external influences on script structure using illustrations from a wide range of scripts rather than a single case study. Chapter 12 discusses the interactions between the long-established activity of writing and new technology. (It was sobering to realize, when I prepared this new edition of my book, that terms such as *computer* and *information technology* were scarcely mentioned in the original edition, written before the advent of word-processing and the Web.) Chapter 13, on English spelling, is not about a particular type of script but largely about the problems of learning to read and write the world's common language.

* * *

Under the "typology" heading, we can assume that there are only a limited number of alternative principles available for reducing spoken language to visible form. Once we have identified that range of theoretically possible principles in Chapter 2, they will serve as a scheme of classification for the hundreds of individual scripts that are, or have been, actually used; but we may expect that actual systems will differ in how far they are "pure" representatives of one particular principle of writing. Many scripts will be characterized as mixtures of different types.

One particularly interesting question relating to typology is whether particular types of script tend to be associated with particular types of spoken language. Are certain kinds of spoken language intrinsically more compatible with one rather than another of the various alternative methods for reducing speech to visible marks, or do the choices of writing system made by various speech communities depend wholly on external historical factors?

Clearly, external factors do play a major role in the adoption of particular scripts. It has been pointed out that, in many cases, "script follows religion": because religions, often, are founded on holy books, and because propagating literacy has often been a function of religious authorities, territorial boundaries between different scripts frequently coincide with boundaries between religions. One obvious case is the use of Roman versus Cyrillic alphabets by speakers of different eastern European languages: Russians, Bulgarians, Serbs use Cyrillic, while Poles, Czechs, Croats use Roman, and the division coincides with that between the Eastern Orthodox and the Western Catholic churches. It has nothing to do with differences between the languages; the nations listed all speak Slavonic languages, indeed Serbs and Croats speak the same language although they write it with different letters.

Nevertheless, the importance of correlations between script and external factors such as religion does not rule out the possibility that there may also be correlations between internal, structural characteristics of spoken languages and types of script used to write them. As this book progresses we shall notice that there do seem to be influences from type of spoken language on script-type, and surely it would be strange if that were not so.

Under the heading "history", obviously, we examine the developments that various scripts have undergone through time. Just as traditional historical linguistics studies the various changes by which, for instance, (spoken) Anglo-Saxon has gradually evolved into modern (spoken) English, or (spoken) Latin has developed into Spanish, French, and the other Romance languages, so we may investigate the processes by which one writing system changes into another over the years and centuries.

There is one major difference between the historical linguistics of spoken language and the historical linguistics of writing, which makes the latter possibly a more rewarding branch of the general study of writing than the former is of general spoken-language linguistics.

Spoken language is a phenomenon that had a beginning. There must have been a time when early humans, or the species out of which humans evolved, lacked anything that we would want to equate with language as we know it today. At some point, perhaps just once or perhaps many times independently among separate communities, language appeared. Those earliest spoken languages must surely have been very different in kind, far simpler and cruder, than their contemporary descendants. However, when we investigate the history of particular spoken languages, the time-span for which we can get any detailed knowledge – a few millennia in the most favourable cases – is very short in comparison with the tens or hundreds of thousands of years over which spoken languages have been developing. Although much of the impetus for the original growth of linguistic science in the early nineteenth century stemmed from the hope that the history of languages would reveal the laws by which sophisticated modern communication systems had evolved out of more primitive antecedents, nowadays we understand that the earliest languages known to us were already "old" languages.

With writing systems, the situation is different. The total history of writing, as already mentioned, is much shorter than that of spoken language; and much of the point of writing is that it is permanent, in contrast to the air-waves that carry spoken utterances, which dissipate as fast as they are produced. Consequently we have access to a portion of the history of various scripts which is large relative to their total history. We may be able to trace right back to the birth of some systems, possibly including the oldest of all.

The study of the typology of writing and the study of its history will not be unrelated enterprises. One obvious question that arises in the historical linguistics of written language is whether there are regularities in the succession of types; do scripts of type *A* regularly or commonly develop eventually into scripts of type *B*, or does one type mutate into another type in an essentially unpredictable fashion? Within the framework of this book it will not be possible to present a definitive answer to this question, but we shall encounter hints that there are indeed regularities of written-language evolution.

The third heading proposed for the study of writing systems was "psychology". By this I refer to questions about how various types of writing work in practice for those who learn and use them. What are the mental processes by which a fluent reader, confronted with a page of written English, extracts the messages which author and printer between them have buried in it? Do these processes differ significantly for users of scripts of other types, for instance the Chinese script?

Until the 1970s psychologists almost completely ignored the topics of reading and writing, for reasons discussed by Rayner *et al.* (2012: 6). There was then an explosion of research on these topics; but the first edition of this book was written so soon after this that many issues which have since been settled by psycholinguistic experiment were still open questions. For instance, it had long been known that, rather than moving our eyes smoothly through a text, we read in a series of fixations on chunks of a few letters linked by leaps ("saccades") to other fixation points (see e.g. Engbert *et al.* 2005). Partly for that reason, as late as the 1990s it was widely believed that the psychology of the reading process could be envisaged as a "psycholinguistic guessing game" (Goodman 1967), in which the reader sampled a text at various points and unconsciously filled in the rest essentially by guesswork and inferences from context. For children in the early learning years, particularly if they are poor readers, this might be a fair picture, but we now know that it is seriously misleading for skilled readers, whose performance is much more systematic (Share and Stanovich 1995). Saccades are cognitively controlled, and mature readers use fixations to build up data that enable them to identify the words on the page correctly with little resort to guessing or contextual knowledge (Rayner *et al.* 2012: 22, 125–33, 333, 397–8).[2] The volume just cited by Keith Rayner and others offers an excellent survey of the current state of knowledge about the reading process.

One subset of questions under the "psychology" heading which are of specially obvious interest are questions about the relative goodness or efficiency of different types of writing, and of individual scripts within single typological categories. What makes a writing system "good" or "bad" is doubtless an issue to which diverse considerations are relevant, but it falls into two main sub-issues:

- How efficiently does the system function for those who have already mastered it?
- How easy is it to learn?

We shall see that these two desiderata are to some extent in conflict.

Questions of this evaluative kind do not normally arise in the linguistics of spoken language. To the contrary, there is a widespread assumption among linguists that all languages are equally "good", equally structurally subtle, equally efficient. This axiom of equal goodness of spoken languages is held partly for ideological reasons. A person's mother tongue is so much a part of his personality that, in an equalitarian age, scholars have wanted to repress any idea that there might be "better" or "worse" among languages. But there are also more respectable justifications for the axiom.

In particular, the very long period of development from which all normal spoken languages (excluding pidgins and creoles) descend might suggest that cultural evolution will have had plenty of time to eliminate inefficient traits and create all the features that languages need (at least with respect to phonological and grammatical structure, if perhaps not with respect to vocabulary, where technological or environmental change may outstrip the ability of a language to provide useful coinages). Also, the concept of "efficiency" in any domain implies that the task to be achieved can be measured independently of the tool whose efficiency is being assessed, but spoken language is in a sense functionally self-defining: its function is often said to be to express ideas or thoughts, yet these can scarcely be identified other than through the language which expresses them. If spoken languages are "tools" at all, they are clearly not tools in the sense of having been consciously fashioned in order to carry out a predetermined job. Both of these considerations might suggest that it is pointless to try to rank languages on evaluative scales.

Neither consideration applies to writing systems. These clearly are tools forged to carry out a task, which they may do more or less well – in the case of early writing systems the task was often much more narrowly circumscribed than in the case of writing in a modern Western community. Writing is felt quite generally to be an aspect of technology, something that people use, rather than part of personality, of what people are. If a foreigner tells me that English spelling is inefficient, I may demur on factual grounds and argue (as I shall argue later in this book) that our spelling has hidden virtues which go some way to compensate for its obvious drawbacks; but I am less likely to raise my hackles in an emotional response than I might be inclined to do if told that the English tense system, or our range of consonant-sounds, was cumbersome and undesirable. Furthermore, we have seen that writing has a relatively short history, most of which is open to inspection; it would be absurd to deny that many of the developments observable in the historical record were cases of evolution from inferior to superior systems. (That is not to suggest that *all* changes in writing systems have been improvements; many changes have had external causes, and some may have led to less rather than more efficiency.) For all these reasons, it is easy to include in the linguistics of written languages an evaluative dimension which scarcely exists in the traditional linguistics of spoken language.

* * *

In the remainder of this introductory chapter I discuss some considerations relating to terminology and notational conventions to be used in the rest of the book.

I shall use the terms *script*, *writing system*, or *orthography* to refer to *a given set of written marks together with a particular set of conventions for using them*. English and German are written with more or less the same set of symbols (more or less, because German but not English writing uses capital and lower-case < ä ö ü > and sometimes < ß > – it is surprisingly difficult to find pairs of European languages written with precisely the same letters); but the "English script", or "English writing system", or "English orthography", is rather different from the "German script/writing system/orthography", because the conventions for using the symbols are rather different. (The conventions differ with respect both to specific matters, such as that < ch > stands for /tʃ/ in the English system, for /x/ and /ç/ in the German, and to general matters such as that each individual symbol or digraph normally corresponds to an actually pronounced sound in the German system while English script is full of "silent letters" such as the < e > of *lake* or the < b > of *doubt*.) Likewise, Latin printed according to modern conventions exemplifies a different script from Latin as classically written with no distinction between upper and lower case letters: both scripts are normally identified imprecisely as "the Roman alphabet", since one is lineally descended from the other, but the modern version is really a different script with twice as many symbols (actually rather more than twice as many) as its ancestor, and correspondingly new conventions for using the symbols, concerning capitalization of sentence-initial letters and proper names.

In everyday speech the term "script" is commonly associated with superficial aspects of visual appearance. Thus the traditional German type style exemplified in the line

Kennſt Du das Land, wo die Zitronen blühen?

is commonly described in English as "gothic script" (the usual German term is *Fraktur*). As linguists, however, we are interested in the structure of writing systems more than in their physical appearance; from the structural point of view we are hardly justified in treating German written in *Fraktur* as exemplifying a different script from German written in roman letters:

Kennst Du das Land, wo die Zitronen blühen?

There is a simple one-to-one correspondence between almost all the symbols used in these two typefaces. The only *structural* differences between the two are that *Fraktur* distinguishes two symbols < ſ s > corresponding to the single roman symbol < s > (compare the first and third words in the two examples), and that *Fraktur* uses a single symbol < ℑ > corresponding to both of the distinct roman symbols < I J >.

In the main, "writing system", "script", and "orthography" will be used interchangeably, though I shall tend to use "writing system" when a script is cited as exemplifying a particular type of writing, and "orthography" in connexion with alternative conventions for using a given set of marks. I do not suggest that there is any precise answer to the question whether two examples of writing represent the same or different scripts. For instance, should the writing system current in the USA be counted as a different script from that current in the British Isles on the ground that, while using the same set of symbols, the American system uses slightly different conventions (exemplified by spellings such as *harbor, defense*)? Or are the two systems merely variants of a single script? German orthographic conventions are much more different from those of (American or British) English than the alternative conventions for English are from each other, but even German and English conventions are strongly related – one could imagine a hypothetical orthography in which the conventions for using the Roman alphabet were far more exotic (by English standards) than German conventions are. So should German- and English-speakers all be said to use varieties of a single script? Such questions are as unanswerable as questions whether two related varieties of spoken language are "different languages" or "dialects of one language". Where we draw the boundaries between related scripts is for us to choose, there is no "right" or "wrong" here.

* * *

One difficulty in talking about scripts is that individual scripts are commonly associated with particular languages, and in common parlance a single name is made to do duty for both the script and the spoken language which it represents. For instance, the Hebrew script is strongly associated with the Hebrew language, and many laymen no doubt suppose that the two invariably go together. In fact they do not. The Hebrew script (the same alphabet of symbols, with roughly the same conventions of usage) is also regularly used to write Yiddish, which is a language quite different from Hebrew, though used by members of the same religious group – Yiddish is a dialect of German. Both Hebrew script and Hebrew language may be colloquially referred to as just "Hebrew", inviting the hearer to forget that there is a distinction. For our purposes this is unfortunate, since it is crucial in the study of writing systems always to bear in mind that *a script is only a device for making examples of a language visible*; the script is not itself the language. One language may be written in different scripts, and the same script may be used to write different languages.

Beginners sometimes find this difficult to grasp. People often say things like "Hebrew originally had no vowels, but acquired them in the Middle Ages". Of course the Hebrew language, like all others, has always had vowels. What happened in the Middle Ages was the invention of an extended version of the script used to write Hebrew; the new script for the first time provided a complete indication of the vowels as well as the consonants of the Hebrew language (but the language itself did not change).

In order to keep languages and scripts separate, it will be important to remember that a language name, such as "Hebrew", "English", "Korean", when used as a noun always refers (in this book, and anywhere where people are being careful about these issues) to a language rather than a script. When a script is intended, phrases such as "Hebrew script" or "the English writing system" are used. Some scripts have their own names, which are not also names of languages: thus Korean is written in a script called "Hangul", and there is no language called "Hangul" – the (sole) language written in this script is called "Korean". So one can use "Hangul" as a noun, rather than resorting to paraphrases such as "Hangul script". But the reader must remember which proper names are names of scripts and which are names of languages.

* * *

Another topic requiring a decision about terminology is the elements used in writing systems. Units of our own script are called "letters"; but this term is not suitable as a general name for the elements of various writing systems, for two main reasons.

In the first place, what we want is a term meaning simply "distinctive written symbol", and even with respect to our own script the term "letter" means more than that. The punctuation marks and (for other languages written with the Roman alphabet) the diacritic marks, or "accents", are not called "letters", yet they are as much part of the writing system as the letters themselves. Furthermore, a pair of symbols such as < g > and < G > are regarded as "the same letter", but the distinction between them is highly significant: it is just wrong to begin a sentence or a proper name with a small letter, for instance.

Second, the term "letter" is used colloquially in a way that ties it to scripts which are fairly similar to our own. An Englishman will be happy to talk of "Russian letters" (or "Cyrillic letters"), and may be willing to refer to "Arabic letters" (though the fact that Arabic words are written continuously makes this phrase less comfortable); almost certainly he would reject "Chinese letters", at least if he knows anything about how Chinese is written. A unit of Chinese script is in English colloquially called a "character" (this term traditionally referred to any script or its elements, but has become specialized recently in connexion with Chinese writing). But the word "character" seems too cumbersome and ugly to revive as a general name for "unit of writing" (even though this usage does live on in the specialized domain of information technology).

The obvious (and usual) choice is to use "graph" as the general term for any unit of any script. Standardly, the citation of a graph, or sequence of graphs, is enclosed in angle brackets. Thus we may write that "German script uses < ü > to represent the vowel /y/" (phonemic transcriptions are enclosed in slashes), or that "/mein/ 'my' is spelled < mijn > in Netherlands Dutch and < myn > in Afrikaans".

When we discuss non-Roman scripts, the signs appearing between angle brackets will often be, not the exotic symbols actually used in the scripts in question, but Roman letters transcribing those symbols. Thus, referring to the Hebrew script, we may write that "the form < ħwh > represents the word /ħawwā/, Eve" – meaning that the three Hebrew graphs conventionally transcribed:

ħwh

and which actually look like this:

חוה

are used to write the Hebrew personal name pronounced /ħawwā/ and for which the English equivalent is "Eve".

* * *

Choice of transcription system for representing the forms of an exotic language in terms of our alphabet is itself an awkward problem. For some languages written in non-Roman scripts there exist several (or many) alternative systems of romanization. Even for languages where a single system is widely accepted, the conventions used with one language often have little in common with those used with another. When words from such languages occur as part of my text, for instance as proper names of institutions or people mentioned in the discussion, I spell them in whatever is the most widely used scheme of romanization for the language in question. When words are quoted as examples, however, small details of transliteration are often important and a more scientific approach is needed. I therefore adopt a practice which may offend readers versed in the traditions of scholarship of some of the languages discussed, but which has the advantage of keeping things simple for readers unfamiliar with these languages. In transcribing examples, I ignore all the standard conventions of transcription for particular languages, in favour of systems based on the alphabet of the International Phonetic Association (IPA). This way, the reader need only be familiar with the IPA alphabet in order to attach some reasonable approximate pronunciation to all the forms quoted from a wide range of languages in this book.

There will be cases where it is inconvenient to use the symbol offered by the IPA alphabet, or where the pronunciation of a vanished phoneme is wholly conjectural; in such cases, if the symbol traditionally used by those who study the language in question is convenient, I shall use it. But the fact that a transcription conflicts with the normal practice of a particular philological tradition will never be treated as a bar to using it, if usage within general linguistics makes it appropriate. (Likewise, I have been ruthless in discarding scholarly conventions that are standard in particular specialist fields whenever it seemed to me that deviating from such conventions makes things clearer to the non-specialist reader without distorting the facts.)

The IPA alphabet is revised from time to time, and this book uses the up-to-date (2005) version.[3] One difference from earlier versions is that various special symbols for fine shades of pronunciation have been dropped; the present IPA alphabet uses a smaller set of basic letters, adding modifying symbols to indicate fine details when necessary. For instance, many languages (though not English) contain "alveolo-palatal" fricatives and affricates; an example is the first sound in the names of the ancient Chinese capital Xi'an and the current Chinese president Xi Jinping, which to English-speakers' ears sounds intermediate between the *s* and *sh* sounds. This voiceless alveolo-palatal fricative, which happens to be written *x* in the standard romanization of Chinese, was written [ɕ] in previous versions of the IPA alphabet. In the 2005 IPA alphabet the same sound is represented as [ʃʲ], i.e. a postalveolar fricative with palatalization. The symbol [ʃ], although it is not a letter of our ordinary alphabet, is a relatively familiar one, needed for transcribing many European languages including English. In a narrow phonetic transcription, the superscript [j] is needed in order to distinguish the Chinese from the English sound (an English-speaker would not mistake one for the other). But phonetic transcriptions in this book will be broad, showing only as much detail as needed to keep the sounds of an individual language distinct (and hence the transcriptions will normally be placed between phonemic slashes rather than phonetic square brackets). *Within Chinese*, there is no contrast between [ʃ^j] and [ʃ], so we shall transcribe the Chinese sound simply as /ʃ/. The difference between English [ʃ] and Chinese [ʃ^j] will never have any significance for our discussion of writing systems, so it is best to keep the transcriptions simple and straightforward.

I have made this point at some length, because readers familiar with earlier versions of the IPA alphabet might otherwise be puzzled by novel phonetic spellings such as /ʃ/ for the Chinese *x* sound, and might feel that the phonetic facts are being distorted. As the years pass, an increasing proportion of readers will have encountered the IPA system only in its new version; it would be a shame to require them to deal with an outdated version.

Unfortunately, the IPA alphabet is not a perfect system. One area where it has always been unsatisfactory is the representation of affricate consonants, such as the *j* sound of English *jam*. Functionally, this is a single English sound, but it has to be transcribed as a sequence of stop + fricative, /dʒ/. That makes little sense: English has no other consonant clusters in /-ʒ/, say */pʒ/ or */lʒ/, and the sound is formed as a single articulatory gesture – the main difference between *dam* and *jam* is that, in the latter, the stop closure is released relatively slowly so that there is an appreciable period while the articulators remain close enough for turbulent airflow to be audible. Yet the only method offered by the IPA system for showing the unitary nature of an affricate is to link the separate symbols with a tie bar, /d͜ʒ/ – as well as being difficult to type or print, this uses three marks to stand for one sound. And the difference between *j* and *dz* lies as much in the stop as the fricative part of the sound, yet the IPA system offers only one symbol [d] for both stops.

Fifty years ago one standard work (Jakobson *et al.* 1961) solved this problem by using a circumflex over a fricative symbol to stand for affrication, for instance /dʒ/ was written /ʒ̂/. Unfortunately this sensible solution never caught on, and it seems too late now to revive it. In this book affricates will be transcribed as pairs of separate letters, e.g. /dʒ/, /ts/, and readers should bear in mind that such letter-pairs stand for single sounds, not clusters of separate consonants.

Another flaw in the IPA alphabet is that it marks long vowels with a colon and usually leaves short vowels unmarked. This is frequently awkward, particularly in languages where short vowels are the less-frequent special case, so I shall indicate long and short by macron and breve: [ē ĕ]. Also, the IPA use of printed [a] and handwritten [ɑ] as contrasting symbols leads in practice to frequent confusion, so I shall write front and back open vowels as [æ a] respectively, using the latter symbol in the many cases where no contrast occurs.

For English, there are alternative traditions for using IPA symbols to represent its vowels and diphthongs (the symbols for English consonants are standard). In this book I shall transcribe Received Pronunciation (the standard speech of England) on the system of Figure 1; the words in small capitals are keywords illustrating the respective vowel or diphthong sounds. (The keywords match those of Wells 1982: xviii–xix, though some of my symbols differ from Wells's.) Note that my English transcriptions will not use any length mark. For Received Pronunciation at least, with marginal exceptions vowel length is allophonic rather than phonemic, so it is not appropriately marked in a broad transcription.

* * *

FLEECE	i	THOUGHT, NORTH	o
KIT	ɩ	LOT	ɔ
DRESS	e	FACE	ei
TRAP	æ	PRICE	ai
*lett*ER, *comm*A	ə	CHOICE	oi
NURSE	ɜ	GOAT	əu
STRUT	ʌ	MOUTH	au
BATH, PALM, START	a	NEAR	iə
GOOSE	u	SQUARE	eə
FOOT	ɷ	CURE	uə

Figure 1

When writing this book I was struck by a difficulty that must have occurred to other authors of works which range over many millennia, namely the inadequacy of the expressions "AD" and "BC". A phrase such as "the fifth century AD" makes no sense (since AD means "in the year of the Lord"), and it is odd to call the thousand years preceding Christ's birth the "first millennium before Christ" when it was the last such millennium. Furthermore the constant referring of events to the birth of Christ is often provincial, for instance in the context of ancient China, and may even offend some readers' religious sensibilities when Hebrew is under discussion. Those of us who acknowledge Jesus as the Saviour have more substantial ways of demonstrating our allegiance. I therefore follow the lead of Joseph Needham (1954–) and use plus and minus signs in the normal mathematical way, omitting the plus sign where no confusion is possible: thus Sumerian civilization arose in the –5th millennium and lasted until the early –2nd millennium, the Olympian Games began in –776 and were abolished in +393. I also write, for example, "–6c", "17c" for "–6th century", "+17th century".[4]

* * *

Having introduced the technical term "graph" earlier, let me close this chapter by drawing attention to a parallel with the linguistics of spoken language.

The analogue, in speech, of a "graph", or elementary unit of written language, is a "phone" or unit of sound. One of the basic principles of linguistics is the notion that, within any given spoken language, not all differences between phones are significant or "distinctive"; in some cases two or more physically distinct phones group into families called "phonemes", in which case the members of a phoneme are called its "allophones". Thus, in English, although the velarized lateral [l^{ɯ}] ("dark l") heard in the word *hill* is physically different from the plain lateral [l] ("clear l") heard in *hilly*, the two phones are not significantly distinct; in English the difference between them is never used to keep different utterances apart (though in other languages, Russian for instance, a similar distinction is). In English the choice between [l^{ɯ}] and [l] is always determined by context: before a vowel only the variant [l] occurs, in other positions only [l^{ɯ}]. The two phones [l^{ɯ}] and [l] are allophones of a single phoneme, /l/.[5]

An analogous phenomenon is found in writing, and it is convenient to use the terms *grapheme* and *allograph* accordingly. An example comparable to that of the /l/ phoneme is offered by the alternative versions of lower-case *s* which were found in the Roman alphabet until the 19c (as we saw on p. 9, a parallel alternation occurred in German *Fraktur*, and Greek sigma displays such an alternation to this day).[6] The two graphs < ſ s > were allographs of a single grapheme. They did not stand for distinct sounds, rather the choice between them was determined by position in the word. At the end of a word (speaking graphically rather than phonetically) < s > was used; elsewhere, < ſ >. Thus:

ſea ſhell meaſure miſt kiſs circus loſe news

More generally, the different appearances of letters in different fonts, or in handwriting as opposed to print, can be regarded as allographic.[7] Such differences are analogous to the slightly differing pronunciations that will be given to the same phoneme by different speakers of a language, or even by a single speaker on different occasions. Thus, the graphs < g g g > would all be allographs of a single grapheme < g >. On the other hand < g > and < G > would *not* belong to a single grapheme; as already noted, the upper versus lower case distinction is significant in our script.[8]

We shall not adopt separate bracketing conventions for graphemic and allographic transcriptions, parallel to the slash/square-bracket distinction used in spoken-language linguistics. Angle brackets will enclose graphemes and allographs, since confusion is unlikely in practice. In examining non-Roman scripts we shall ignore minor differences comparable to font differences in print, and we shall illustrate the scripts via single standardized varieties. Where allographic differences comparable to the < ſ s > distinction are important enough to consider, attention will be drawn to them explicitly.

Notes

1. For reasons why Chomsky's and Pinker's ideas about this were wrong, see Sampson (2005a), Sampson and Babarczy (2014).
2. There are some hints that in old age we may revert to using guesswork to compensate for cognitive decay (Laubrock *et al.* 2006).
3. See www.langsci.ucl.ac.uk/ipa/ipachart.html (accessed 29 March 2014). Note particularly that, as a phonetic symbol, [j] represents the *y* sound of English *yet*, *yoke*, etc.; [y] is the close front rounded vowel of French *tu* or German *kühn*.
4. Recently a new convention has appeared which replaces AD, BC by "CE, BCE". This seems unnecessarily obscure (I note that leading academic publishers avoid using it), and I have preferred to stick with Needham's logical system.
5. Morris Halle (1959: 20–24) argued convincingly that the theoretical "pho-

neme" entity envisaged by many mid-20c linguists does not work. Nevertheless, as Michael Cahill points out (2014: 16), "Speakers of a language are generally aware of phonemic differences but not of allophonic variation"; as a practical rule-of-thumb construct the phoneme is indispensable, though theoretically minded linguists may prefer to see it as shorthand for a bundle of distinctive feature values rather than an atomic unit.

6. The long *s* was first given up in roman type by John Bell in about 1775. It would be hard to establish just when it finally died out in handwriting; a clue is offered in Winifred Holtby's novel *South Riding* (1936), in which one of the older characters is described as the last man to make the distinction.
7. The traditional British term for a stock of type in a given style was *fount*; "font" meant exclusively a container for baptismal water, and its use for "fount" was an Americanism. However, the spread of American word-processing software has now made this terminology usual in Britain, and this book will follow the American usage.
8. On problems that arise with the concepts "grapheme" and "allograph", see Bazell (1956), Minkoff (1975: 195–6).

2 Theoretical preliminaries

What is writing? To "write" might be defined, at a first approximation, as: to communicate relatively specific ideas by means of permanent, visible marks.

The term "permanent" is included in this definition because we would not normally count, for instance, the sign language used by the deaf and dumb as an example of "writing". More problematic is the term "specific". This word is included in order to eliminate cases where ideas are conveyed through a durable visible medium which no one would want to call writing: most obviously, artistic drawing or painting. Picasso's painting "Guernica", for instance, succeeds well in communicating ideas of horror, carnage, cruelty, without being an example of writing. The definition of "writing" given above excludes "Guernica": the ideas it communicates, while powerful, are vague rather than explicit. A "translation" of the message of "Guernica" into English would hardly be open to correction, as a translation of a passage of Spanish or German would.

What makes a visible communication medium explicit enough to describe as writing is very hard to say. Perhaps it was a mistake to include this in our first attempt at a definition; one might suggest that the characteristic property of writing is not that it communicates *specific* ideas but that it communicates ideas in a *conventional* manner. A script can be understood by its readers only because they have learned the conventions for interpreting it, and it might seem that graphic art, by contrast, is independent of convention – you just look at it and see what it expresses. But the truth is that the arts are full of convention: consider how differently Breughel, Cézanne, or a Chinese painter would render the same landscape on canvas or paper. It is difficult to use the concept of convention in order to distinguish writing from art.

The reader may object here that neither specificness of ideas communicated nor conventionality of the means of communication is the crucial factor, and that I am missing the point of my own statement, in the previous chapter, that a script is a device for representing a language (rather than a language itself). The proper definition of "writing" is that it is a system for representing utterances of a spoken language by means of permanent, visible marks. However, this definition too is problematic.

In the first place, written language is not straightforwardly a transcription of spoken language. Our own script is capable of being used to represent spoken English directly, but it is fairly unusual for people to use it that way. By this I mean not merely that written messages are commonly composed on paper or screen, rather than being taken down from oral dictation, but that the language in which written messages are couched is somewhat different from the language which Englishmen and Englishwomen speak. For instance, the contracted forms *don't*, *I've*, *he's* and the like are for written English merely optional variants of the full forms *do not*, *I have*, *he is*, etc., and it is more usual to write the full forms. In spoken English, on the other hand, it is compulsory to use the contracted forms except in certain special environments – to *say* "I have got your book" rather than "I've got your book" would sound absurdly stilted (unless *have* is given special contrastive stress). There are many other small differences between spoken and written English.

In many other language communities the analogous differences are much greater than for English. In the Arabic-speaking world, for instance, there are considerable differences in vocabulary, grammar, and phonology between written and spoken varieties of Arabic. It is possible to transcribe Arabic speech directly into Arabic script, but such writing strikes Arabs as bizarre – the forms of spoken Arabic are perceived as inappropriate for writing down. Written Arabic can be spoken, but this will be done only in unusually formal speech situations such as public lectures. In China the situation as it existed until the early 20c was yet more extreme: the language used for written communication not only was not normally spoken, but (for reasons having to do with special characteristics of the Chinese language, to be discussed in due course), if it was spoken – for instance, if a document was read aloud – it could not be understood by even an educated man without sight of the written text.

If written and spoken languages can diverge as far as this, can we define writing in general as a system for representing spoken language? In fact I believe we can, but only provided we understand the phrase "spoken language", paradoxically, as something that is not necessarily spoken. The kind of English that we use in writing and the kind we use in speech are, in the linguist's technical sense, closely related dialects – that is, they both descend from a single ancestor language, which was a spoken language. But, just as some dialects, once they have diverged sufficiently for their separate identity to be recognized, are used in one restricted area of territory, so the dialect which we may call "literary English" is used in one restricted area of behaviour, namely writing. Literary English inherits all the apparatus of a spoken language, including phonology, from its spoken ancestor, but it happens that this particular dialect is not normally spoken (except when written documents are read aloud). Similar remarks apply in cases where literary and colloquial languages exhibit greater divergence. The reader will have noticed, for instance, that I included phonology as one of the respects in which Literary Arabic differs from the various regional varieties of Colloquial Arabic; Literary Arabic has its own phonology, including one or two phonemes that do not appear in some versions of Colloquial Arabic (an Arabic speaker has to use the special Literary phonemes if he reads a written document aloud). Even Literary Chinese can be spoken, in the sense that a text written in it has a definite pronunciation, though it happens in this case that there is very little point in speaking the language since it cannot be understood by a hearer. If we think of a "language" (as linguists often do) as a system of relationships between meaning and speech-sound, then a script will be a device for representing a language in this sense, even though it often happens that languages or language-varieties which are commonly written down are not spoken (except in artificial circumstances such as reading aloud), and that languages or language varieties which are spoken are not written down (except, for example, when sound recordings are transcribed verbatim).

* * *

But there is another difficulty about defining writing as essentially parasitic on spoken language: there are forms of communication which one might want to describe as "writing" but which are not in any sense dependent on spoken language.

Take for instance the international system of garment-care symbols; a few examples are shown in Figure 2. These symbols communicate specific ideas in a highly conventional manner, but they are not tied to any particular spoken language. Someone asked to say what the top left symbol means might answer "Hand wash only", but another form of words such as "Launder by hand" would be equally correct, and so would a response in some other language. This particular sign is motivated, so that a newcomer might guess its meaning, but many other signs are not. One surely could not guess that the horizontal below the tub at top right means "reduced washing conditions", or that (at lower right) parallel diagonals across a triangle mean "non-chlorine bleach" but across a square mean "dry in the shade".

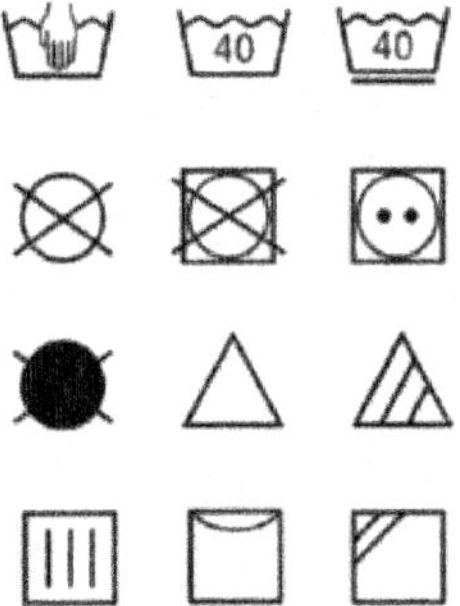

Figure 2

Since the onset of globalization, this type of writing that is independent of any spoken language has become much more widespread than it was a hundred years ago – another example is the international system of road signs. Writing of this type can be called *semasiographic*, as contrasted with *glottographic* writing, which represents forms of some particular spoken language. (These terms, and others to be introduced in this chapter, are adapted from Haas 1976a.)

One might of course question whether these systems should be called "writing". Some scholars who believe that all the world's writing systems are essentially similar have argued that systems which are not created in order to record spoken language cannot count as writing. If this is put forward as a matter of definition, it does not tell us much; obviously, if one defines "writing" as representing speech in visible form, then all writing systems must be based on spoken language. But one can argue that systems like washing instructions and road signs amount to much less than what we mean by writing, without making this a matter of definition. Both systems are extremely limited in what they can express. One cannot use a road sign or a garment-care symbol to ask a question; and one cannot use them to give information about anything outside the domains of clothes care or traffic conditions. One might well wonder whether there could possibly be a semasiographic system with the ability to communicate the comprehensive range of ideas that any spoken language can express. Some have claimed that this is not possible. John DeFrancis (1989: 7) held that "all full systems of communication are based on speech. Furthermore, no full system is possible unless so grounded."

Perhaps surprisingly, DeFrancis was wrong about that. There is a system of the kind he calls impossible, named Blissymbolics. Blissymbolics was invented by a chemical engineer born Karl Blitz in 1897 in the town best known in English as Czernowitz (which, when Blitz was born, lay in the extreme east of the Austro-Hungarian Empire – it is currently in the Ukraine and called Chernivtsi). After escaping from Nazi concentration camps Blitz emigrated to Australia, changed his name to Charles Bliss, and invented Blissymbolics in the 1940s. Bliss seems to have been motivated by the hope that his system would foster inter-ethnic harmony. (There are striking parallels between Bliss and the ophthalmologist Ludwik Zamenhof, creator of Esperanto: both came from eastern European areas riven by animosities between communities speaking several different languages, and both believed that a neutral communication system might help to resolve these.) In practice the chief application of Blissymbolics has been as an auxiliary mode of communication for people suffering disabilities such as cerebral palsy; groups in Canada and in Sweden claim to have achieved considerable success with it.[1]

Blissymbolics aims to be a full-scale "language" allowing users to discuss whatever they want to discuss. I approached a member of Blissymbolics Communication International to ask for an example to display in this book, and in return I received Figure 3 – part of my request message, translated into the system. While not necessarily what I was expecting, this is actually a good way to show the versatility of the system: it is spontaneous rather than a pre-planned demonstration, and my message was linguistically complex, including clause subordination, abstract as well as concrete concepts, a complex proper name, and so forth. This surely is written language in the full sense, but not based on any spoken language.

Those who feel sceptical about the semasiography idea might object that, even if comprehensive, Blissymbolics is an artificial system. One answer is that *all* writing systems are artificial – writing, and reading, are not natural behaviours like eating or sleeping. But what is true is that all the semasiographic systems I have mentioned were created by people who were already thoroughly familiar with glottographic writing. No human society to my knowledge has created a system comparable to Blissymbolics as its first writing system. Various ethnic groups in the Americas and Siberia with no other kind of writing have developed limited semasiographic systems (see e.g. Boone and Mignolo 1994), but it remains an open question whether these could ever have been expanded into comprehensive written communication systems. By now the world is too interrelated for that question ever to be answered in future. In that sense we might say that semasiography as a full-scale writing system is a theoretical possibility rather than an actually occurring type of script.[2]

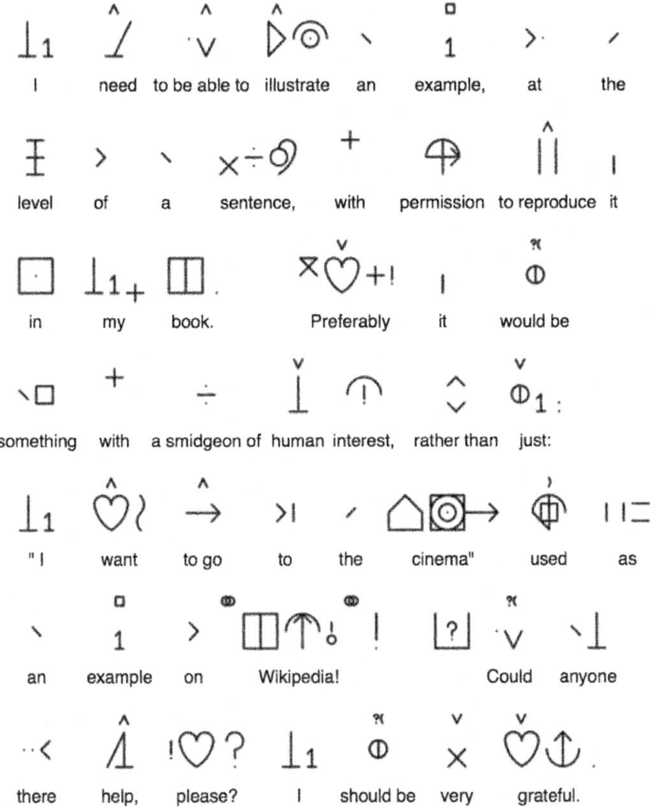

Figure 3

Within limited domains, though, semasiography can fulfil important, high-level functions. The written "language" of mathematics, for instance, is one highly sophisticated example of semasiography. The way in which a mathematical statement is formulated in written symbols does not depend on the way that the equivalent statement is formulated in any particular spoken language, as it would if the system of symbolization were glottographic. Thus the equation < $4^3 = 64$ > translates into English as *four cubed equals sixty-four* and into German as *Vier hoch drei gleicht vierundsechzig*. The English and German expressions have rather different structures, and the structure of the mathematical equation is quite different from either. Mathematical symbolism is a "language" crucial to modern civilization which articulates (certain kinds of) thought directly and independently, rather than merely standing for its spoken articulation.

* * *

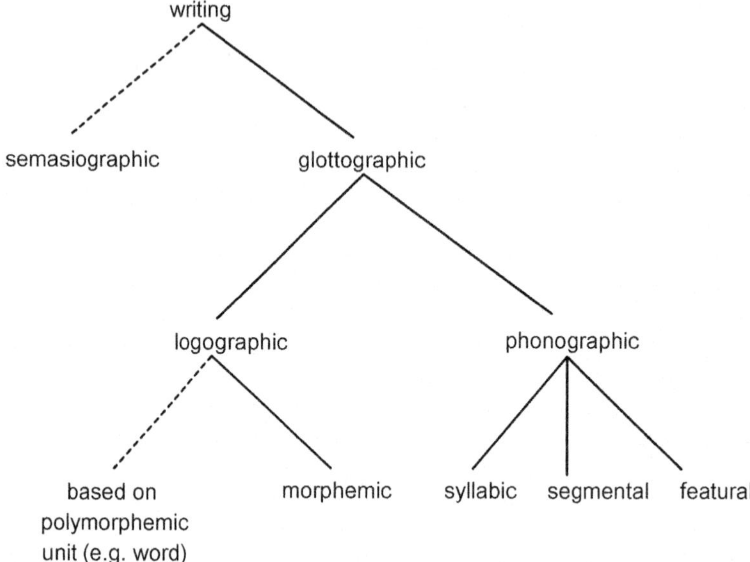

Figure 4

Let us now examine the various glottographic systems of writing – "writing proper", if semasiography is deemed not to be true writing. Figure 4 displays a classification scheme.

At the top of Figure 4, writing as a whole is divided into semasiographic and glottographic systems, the former dominated by a dotted line to show that their inclusion under "writing" is open to question. Among glottographic systems, the major division is between *logographic* and *phonographic* writing.

The basis of this distinction is a phenomenon called by the French linguist André Martinet the "double articulation" of language. Any language is a system which articulates thought into a large range of units and provides vocal symbols for those units – words, or meaningful components of words known as "morphemes", such as the *un-* and *-ing* of a word like *uncaring.* Things would be simple if a language could provide a separate unit of sound to symbolize each unit of thought that the language isolates. But the range of possibilities provided by the human vocal organs, though quite large, comes nowhere near offering enough separate sounds for the several thousands of meaningful units contained in a typical language. Instead, a language imposes a quite independent articulation on the sound-medium, analysing it into a relatively small and manageable set of phonological units having no relationship with the first articulation with respect either to number of units or to the principles by which units combine into larger phonological wholes. Then the various meaningful units of the first articulation are associated with *groups* of phonological units. Although there are relatively few individual sound-units, enough combinations are available to provide pronunciations for all the many meaning-units.

Since languages are "doubly articulated", the possibility exists for a writing system to represent either units of the first articulation or units of the second articulation. Logographic systems are those based on meaningful units, phonographic systems are those based on phonological units. Thus, if one were to invent a logographic writing system for English, it might represent the sentence *The cat walked over the mat* as in Figure 5, say, in which the pointing hands are being used to represent the word *the*, the walking legs represent the root *walk* and the clock with anticlockwise arrow represents the past-tense morpheme *-ed*, the horizontal arrow over a block represents *over*, and the symbols for *cat* and *mat* are self-explanatory.

On the other hand, one particular phonographic system (the IPA alphabet) represents the same English sentence as:

ðə kæt wokt əuvə ðə mæt

– in which individual symbols represent "segments" of sound.

Here and there on the periphery of our own writing system are some clearly logographic elements. A standard computer keyboard, for instance, includes the graphs < & % >, which represent respectively the word *and* and the phrase *per cent*. (We might add < @ > for *at*, though this is a less straightforward example because the cases of *at* which can be written < @ > are strictly confined to certain positions in particular commercial documents – one would not encounter < @ > in a novel; and the logographic nature of < £ > for *pound* is still more questionable, because of the difference in order between, for example, *one pound* and < £1 >, and because the same graph < £ > is used whether the spoken name for a sum of money includes *pound* or *pounds* – it might be preferable to regard < £ > as belonging to the semasiographic notation of mathematics.) It would be

Figure 5

quite wrong to think of < & > as a phonographic symbol which happens to stand for a sequence of three sounds /ænd/ (as < x > stands for a sequence of two phonemes /ks/); in ordinary English writing (leaving aside children's puzzle-page rebuses or the like) words such as *land*, *Andrew* would never be written < l& >, < &rew >, whereas that ought to be possible if the symbol were phonographic.

(In everyday usage, people commonly describe some exotic writing systems as "ideographic" – and I introduce this term here in order to stress that we shall not be using it at all. The reason for avoiding this term is that the meaning people attach to it is quite unclear, indeed it seems to be used in a way that blurs the distinction between semasiographic and logographic systems.)

* * *

Before moving on to consider the lower branches of the classification-scheme in Figure 4, it will be convenient to introduce two further principles of classification which cut across the distinction phonographic/logographic/(semasiographic), as well as across each other. These are the contrasts of *motivated* (sometimes called *iconic*) versus *arbitrary* systems and of *complete* versus *incomplete* (or *defective*) systems.

The terms "motivated" and "arbitrary" refer to the relationship between the graphs of a writing system and the spoken-language units they represent. If there is some natural relationship, the system is motivated; if not, it is arbitrary. For instance, the graphs of Figure 5 above are clearly motivated: the graphs for *cat* and *mat* look like a cat (or at least a cat's head) and a mat respectively, and the graphs for morphemes not referring to physical objects display some logical connexion with the respective ideas. On the other hand the IPA transcription is entirely arbitrary – there is no natural connexion between the shape of the graph < k > and the consonant which begins *cat*, or between the shape of < æ > and the vowel of *cat*: one just has to learn which shapes go with which sounds.

From the examples given so far, one might suppose that logographic scripts are always motivated and phonographic scripts always arbitrary. But this is by no means necessarily so. For instance, the shape of < & > betrays no resemblance to the idea of addition or conjunction; and although the hypothetical logographic system of Figure 5 used motivated graphs, another system might assign arbitrary symbols to the same words *The cat walked over the mat*. Indeed, Chinese script in its modern form is such a system. The Chinese for *The cat walked over the mat* would be written 猫走過席子. Can the English reader correlate any of these graphs with the ideas in the sentence on the basis of visual appearance? I hardly think so. Conversely, it would be quite possible to design a phonographic script in such a way that the shape of the graphs was related to the positions of the vocal organs when making the corresponding sounds. Indeed, "motivated" phonographic scripts exist, both as technical systems of transcription within scientific phonetics (cf. Abercrombie 1967: 116–20) and, in one case, as an ordinary national system of orthography (see Chapter 8).

The properties "motivated" versus "arbitrary" are primarily properties of individual graphs; a writing system might include some motivated graphs and others which are arbitrary (as, for instance, in the Arabic numeral system the graphs < 0 1 >, portraying respectively an empty hole and a single stroke, are motivated while the other digits are arbitrary). Furthermore, "motivatedness" is a matter of degree rather than a yes-or-no matter. The symbol for *cat* in Figure 5 is highly motivated, but a symbol , alluding just to the whiskers, would be a possible alternative that could still be regarded as somewhat motivated, though less so. No doubt, within any single writing system, there is a tendency for the various individual graphs to be roughly similar in their degree of motivatedness, so that often it will be appropriate to describe a script as a whole as "highly motivated", or as "almost wholly arbitrary".

Another term from everyday language which is worth mentioning here in order to reject it is "picture-writing" or "pictography". When people describe something as "picture-writing" it is not clear whether they mean that it is a relatively clearly motivated script of some kind, or that it is a semasiographic rather than glottographic system. It may be that to some extent the two go together, but this tendency is not absolute. We saw that there is a great deal of arbitrariness in the system of garment-care symbols, as there is in road signs – consider for instance the "give way" sign, consisting of a downward-pointing triangle. The symbolism of mathematics contains scarcely any motivation. Conversely, while the more familiar glottographic systems, including our own script, are highly arbitrary, we shall encounter other glottographic scripts which display a great deal of motivation. Like the term "ideographic", the terms "pictographic" or "picture-writing" should be shunned because they blur distinctions which the student of writing needs to keep carefully apart.

* * *

The dimension "complete" versus "incomplete/defective" – again a gradient rather than all-or-nothing dimension – refers to the extent to which a script (whether logographic or phonographic) provides representations for the whole range of units of the relevant level in the language concerned. To what extent does the script leave out material that exists in the spoken language? Probably no script in everyday use attains total completeness, but scripts differ considerably in degree of defectiveness.

Scripts that are historically early are often quite incomplete. To understand why this should be so, we need to bear in mind that relatively early scripts tend to be logographic rather than phonographic, a fact for which two reasons can be given. In the first place, the units of the "first articulation" of a language tend to be relatively apparent to speakers of the language – a child does not need to have learned to read and write in order to be able to split up a spoken sentence into words – while the units of the phonological "second articulation", particularly phonological units smaller than syllables, are not obvious. A child has to be taught to hear the word *cat* as "ker-a-ter"; there is nothing self-evident or natural in the splitting of a speech-chain into separate vowels and consonants (cf. Rayner *et al.* 2012: 311, 321–4). Also, many units of the "first articulation" of a language have meanings for which it is easy to invent motivated symbols, and when a script is being created from scratch, the iconicity principle is a particularly obvious way to facilitate the task of inventors and first learners. If a script is invented by providing motivated symbols for the meaningful units of a language, however, a problem arises in that some of these units are much easier to represent pictorially than others. Sticking to our example *The cat walked over the mat*, the words *cat* and *mat* lend themselves far more readily to graphic representation than *the* or the inflection *-ed*. However, it is also true that the less "picturable" units are also often less crucial to the message than the more easily picturable parts; so a script may simply leave them out – an incomplete logographic script for English might write our sentence as in Figure 6.

Figure 6 fails to distinguish *The cat walked over the mat* from *A cat walked over the mat*, *The cat is walking over the mat*, and so forth, but it might be unnecessary to make these distinctions explicit for the purposes for which the script is used. An incomplete script is a great deal better than no script at all.

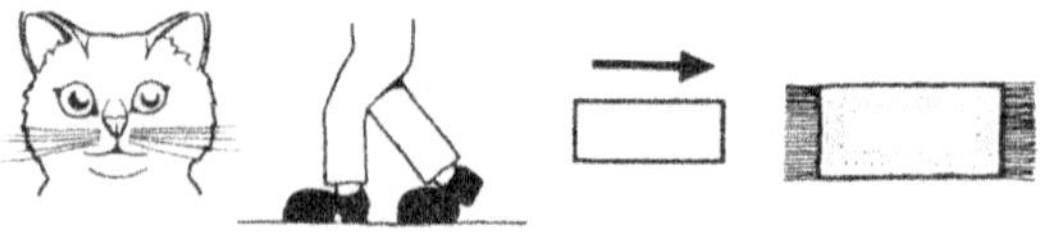

Figure 6

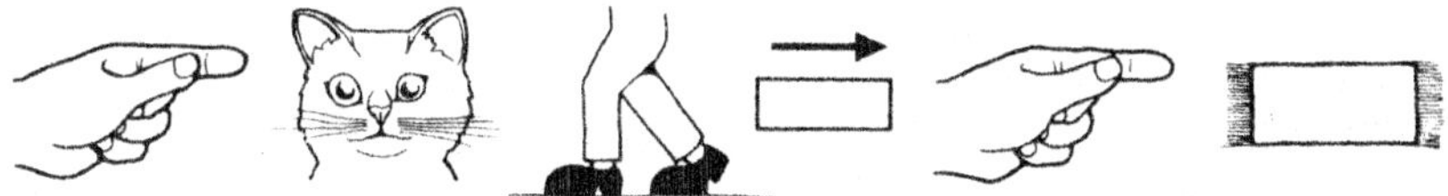

Figure 7

A script can be "incomplete" not only by failing to provide any representation for some linguistic units but also, or alternatively, by providing representations that are ambiguous. Thus, a more complete version of the logographic system of Figure 6 might include the "pointing hand" graph, but use it not merely for *the* but also for *this* and *that* – so that the inscription of Figure 7 would, unlike Figure 6, succeed in eliminating the interpretation *A cat walked over the mat* but still fail to distinguish *The cat walked* ... from *This cat walked* ....

Even if they are phonographic, scripts will often fail to mark all the distinctions of sound which are significant in the language they are used to write. Latin of the classical period, for instance, had an important contrast between long and short vowels. *Mălum* "an evil, a disaster" was different from *mālum* "an apple", and so on. But nothing in Latin orthography expressed that contrast. The breve and macron symbols which classicists add to the vowel letters nowadays are a modern invention; a Roman wrote both words identically as MALVM, and a reader had to rely on context to select the relevant word. (Classical Latin had no /v/ sound; its letter V corresponded to our /u/.)

There is one notable respect in which modern English orthography is highly incomplete, namely intonation. To some extent punctuation gives clues to intonation, but it is easy to show that the indications provided by punctuation fall far short of a complete representation of English intonation distinctions. Consider a group of utterances which comprise the same sequence of words spoken on different intonation patterns, indicated here in the transcription system of Michael Halliday (1967), which was one attempt to fill the gap in completeness that we are discussing (in this system, // and / represent "tone-group" and "foot" boundaries respectively, underlining represents the "tonic syllable" of a tone-group, and numerals represent various English "tones" or patterns of pitch):

> //2 is he / sure of it// – rising to high pitch: a neutral question
> //-3 is he / sure of it// – low level pitch rising to mid: "I'm asking 'Is he sure of it?', not that it really matters ..."
> //5 is he / sure of it// – rising to high, then falling: "Is he sure of

it, because if he *isn't*, ..."
//4 is he / sure of it// – falling to low, then rising: "You ask whether he's sure of it? Of course he is!"

These four utterances are quite distinct in pronunciation and in meaning in spoken English. Yet in English orthography they cannot be distinguished. Perhaps the third example might be differentiated from the others by italicizing *sure*; but that would normally imply not merely that the utterance was said on tone 5 but also that the word *sure* bore contrastive stress – in reality it is perfectly possible to have the intonation contour without special stress on *sure*. And apart from that, all the sentences must be written alike as < Is he sure of it? >.

These examples of phonographic incompleteness – length in Latin vowels, and the various phonetic features such as pitch and loudness which jointly realize English intonation patterns – are cases of what phoneticians call "suprasegmental" features, as opposed to features of vocal-tract closure, tongue position, and so forth which determine the qualities of individual vowel and consonant segments. It is generally true that suprasegmental features tend to be less psychologically salient to users of a language, even if they are contrastive in the language (as vowel length was in Latin), than segmental features; so it is no surprise if orthographies are often particularly incomplete with respect to suprasegmentals. But a script can be incomplete in the way it records segmental phonetics also. In Chapters 4 and 5 we shall look at scripts which are highly ambiguous in the way they record consonants and vowels respectively.

Incidentally, my statement that some types of phonetic contrast are in general less salient than others might jar with some readers, because for a long time it was an axiom of linguistics that "Such a thing as a 'small difference of sound' does not exist in a language" (Bloomfield 1926: 157). It was believed that, to speakers of a given language, sounds in that language were either the same or sharply different, and "almost the same but not quite" was meaningless. But we know nowadays that things are not so straightforward. Even with respect to segmental phonology, two phonemes can be almost but not completely merged into one (Labov 1994: 349–90). Phonological contrasts do differ in degree of salience, and an incomplete phonographic script is more likely to ignore contrasts which are less salient.

Of course, for someone who can read and write, the script itself largely determines what phonetic features he notices and which he overlooks. Some readers may have felt that I was in a sense cheating when I offered the example of English intonation in support of the claim that English orthography is incomplete; they might object that intonation patterns are not "really" part of sentences in the way that the words they contain are – so that the question of completeness scarcely arises with respect to intonation. But this would be circular. The reason why we instinctively feel that intonation-patterns are not "of the essence" of sentences, while words are, is that our instinctive ideas about our language are heavily coloured by the orthographic system we have learned for reading and writing it, and this happens to neglect intonation. True, intonation-patterns are usually not the most significant elements of sentences, but often they are far from the least significant. The intonation differences between my four example sentences carry far more significance than the choice of *it*, rather than *this* or *that*, as the last word in the respective sentences; the fact that the latter distinctions are consistently recorded by our orthography, while the former distinctions are consistently overlooked, is surely merely a fact about the arbitrary limits to the completeness of our particular script, rather than something that one would naturally expect to be the case for any practical script for English.

All this is not to suggest, however, that the best script for a language will necessarily be the most complete script. Halliday's notation was invented for specialized linguistic purposes – Halliday certainly does not propose that anything like his notation ought to be used in everyday writing. Completeness is one desideratum in a script, since it permits the largest possible number of thought-distinctions to be transferred from speech to paper; but there are other desiderata which will often conflict – notably economy, in the sense both of fewness of different symbols to be learned and of fewness of symbols used to represent any given utterance. It may perhaps be that the kind of incompleteness found in English script represents a good compromise between these conflicting desiderata; although in the cases quoted above intonation patterns are crucial, there will be many cases where, in context, intonation could be predicted from word-sequence – sufficiently many, perhaps, that it is just not worthwhile for our script to include detailed representation of intonation. Likewise, the relatively extreme incompleteness of some early scripts may not always be merely a flaw of immaturity; if a script is used only for highly specific purposes, so that much of any utterance is predictable from context, a highly incomplete script might actually be the *best* script since the balance of advantage would tip away from completeness towards economy.

* * *

Let us return to the classification scheme of Figure 4 (p. 24). We have yet to deal with the subclassification of logographic and of phonographic systems.

At each of Martinet's two levels of articulation, a language has units of different sizes. The smallest elements of the "first articulation" are morphemes, but in most languages there are also "words" – some words will consist of a single morpheme but many will be polymorphemic. In all languages morphemes (and/or words) will be grouped into larger syntactic units: phrases, clauses. Likewise, for the second articulation the smallest units are phonetic features – elements such as "consonantal", "labiodental contact", "fricative", "voiced"; but phonetic features combine into "segments" or "phones" (e.g. the set of features just listed add up to the segment [v]), and into the larger units called "syllables".

It is a commonplace of modern linguistics that the number of potential well-formed sentences in any human language is infinitely large; clearly, then, it would be out of the question to invent a script which represented whole sentences by single graphs. The same consideration rules out the possibility of basing a logographic script on the clause or the phrase. In principle it might be possible to use the word as the unit of graphic representation: the number of words in the vocabulary of a language is larger than the number of its morphemes, but it is only finitely large. Thus, one might imagine a logographic script for English in which, say, the words *walk, walked, walking* were represented by three distinct and unrelated graphs, rather than being split into their constituent morphemes as in Figure 5 (p. 25). In reality, though, I know of no logographic systems based on units larger than single morphemes (which is why the left-hand line descending from "logographic" in Figure 4 is dotted – it is a hypothetical rather than an actual possibility). This is not surprising: one drawback of logographic systems in general is that they are uneconomical in terms of the number of graphic units which must be invented and remembered by readers. To use separate graphs for various words derived from the same roots would greatly increase this burden.

At the level of the second, phonological articulation, on the other hand, everything is finite. In any language there are only finitely many phonologically admissible syllables (in many languages this range will be considerably smaller than in English, whose complex consonant clusters, diphthongs, and triphthongs make for an unusually large syllable inventory). The syllables of any language can be analysed as sequences of elements drawn from a much smaller set of consonant and vowel segments, which in turn can be treated as bundles of simultaneously occurring phonetic features: the inventory of features used by a language will usually be smaller than its inventory of segments.[3] So it is possible to base a phonographic system on any of these units, and there are real examples of all three categories.

The notion of a script based on segments scarcely needs illustration, since European orthographies are (at least approximately) segmental. The notion of a syllabic script perhaps deserves a word or two of clarification (before actual examples are discussed in detail in Chapters 4 and 11). Looking back to the hypothetical script of Figure 5, one might well ask whether this is clearly distinct from syllabic writing: most of the graphs of Figure 5 represent syllable-sized elements of English – *the*, *cat*, etc. However, in the first place there are exceptions: the fifth graph stands for a disyllable, *over*, and the fourth graph stands for the past-tense morpheme which is pronounced as part of a syllable. In a syllabic script the number of graphs in an inscription depends on the phonology of the utterance transcribed – words which are long in terms of pronunciation will be represented by more graphs than are needed to write short words. In a morphemic script, on the other hand, the number of graphs in an inscription is independent of pronunciation: even a long word like *catamaran*, being only one morpheme, will be written with just one graph. Furthermore, in a morphemic script elements will not be written alike merely because they sound alike, provided they are in fact distinct meaning-units: the last graph in Figure 5 represents the word *mat*, and if the script is logographic a different graph would be used for the semantically unrelated word *matte*, even though it too is pronounced /mæt/. In a syllabic script, *mat* and *matte* would be written alike, and the graph which writes *cat* would also appear as the first graph in the writing of *catamaran*.

Turning to "featural" script (an ugly term, but no better alternative is available): again we shall be examining in detail (in Chapter 8) a standard national orthography which works on this principle, but meanwhile the reader might be interested in examples which are drawn from closer to home and may be more familiar. A pure, scientific featural script is the notation used by "generative phonologists" (e.g. Chomsky and Halle 1968), in one version of which the English word *cat*, for instance, would be transcribed like this:

consonantal	+	–	+
vocalic	–	+	–
sonorant	–	+	–
anterior	–	–	+
coronal	–	–	+
close	–	–	–
open	–	+	–
back	–	–	–
round	–	–	–
voiced	–	+	–

The rows of such a table stand for various phonetic features which may take plus or minus values (e.g. "+voiced" means voiced, "–voiced" means voiceless); the columns stand for successive segments of the utterance transcribed.

This notation was designed for scientific purposes and would be too cumbersome for everyday use. As an example of a more practical featural script for English, consider Pitman's Shorthand. Figure 8 shows the basic elements of this system. (Pitman's system as a whole contains many complexities designed to reduce the written shapes of words to the simplest possible outlines for speed of writing; we shall examine only the basics of the system.) The script does not represent phonetic features by assigning them individual graphs which are written separately; rather, a graph represents a whole segment, but the various visual properties of the graph correlate with the different phonetic features making up the segment. The major contrast between consonants and vowels is represented as a contrast between extended lines versus small dots and dashes in different positions adjacent to consonant-lines. (Figure 8 uses the line for /k/ to illustrate positioning of the vowel signs; thus the grouping of marks shown for /i/ stands for /ik/ *eke*.)

Among the graphs for obstruent consonants, the contrast between thick and thin represents the voiced/voiceless contrast; place of articulation is shown by orientation (left-leaning = labial, vertical = apical, right-leaning = palato-alveolar, horizontal = velar); curved lines stand for fricatives, straight lines for stops (including affricates). Among the vowel signs, the heavy/light contrast distinguishes "tense" vowels (those that do not require a following consonant in the same syllable) from "lax" or "checked" vowels. Dot versus dash stand for front versus back; position in relation to the adjacent consonant sign represents the close versus mid versus open contrast. (The system slightly distorts the phonetics of standard English by treating /ei əu/ as if they were pure vowels [e o] – as, in some regional dialects, they are.) The alternative signs for /r/ and /h/ are allographs, choice between which is determined by convenience in joining the signs to those that precede and follow. A few of Pitman's basic graphs, notably that for /h/ (which is difficult to analyse into features from the phonetic point of view) are unitary segmental signs; in the main, though, his system is clearly featural.

These, then, are the principal categories of glottographic script in terms of the type of unit represented. But it must be stressed that the actual orthographies used in real life are not usually pure, textbook examples of one or another of these categories. When a speech-notation system is invented and used for scientific purposes it may be all of a piece and pure, but we shall see as the book proceeds that scripts which have evolved over long periods as everyday writing systems are almost always something of a mixture. In some cases the different types of writing are mixed in such proportions within a given script that one cannot say which predominates; thus in Chapter 11 we shall see that Japanese writing cannot be called "essentially logographic" or "essentially phonographic", it is partly one and partly the other. Perhaps more commonly, one of the various principles will control the majority of components within an orthographic system, but there will almost always be an admixture of elements inconsistent with that principle.

* * *

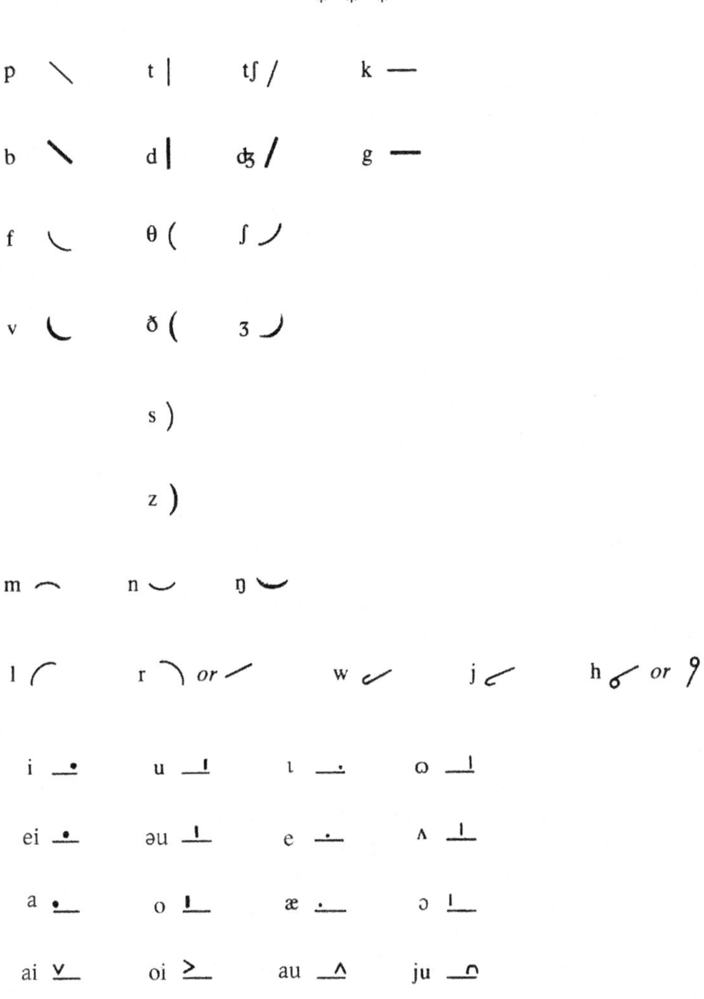

Figure 8

Apart from the distinctions between different kinds of linguistic unit represented, between complete versus incomplete systems, and between motivated versus arbitrary graphs, one further classification principle for glottographic scripts must be introduced before we close this chapter. This last distinction, between *deep* and *shallow* orthographies, is more technical than those discussed earlier, but it is quite important for understanding the linguistics of writing.

Students of linguistics are familiar with the idea that analysis of a linguistic structure frequently leads one to set up "underlying" levels of description at which a given utterance comprises a rather different sequence of units from those it contains at the "surface". The point is most easily exemplified from phonology. In the first place, we know that various families of two or more sounds in a given language will often function as replacements for one another in different phonological environments, so that, although the sounds are physically distinct, they are conveniently regarded as different manifestations of a single phoneme at a "deeper" level. Familiar examples in English are the plain and velarized laterals [l l^{ɯ}], of which the former occurs before a vowel and the latter elsewhere, and the pairs of plain and aspirated voiceless stops, such as [p p^{h}], [t t^{h}], of which the former occur in clusters following /s/ and the latter elsewhere. In each of these cases English orthography is "phonemic rather than phonetic": it uses an invariant graph, < l >, < p >, etc., for the phoneme as a family of sounds, rather than using different graphs for the different allophones. We could easily imagine a variant orthography for English which resembled the standard system except that it used different graphemes, say< l λ >, for the plain and velarized laterals. In such an orthography, words such as *lip, lily, Lil, hill, hillock* would be written < lip lily Liλ hiλλ hillock > respectively (I assume that other orthographic rules, e.g. those governing the use of single versus double consonant letters, are unchanged). An orthography which used < l λ > in this way would be slightly "shallower" than ordinary English orthography. As we shall see in later chapters, scripts actually used in practice sometimes do provide separate graphs for distinct allophones in this way.

Notice that, in this hypothetical orthography, it would be incorrect to call < l λ > "allographs" of one "grapheme", like the graphs < ſ s > discussed on pp. 15–16 above. The signs < l λ > would be distinct graphemes, used to represent distinct elements of the spoken English language, although elements at a particularly shallow level within the structure of spoken English. The signs < ſ s >, on the other hand, were not used to represent separate allophones of the /s/ phoneme; there was no systematic difference in spoken English between the sounds written < ſ > and those written < s >, and the choice between the two allographs was determined by a purely graphic consideration (word-final versus non-word-final position), so that both allographs would appear for a single instance of the /s/ phoneme in words such as < miſs loſs >, and a term which could be written as one word or two would appear now with one allograph, now the other: < bees wax >, < beeſwax >.

The phonemic level of English phonology is deeper than the surface phonetic level, but it is not very deep. Linguists argue that we must recognize levels of "morphophonemic" representation which are yet more abstract, further removed from the physical facts of pronunciation, than the phonemic level. Consider, for instance, the formation of noun plurals in English. Regular plurals take one of three suffixes, phonemically speaking: /ɪz/ if the noun stem ends in a sibilant such as /s/ or /dʒ/, /s/ if the stem ends in a voiceless sound other than a sibilant, and /z/ otherwise. Thus we have:

pɪtʃ pɪtʃɪz *pitch pitches*
lɔs lɔsɪz *loss losses*

kæt kæts *cat cats*
mɪθ mɪθs *myth myths*

fɔg fɔgz *fog fogs*
həu həuz *hoe hoes*

Clearly there is phonetic logic in the distribution of the three allomorphs of the plural morpheme; the variation between the three is not just a matter of arbitrary irregularity (like the use of the allomorph /ən/ after *ox* and the zero allomorph after *sheep*). A linguist would analyse this situation by saying that, "underlyingly" (or "morphophonemically"), there is just one regular plural suffix, which has the form /z/. Thus the underlying forms of the words *pitches, cats, fogs* are | pɪtʃz kætz fɔgz | ("underlying" forms are standardly written between vertical bars). The phonemic forms are derived by the application of two rules:

1. An epenthetic /ɪ/ is inserted between two sibilants (thus | pɪtʃz | becomes /pɪtʃɪz/).
2. A voiced consonant is devoiced following a voiceless consonant (thus | kætz | becomes /kæts/).

These rules must apply in the order given; if rule 2 applied before rule 1, | pɪtʃz | would be changed by rule 2 to /pɪtʃs/ which by rule 1 would then become */pɪtʃɪs/, which is not the correct pronunciation of *pitches*.

How does ordinary English orthography treat this situation? Interestingly, it represents a level intermediate in depth between the phonemic and the morphophonemic level – namely, the level at which rule 1 has already applied but rule 2 has not. The epenthetic /ɪ/ produced by rule 1 is written, as < e > (which is the standard spelling of this phoneme in grammatical suffixes, cf. Albrow 1972: 29–30); on the other hand, the distinction between /s/ and /z/ produced by rule 2 is ignored, so that the suffixes of *cats* and *fogs* are both written < s >, which standardly represents the sound /z/ in this position (*ibid.*: 25). If English orthography were maximally "deep", it would write < pitchs cats fogs >; if it were maximally "shallow" it would write < pitches catss fogs > (since < ss > is the standard spelling of /s/ in non-initial position).

The analysis of "underlying" levels in phonology is a controversial aspect of linguistics; many linguists believe that any phonological analysis which departs significantly from the brute facts of pronunciation is an artificial linguists' invention and irrelevant to the processing of utterances by ordinary speakers. The fact remains that, as we shall see in later chapters, phonographic scripts often seem to be considerably "deeper" than the allophonic or even phonemic level. (Like the motivated/arbitrary contrast, the deep/shallow contrast is a gradient rather than all-or-none distinction, and one which applies to different components of an orthography separately – a given writing system may be deep in its representation of one aspect of a spoken language but shallow in its representation of another aspect.)

The points I have been making about a deep/shallow distinction in phonology are in principle equally applicable to grammatical analysis. Consider, as a very simple example, the word *du* in French: this would commonly described as the "surface" manifestation of an "underlying" sequence of morphemes *de le*. In standard French orthography, a phrase such as /aʃte dy pɛ̃/ "to buy bread" is written < acheter du pain >. But it is easy to imagine a hypothetical orthography which recorded the underlying morphemes, and wrote the same phrase < acheter de le pain >. Such an orthography would be grammatically "deeper" than standard French orthography, and the grammatical depth of a script would be an issue independent of its phonological depth – even a logographic script could be deep or shallow in this sense.

In practice, however, the depth issue arises only with respect to phonology. I know of no script, whether phonographic or logographic, that is at all deep grammatically, though phonographic scripts differ considerably in their phonological depth.

We have now drawn all the theoretical distinctions needed to investigate the linguistics of writing. The chapters that follow will apply these conceptual tools in a series of case studies.

Notes

1. On Blissymbolics see the Wikipedia article "Blissymbols" (accessed 31 March 2014).
2. The first edition of this book described an artefact produced by a member of the Yukaghir tribe of Siberia that has often been cited by anthropologists and linguists as an example of sophisticated semasiographic writing. But DeFrancis (1989: 24–35) has researched the example and has established convincingly that this so-called "Yukaghir love letter" is something much less than it was taken to be, and not really writing at all.
3. From a theoretical point of view it is misleading to describe phonetic features as elements of segments; features overlap with one another and co-occur with sequences of other features in complex ways within a syllable. But we need not enter into that matter here.

3 The earliest writing

As already mentioned, one distinction between the linguistics of writing and the linguistics of speech is that for the former we can delve far enough back into the past to come close to its beginning. In this chapter we examine the development of one early writing system, the Sumerian system whose later stages were known as "Cuneiform". This is a specially interesting case, because it appears to be the oldest writing system in the world.

Indeed, the fact that Sumerian writing is older than any other scripts has led some scholars in the past to suggest that all writing systems in the world might ultimately be related to one another, with the earliest version of Sumerian writing being the ancestor of all other scripts. However, we shall see that this "monogenetic" hypothesis is not seriously tenable in the light of current knowledge.

For our purposes in this book, the monogenesis issue is not centrally important. Even if other scripts originated independently, looking at the origins of Sumerian script may well give us clues about how those other systems first came into being. The evolution of Sumerian script certainly reveals strong parallels with developments that occurred independently in other writing systems, and this is another reason for beginning our case-studies with a sketch of this system: it makes a convenient introduction to ideas that will be examined in more detail in later chapters.

* * *

The culture called "Sumer" flourished from perhaps –4500 to about –1750 (when it was absorbed by the Babylonians), in lower Mesopotamia – southern Iraq, in 21c terms. Sumer was probably the first civilization in world history, in the sense that it produced the earliest cities (the ideas of "city" and "civilization" are commonly taken to be related by more than etymology). It is not surprising, then, if the Sumerians were the world's first scribes. The Sumerians spoke an agglutinating language comparable in type to Turkish or Hungarian, but apparently unrelated to any other known language of past or present. Their alluvial terrain had little wood or stone, so the Sumerians wrote on what they had: clay, which they formed into tablets (frequently squarish in shape, and convex rather than flat), and on which they made marks with a stylus cut from a reed. The earliest Sumerian writing, as such, is believed to date from the late −4th millennium, possibly as late as −3000; most extant examples are from the Sumerian capital Uruk (the biblical Erech, modern Warka). This “archaic” stage of Sumerian script is not wholly understood by modern scholarship, but we do know its general nature.

Archaic Sumerian writing was used for administrative purposes, in particular for recording things like tax payments or distribution of rations. Figure 9 shows a typical archaic tablet. G.R. Driver (1954: 40) translated it: “Ḫegiulendu [the priest of] the god Ensarnun: 600 *bur* of (?) land”, with the question-mark alluding to the fact that one graph is not now understood.[1] The relationship between Ḫegiulendu and Ensarnun, which Driver gave in brackets, is not spelled out on the tablet since the writer took it for granted. Records were tied to a particular administrative context; it would have been as pointless for the Sumerian scribe to write out “the priest of” explicitly (assuming that the script allowed him to do so) as it would be for me to expand the jotting in my diary, *Noon - Vice-Chancellor*, into *At noon I go to see the vice-chancellor.*

Figure 9

A first point to make is that archaic Sumerian writing was quite typical of early scripts in being primarily or exclusively used for somewhat humdrum administrative purposes. Modern Western education commonly links the study of languages with that of literature, and this often leads people to imagine that writing of high aesthetic value is the central use of writing, so that they expect early scripts to have been used for literary production. That is misleading. Even in the 21c West, where literary writing is widespread, it is surely swamped in quantity and importance in people's lives by the mass of documents we deal with of a more practical nature – job advertisements, tax returns, newspapers, hobby magazines, etc. etc. Writing in Sumer was an advanced technology developed, as new technologies commonly are, to solve pressing material problems; we might not too fancifully draw an analogy between writing in Sumer and information technology in our own culture, and liken the Sumerian scribe, who was a respected "white-collar worker", to the systems analyst or data-processing engineer. In the 21c, computers have come to be used for social networking and various lighthearted activities, but their original applications were in more technical or practical fields such as science, business, and defence, and that is the type of application that might be compared to early writing. According to Marcel Cohen (1958: 7–8):

> Practically everywhere, the first use of writing must have been for more or less official messages. The next uses would have been commercial and legal: accounting and the drawing up of contracts. [Various magical or religious uses] often occur at an early stage. Then one finds increasing numbers of governmental proclamations and edicts, or texts of treaties ... Chronicles or ritual texts only appear later. Writing designed for instruction or entertainment, later still.

Postgate *et al.* (1995) offer a cross-cultural survey of the uses writing has been put to in newly literate societies.

Because archaic Sumerian writing consisted of brief, context-bound administrative inscriptions, it used a limited vocabulary. Many inscriptions mentioned only quantities of goods of various sorts together with the people concerned in transactions, so that we find mostly graphs for numerals, units of measurement, personal names, and material objects such as "sheep", "cow", "cloth", "land", and so forth. The numeral graphs were unmotivated, geometrical shapes; the graphs for material objects were in many cases stylized but recognizable pictures of the things in question. There were quite a large number of different graphemes – Margaret Green (1981: 356) counted nearly 1200 at the early period – but the system represented only a limited range of the elements that spoken Sumerian must have contained: we find little in the way of grammatical elements akin to English *the*, *was*, for instance.

The extreme austerity of the early inscriptions has made some scholars reluctant to categorize archaic Sumerian writing as a logographic system. Thus Marvin Powell (1981: 421) prefers to call the writing "mnemonic" rather than "logographic". This strikes me as a false opposition. My diary jotting, *Noon – Vice-Chancellor*, is mnemonic, in the sense that it suggests a thought whose full expression requires a complete sentence by recording just its most salient elements. But those elements are written in a specific script of a particular type (in this case, approximately phonographic). Likewise, archaic Sumerian writing appears to be a genuine writing system, of the logographic type: graphs of the script stand for morphemes of spoken Sumerian.

It may be that, by calling the script "mnemonic", Powell meant to suggest that it should be seen as semasiography, in our terms, rather than as true glottographic writing. When inscriptions are limited to abbreviated jottings rather than full sentences, the distinction between semasiography and logographic writing blurs. If I write < Noon > in my diary in a phonographic script like ours, there is no doubt that I am writing English – despite the lack of grammatical material – because only in English does the sequence of sounds /nun/ stand for a time of day. If, on the other hand, we used a logographic script in which *noon* was written, say, < 🕛 >, then it would be difficult for an outsider to know whether an inscription involving just this sign and a sign for *Vice-Chancellor* was to be interpreted with < 🕛 > standing specifically for *noon* as opposed to *Mittag* or *midi*, or rather whether it directly represented the idea common to all these words. (On the other hand, if the whole sentence *At noon I go to see the Vice-Chancellor* were written out logographically, the grammar would make it clear that the graphs were to be read as English rather than German or French words.) In the oldest Sumerian tablets, furthermore, even when phrases more complex than a single word were written, the corresponding graphs were not arranged in a systematic order. (In Figure 9, the group of signs for "the god Ensarnun" are grouped together within the box at lower left, but "H̱egiulendu" is spelled out across the top and down the right-hand side, interrupted by the circular mark at top centre representing "600".) However, linear ordering and other formatting conventions were soon adopted (Driver 1954: 39ff.; Green 1981: 348ff.). Once a script uses linear ordering consistently its glottographic status seems indisputable. The only reason to introduce systematic linear (horizontal or vertical) placement of graphemes is to mirror the sequential utterance of spoken forms.[2]

Another characteristic of early Sumerian writing which might seem to establish decisively that it was glottographic (cf. Gelb 1952: 279 n. 11) was the separation of numeral graphs from graphs indicating the objects enumerated. In a semasiographic system, one would expect to find an idea such as "four sheep" expressed by a set of four "sheep" graphs. But no spoken language would express the idea by four repetitions of a word for "sheep", so in a glottographic script we expect to find the idea written with a single sheep graph associated with a separate graph (or group of graphs) standing for the number "four". This is what we find from the time of the earliest Sumerian inscriptions. Likewise, one would expect to find an adjective–noun combination, say "black cow", expressed by one graph in semasiography – a "cow" sign with some modification such as cross-hatching to indicate blackness – but by two graphs in a glottographic system: an unmodified "cow" graph together with a separate graph standing for the word "black". (Unfortunately, it is not clear whether archaic Sumerian script included any phrases of this latter kind.)

Perhaps one should conclude that the oldest known stage of Sumerian script occupies an ambiguous middle ground between clear semasiography, comparable to Blissymbolics, and the clear glottography into which Sumerian script eventually developed. Later Sumerian writing is well understood, and it is unquestionably glottographic. From about –2400 onwards it was used for extended texts: myths and other literary genres, legal judgements, letters, and so on. The script was written in a linear sequence with word-order reflecting consistent rules of syntax, and it was complete, in the sense that it included a range of devices that were capable of recording all lexical and grammatical elements of the spoken Sumerian language. It is true that elements which would have appeared in a given spoken Sumerian utterance often failed to occur in practice in the written version of the utterance: Sumerian orthographic conventions encouraged scribes to omit grammatical items whenever they were predictable from context, rather as telegraphic style in English leaves out many instances of words like *the* (Civil and Biggs 1966: 13). But, as Civil and Biggs rightly add, this practice does not affect the status of the system as a full-scale glottographic script. Whenever a scribe chose to write out a phrase in full, the system offered him the means to do so.

* * *

The development of archaic Sumerian script into this later version can be described from two points of view: the outward shape of the graphs, and the inner logic of their structure and values. In this book we are chiefly concerned with the inner structure of writing systems. However, the history of the graph shapes is also worth spending a little time on, since it is characteristic of developments which have happened in the history of many other writing systems.

A few examples of Sumerian graphs are shown in Figure 10 (after Kramer 1963). Column I gives their original form, in which most are recognizable pictures. Graph 1 stood for /sag/ "head"; graph 2, in which the mouth area was picked out by hatching, for both /ka/ "mouth" and /dug/ "speak". Graph 3 stood for /a/ "water", and graph 4, combining "head" and "water", for /nag/ "drink". The foot depicted by graph 5 stood for all of the following words: /du/, /ra/, /gin/, which are approximate

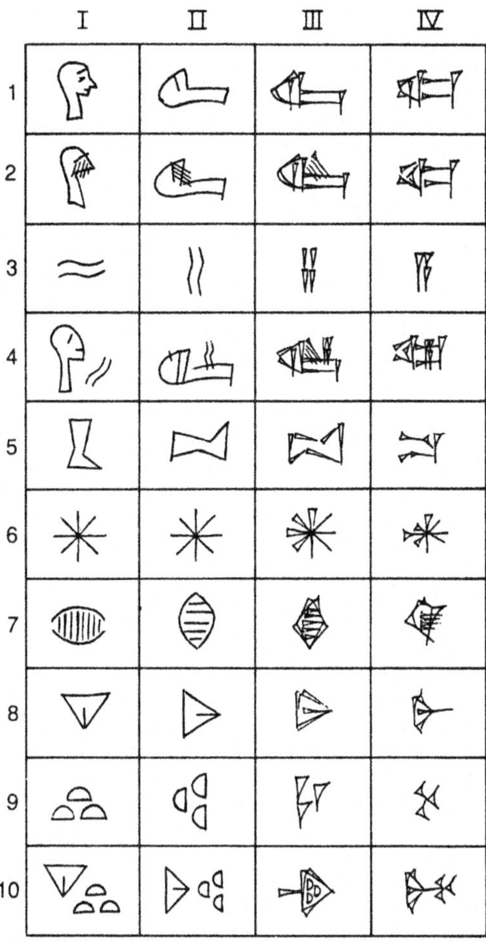

Figure 10

synonyms for "go", /gub/ "stand", /tum/ "bring". Graph 6, a picture of a star, stood by association of ideas for /an/ "heaven" and hence also for /dingir/ "god". (The word /mul/ "star" itself was written with a slightly different graph having more rays.) Graph 7 is known to have stood for /ki/ "earth, land"; in this case, as in many others, the motivation of the graph is not clear – after so many millennia it would be surprising if there were no signs whose logic is obscure to a modern reader, though it may have been obvious enough to a participant in Sumerian culture. Graph 8, a picture of the female pudendum, stands for /sal/ "pudendum" and for /munus/ "woman". Graph 9 is /kur/ "mountain". Graph 10, combining "woman" and "mountain", stands for /geme/ "slave-girl"; the reason for that is that the Sumerians took female slaves from the tribes inhabiting the mountainous area to the east.

Soon after the script was first used, all the signs were rotated 90° anticlockwise, as in column II. A development of this kind may well look gratuitous and bizarre. The fact is, though, that comparable changes have happened over and over again in the history of scripts: individual graphs, or (as here) whole inventories of graphs, have been turned on one side or the other, inverted, or replaced by their mirror-images. The reasons for such developments are no doubt various. The systematic 90° rotation of Sumerian script may have been linked with the way that scribes found it convenient to hold tablet and stylus when writing (M.A. Powell 1981: 425; Green 1981: 370 n. 19).

Another development during the first half of the –3rd millennium involved the change from a pointed stylus, which was used to draw lines in the clay rather as one draws with pencil on paper, to a blunt stylus with which the scribe pressed lines into the clay with minimal lateral movement. There was a practical reason for this: moving a point through clay causes it to heap up and clog the lines already written, so that graphs were easier to form legibly with the new technique. But it naturally led to modification of the shapes of the individual graphs, as continuous curved lines were replaced with straight segments. Each single impression made by the new stylus was shaped like a wedge or nail, hence the name "Cuneiform" (from the Latin for "wedge-shaped") for the script as a whole. Again it is entirely characteristic of the history of writing for a change in the materials employed to lead to a large change in the form of the script.

Once the cuneiform technique had been adopted, there was a tendency to use wedges only in orientations which could be made without bending the wrist too much; in practice this meant that the head of the wedge must point in some direction on the arc running from southwest clockwise to north – that is, the set of wedges used to form graph 6 in columns III and IV was the favoured inventory. Column III displays the early cuneiform version of the script, from about –2500: some graphs still involve dragging the stylus through the clay (e.g. to form the line representing the back of the head in graph 1) or placing the stylus in an awkward orientation (e.g. the line representing the forehead in that graph). By the period about –1800 when most of the Sumerian literary documents were written (represented by column IV) these elements had been eliminated.

These changes in graph shapes entailed a change in their status from motivated to arbitrary. Even at the stage represented by column I, the graphs were highly conventional; Green (1981: 356–7) pointed out that graph 1, for instance, "may be realistically drawn with clearly delineated eye, nose, and chin, but it has to be a right side-view and include both head and neck but not hair, mouth, or ears". Still a user of the script might at this stage perceive the graphs as pictures, even if heavily stylized pictures. Once the graphs were rotated, as in column II, one would suppose that literate Sumerians must have thought of them most of the time simply as conventional shapes; even if they knew that they were pictures laid on their sides, presumably it would have taken an effort of will to see them as pictures during fluent reading or writing. After the move to cuneiform writing in column III, a new learner without access to historically earlier versions of the script could scarcely have detected any motivation at all in most graphs. At this stage, graph 1 for instance must surely have looked like an entirely arbitrary collection of wedges. And once that was true, nothing would have restrained scribes from saving work by replacing difficult stylus strokes by easy ones and reducing the total number of wedges in a graph (as in the column IV versions of graphs 3 and 5).

I have examined these developments in some detail, in order to make clear, to readers used to the high degree of standardization and long-term stability in letter shapes that comes with printing, just how natural it was for graph shapes to change drastically before that technology was invented. There were few mechanisms making for stability of graph shapes before printing, so it would be surprising if graphs did not change shape. In Chapter 7 we shall look at some of the many factors involved in the changing outward appearance of various scripts. We shall not investigate all the individual changes that have occurred in the scripts used in future case-studies – that would be too time-consuming, and tedious for the reader. But, as the book progresses, readers should not be surprised when they notice graph shapes changing.

* * *

While it was evolving in its outward appearance, the Sumerian script was undergoing equally radical changes in its internal logic. In its initial state, many words of the Sumerian language had no written form, and many of the graphs which did exist were ambiguous between quite different words (as graph 2 in Figure 10 stood for both /ka/ "mouth" and /dug/ "speak", and indeed also for /zu/ "tooth" and /inim/ "speech"). According to Cohen (1958: 83) some graphs had as many as twenty distinct values. These deficiencies were met by the introduction of a phonographic principle into the script (Driver 1954: 56ff.).

One of the first ways in which phonological relationships were exploited lay in the extended use of certain graphs to stand for words homophonous with their original values. Thus graph 3 was invented to stand for /a/ "water", but was then also used for /a/ "in", a word whose abstract meaning made it difficult to picture; and a graph for /ti/ "arrow" was extended to stand also for the near-homophone /til/ "life", again a less picturable concept. Cases of this kind, which occurred within the earliest centuries of the existence of the script, were not yet true phonography; the "arrow" graph did not stand for *any* occurrence of the syllable /ti/, but only for certain specific morphemes which had those sounds in common. But, a short while later, graphs began to be used to indicate grammatical affixes. For instance, the graph for /me/ "oracle" (the original shape of this graph was a simple T, the motivation of which is now obscure) was adapted to stand for the plural suffix /-me/ or /-meʃ/, and other graphs were similarly used to represent case and conjugation affixes.

When graphs stand for relatively "meaningless" grammatical elements it is difficult not to perceive them as having purely phonological value. Later in the –3rd millennium phonographic use of the symbols of Sumerian script became more widespread. Most Sumerian roots are monosyllables, of CV (consonant + vowel) or CVC shape, so individual graphs represented syllables (rather than, for instance, separate segmental sounds or phonemes).

What led to the adoption of the phonographic principle, according to Gelb (1952: 66–7), was less the problem of writing grammatical elements than the problem of writing proper names. In the early period when the script was used only for accountancy, grammatical niceties were unimportant, but names were crucial; and Sumerian personal names were typically composed of morphemes from outside the set of numerals and names of goods which sufficed for the rest of the work of recording accounts. As for place names, these were often quite meaningless sequences of sounds for the Sumerians, as *London*, *Glasgow* are for us, and for a similar reason

– the Sumerians had inherited place names from earlier inhabitants of the same territory who spoke a different language. If a proper name is a meaningless sound-sequence, it can be written only phonographically, unless one invents a special logographic sign just for that name (which gets very cumbersome when many names have to be written). Very early Sumerian writing does contain graphs which appear to stand logographically for proper names, but names were soon regularly written phonographically, well before it became normal to give a full written indication of the grammatical elements of a sentence.

The phonographic use of Sumerian writing fell far short, though, of amounting to a "complete" syllabic script. Many phonologically possible syllables had no graphs; and devices were adopted to indicate them, either by graphs for words of similar sound, or by combining existing graphs (for instance the syllable /raʃ/ was spelled with graphs for /ra aʃ/). On the other hand, individual graphs did not have unique phonological values; as we have seen, many graphs originally stood for a range of different words all of whose meanings were connected with the object depicted, and these different words would often give rise to very varied phonographic values for the graph in question. Thus graph 5 might be used not only for the syllable /gub/ and possibly for phonetically similar syllables, but also for /du/, /gin/, etc., and for syllables phonetically similar to these.

Words which had logographic writings continued to be written logographically (and far more words were in due course provided with logographic signs than the few which had sufficed for keeping early accounts). The Sumerians tended to use signs phonographically only when the limitations of their logographic system forced them to do so. Another way in which the phonographic principle was exploited, though, was in disambiguating logographic signs. Thus, in order to establish that graph 6 stood on a given occasion for /dingir/ "god" rather than /an/ "sky", the scribe would write a graph with the phonetic value /ra/ after it, to indicate the last consonant of the required reading; a suffixed /na/ would indicate that the reading should be /an/. Graphs functioning in this way are called "phonetic complements".

Conversely, a few key graphs were used as so-called "determinatives" in order to disambiguate other graphs by reference to the *logographic* values of the former. For instance, a graph showing blades of a marsh plant had the logographic values /naga/ and /te/, which were names of two such plants, and also /nidaba/ and /ereʃ/, the latter being names respectively of a goddess and a town both of which were associated with marshes. When the graph was used for /te/ it had the graph for /u/ "plant" written before it as determinative; when it stood for /nidaba/, graph 6 ("god") was prefixed; when it stood for /ereʃ/, graph 7 ("land") was written after it.

The fact that, in the earliest period, one Sumerian graph could stand for a range of semantically related words is another reason why some writers have felt that the system was semasiographic rather than logographic. But Gelb (1952: 107) made the point that, as soon as the Sumerians invented devices for distinguishing between the various readings possible for a graph, they applied these rather consistently; and he suggested that this gives us good reason to interpret the system, even as it was before those devices were invented, as an – admittedly very defective – logographic rather than semasiographic system (cf. Civil 1973: 21).

When graph 6 was used as a determinative, the potential confusion between "god" and "sky" was not troublesome: "god" is used as a determinative, "sky" is not. However, when one reads a Sumerian inscription, nothing indicates explicitly which graphs are to be treated as determinatives, which as phonetic complements, and which stand directly for Sumerian words either logographically or phonographically.

Perhaps halfway through the –3rd millennium, the Akkadians, a neighbouring people to the north who spoke a Semitic language unrelated to Sumerian, adapted the Cuneiform script to their own language, developing it greatly in the process. Since the culture of the Akkadians (or, as the relevant sub-group was later called, Babylonians) came to dominate Mesopotamia, eventually extinguishing Sumer as a political entity and Sumerian as a language, far more of the Cuneiform writing that has come down to us is in Akkadian than in Sumerian. (In due course Cuneiform script came to be used for other languages too.)

The Akkadians greatly extended the use of the phonographic principle. Akkadian was an inflecting language, in which the chain of spoken sounds could not be neatly divided up into morphemic meaning-units (compare the way that English *men* collapses the ideas of "man" and "plural" into a single sound shape). Pure logography was less practical for such a language than it was for an agglutinating language like Sumerian, where each spoken syllable could be identified unambiguously with some one particular unit of lexical or grammatical meaning. Having been forced by the nature of their language to develop the phonographic aspect of Cuneiform script, the Akkadians extended the principle to aspects of writing where they could have managed without it. Sumerian Cuneiform, to the end, was an essentially logographic script with a limited admixture of phonography.[3] In Akkadian, almost any linguistic form might be written either phonographically or logographically, and which writing was chosen for a given word on a given occasion would depend on the stylistic effect aimed at, or the whim of the scribe.

Furthermore, the relationship between sounds and graphs used phonographically became much more complicated in Akkadian script. We have hinted that the Sumerians would on occasion use a graph invented for a word with one particular pronunciation to represent a slightly different syllable: this happened much more extensively in Akkadian writing, partly because Akkadian contained sounds which did not occur in Sumerian. Moreover, the Akkadians derived phonographic values for a given graph not only from the pronunciations of the various Sumerian words for which the graph stood, but sometimes also from their own Akkadian names for the same things.

When one adds that Akkadian scribes sometimes deliberately cultivated archaism and gratuitous obscurity in their orthography, it will be seen that the study of Akkadian Cuneiform is a highly complex discipline.

We shall pursue it no further. Our main purpose in examining Cuneiform was a historical one. To examine in detail the workings of various phenomena of writing in scripts considered as synchronic systems it will be more fruitful to look at modern (or at least more recent) scripts, for which the facts are more accessible. Readers may notice that many themes which will become relevant with respect to other scripts from diverse parts of the world discussed in later chapters are prefigured in the development of this one earliest of all writing systems.

* * *

If Sumerian script was the world's earliest true writing, one would very much like to know how it originally came into being. For most of the period that modern scholarship has investigated it, no real answer to that question was available. However, a theory has been put forward which in recent decades has achieved considerable traction. This theory, let me say straight away, is highly problematic; but the question it attempts to answer is so acutely interesting that it would be a pity to ignore the idea here out of excessive scholarly caution.

The idea I am referring to was originally put forward by Pierre Amiet of the Louvre Museum (Amiet 1966).[4] Subsequently, Amiet's idea has been elaborated in numerous publications by Denise Schmandt-Besserat of the University of Texas (e.g. Schmandt-Besserat 1992, 1996). The point of departure of these scholars is the observation that excavations in Mesopotamia have yielded large numbers of small clay objects of various simple geometrical shapes (spheres, discs, cones, tetrahedra, etc.), some of which have lines incised in set patterns (for instance there are discs with a cross on one face), or have small pellets or coils of clay added to them. For want of a more neutral term these objects are referred to as "tokens". They are commonly found in the storage areas of dwellings. Archaeologists have often paid them little attention, dismissing them briefly as "gaming pieces", "amulets", or the like.

Late in the –4th millennium, as urban life was beginning, the inventory of token shapes increased. Some of the new shapes were more naturalistic, for instance they included highly stylized models of animal heads and jars. At this same period we find examples of sets of tokens being enclosed in clay envelopes or "bullae", balls of clay which were hollowed out and sealed after the tokens were inserted. In many cases the envelopes carry rows of marks on the outside, which could have corresponded to the tokens inside, though since the envelopes when excavated were almost always broken it was hard to be sure of this. Sometimes (though rarely) the marks on the outside of the envelopes appear to have been made by pressing tokens themselves into the envelope surface; more usually, shapes were simulated by hand. Amiet argued that the clay tokens must have been used to stand for goods in a system of accountancy. He treated this system as having been invented in the –4th millennium by the inhabitants of Elam (a civilization neighbouring Sumer to the east, based on Susa, modern Shūsh).

Amiet then suggested that, if people were accustomed to marking the outside of bullae as a record of their contents, the inevitable next step was to simplify matters by dispensing with the contents of the envelope and exchanging just marked clay surfaces: in which case one has writing, or something very like it.

This is on the face of it a very attractive and plausible idea about how writing might first have developed out of non-writing. However, after pioneering the theory, by the 1980s Amiet backtracked. When radiography was used to compare the contents of some unbroken bullae with their surface markings, they proved not to match. Amiet concluded that the bullae cannot have been intended to convey information in their own right, but at most to serve as aide-memoires to prompt people who passed information on by word of mouth (Jasim and Oates 1986: 350).

Denise Schmandt-Besserat was not put off, though. She makes considerable play with a case of a bulla that was excavated whole in the 1920s and, when broken open, is claimed to have contained a set of tokens that did match the markings on the exterior. (But those markings were in Cuneiform, so the date of this bulla must have been far too late to be relevant to the birth of writing, and in any case the claim cannot be checked because the tokens were lost long ago.) Schmandt-Besserat casts her net wider than Amiet, and she has succeeded in publicizing the theory remarkably widely. She notes that similar tokens are found not just in Mesopotamia but at many sites over a wide area of the Middle East, and that at some sites they go as far back as the -9th millennium, when the hunting-and-gathering way of life was first giving way to farming. The tokens appear to represent the earliest use of fired clay for any purpose. Similar tokens continue to appear in the archaeological record up to the -3rd millennium, the peak of production seemingly being about -3500.

Schmandt-Besserat argues that the coincidence of the earliest tokens with the beginnings of farming is understandable. Whereas hunter-gatherers live literally from hand to mouth, agriculturalists need to make long-term plans of things like the division of the harvest into grain for current consumption versus seed-corn. Before the invention of writing, it might have been very useful to have a system in which crops and livestock were represented by small tokens which would perhaps be shifted from one tray to another in order to model activities on the farm. With the growth of towns, the range of goods available would have increased, and this may be reflected by the increase in number of token-types.

Urban life also implies the beginning of large-scale trade, and this may explain the bullae. The farmer now needs not only to maintain a model of the disposition of his working capital; he must also exchange documentation with others. A bulla could have been a bill of lading, recording consignments of stock or goods sent to market in the charge of a servant. The envelope would function not only to keep the tokens together but to protect them from fraudulent alteration; and, since they could be inspected only by breaking the bulla, it would have been convenient to keep a record of the contents on the outside for casual checking. (A proportion of tokens are perforated, suggesting that they were held on strings. Schmandt-Besserat at one point suggested that this might have been done to enable the tokens to stand for linear word-sequences, but this daring idea was not pursued.)

Schmandt-Besserat believes that the token system represents the origin not merely of the general principle of communicating by marks on clay, but of the details of Sumerian script. She notes that a number of the earliest logographs of the Sumerian system (whose values are established by their continuity with later, better-documented forms of the script) seem thoroughly unmotivated – contrary to the natural assumption that any script will begin pictorially and gradually evolve into a less-motivated form. For instance, "sheep" was written with a cross in a circle, ⊕; and, as we have seen, there were tokens shaped like small discs with a cross on one face. More motivated early Sumerian graphs tend to be either names of *wild* animals (e.g. "wolf") or items of advanced technology (such as "chariot"). Others have explained this by supposing that the oldest known examples of Sumerian writing themselves emerge from an earlier period of development which is lost to the record, at the beginning of which even a graph like "sheep" would have been more motivated. But Schmandt-Besserat finds it surprising that all trace of the postulated earlier stages should have been lost, and (following a suggestion of Amiet's) she suggests that the unmotivated shapes would be understandable if they were created as two-dimensional imitations of already-existing three-dimensional tokens (because small clay tokens would as a matter of practicality have had to be made in simple shapes). Wild animals would have been irrelevant to the token system, and technological advances such as chariots might have postdated that system, so words for these things would have been written two-dimensionally from the start and hence would naturally have been given motivated graphs.

Schmandt-Besserat even argues that this theory explains why the Sumerians wrote on clay, which she regards as a relatively inconvenient medium, and why their tablets were usually somewhat convex – this could have been a hangover from the convexity of the hollow bullae. (But it is not clear that the Sumerians had any alternative to clay; and Driver (1954: 9) suggested that convexity protected the tablets from the risk of cracking.)

Schmandt-Besserat's theory has encountered serious criticism. An obvious problem is that it is dangerous to equate signs from widely different sources merely on the basis of similarity of appearance, particularly when the shapes in question are simple geometrical ones. There are only so many possible shapes, so coincidences will happen by chance. (We have no reason to assume that all the so-called "tokens" were signs at all – cf. the earlier suggestions of "gaming pieces" or "amulets".) Furthermore, if we do accept Schmandt-Besserat's identifications, we must assign meanings to some of the "tokens" which are hard to reconcile with her notion of how the token-system was used: what use would there have been for clay tokens meaning "good", "legal decision", or "heart"? Stephen Lieberman (1980) claimed that Schmandt-Besserat has greatly exaggerated the extent of coincidence between token-system and early Sumerian script, both by equating two or more distinct Sumerian graphs with one token-type and vice versa, and by casting her net unreasonably wide in investigating the tokens, ignoring the fact that many token-types which look most like Sumerian graphs have never been found at Mesopotamian sites (cf. also Le Brun and Vallat 1978).

A large problem with Schmandt-Besserat's theory is that over several decades she has rarely or never responded to such objections (Michalowski 1993: 996), so that many of her readers may be unaware that the theory is anything less than established truth. Indeed, by now it is often treated as established truth in non-specialist publications, and meanwhile Schmandt-Besserat's claims have grown increasingly grand. By 1999 she was invited to contribute the entry on "Artifacts and Civilization" to the *MIT Encyclopedia of the Cognitive Sciences*, in which she claimed that her findings were the key to understanding how mankind first developed the cognitive ability to "manipulate data abstractly" (Schmandt-Besserat 1999).

However, when Schmandt-Besserat published the catalogue of raw evidence on which she bases her conclusions (Schmandt-Besserat 1992), Paul Zimansky (1993) found that the conclusions fail to match the detailed evidence. Furthermore, Schmandt-Besserat's assumption that similarly shaped "tokens" had the same significance for diverse cultures spread over a huge area of western Asia over many millennia turned out to entail absurd implications. For instance, the fact that the pre-Cuneiform symbol ⊕ for "sheep" occurred also as a token shape played a large part in winning converts to Schmandt-Besserat's theory; but, although sheep were central to Middle Eastern economies, it turned out that only a few putative "sheep" tokens have ever been found. A token shape which occurs frequently in the archaeological record, on the other hand, is claimed by Schmandt-Besserat (who does not discuss statistics) to refer to "nails". As Zimansky asked (1993: 516), "Is it really credible that these early villages would leave more evidence of keeping accounts o[f] nails ... than livestock?"

It is not credible. In the 21c, our conclusion must be that Pierre Amiet's idea about how writing first evolved out of non-writing was reasonable, and could have been correct; but the evidence just is not there. Regrettably, we shall probably never know just how the earliest writing system first emerged. Very possibly, writing may have evolved in different ways at different places.

* * *

Finally, what about "monogenesis"? As we saw on p. 40, some have suggested that Sumerian script was ancestral not only to Akkadian script and, less directly, to other scripts of western Asia, but that every script in the world might ultimately stem from this one earliest writing system. This monogenetic hypothesis was advocated for instance by Ignace Gelb (1952: 218–20), who argued that "all Oriental systems outside of Sumerian came into existence in periods of strong cultural influences from abroad".

It is not controversial that many Middle Eastern scripts, even though they are sometimes structurally and visually very different from one another, are linked by chains of cultural borrowing (and the Roman and other European alphabets certainly came from the Middle East). We shall often encounter such relationships in later chapters. Standardly, Chinese writing would be seen as a clear case of a system that developed quite independently of western Asia. However, the two ends of Asia are connected by land and we know that there was coming and going between them from an early date (see e.g. Mair 1990: 43–4), and furthermore the beginnings of Chinese script are completely lost from the archaeological record. So, even though the nature of Chinese script seems very different from Middle Eastern systems, conceivably it might ultimately have derived from one of them.

Until late in the 20c, the debate would have had to be left there. By now, though, the argument against monogenesis is conclusive. What has changed the situation is the decipherment of the Maya script of Central America.

The inscribed stone monuments of the Maya civilization, which peaked in the period from about +200 to +900 and was based in and around the Yucatán peninsula, have been known for centuries. An example is illustrated in Figure 11: "Stela 3" at Piedras Negras, on the Guatemala–Mexico border. But although attempts at decipherment began at an early date, until recently there was not even a consensus that these carvings were writing at all. Recognition of them as such was long delayed particularly by the influence of the British Mayanist Sir Eric Thompson, who until his death in 1975 insisted that they were merely stylized illustrations of Maya gods and myths.

Thompson was mistaken. While not every last detail of Maya script is yet understood, so much has now been successfully deciphered that there is no doubt left that this is indeed writing.[5] The inscription of Figure 11, for instance, is an account of events in the life of a powerful queen, Lady K'atun Ahaw, born 7 July +674 at a place called *Man*. (Classical Maya culture was obsessively concerned with dates and calendrical matters. They used a very elaborate calendar whose "Day 1" fell as far back as 13 August −3114 in our terms – some readers may remember that the Maya Great Cycle which began on that day ended on 23 December +2012, leading some gullible people to expect an apocalypse which did not materialize.) Furthermore, although Maya script was the most fully developed writing system of Central America, its ancestry can be traced much further back in that region. According to Julia Guernsey (2006: 10), the original development of the script tradition "must have taken place ... during the Middle Preclassic period [about −900 to −300] at the very latest".

Maya script used a mixture of logographic and syllabic (CV) symbols, grouped into squares (identified in Figure 11 by letters and numbers) which are arranged left to right and downwards in pairs of columns. Take for example the clause which is written in squares E1 F1 E2 F2 E3 F3 E4. The clause runs, in Maya:

> Holuhum, waxak winikihi, ux tuni, iwal ut buluch imix chan-luhum yaxk'in u ch'amuwa lom na k'atun ahaw nana man ahaw.[6]

In English:

> Day-count 14 k'ins, 8 winals, 3 tuns: it came to pass on day 11 Imix 14 Yax that Lady K'atun Ahaw, Matron from *Man*, grasped the staff.

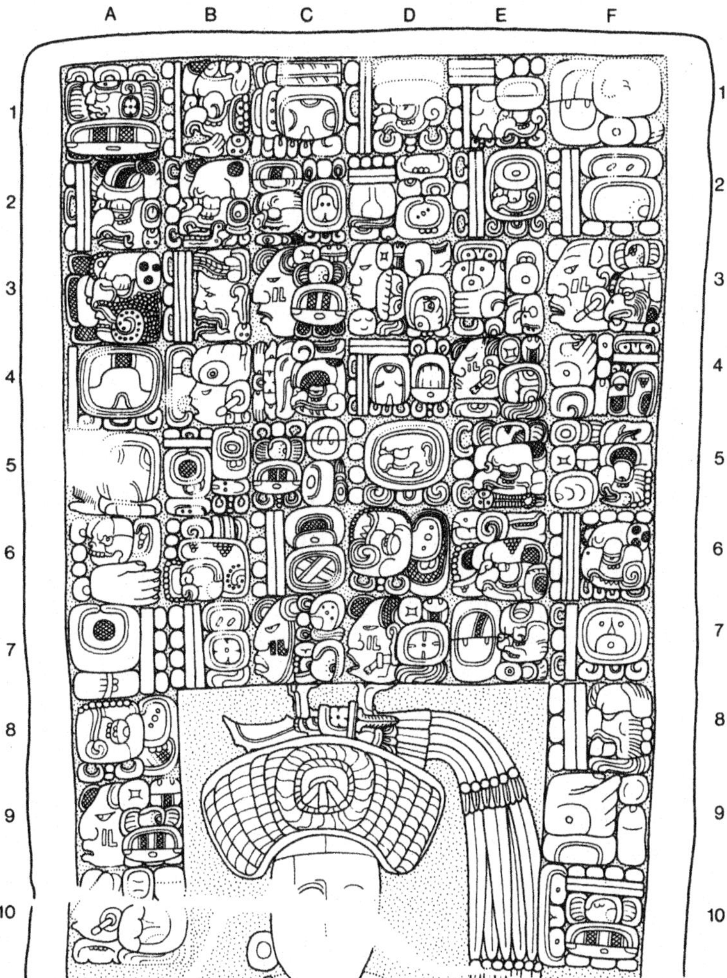

Figure 11

"Grasping the staff" was a ritual ceremony. The date given corresponds to a day in year 711 of our era.

Square E3 reads *u ch'amuwa lom*, "she grasped the staff". (The conventional spelling *ch'* represents an ejective affricate, in the IPA system [tʃ'].) Within this symbol group, the recognizable open-hand element with a face squeezed between thumb and fingers is a logograph for the root *ch'am-*, "grasp", but other elements are phonographic. At top left, stands for /u/, a syllable with zero consonant. is /mu/; is /wa/. In the right-hand section of the group, the word *lom*, "staff", is written purely phonographically: is /lo/, is a fuller version of the sign for /mu/. (The script had no signs for closed syllables, i.e. ones ending in consonants, so a final consonant had to be written by supplying a redundant extra vowel.) Thus we have /u CH'AM-mu-wa lo-m(u)/. (It is conventional to transcribe logograms in capitals and phonographic elements in lower case.)

This is a sophisticated system, which probably enabled Maya scribes to write anything in their language that they wanted to write. And it is not seriously possible to suggest that writing could have been taken from the Old World to Central America in the middle of the –1st millennium, more than a thousand years before anyone is known to have crossed the Atlantic. Clearly, writing arose independently in Central America. The monogenetic hypothesis is wrong.

* * *

If writing has been invented more than once, then there is little reason to doubt that there have been some independent inventions even in cases where geography did not rule out the possibility of cultural contacts. The Linear B script examined in the next chapter, for instance, was used in the eastern Mediterranean, not far from where other writing systems were in use; but it appears quite separate from them, and very likely it was.

Nevertheless, the situation with scripts is different from the situation with spoken languages. Even in the modern world there are thousands of living languages, and they belong to dozens of unrelated language families. Spoken language seems to have emerged on many separate occasions in the prehistory of our species. (A few scholars have argued for monogenesis with respect to spoken language, but that idea is purely speculative; if it was so, then language-families have diverged so much since the hypothetical common origin that all traces of relationship have been lost.) On the other hand there are far fewer different scripts than different languages, and although writing has evidently been invented more than once it may not have been independently invented very many times.

This creates what is probably the largest problem in extending the techniques of scientific linguistics to the study of writing. In linguistics we would like not just to examine individual facts for their own sake but, where possible, to draw generalizations. With the linguistics of spoken language that is fairly easy to do. If something seems to be generally true among the widely studied European languages, that might be merely because the ancestral Indo-European language just happened to possess that property and it has survived in the present-day descendant languages. But there are plenty of other language families to check the generalization against. If we find that the generalization also holds for Chinese, and Fijian, and Zulu, and Cherokee, then (provided the feature in question is not something borrowed between languages recently, such as a word for a piece of modern technology) we may be pretty safe to infer that it is a true linguistic generalization. In the case of writing systems we can hardly ever do this: there are too few independent examples to make generalizations thoroughly reliable.

That is an unavoidable constraint on this branch of linguistics. But any scholarly endeavour has to contend with limitations. The study of writing systems is too interesting a topic to give up on just because the data are not as ideally rich as we might like. As this book develops, I believe readers will not feel any shortage of worthwhile findings.

Notes

1. Another Sumerologist, Dietz Otto Edzard (1968: 167), did not believe it was possible to give such a precise translation, but Edzard did not call into question Driver's account of the general nature of the script.
2. It is true that Blissymbolics, which I quoted as the best example of semasiographic script, is itself written in linear sequences. But that is surely a consequence of the fact that it was invented by someone who was already thoroughly accustomed to linear alphabetic writing.
3. Arno Poebel (1923: 10–11) argued that the role of the phonographic principle in Sumerian Cuneiform was much greater than this, but his interpretation has not found favour with more recent experts. Civil (1973: 26–7) gave statistical details of the relative proportions of logographic and phonographic writing in various Sumerian texts.
4. Zimansky (1993) also credits a paper published in the same year by Maurice Lambert, which I have not seen.
5. For a highly readable account of the decipherment, see Coe (1992); for detail on how the script works, see Kettunen and Helmke (2011).
6. Maya is a living language today, although the script was suppressed when Maya civilization was destroyed by the Spanish conquistadores in the 16c. This transcription is given in modern Chol Maya; some details of pronunciation will have differed in the Classical period.

4 A syllabic system: Linear B

Cuneiform script was a complex system which rather untidily combined various orthographic principles in differing proportions at different stages of its history. In this chapter we shall look at an orthography that was much more neatly logical: the "Linear B" script used to write an early form of the Greek language during part of the –2nd millennium, well before the Greeks first encountered alphabetic writing. Linear B is an interesting script for two reasons: first, because it is a relatively pure example of syllabic writing, and second because it is a highly "incomplete" script (in the sense defined on pp. 27–8), while at the same time being quite systematic and consistent within its own limitations. (Linear B is also the earliest European script that we know how to read.)

Linear B was used, probably from about the –16c to the –13c, for record-keeping purposes by the civil service of the "Mycenaean" civilization which then flourished in southern Greece. Early in the –2nd millennium a civilization now called "Minoan", speaking an unknown language, had grown up in Crete, and used a script known as "Linear A" (which remains largely unintelligible). The Mycenaeans derived much of their culture from the Minoans (until they conquered Crete in about –1450), and the Linear B script seems to have been created as an adaptation of Linear A to the Greek language. Linear B ceased to be used when the Mycenaean cities were destroyed in about –1250, possibly by invaders from the sea. (However, a syllabic script distantly related to Linear B was used to write Greek on Cyprus in the Classical period.)

Linear B was written on unbaked clay tablets – the examples we have are those that were baked when the palaces burned down around them. From the subtle, curvilinear shapes of the graphs (contrast Cuneiform) it seems possible that Linear B may also have been written with pen and ink or the like, but if so no direct evidence survives. It appears that the tablets which have come down to us are temporary files dating to the last year before the destruction of each archive, and the information would perhaps have been transferred annually to more permanent records which have not survived. It is fascinating to observe that some of the tablets appear to record troop movements and civilian evacuation measures in anticipation of an invasion.

Linear B was deciphered in 1952 by an English architect, Michael Ventris, with the help of a classics scholar, John Chadwick. It had previously been thought unlikely that the language of Linear B was Greek; Ventris discovered that it was, although (naturally) an archaic form of Greek. (For comparison, the oldest Greek literature, the Homeric *Iliad* and *Odyssey*, is thought to have been fixed in the form we know towards −700, and the classical Attic Greek that modern schoolchildren are taught represents a period eight to ten centuries later than the Linear B tablets.)

The story of the decipherment has much of the excitement of a detective thriller – it has been recounted for a general readership by Chadwick himself (1958), and more recently by Margalit Fox (2013).[1]

All the Linear B inscriptions we have are administrative records. To give the reader an impression, the best thing will be to display a sample. Figure 12 shows the first line of tablet PY Ta722, which inventories a series of four footstools decorated in various ways. In the Figure the actual inscription is set in a regularized modern Linear B font (writing on the real-life tablets is not so neat); words are separated by short vertical ticks. The next line gives the conventional transliterations of the individual graphs, and the third line is a phonemic transcription of the Mycenaean Greek words which the graphs represent. The English translation is *A footstool inlaid with a man and a horse and an octopus and a palm-tree in ivory: FOOTSTOOL 1.* One of the Mycenaean Greek words, < a-ja-me-no >, is not known independently though in the Linear B corpus it is frequent; the meaning "inlaid" is deduced from context, but the precise pronunciation lying behind the spelling can only be conjectured. However, all the other words are known – not only from Classical Greek, but indeed from English too. The first word is related ultimately to *throne*; the other words result from adding a case ending and (in the latter words) a suffix meaning "and" to roots which, in their Classical form, give English *elephant*, *anthrop-* (as in *anthropology*), *hippo-* (as in *hippopotamus*, "horse of the river"), *polypod-* (many feet), and *Phoenic-* (the Greeks associated date palms with the Phoenicians).

* * *

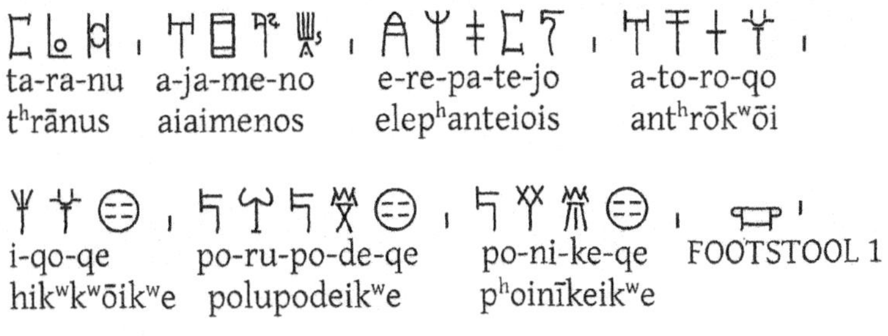

ta-ra-nu	a-ja-me-no	e-re-pa-te-jo	a-to-ro-qo
t^{h}rānus	aiaimenos	elep^{h}anteiois	ant^{h}rōk^{w}ōi

i-qo-qe	po-ru-po-de-qe	po-ni-ke-qe	FOOTSTOOL 1
hik^{w}k^{w}ōik^{w}e	polupodeik^{w}e	p^{h}oinīkeik^{w}e	

Figure 12

A first point to explain is that as well as phonographic script, Linear B used a range of logographic symbols (Mycenaeanists call them "ideograms"). These are graphs standing individually for objects of the kinds inventoried by the tablets, such as "footstool" here (other logograph values include "sheep", "man", "barley", "gold", etc.), or for units of measurement comparable to our "gallon", "bushel", etc. They are used, in conjunction with numeral signs, to enable the reader to take in at a glance the general category of items described in detail in the phonographic text. Linear B "ideograms" seem to serve the same function as the modern military habit of listing items with the head noun at the beginning of its phrase: where we might write "6 cups, blue, china, tea, officers for the use of", a Mycenaean scribe would have written something like "Blue china teacups for the use of officers: CUP 6".

Our concern is with the phonographic side of the script, which accounts for the overwhelming bulk of the inscriptions. This uses a set of about ninety graphs, a few of which are too rare for their values to be known for sure; most stand for CV syllables, where the C and the V are drawn from sets conventionally represented respectively as /d j k m n p q r s t w z Ø/ and /a e i o u/. There are also a few exceptional graphs standing for other values, to be discussed later.[2] Unlike the ideograms, many of which (like FOOTSTOOL) are clearly motivated, most of the Linear B syllabic graphs seem purely arbitrary. Where a pictorial motif is recognizable, it does not link in any obvious way to a Greek word for the thing pictured, which is unsurprising if the values of the graphs derive from an earlier script (Linear A) used for another language.

The script is syllabic in the full sense – that is, there is nothing in common among the shapes of graphs for different syllables sharing the same consonant, or sharing the same vowel. Note, in Figure 12, that the graphs labelled /ta te to/ do not resemble one another, and likewise for those labelled /pa/ and /po/. To strengthen the point, Figure 13 displays the full set of /k-/ graphs, and the full set of /-i/ graphs. (There are no known graphs for /ji/ or /zi/, probably because these were not possible syllables in Mycenaean Greek – /ji/ might not have been heard as distinct from /i/.)

ka ke ki ko ku

i di ki mi ni pi qi ri si ti wi

Figure 13

The point that Linear B is fully syllabic is worth making, because scripts are often called "syllabic" which in terms of Chapter 2 are nothing of the kind. Thus, compare Figure 14, which shows a sample of the 182 graphs of the Ethiopic script. The Ethiopic graphs are "syllabic" rather than segmental in the sense that each physically continuous written mark stands for a syllable; but the shape of the graphs is determined by the segmental composition of the syllables, so that syllables beginning with a particular consonant share the same basic outline and each vowel is indicated by a consistent method of modifying the consonantal outline; /a/ is indicated by absence of modification. In the full inventory of Ethiopic graphs there are a few exceptions to this system, but in essence the Ethiopic writing system is a segmental script in which segments are encoded as features of graphs rather than as independent, spatially disconnected marks.

* * *

Mycenaean Greek had considerably more than just twelve consonants and five vowels. The script ignored many of the distinctions that were contrastive in the language for which it was used. That is what I meant by calling it an "incomplete" system. The phonographic components of Sumerian or Akkadian Cuneiform, for that matter, were "incomplete" in the sense that many syllables had no graph and were written with combinations of graphs for other syllables, and that various groups of phonologically similar syllables were written with the same graph. But in Cuneiform script there was no particular logic that decided which syllables had graphs and which did not, and the methods used to spell syllables lacking their own graphs were fairly ad hoc and diverse. Linear B was not like that. The range of phonological contrasts encoded in the script was a neat,

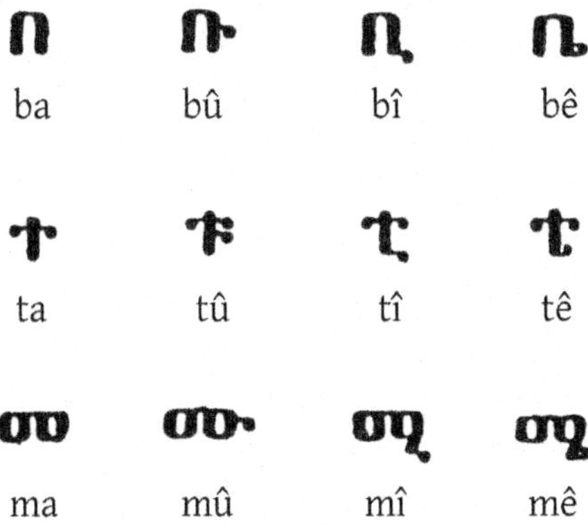

Figure 14

logical subset of the range of contrasts found in the spoken language, and the orthographic rules were likewise rather simple and straightforward.

Figure 15 offers a reconstruction of the phonological inventory of Mycenaean Greek (about which much was known independently of the Linear B evidence). "Suprasegmental" matters such as stress are necessarily ignored; and various details of the segmental phonology are open to question – for instance Mycenaean Greek may already have had the distinction between half-open and half-close long vowels which developed in Attic (that is, the dialect of the Athens region), and it probably had a long/short contrast in some but not all diphthongs. The symbols /k^{wh} k^{w} g^{w}/ stand for "labio-velars" – probably realized as velar stops co-articulated with lip rounding. In later Greek these changed into other consonants (labials or dentals, depending on environment), and /w/ disappeared; thus we have Mycenaean /hi$k^{w}k^{w}$os/ "horse" (cf. Latin *equus*) corresponding to Classical Greek *hippos*, Mycenaean /wanaks/ "king" corresponding to Classical *anax*, etc.[3] The symbol /z/ is used conventionally for the phoneme symbolized in the Greek alphabet as zeta, ζ. In Modern Greek this is pronounced /z/ but in Ancient Greek it was probably a more complex sound, perhaps the affricate /dz/.[4] The symbol Ø is included in the consonant table in order to make the point that a word can begin with no consonant at all, as in English. (The /h/ symbol in the same column also relates only to word-initial position; because [h] occurred nowhere else in Greek, it was not regarded by Greeks of the Classical period as a separate phoneme but rather the h/Ø contrast was treated as a distinction between two ways of pronouncing words beginning with vowels.)

Except possibly for the distinction between [j] and Ø, all the distinctions in Figure 15 were contrastive; no pairs of sounds listed were mere allophonic variants of one another. When [j] occurred, it was commonly just a glide produced automatically by the transition from an /i/ to a following vowel (e.g. /hiereus/ "priest" was heard as [hijereus]). There are a few cases where [j] seems to have occurred other than following /i/, in which case it would have had phonemic status (e.g. /jō/ "thus", /mewjōn/ "lesser"); but the uncertainties of the transcriptions are such that it might be rash to claim a phoneme /j/ on the basis of these few examples. In English, unaspirated voiceless stops are allophonic alternants of aspirated stops; but in Mycenaean Greek, as in Classical Greek, /p^{h}/ and /p/, and the other aspirated/unaspirated pairs, were entirely separate phonemes (e.g. a minimal pair from Classical Greek is /ponos/ "toil" versus /p^{h}onos/ "murder").

The set of Linear B syllable symbols was mapped onto the much larger range of Mycenaean Greek syllables in accordance with the following

Vowels

pure

ĭ ī		ŭ ū
ĕ ē		ŏ ō
	ă ā	

diphthongs

ei eu		oi ou
	ai au	

Consonants

p^h	t^h	k^h	k^{wh}	h
p	t	k	k^w	Ø
b	d	g	g^w	
m	n			
	(j)			w
	s			
	l			
	r			
	z			

Figure 15

conventions. Normally, the aspirated/unaspirated contrast was ignored (in Figure 12, notice that both /t^h/ and /t/ are spelled with graphs transliterated with < t >, and similarly for /p^h/ and /p/); and similarly the sound /h/ was ignored. (This rule had minor exceptions: one of the exceptional graphs could optionally be used instead of < a > to represent /ha/, and another could optionally be used instead of < pu > to represent /p^hu/.) Also, the voiced/voiceless distinction was unrecorded except among the dentals – /d/ syllables were distinguished from /t, t^h/ syllables, but /b g g^w/ were equated with /p^h p/, /k^h k/, and /k^{wh} k^w/ respectively. (The two phonemes /s/ and /z/ were kept separate, but we saw above that /z/, however it was pronounced, was not a voiced counterpart to /s/.) The distinction between the liquids /l r/ was ignored. Length was ignored both in vowels (e.g. /ĕ/ and /ē/ were treated as identical) and in consonants (e.g. the geminate /ss/ was not distinguished from /s/).

Thus when, in Figure 12, three graphs are shown with the conventional transliterations < a, pa, ra >, this really means that the first stands for an open vowel of unspecified length with or without a preceding /h/; that the second stands for an unspecified bilabial stop followed by an open vowel; and that the last stands for an unspecified liquid followed by an open vowel. It would be equally appropriate to transliterate the two latter signs as < ba la >, but it happens to have become conventional in Mycenaean scholarship to represent stops of unspecified manner of articulation as voiceless unaspirated stops, and unspecified liquids as < r > rather than < l >. Likewise, < q > is conventionally used to represent any of the three labio-velar stops.

Furthermore, although almost all the graphs stand for simple CV syllables, the language had many syllables that were more complex. Consequently, there had to be rules for converting spoken words into written form.

As one might expect, there was some variation among alternative scribal conventions, and the extant texts also contain cases that seem to have been downright mistakes on the scribe's part. But the following rules come fairly close to being a complete and general statement of the Linear B orthographic conventions.

Consider first the treatment of diphthongs. This depends on their final vowel. Diphthongs in /-u/ are treated as sequences of two vowels; for example, /g^{w}asileus/ "chief" (Classical Greek *basileus*, "king") is written < qa-si-re-u >. With diphthongs in /-i/ the /i/ is ignored (e.g. /poimēn/ "shepherd" is < po-me >). But that does not mean that /-i/ diphthongs are never distinguished in writing from pure vowels; whenever such a diphthong is followed by another vowel, this is written with the graph for the corresponding /j-/ syllable, e.g. /palaios/ "old" is < pa-ra-jo >. (Likewise /-u/ diphthongs followed by a vowel give writings in < w- >, e.g. /kuanos/ "lapis lazuli" is < ku-wa-no >.) Two of the exceptional graphs can be used for the diphthongs /ai/, /au/ just when they begin a word, so /aiwolos/ "nimble" can be written either < ai-wo-ro > or < a-wo-ro >. (Oddly, there is also a special graph for the syllable < rai >.)

The spelling of a consonant which immediately precedes a vowel is straightforward. But when a consonant in speech either precedes another consonant or is word-final, its treatment depends on whether it is a continuant (one of /s m n r l w/) or a stop.

If it is a stop, it is written by "borrowing" the next vowel to make a CV syllable; e.g. /ktoinā/ "plot of land" is < ko-to-na >, /ptelewās/ "of elm-wood" = < pe-te-re-wa >, /aksones/ "axles" = < a-ko-so-ne >, /tripos/ "tripod" = < ti-ri-po >, /alektruōn/ "cock" = < a-re-ku-tu-ru-wo >. If there is no following vowel, then it seems (though examples are too few to be sure that this is a general rule) that the preceding vowel is used: /wanaks/

"king" = < wa-na-ka >, /ait^{h}iok^{w}s/ "sunburnt" (the root from which we get the name *Ethiopia*, after the labiovelar had become a bilabial – Greeks took Africans to be heavily suntanned) = < ai-ti-jo-qo >.

On the other hand, when a continuant consonant has no immediately following vowel, it is written with a "borrowed" vowel only if the next sound is a sonorant (one of /m n r l w/). A continuant consonant at the end of a word, or followed by an obstruent (a stop or /s/) is simply omitted. The only consonants which can occur word-finally in Greek, namely /n r s/, are continuants, so no consonant that is word-final in speech is noted in Linear B. (See "tripod" and "shepherd" above, or /patēr/ "father" = < pa-te >.) Examples of continuants omitted before obstruents are: /p^{h}asgana/ "swords" = < pa-ka-na >, /worzōn/ "performing" = < wo-zo >, /k^{h}alkos/ "bronze" = < ka-ko >, /aiksmans/ "points" = < ai-ka-sa-ma >. (In the last example /n/ is omitted as preceding the obstruent /s/, which is itself omitted as word-final.) Examples of continuants written with borrowed vowel before sonorants are: /amnīsos/, a place name = < a-mi-ni-so >, /dosmos/ "contribution" = < do-so-mo >, /wrīnos/ "leather" = < wi-ri-no >, /ksenwios/ "intended for guests" = < ke-se-ni-wi-jo >.

One would obviously like to know whether there is any rationale for the rules about when a consonant is omitted and when it is written with a borrowed vowel. A rule which comes close to matching the diverse data would be: consonants are written (if necessary, with borrowed vowels) whenever they precede the vowel of their syllable, and are omitted whenever they follow the vowel of their syllable. Greek permits stops to cluster rather freely with other following consonants, so in a sequence "vowel + stop + consonant + vowel" the syllable-boundary will normally precede the stop, hence this will be included in the Linear B spelling. (For instance, /aksones/ "axles" is syllabified /a\$kso\$nes/ because in Greek /ks-/ is a permitted, indeed common, initial cluster – hence the many Greek-derived words in English that begin with *x*, e.g. *xylophone* from /ksulon/ "wood".) One might query the spelling < a-re-ku-tu-ru-wo > for /alektruōn/: it is true that /ktr-/ is not a possible Greek initial cluster, but on the other hand /kt-/ is possible (e.g. /ktoinā/ "plot of land"), whereas /-k -kt -ktr/ are all quite impossible in word-*final* position, so /a\$le\$ktru\$ōn/ seems the most appropriate syllable-division, and this correctly predicts the Linear B spelling < -ku-tu-ru- >.

There are two things wrong with this rule as it stands. It predicts that no element of word-final consonant clusters should be written, but we have seen that e.g. /wanaks/ "king" is < wa-na-ka >, not *< wa-na >. A possible explanation is that, since the general rule led to the overwhelming majority of stops being written, the rule was expanded to require all stops to be written – the only stops which would have been omitted under the simpler rule are those in the word-final clusters /-ks -k^{w}s -ps/. Also, the rule does not explain why /s-/ is ignored before an obstruent, as it consistently is: e.g. /sperma/ "seed" = < pe-ma >, /stat^{h}mos/ "farmstead" = < ta-to-mo >, or /ksunstrok^{wh}ā/ "aggregate" = < ku-su-to-ro-qa >, where the syllable division must surely be immediately after the /n/. These two points must be accepted as departures from the rule in its most general form. Thus, the rule I would actually defend is: a consonant other than a stop is omitted if it occurs after the vowel of its syllable, and /s/ is omitted if it immediately precedes a stop. All other consonants are written, with a borrowed vowel if necessary.

There are exceptions even to this more complex rule in the corpus of Linear B inscriptions. For instance /ararmotmenā/ "fitted together" is written < a-ra-ro-mo-te-me-na >, but there is a syllable boundary after /arar-/, so the < ro > graph should not appear. I assume that cases like this were exceptions or "mistakes" (if the concept of spelling mistakes was meaningful for Mycenaean scribes).

* * *

One thing that has struck scholars about the Linear B script is that it seems oddly ill-adapted to write the Greek language for which it was used. Not only does it ignore many phonetic contrasts which were central to the phonology of Mycenaean Greek, but (as mentioned above) it has additional graphs which seem redundant. Some of these, representing < ai au rai ha p^{h}u >, do at least fit the sound pattern of the language, though it is not obvious why these particular syllables should merit having special graphs provided for them. But the majority of the known exceptional graphs do not even seem as Greek-oriented as this. Their values are < nwa pte tja twe two dwe dwo rjo rja >: all except /pte/ are combinations of a consonant with a /j/ or /w/ semivowel (and it is known that Greek /pt/ often developed from an earlier /pj/, so perhaps < pte > originally had the value < pje >). In Greek [j] was normally just an automatic glide between vowels with marginal phonemic status, and it is not clear whether Mycenaean Greek actually had /Cj/ clusters; the graph transcribed < tja > seems to have been used in practice to transcribe pairs of syllables as an alternative to < ti-ja >. And even in the pre-Classical Greek which still contained a /w/ sound, it was a rare one.

Our own alphabet has a redundant letter X standing for a pair of consonants /ks/ which do not function as a unit (and do not occur particularly frequently together) in western European languages, because we inherited the letter from an earlier alphabet used for a different language. It may be that the odd fit between the Linear B syllabary and Mycenaean

Greek phonology stems from the fact that Linear B was not created from scratch as a script for that language, but was developed from a pre-existing system (Linear A, or some lost common ancestor-script) which had been developed to write the sounds of a quite different "Minoan" language. L.R. Palmer (1963: 36ff.) suggested that much of what seems puzzling in the Linear B system would fall into place if we suppose that the unknown Minoan language was one in which the important manner distinctions among consonants involved secondary articulations of palatalization and lip-rounding, rather than voice and aspiration. That is, Minoan would have been a language in which each plain consonant, for instance /t/, contrasted with a palatal counterpart /tj/ and with a labialized counterpart /tw/ – whereas voicing and aspiration either did not occur at all, or were mere subphonemic "noise" playing no distinctive role in the language. (Palmer also urged that a good guess for the pronunciation of the phoneme transcribed as /z/ would be a palatalized velar, /k^j/, which would strengthen this idea.) Someone designing a syllabic script for Greek from scratch would scarcely have provided a graph for /tia/, but if a < t^ja > graph existed ready-made it is understandable that scribes would have used it on occasion as an alternative to < ti-ja > in order to write /tia/.

Partly for these phonological reasons, Palmer suggested that a plausible hypothesis about the identity of "Minoan" would identify it with Luwian; and this suggestion is broadly supported by recent research (e.g. Finkelberg 2005: 52–4). Luwian was a member of the long-extinct Anatolian branch of the Indo-European language family; in historical times it was spoken in various parts of what is now Turkey, but it is believed to have been spoken earlier over a much wider area of the eastern Mediterranean (on Luwian people and language, see Mouton *et al.* 2013). The suggestion is that the population who inhabited what became Greece, before the Greeks arrived from the north, were Luwian speakers.

* * *

Whether or not that is right, it remains true that Linear B was a particularly "incomplete" script with respect to the contrasts which were important to the phonology of Mycenaean Greek. As a result, there are usually many different ways of reading any short sequence of Linear B graphs. Consider e.g. the pair < pa-te >. This occurs in the tablets with at least two readings: /patēr/ "father", /pantes/ "all". Many other readings are phonologically possible: /bat^{h}ē/, /p^{h}antes/, /pāstēn/, and so on; probably one or two at least of the further possibilities would correspond to actual words of Mycenaean Greek. How could such an incomplete script have been usable in practice?

It may be that a system incorporating the degree of ambiguity found in Linear B would not be usable as the general purpose tool of communication which written language became in later ages. Certainly, so far as our knowledge of it extends, Linear B was used only for specialized administrative purposes, and would have been read in circumstances which supplied strong contextual clues to meaning. The reader knows that a tablet will describe tenancies if he takes it from a basket full of tenancy records. Given the "ideogram" for FOOTSTOOL in Figure 12, it is evident that the reader of that tablet would have had no difficulty in reading < ta-ra-nu > as /t^{h}rānus/ "footstool" rather than any of the other theoretical possibilities. Some of the other words might seem less predictable; but even there, if the function of this tablet was as a check on a set of objects meant to be kept in a certain place, presumably one would normally inspect the objects and then check them off against the tablet, which would greatly reduce the problems of interpreting the latter.

For many years after Ventris's decipherment, the incompleteness of the script led a number of sceptics to reject it. They felt that Ventris and Chadwick were playing a hand with too many jokers; if the proposed decipherment allowed a given Linear B graph to represent so many different Greek syllables, they argued that it would always be possible to twist some Greek meaning out of a given sequence of graphs, even if the graph-values were assigned at random. That type of scepticism later faded away, because an objection which might have some force when only a few inscriptions had been read loses that force as more and more inscriptions turn out to yield good Greek, saying things that made sense in terms of the "ideograms" which accompany the phonographic writing. But although the decipherment is now firmly established, it remains true that the script is strikingly "incomplete".

However, it is dangerous to assume, because Linear B was much less complete than modern scripts, that it must have been impractical for speakers of Mycenaean Greek to use it except in circumstances where context gave many clues to message content. After all, Ventris and Chadwick succeeded in reading the inscription of Figure 12, and they not only did not have the footstool to help them but were not even familiar with the language except via dialects of it which were many centuries younger. Chadwick (1958: 131) mentioned that he and Ventris succeeded in writing postcards to one another in Linear B. A.J.B. Wace, in a foreword to Ventris and Chadwick (1956), went so far as to say that "so elaborate a system of writing cannot have been employed only for recording inventories of goods or payments of taxes ... the Linear B script was probably also used for letters, treaties and even literary texts".

If so, sixty years later no trace of such uses has yet shown up. And it is not as clear to me as it was to Wace that the complexity of the system supports the view that Linear B actually was used for a wide range of communicative purposes. There are too many known examples of communities that possess quite sophisticated scripts while using them only for very limited purposes to make that conclusion safe. But I am inclined to agree with Wace that Linear B *could* potentially have been used more widely, despite its incompleteness. It is just not clear how complete a writing system has to be, in order to be usable as a general-purpose communication medium.

Some would argue that we only see Linear B as an impoverished system because we compare it with the strikingly sophisticated alphabetic script later used to write the same language. Barry Powell (1991: 68 n. 2) sees Linear B as "an advanced writing system ... [it] may not do the job that we expect of writing, but it did a far better job of recording Greek than, for example, Egyptian hieroglyphic did of recording Egyptian."

My guess, for what it is worth, is that we can manage with much *less* completeness than one might naively suppose. Readers are skilled at resolving ambiguities in a written text by reference to the rest of the text, without needing to refer to features of the external world within which the text is located. We shall see in the next chapter that Semitic writing, which is in widespread use for general purposes in the 21c, is strikingly incomplete by comparison to modern European orthographies (though less so than Linear B). It would not surprise me to find that novels could be written and read in Linear B (though perhaps the reader of a Linear B text might need to put rather more unconscious mental effort in than the reader of an alphabetically written equivalent, just as reading handwriting is presumably harder work than reading print). Unfortunately, there seems to be no way to test how much incompleteness in a writing system is tolerable in practice. Becoming a skilled user of a script takes years, and one cannot ask people to acquire such skills merely for the purpose of a psycholinguistic experiment.

If my guess about the usability of Linear B is correct, it suggests a sobering thought: our own writing system is inherited from the Greeks. If Mycenaean civilization had not collapsed in the −13c, and if Greece had been spared the several-centuries-long Dark Age which followed, perhaps the Greeks would have had little use for the Semitic alphabet when they eventually encountered it. I might now be writing this book, and you reading it, in a syllabic script derived from Linear B. The idea of an alphabetic script of just a couple of dozen graphs could have been a curiosity restricted to the Middle East.

Notes

1. On Michael Ventris, who died in a car crash not long after achieving the decipherment, see Robinson (2002). A concise account of the script is Chadwick (1987), and his "Bibliographical note" is a guide to the leading items in the fuller scholarly literature. On Mycenaean civilization in general see Chadwick (1976).
2. For the complete range of Linear B syllabic graphs see e.g. www.omniglot.com/writing/linearb.html (accessed 22 March 2014).
3. Since short vowels are much commoner than long vowels in Greek, when quoting examples I shall mark long vowels but leave short vowels unmarked in this chapter and in Chapter 6.
4. Alternatively, rather than /dz/ this element may have been a consonant cluster /zd/. The debate about this is summarized in the Wikipedia article "Zeta" (accessed 22 March 2014).

5 Consonantal writing

We saw in Chapter 3 that monogenesis – the idea that all scripts everywhere in the world derive ultimately from a single common ancestor – cannot be true. However, if we restrict our vision to the segmental subtype of phonographic writing, then monogenesis becomes the correct theory. All "alphabetic" scripts derive from one ultimate ancestor: the Semitic alphabet.

The term "Semitic" refers to one of the branches of the larger "Afro-Asiatic" or "Hamito-Semitic" family of languages, members of which are spoken from the Levant westwards to the Atlas and southwards as far as Nigeria, Ethiopia, and Somalia. The Semitic branch itself (on which see Goldenberg 2013) includes a number of individual languages, two of the best-known being Arabic and Hebrew. The script from which all alphabets descend is called "Semitic" because the main thing we know about its creators is that they spoke a Semitic language (possibly Phoenician), and because certain structural properties of the script were influenced by properties of Semitic spoken languages.

The most important of those structural properties is that the original version, and some modern descendants, of the script have graphs for consonants but no vowel letters. We shall see why the nature of Semitic languages makes that appropriate. Obviously, many alphabets which ultimately descend from the original Semitic alphabet, including our Roman alphabet, do now have vowel letters. It will be convenient to reserve the term "Semitic script" for the original Semitic alphabet, together with those of its descendants which still lack letters for vowels (of which the main ones are the modern Hebrew and Arabic scripts). Hebrew and Arabic scripts remain very similar to their common ancestor, except for the outward shapes of the graphs (in the latter respect Hebrew and Arabic scripts have diverged greatly from their ancestral form and from each other). In this chapter we shall be examining "Semitic script" in this sense. But bear in mind that, applied to a form of writing, the term "Semitic" is only a handy label. There is no implication that Semitic languages are all written in "Semitic" script, or that "Semitic" script is used to write only Semitic languages. Akkadian was a Semitic language, but (as we saw in Chapter 3) it was written in Cuneiform, which was not an alphabetic script. Maltese is a modern Semitic language written in the Roman alphabet. Conversely, Arabic script is used to write many non-Semitic languages, such as Persian (an Indo-European language) and, until 1928, Turkish (an Altaic language); and Hebrew script is used to write Yiddish, a dialect of German.

To investigate the detailed workings of Semitic script we must choose one particular Semitic language as an illustration. I do not want to give readers the impression that the various types of script discussed in this book are of mainly antiquarian interest. Vowel-less Semitic writing is widely used in the 21c world, being the normal form of writing in many nations including some of the wealthiest. It is tempting, therefore, to choose modern Arabic or modern Hebrew to exemplify the system.

However, our natural inclination to focus on present-day languages is counterbalanced by the fact that orthographies tend to be "cleanest" and most straightforward to expound when recently devised. In the Semitic case, to choose modern Israeli Hebrew as our example language would require us to deal with many complexities stemming from the complex history of Hebrew since Biblical times. As a colloquial spoken language, Hebrew died out around −250, though it continued (and has never ceased) to develop as a literary language; it was artificially revived as a spoken language in the 19c by members of the Zionist movement. Modern Hebrew (on which see e.g. Schwarzwald 2001) is phonetically simpler than Biblical Hebrew (it has fewer sounds), but phonologically it is arguably more complex, and it is certainly much more complex in terms of the relationship between spoken sounds and orthography (since it has retained Biblical orthography largely unchanged despite major changes in the spoken language). Readers would not wish to be burdened with unravelling the many complications in modern Hebrew orthography which can be explained only with respect to an earlier form of the language. And to opt for Arabic would introduce other unnecessary complications.

I have therefore chosen to discuss Biblical Hebrew, as the best available compromise between these considerations. By "Biblical Hebrew" I refer to the pronunciation of written Hebrew as fixed about +900 by the "Masoretic" editors of the Old Testament. Biblical Hebrew in this sense represents an attempt to analyse and record the pronunciation of spoken Hebrew as it was before it became extinct. (On the status of Biblical Hebrew as a language see Ullendorff 1971.)

Although Biblical Hebrew is in a sense a somewhat artificial language, there is nothing artificial or unrealistic about the general kind of writing to be discussed here. As a written language this language is in daily use as the standard language of Israel, though Israeli pronunciation is different from the pronunciation we shall examine.[1] The orthographic principles of written Arabic are fundamentally the same as those of Hebrew, although different in detail. Biblical Hebrew – which from now on I shall call simply "Hebrew" and discuss in the present tense – happens to offer a pedagogically convenient example of a type of writing which is one of the most significant types in use today.

* * *

The Semitic alphabet seems to have originated in the Palestine area some time in the −2nd millennium (though see p. 100 below); the earliest readable inscription of more than two or three words in this alphabet is now thought to date to about −1000 (Millard 1986: 390). In its Hebrew version the alphabet is a set of 22 symbols which represent consonants on the *acrophonic* principle: each symbol appears to have begun as a simple sketch of a concrete object, and the phonetic value of the symbol is the first sound in the name of that object, as if in English we used, say, a sketch of a fish to stand for the phoneme /f/. (In some cases we no longer understand what a letter was intended to picture and hence how it fits its sound-value.)[2]

Figure 16 shows, in the leftmost column, an early form of each letter, and in the second column their forms in the Hebrew alphabet. The third column gives the Hebrew names of the letters, and the fourth column their phonetic values. The last column gives the Hebrew form of the Semitic word, with gloss, from which the letter shape seems to have derived, if we can tell what that was. (In most cases the letter name differs in details of vocalism from the word which gave rise to the letter; this is explained by Diringer (1968: 169) as due to borrowing of letter names from one Semitic language to another.) Sequences of letters were written from right to left, and this continues to be the direction of writing in the modern Hebrew and Arabic scripts.

Five Hebrew letters, < k m n p sʼ >, each have two allographs. The difference between these shapes has no phonetic significance: the right-hand forms are the basic letter shapes, the left-hand forms are used at the end of a word.

In connexion with the phonetic transcriptions, I should mention some features of the Hebrew consonant system which make it very different from European languages; many of these features are common to other Semitic languages.

First, alongside voiced and voiceless obstruents, the Proto-Semitic ancestor language from which Hebrew descended had a third series of

𐤀	א	ʔālep	ʔ	ʔelep "ox"
𐤁	ב	bēt	b	bajit "house"
𐤂	ג	gīmel	g	gāmāl "camel"
𐤃	ד	dālet	d	delet "door"
𐤄	ה	hē	h	?
𐤅	ו	wāw	w	wāw "hook"
𐤆	ז	zajin	z	zajin "weapon"
𐤇	ח	ħēt	ħ	?
𐤈	ט	t'ēt	t'	?
𐤉	י	jōd	j	jād "hand"
𐤊	כ ך	kāp	k	kap "cupped hand"
𐤋	ל	lāmed	l	lāmad "to study" (picture of teacher's cane?)
𐤌	מ ם	mēm	m	majim "water"
𐤍	נ ן	nūn	n	nūn "fish" ? (but see p.100)
𐤎	ס	sāmek	s	sāmak "fulcrum" ?
𐤏	ע	ʕajin	ʕ	ʕajin "eye"
𐤐	פ ף	pē	p	pe "mouth"
𐤑	צ ץ	s'ādē	s'	?
𐤒	ק	k'ōp	k'	k'ōp "ape"
𐤓	ר	rēʃ	r	rōʃ "head"
𐤔	ש	šīn	ʃ, ś	ʃēn "tooth"
𐤕	ת	tāw	t	tāw "mark"

Figure 16

what phoneticians know as "ejective" consonants (Goldenberg 2013: 65), and three of these, /t' s' k'/, survived as separate phonemes in Hebrew. (Whether in the Biblical period they were still pronounced as ejectives or in some other way is not known, but they were distinct from the plain obstruents /t s k/.) Secondly, unlike European languages Hebrew had phonemes at the pharyngeal place of articulation: a voiceless fricative /ħ/, and an approximant /ʕ/. It also had a lateral sibilant, which I represent as /ś/; this may have sounded much like the Welsh *ll* sound, IPA [ɬ], but for Hebrew it makes better sense to transcribe it with a symbol based on *s* rather than *l* – it was evidently heard as a kind of sibilant rather than as an /l/-like sound.

Finally, the pronunciation of most of the consonants alternated between allophones which, in European languages, would typically represent contrasting phonemes. All consonants except /ʔ h ħ ʕ r/ could occur either single or geminated (doubled). In those few European languages which distinguish geminated from single consonants, the distinction is phonemic (e.g. Italian *cita'* "quote!" versus *città* "town", with a long [tː]). But, in Hebrew, gemination is determined by the surrounding sounds. If a consonant occurs between two vowels of which the former is short and the latter stressed, then the consonant is geminated; otherwise it is single: [kaˈmmōn] "cumin" versus [kāˈmūs] "hidden", [ˈkeleb] "dog".[3] (The definite-article prefix /ha-/ also causes gemination of the following consonant: [hakkaˈmmōn] "the cumin".) Furthermore, when preceded by a vowel and not geminated, the obstruent phonemes /p t k b d g/ are realized as fricatives [f θ x v ð ɣ], while otherwise they are stops [p t k b d g]. Consider for instance the name of Bathsheba, the woman whom King David spied bathing and fancied so much that he arranged for her husband to be killed in battle. (The story is in the second book of Samuel.) Phonetically, the name is pronounced [baθʃevaʕ], but phonemically it is /batʃebaʕ/. In a European language it would be quite unusual for stop versus fricative to be a merely allophonic distinction.

Readers might wonder why the English spelling "Bathsheba" represents one of the sounds in question as < th > but the other as < b > rather than < v >. And, if they are Jewish, they may be further confused because they are used to hearing the first syllable (which is Hebrew "daughter") said as [bas] (as in *bas mitzvah*, a Jewish girl's coming-of-age ceremony). These things result from the complex fate of Hebrew language and literature since Old Testament days. On the one hand, the Christian scriptures came into English not directly from Hebrew but via translations into Greek and Latin, and spellings of names have been heavily influenced by accidental features of the sound-systems and orthographies of all these languages. Also, for many centuries Hebrew was spoken aloud only for liturgical purposes by Jews whose native language was often German, so they adapted its pronunciation to the sounds available in that language. Both of these considerations explain, for instance, why the English spelling "Bathsheba" entirely ignores the final pharyngeal /ʕ/: European languages have no pharyngeal sounds, and the Roman alphabet offers no way to write them. It would be extremely confusing to go into the ins and outs of all those developments here, and we shall not try to do so. What matters for present purposes is just that readers who are familiar either with the English Bible or with Jewish liturgy should understand that there are good reasons for discrepancies between my Hebrew transcriptions and the forms they are familiar with. I am keeping things simple by discussing the language as it was spoken when (or not long after) its script was devised.

Hebrew script is phonemic rather than phonetic, writing fricatives, single stops, and geminated stops as the same single letters. (When quoting Hebrew examples between phonemic slashes, I shall do likewise.) With respect to the fricative/stop alternation, though, that does not imply subtle phonological analysis by the script inventors; when the alphabet was created, the fricative allophones had not yet developed in speech. (In *modern* spoken Hebrew some of these fricative sounds have been lost, but those that remain are no longer mere allophones of stops; Rosén (1977: 65) argues that "the spirant : stop opposition may well be one of the most heavily loaded in Israeli Hebrew". This is one reason why, for simplicity, it is preferable to avoid discussing modern Israeli pronunciation.) The alternation between geminate and single stops may have been older, but it seems to be universally true that phonetic contrasts relating only to length rather than sound quality are less noticeable to speakers.

Thus the alphabet represented the set of Hebrew consonant phonemes in a one-to-one correspondence, ignoring allophonic variation, with the sole exception that the same letter šīn does duty for both of the phonemes /ʃ ś/. (I shall transcribe the letter, neutrally, as < š >.) Presumably, while /ś/ was a separate phoneme, it was heard as relatively similar to /ʃ/, though the two sounds certainly contrasted (there were plenty of minimal pairs, e.g. /ʃārā/ "soak" versus /śārā/ "struggle"). However, in due course a sound change merged /ś/ not with /ʃ/ but with /s/, so that in the historical period the letter šīn has been ambiguous between /ʃ/ and /s/, and the phoneme /s/ in different words has been written either by that letter or by sāmek.

Some experts are unwilling to accept that the Semitic letters began as pictures which derived their values acrophonically, as I described them above. At most, they have suggested, the letters were invented as abstract shapes but then had names assigned by reference to vague similarities to real objects (e.g. Gelb 1952: 140–41; Goldenberg 2013: 35). According to those scholars, the Semites did not invent the letter < ʔ > by thinking of a picturable object (the ox) whose name began with /ʔ/ and drawing a stylized picture of an ox head; rather, they designed the letter at random and assigned it the value /ʔ/ arbitrarily, but then called it "ox" as a name beginning with the right sound which they found satisfying because they noticed a loose similarity between their arbitrary letter shape and the appearance of an ox. According to Ignace Gelb (1952: 140–41), "None of the Semitic signs was drawn in a form which would immediately betray its pictorial character." We shall see on p. 100 below that many people now believe the Semitic script was created by radically simplifying an older writing system, with the acrophonic principle being one of the leading features linking the two systems. If the Semitic alphabet was not in fact derived via the acrophonic principle, the case for seeing it as a borrowing from elsewhere would be greatly weakened, so that idea may be attractive to people who for cultural reasons would like to magnify the originality of the Semitic achievement. I find it implausible.

Gelb's remark just quoted seems not to be to the point. The fact that a script has been *created* by drawing pictures of objects is not a reason for *maintaining* its motivated character, once it has come into use; so the fact that the earliest known Semitic graphs at best hinted at the shapes of objects, rather than being careful portrayals, does not argue against the graphs having originally been motivated. The first Semitic scribes may well have valued speed and convenience over artistic detail in their writing system, in which case they would rapidly have stripped down their graphs to the minimum needed for distinctiveness and distorted the shapes for ease of writing.

Also, Gelb seems unimaginative in denying that some early Semitic letters have any iconic value. Thus he singles out gīmel and k'ōp as names which do not in any obvious way fit their graphs. Yet anyone asked to pick out the most distinctive visual feature of the camel would surely name the hump – the shape of gīmel could easily be seen as a stylized camel's hump.[4] The version of k'ōp in the first column of Figure 16 strikes me as quite reminiscent of the face of an ape, with heavy simian eyebrows.

It is true that some of the early letters show considerable variety of shapes, and in Figure 16 I have selected variants which make acrophony look plausible. The upper part of k'ōp is sometimes a circle rather than a D shape on its side, reducing the resemblance to an ape. Some variants of ʔālep have the crosspiece meeting the V at its apex, so that the whole looks like a K and cannot be seen as an ox head. I assume that the more-iconic shapes were original and these less-iconic variants came later, but it might have been the other way round. Furthermore, not all the letter names can easily be explained. Sometimes this may be due to differences of culture: the triangle might not be such an odd shape for "door" if the creators of the script lived in tents with triangular door-flaps. Other letter shapes and names are more mysterious, though tentative explanations have been offered for all of them (Diringer 1968: 169). Gideon Goldenberg (2013: 35) believes that some of the hard-to-explain letters may have been modifications of others, for instance t'ēt might have been a combination of tāw and ʕajin, with the pharyngeal /ʕ/ suggesting the ejective quality of /t'/. At such a distance in time we cannot expect everything to be clear, but enough of the letters are transparently iconic to make the explanation in terms of acrophony, to my mind, fairly cogent.

What has *not* been explained is the ordering of the letters of the Semitic alphabet. This has been fixed from the beginning, and – allowing for certain losses of letters and additions of new letters – is the order of our Roman alphabet today; but no phonetic logic is apparent in it, and there are no theories about how it was originally settled upon (Jensen 1970: 282.)

* * *

The Semitic alphabet was not invented from scratch – its creation was almost certainly inspired by an earlier script. But the creators of the Semitic alphabet were unquestionably innovators in producing a script in which individual graphs consistently stand for single phonemes, and in which – if we overlook the problem about /ś/ and /ʃ/ – each phoneme of the category recorded by the script has one unambiguous graph.

Some linguists have argued that Semitic script ought to be called syllabic rather than segmental (O'Connor 1996: 88), on the ground that a single Semitic letter stood for syllables such as /ba be bi bo bu/.[5] But the vowel-less Semitic script is very different from a true syllabic script such as Linear B, in which the vowel of a syllable is as relevant as the consonant in determining which graph will be used to write the syllable. In early Semitic writing only the consonants of a spoken form were relevant to the orthography, so this script is not a syllabic script: it is a segmental script which ignores vowel segments.

The assumption that the Semites created their graphs by the acrophonic principle explains why the script provides graphs only for consonants – which Diringer (1968: 165), who did not make that assumption, treated as inexplicable. All words in Semitic languages begin with consonants, so if letters are invented acrophonically there is no possibility of getting letters for vowels.

Words which we might hear as beginning with a vowel are perceived by Semitic speakers as beginning with a glottal stop. In English a word like *ever* will often be said with a marked initial glottal stop, [ʔevə]; but we do not normally treat this as a phoneme of English, partly because it will often be missing even at the beginning of a word (a phrase like *he admits* would commonly be said [hiədmɪts], with the diphthong of *here*, rather than [hiʔədmɪts]), and partly because in standard English the distribution of the glottal stop is extremely limited: it essentially occurs only at the beginning of words. In a Semitic language such as Hebrew, the glottal stop is as compulsory a feature of a word in which it occurs as any other consonant. A word beginning with a glottal stop will not lose it if a prefix is added (/w/ "and" + /ʔīʃ/ "a man" gives /wəʔīʃ/ "and a man", not */wīʃ/), and glottal stops occur at various places in a word (e.g. /jāʔab/ "long for" contrasts with /jāhab/ "give" or /jās'ab/ "stand").

The acrophonic principle, and the lack of initial vowels, may explain why the Semitic alphabet was not originally equipped with vowel letters. To understand how such an alphabet functioned satisfactorily, we need to examine the structure of the spoken languages for which it has been used. Vowel letters are not as useful when writing a Semitic language as they are when writing Indo-European languages.

Taking Hebrew as our sample Semitic language, the issue is not that it has a shortage of vowel sounds. The system is actually rather rich; it has five long vowels, five short vowels, four "reduced" (very short) vowels including shwa, and a number of diphthongs. (In my transcriptions, [ā a ă] will indicate long, short, and reduced respectively.) Many differences among these vowels are only allophonic, for instance the diphthongs in [-a] are automatic variants of long vowels before pharyngeal consonants. (The name [nōaħ] "Noah" is phonemically /nōħ/.) Reduced vowels are either allophones of fuller vowels in unstressed positions, or inserted to break up a consonant cluster. Even the short vowels other than /a/ are close to being allophonic variants of the long vowels. Minimal pairs can be found, e.g. [mīʃōr] "a plain" versus [miʃʃōr] "from an ox" (if the single versus geminate consonant difference is allophonic, [ī] versus [i] must be a phonemic contrast); but such cases are somewhat rare and freakish, and in many cases VCC and V̄C are interchangeable (e.g. [giggīt], [gīgīt], alternative forms for "tub"). Probably we should recognize all ten short and long vowels as phonemes, but the "functional yield" of the short/long opposition is very low except in the case of the pair /a ā/. In stressed monosyllables, the only vowels we find are the five long vowels and /a/. It is easy to find examples to demonstrate contrast for any pair of these (e.g. /dīr/ "a stable", /dar/ "mother-of-pearl", /dār/ "to dwell", /dōr/ "generation", /dūr/ "rim", etc.).

Of course, the fact that a large range of vowel phones can be resolved into a smaller set of contrasting phonemes would not in itself be a reason against recording the vowels in writing. But two other considerations about the role of vowels in Hebrew and other Semitic languages would have made it unattractive to include them in the script.

First, there is a great deal of "meaningless" alternation among vowels, which extends beyond alternations between allophones of one phoneme to include many cases of alternation between separate phonemes. Secondly, when vowel differences are used meaningfully, the meanings expressed are very commonly only grammatical – not lexical, as they are in the "dīr/dar/dār/..." case.

By "meaningless" vowel variation I am thinking of cases analogous to the varying pronunciation of the root < metr > in English words like *metre, metric, telemetry*. All these words derive from the same Greek word meaning "measure", but in English the < e > is pronounced respectively /i/, /e/, /ə/. In English, this kind of variation occurs mainly in words derived from Classical languages; but, in Hebrew, comparable variation runs through the whole vocabulary, and a given root will commonly exhibit more than three different forms.

For instance, the noun for "way, road" in its basic form is /derek/. But when the word happens to be the last in its sentence or other major grammatical unit, it takes the "pausal form" /dārek/. With a possessive suffix it is /dark-/ with a short /a/, e.g. /darkī/ "my way". With the plural suffix /-īm/ it is /dərāk-/, i.e. /dərākīm/ "ways", but in the "pregenitive" plural it is /darək-/: /darəkē hamelek/ "the ways of the king". And the same root can be used verbally with the meaning "tread" (the noun for "road" will originally have derived from this verbal root): the simplest form of the verb is /dārak/. Nothing is constant except the consonants, d-r-k, and this is the normal situation with a Hebrew root. A native speaker who reads a written text wants to know what the words are; once the words are recognized, he already knows how to pronounce them in the relevant grammatical form, so spelling out those varying vowels might make word-recognition harder, by introducing meaningless visual variation, without any compensating gain.

I can illustrate what I mean by grammatical rather than lexical use of vowel contrasts by listing a few inflected forms of two verbal roots; my examples will be the roots k-t-b, standing for the concept "write", and d-r-ʃ, standing for the concept "seek, enquire". The numerous inflected forms of these verbs are realized by choice of vowels replacing the hyphens in the root forms, together in some cases with prefixes or suffixes. Any given pattern of vowels, together with affixes if any, will conjugate either root in the same way:

kātab "he wrote" dāraʃ "he sought"
kātabtī "I wrote" dāraʃtī "I sought"
kātəbū "they wrote" dārəʃū "they sought"
etc.

jiktōb "he will write" jidrōʃ "he will seek"
ʔektōb "I shall write" ʔedrōʃ "I shall seek"
etc.

kətōb "write!" dərōʃ "seek!"
kōtēb "writing" dōrēʃ "seeking"
kātūb "being written" dārūʃ "being sought"
etc. etc.[6]

Given the limited role of vowels as distinctive elements in Semitic languages (and given that many inflected and derived forms include affixes containing consonants), a script which indicates only consonants is not unreasonably ambiguous in practice. If we were told in English that a verb with the consonants /l ... k/ fits into the context *Did the dog ___ the bone?*, it would be hard to know whether *lick* or *like* was intended; but if we were told that the verb is *lick* and the only question is what form of the verb is appropriate, it is easy to choose *lick* rather than *licking* or *licked*. A better analogy might be with a more inflected language such as French. Given a French sentence with all the inflexions removed, say:

> Ecouter, Israël, moi être l'Eternel ton Dieu, qui toi avoir tirer du pays d'Egypte

it is not hard to see that this must mean:

> Ecoute, Israël, je suis l'Eternel ton Dieu, qui t'ai tiré du pays d'Egypte.

Accordingly, in early written Hebrew, no indication whatever was given of vowels; the orthographies of some other Semitic languages never throughout their history developed any method of giving information about vowels.

* * *

However, there are real disadvantages even for a Semitic language if vowels are completely ignored in writing. Distinctions such as those between "he wrote" and "they wrote", or "he wrote" and "he is writing", are less crucial for communication than the differences between one lexical item and another, but they are not trivial. Furthermore, we have seen that cases where distinct lexical items differ only in vocalism are by no means absent. Noun roots in particular often have fixed inherent vowels.

This problem was addressed, for some Semitic languages including Hebrew, by making certain consonant letters do double duty and serve also to indicate vowels. Letters functioning this way are called *matres lectionis*, "mothers of reading" (on the beginning of the *matres* system, see references in Sass 2005: 52).

The use of *matres* for Hebrew evolved gradually as Biblical texts were written down by many different scribes, so that it is possible to find exceptions to almost any statement one makes on the subject. Furthermore, because of the status of the written Old Testament in the life of Israel, many such individual exceptions became entrenched and remain part of current usage. Nevertheless, it is possible to state rules which are valid for the great majority of words.

Rule 1 Short (and reduced) vowels are ignored, with one exception to be discussed below.
Rule 2 Among the long vowels, /ī ū/ are obligatorily written < j w > respectively.
Rule 3 The vowels /ē ō/ can optionally be written < j w > respectively.

Thus the words /dīr dar dōr dūr dār/ will be spelled < djr >, < dr >, < dwr > or < dr >, < dwr >, < dr >.

These rules, clearly, are motivated by the phonetic similarity of approximants /j w/ to close front spread and back rounded vowels. Indeed, Hebrew scribes may perhaps have heard these vowels as diphthongal, [ɩj ej ɷw ow]. Note that the use of < j w > as *matres* was phonetic rather than phonemic. The distinction between e.g. /ī/ and /ē/ was clearly contrastive, but the same *mater* had to do duty for both. On the other hand, the distinction between /ī/ and /i/ was at most marginally contrastive, but /ī/ was written as < j > while /i/ was ignored – perhaps because it was a lax, [ɩ]-like vowel lacking a timbre reminiscent of [j].

Rule 4 Unlike in English, the consonant /h/ did occur word-finally, but < h > was also used to indicate word-final vowels not representable by < j > or < w >, most commonly /ā/.[7] Thus e.g. /malkā/ "queen" is < mlkh >.

The writing of word-final /ā/ as < h > is obligatory, as a special case of a further rule:

Rule 5 Word-final vowels must be indicated by a *mater.*

Rule 5 overrides Rule 1: one of the short vowels, /e/, does occur word-finally, and a word like /śāde/, "field", is written < šdh >, not *< šd >. Rule 5 has a clear rationale. Provided one knows that some vowel occurs in a given position, familiarity with the morphological patterns of Hebrew will commonly tell one which vowel it is; and the presence of a consonant letter will normally reveal the presence of a following vowel, since consonant clustering is very limited in Hebrew. However, it is quite usual for a word to *end* with a consonant, so without Rule 5 the reader could overlook an entire syllable.

Internally in a word, /ē ō/ are sometimes written and sometimes not: e.g. /lōt'/ "wrapper" can be < lwt' > or < lt' >, /ħēk'/ "lap" can be < ħjk' > or < ħk' >. But there are conventions settling the matter for particular vocabulary items or particular inflexional patterns: thus /ʃēm/ "name" is always < šm > rather than *< šjm >, and the -ō-ē- vowel pattern which marks the active participle is regularly written with < w > for /ō/ but with

/ē/ unmarked. The vowels /ī ū/ are always written, irrespective of their position in a word; /ā/ cannot be written except when word-final.

A further letter, < ʔ >, is used in a way that makes it resemble a *mater* although historically it was not one. At an early stage in the development of Hebrew as a spoken language, word-final glottal stops were dropped: /lōʔ/ "not", /nābīʔ/ "prophet", /dūdāʔ/ "basket" came to be pronounced /lō/, /nābī/, /dūdā/. However, the glottal stop is still "underlyingly" present in such words if they can take a suffix beginning with a vowel (such as the masculine plural suffix /-īm/), since in this case the glottal stop, not being word-final, is retained in the pronunciation: /nəbīʔīm/, /dūdāʔīm/. (Compare /nābī/, /nəbīʔīm/ with /nōs'rī/ "Nazarene, Christian", plural /nōs'rīm/, which never had a glottal stop in its pronunciation.) Partly for this morphophonemic reason and partly because of the conservatism of Hebrew orthography, < ʔ > continued to be written in words from which it had been dropped in speech: "prophet" and "basket" are written < nbjʔ >, < dwdʔ >, and "not" is written < lʔ > even though the glottal stop is never pronounced in this word since it takes no suffixes. (Compare the many word-final consonants in written French which in modern spoken French are pronounced only in liaison or not at all.)

The system of *matres* resolves some graphic ambiguities only at the cost of introducing others. The use of < j > as a *mater* enables e.g. /ʕīr/ "city" to be distinguished from /ʕār/ "enemy", but creates the new possibility of confusing /ʕīr/ with /ʕajir/ "donkey foal". On balance so-called *plene* writing – writing with *matres* – is less phonologically ambiguous than writing without *matres*, but plenty of ambiguity remains.

Nevertheless, users of Hebrew script have never felt a need to adopt a more complete phonographic system for everyday purposes. For certain special purposes – originally, for preserving the language of the Bible itself as accurately as possible when Hebrew was no longer a living colloquial language – a system was invented of "pointing" the consonantal script, that is of supplementing it with tiny dots and dashes below, above, and within the consonant letters, to indicate those aspects of the pronunciation which are left vague by the consonantal orthography. This system gives a very precise indication of pronunciation, extending even to matters such as primary and secondary stress, which is phonologically determined in Hebrew. The pointing system currently used was evolved in the +9th and +10th centuries.

But, apart from the Bible, the only written materials which are normally pointed in modern Israel are reading-books for young children (who are not yet familiar enough with the structure of the language to identify words from the clues given by unpointed consonantal script), and, interestingly, poetry. In poetry words are put together in creative, unexpected ways, so that familiarity with the usual patterns of the language apparently does not always allow a Hebrew-speaking reader to identify words in a poem conveniently from the consonantal script alone.[8] An isolated name, say over the door of a café, might be pointed because, out of context, there is no basis for predicting its vowels. But ordinary handwritten or printed Hebrew prose contains exclusively the consonantal script, with vowels indicated only by *matres*. The reader identifies the words using the information supplied by the consonant letters, by his understanding of the subject-matter (which makes some words more probable than others in a given context), and by knowing the characteristic morphological and syntactic patterns of the language, which impose constraints on the possible distribution of vowels.

Barr (1976: 89–90) remarks that the Hebrew reader's need to recognize word-patterns was allowed for by the practice of leaving spaces between words from a very early period, while in European orthographies word-spacing became usual only about +1000 (Cohen 1958: 423). Biblical Hebrew orthography even uses a hyphen to mark cases where "phonological words" (i.e. the domains relevant for application of the stress and allophony rules) comprise more than one word in the morphological sense – though this hyphenation is not carried out with complete consistency.

Figure 17 shows a sample of ordinary modern vowel-less Israeli script: the beginning of a sports report from January 2014, which translates as:

ספורט כדורגל בעולם

שבת אירופית ||
אתלטיקו וברצלונה
נפרדו ללא שערים,
צ'לסי בראש
הפרמייר-ליג

תיקו מאכזב במשחק העונה בספרד;
שתי הקבוצות נותרו דבוקות בצמרת.
הבלוז גברו 2-0 על האל סיטי,
מנצ'סטר יונייטד חזרה לנצח

Figure 17

Sport: World Football
Saturday in Europe:
Atlético versus Barcelona ended in goalless draw,
Chelsea at head of Premier League
Disappointing draw in Spain's match of the season;
two clubs neck and neck at the top.
The Blues beat Hull City two–nil,
Manchester United back on winning form

Vowels are indicated only by *matres*; but the many foreign words, whose vowels cannot be predicted on the basis of Hebrew word-patterns, force the *mater* system to be used more extensively than in Hebrew vocabulary. For instance the name *Hull City* (at the end of the penultimate line) is written < hʔl sjt'j >: the letter < ʔ > indicates a word-internal open vowel, in a way that would be very unusual in a Hebrew word.

As an example of pointed Biblical Hebrew, Figure 18 shows the opening lines of the 23rd Psalm. The first two lines (labelled 2 and 3 in the figure) run, in phonetic transcription, in word-for-word gloss, and in the English of the Authorized Version:

JHWH	rōʕî	lōʔ	ʔeħsār
LORD	shepherd.my	not	I.shall.want

The LORD is my shepherd; I shall not want.

binʔôθ	deʃeʔ	jarbîs'ēnî
in.pastures	fresh.grass	he.makes.me.lie.down

He maketh me to lie down in green pastures:

ʕal-mê	mənuħôθ	jənahălēnî	nafʃî	jəʃôvēv
by.waters	still	he.leads.me	soul.my	he.refreshes

he leadeth me beside the still waters. He restoreth my soul

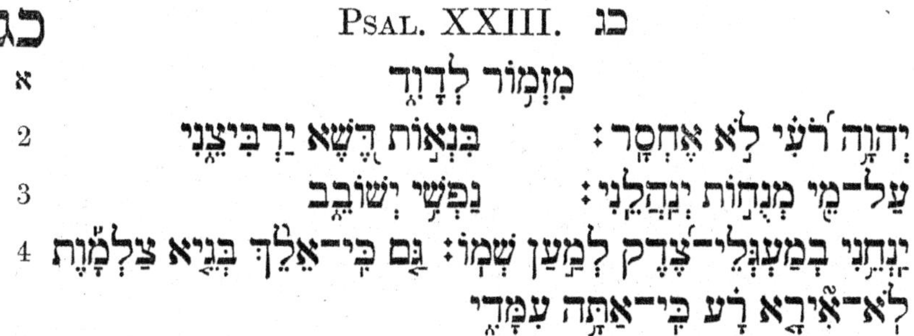
כג Psal. XXIII. כג
א מִזְמוֹר לְדָוִד
2 יְהוָה רֹעִי לֹא אֶחְסָר׃ בִּנְאוֹת דֶּשֶׁא יַרְבִּיצֵנִי
3 עַל־מֵי מְנֻחוֹת יְנַהֲלֵנִי׃ נַפְשִׁי יְשׁוֹבֵב
4 יַנְחֵנִי בְמַעְגְּלֵי־צֶדֶק לְמַעַן שְׁמוֹ׃ גַּם כִּי־אֵלֵךְ בְּגֵיא צַלְמָוֶת
לֹא־אִירָא רָע כִּי־אַתָּה עִמָּדִי

Figure 18

The first word, < jhwh >, is the name of God; it is transcribed in capitals and without vowels, because uttering this name is forbidden, so in reading aloud it is customary to substitute the word /ʔădōnāj/, "lord", and the pointing provided by the Bible text relates to that word. In line with a standard Hebraist convention, my transcription uses circumflex to show that a long vowel is spelled with a *mater*: thus the second word is transcribed rōʕî because the /ō/is indicated solely by the dot over the left-hand corner of the < r > (there is no < w >) but the /ī/ vowel is indicated by a < j >.

The pointing uses dots and short straight-line marks for three purposes:

1. Most of the marks identify vowels, for instance the vowel /ā/ is represented by a small T shape below a consonant.
2. A dot in the centre of a letter shows that the consonant is a stop rather than fricative, and/or geminate rather than single. Thus, in the word which begins the second half-line, the initial < b > has a dot because it is phonetically [b] rather than [v], the final < t > lacks a dot because it is phonetically [θ].
3. The alternative values of the ambiguous letter < š > are distinguished by a dot above the right-hand side for /ʃ/ and above the left-hand side for /ś/ (Figure 18 happens to include several cases of the former but none of the latter).

There are also "cantillation marks", such as the curved line above and to the right of the second word. These are musical notations, showing how the psalm is to be sung. In modern times the cantillation marks have not been well understood, but for recent ideas about how the system worked see Mitchell (2013).

* * *

To give the reader a sense of how far in practice the vowel-less nature of the script creates difficulties for the reader of Hebrew, I illustrate the problems of interpretation posed by ten words chosen at random from a passage of modern written Hebrew (I selected the penultimate word in each of ten successive lines from an advertisement for a dictionary). For each sample word I begin by transliterating its written form.

1. < nwšʔjm > The letters < -jm > at the end of a word will almost always stand for the masculine plural suffix /-īm/. Although /n/ occurs in some prefixes, /w/ is vanishingly rare as the first consonant of a root; therefore < w > is likely to be a mater. The only

stem spelled < nwšʔ > is /nōśē/ "topic", active participle of the root n-ś-ʔ "to lift", so the word is /nōśəʔīm/ "topics".

2. < hwʔ > This is /hū/ "he", so common a word that no problems of recognition arise.
3. < hmlwn > In a word of several letters beginning with < h > the probability is high that, as here, < h > represents the definite-article prefix /ha-/. (If several words together begin with < h > this interpretation becomes virtually certain, since Hebrew adds the prefix to each element of a definite noun-phrase – "this good man" is expressed in Hebrew as "the-man the-good the-this".) In the present case the correct reading is /hamilōn/ "the dictionary", which in context is obvious enough (the succeeding words translate as "... contains 30,000 entries in alphabetical order"). Out of context < hmlwn > could equally well read /hamālōn/ "the hotel", or /hamēlōn/ "the melon".
4. < mk'jp > This is /mak'īp/ "circle", derived from the root m-k'-p "concave". Often < m > is a prefix, but it cannot be one here because there is no root *k'-j-p or *k'-p.[9]
5. < hpʕljm > Again < -jm > shows that we are dealing with the plural of a noun or adjective, so < h- > is likely to be the definite article. The root p-ʕ-l is a frequent one, meaning "do". The only noun or adjective derived from it which requires no further letter is /pōʕal/ "deed". (The root also gives e.g. /pāʕīl/ "active", but that requires a < j > *mater* in the second syllable; /pōʕēl/ "worker" is an active participle, the -ō-ē- pattern of which is conventionally always written with a < w > *mater* for the /ō/; and so on.) Therefore word 5 is /hapəʕālīm/ "the deeds".
6. < lrʔšj > In a five-letter word some of the letters are almost sure to be prefixes or suffixes, and < l > is a good candidate because it represents the common prefix /l-/ "to"; in any case, there are restrictions on the consonants which may occur in adjacent positions in Hebrew roots, and these rule out the possibility of a root with l-r- in the first two positions. Final < j > is often a *mater* representing a suffix /-ī/ or /-ē/ (or, less commonly, a suffix diphthong). The root spelled < rʔš >, "head", is one of the rare Hebrew words in which a word-internal /ʔ/ has been elided ("head" is /rōʃ/); word 6 is /lərāʃē/, the pregenitive form of /lərāʃīm/ "to the heads".
7. < mt'bʕwt > Just as final < -jm > indicates the masculine plural /īm/, so final < -wt > indicates the feminine plural /-ōt/. That leaves four letters, none of which can be a *mater*. Since roots

usually contain at most three consonants, probably either < m > represents a prefix or < ʕ > a suffix. There is no suffix spelled < ʕ >; but nominalizing prefixes frequently begin with /m-/, so we expect this word to be formed from the root t'-b-ʕ "to sink, to coin". That gives three possibilities: /mat'bēʕ/ "a coin", plural /mat'bəʕōt/; /mit'bāʕā/ "a mint", plural /mit'bāʕōt/; /mat'baʕat/ "a die", plural /mat'bāʕōt/. All of these plural forms would equally be spelled < mt'bʕwt >, and only the context shows that in this case the first of them, "coins", is intended (the word occurs in the phrase /mat'bəʕōt wūkəsāpīm/, literally "coins and monies", i.e. "currency").

8. < hlšwn > The root l-ʃ-n means "to slander", and < h > can be a verbal prefix; but no form taking that prefix has an /ū/ or /ō/ in the last syllable. In any case the context calls for a noun. Therefore the correct reading is the frequent noun /halāʃōn/ "the language"; no alternative reading is possible.
9. < šl > The very common word /ʃel/, "of". Out of context the word could also be /ʃal/ "error"; but "of" is so much more frequent that no reader is likely to think of "error" unless the context is incompatible with the reading "of".
10. < wbmjħd > Word-initial < w > is virtually always the prefix "and". The range of consonants found in Hebrew suffixes is quite limited and does not include /d/, so that letter must be part of the root – in which case < b > is likely also to be a prefix (it means "in"). The possibility that < j > is a *mater* need not be considered, because there happens to be no root m-ħ-d. The root is j-ħ-d, which (strangely) combines the opposite meanings "together" and "apart", and the stem is the word /məjuħād/ "particular" (i.e. "set apart"), formed by adding the nominalizing prefix /m-/ to this root. No alternative reading is possible. The word as a whole is read /wūbimjuħād/, "and in particular" ("and" takes the vowel /ū/ before labial consonants).

Needless to say, the fluent reader will not consciously go through the deductive reasoning spelled out in detail for our ten example words. What it means to be a fluent reader is that one has learned to carry out such reasoning unconsciously and rapidly, so that the process of translating from graphs to sense appears subjectively to be quite direct and effortless. Compare the problem of reading an English word such as < gaping >, as in *It was gaping open*. The form is not so common that a reader will necessarily have encountered it in writing before, but a literate English-speaker is unlikely to have trouble with it. If we had to spell out the reasoning by which a reader understands the word, it might run more or less as follows. The last letters < -ing > are almost certainly the common participial suffix /ɪŋ/. The letters < gap > in isolation represent /gæp/, and this root can take the /ɪŋ/ suffix. However, an English orthographic rule requires consonant letters other than < v > to be written double when, as here, they occur in words of the native Germanic vocabulary between a checked vowel such as /æ/ and a following vowel. (*Apical* /æpɪkəl/ is not written with double < pp >, because it derives from Latin, but *gap* is a native root.) Therefore < a > in < gaping > must be given its alternative (non-checked) value /ei/: the word is /geipɪŋ/. This identification is reinforced by the fact that *to gape open* is a standard phrase, whereas *to gap open* is less common (though it is meaningful in the finance industry). But this reinforcement is not crucial; the word < gaping > is quite readable in isolation.

Of course no fluent reader of English is aware of going through steps like these before understanding the word on the page. The same applies to the reader of Hebrew.

* * *

Although the idea of writing without vowels seems strange to Europeans, plainly it works. Readers of Hebrew do not find themselves floundering indecisively between one interpretation of a written word and another; where alternative readings are possible for a given letter-sequence, normally the context will settle the matter straightforwardly enough. To say this is not to say, though, that Hebrew script is fully as convenient in practice, for speakers of the Hebrew language, as our script is for English-speakers. By contrast with the orthography of any European language, Hebrew script is strikingly lacking in redundancy.

"Redundancy" is a technical term referring to a measurable property of any system of communicable messages or "signals" (Shannon and Weaver 1949: 25–6). A system possessing relatively high redundancy is one where, in an average signal, the identity of any given part of the signal is relatively easy to predict given the rest of the signal. Suppose that a policeman telephones to give you details of a suspect who needs to be looked out for, but because the line is bad you hear only some of the letters and numbers as they are spelled out: you hear that the suspect's name is F*ANK DAW*ON and his car registration is GY14 *WY. You will have little difficulty guessing that the name is "Frank Dawson"; but you will be completely stumped when it comes to filling in the missing element of the registration. This is because English personal names form a system with high redundancy, whereas car registration marks form a low-redundancy system.

The absence of vowel letters means that, of ten written Hebrew words picked at random, at least three could be read as any of two or more phonologically different spoken words. Comparable written words exist in English (for instance < lead > can be the verb /lid/ or the noun /led/) but they are rare; it is quite unlikely that even one such word would occur in a random collection of ten words. Of course the context will normally settle the ambiguities in Hebrew, but the point is that the existence of such words forces one to examine the context more carefully than one would otherwise need to. When a word is graphically unambiguous, it can act as a fixed datum from which parts of the context can be predicted so that they need not be physically examined.

Then, the idea that one reads by sampling parts and inferring the whole is likely to apply not just between words but within them. Whether or not a fluent English reader looks at every word in a text, it is likely that he does not focus on every letter in a word, unless the word is so short that all its letters are focused in a single fixation.[10] But it is much harder in Hebrew than in English to predict the identity of an unexamined letter from the identities of the other letters in a word.

Let me illustrate this by a small experiment. I picked a random set of ten English words from a running text, to act as a comparison with my sample of ten Hebrew words; in each word of either language I deleted one letter chosen at random, and then worked out for each language what proportion of the missing letters could unambiguously be restored if the word were taken in isolation. Ten-word samples are too small to place great reliance on the numerical results, but the general trend is clear. In the English case only the three shortest words of the ten yielded ambiguities: < *y > could be *my* or *by*, < *he > could be *the* or *she*, < *f > could be *if* or *of*. The seven longer words, < *riting, g*ographic, wer*, thro*gh, resul*ing, inacces*ible, C*erokee >, all remain unambiguous. In the Hebrew sample the situation is reversed: only three of the longest words failed to yield ambiguities (even leaving aside the ambiguities which already existed for some of the words before any letter was removed). I cannot find any second reading for the words < *wšʔjm, hpʕl*m, wbm*ħd >. But < h*ʔ > could be < hjʔ > /hī/ "she"; < mk'j* > could be < mk'jk' > /mik'īk'/ "from a castor-oil plant"; < *t'bʕwt > could be < ht'bʕwt > /hat'abaʕōt/ "the rings"; and so on.

Another way of looking at this is to notice that the paragraph from which my ten Hebrew words were chosen, which is an advertisement printed in Hebrew and English, contains 70 words in the English version totalling 407 letters, while the Hebrew version contains 60 words totalling 285 letters. The difference in number of *words* is merely a trivial consequence of the fact that elements such as "the" and "to" are separate words in English but prefixes in Hebrew. But the difference in number of *letters* means that each occurrence of a Hebrew letter is on average almost half as important again in determining the meaning of the text in which it occurs as is the occurrence of an individual Roman letter in the English text. It is therefore less easy for the reader of Hebrew than it is for the reader of English to skim a text and reconstruct its contents from observation of a small proportion of its letters.[11]

Modern Israeli Hebrew is still a young language, and some aspects of its orthography have been changing. For instance, contemporary Hebrew spelling has taken to using more *matres* than was normal in standard Biblical Hebrew, not just in foreign words (such as *Hull* in the football example) but in words of the native vocabulary. Thus, the word /milōn/ "dictionary" (example 3 on p. 89 above) would nowadays be spelled < mjlwn > rather than < mlwn >, and /məjuħād/, "particular" (example 10) would be spelled < mjwħd > rather than < mjħd > (the text I quoted my example words from was printed back in 1961). Although, as we have seen, *matres* create ambiguities as well as resolving them, on balance more *matres* mean less ambiguity.

Nevertheless, even taking these developments into account it seems fair to describe Hebrew script as a somewhat cumbersome writing system. Its adoption by the founders of a highly developed nation, all of whom were familiar with other forms of writing, must be explained in terms of emotional considerations to do with history and religion. In the linguistics of spoken as well as of written language such non-rational factors often weigh heavily.

* * *

We have seen that the distinctive, consonant-only nature of Semitic writing is linked to special properties of spoken Semitic languages. It is interesting to ask how well such a script can be made to work if it is adapted to writing a language in which vowels are "first-class members" of the phoneme inventory.[12]

Our Roman alphabet itself represents one such adaptation, and we shall look in detail at how European scripts developed out of Semitic writing in Chapter 6. But in that case the adaptation amounted to a decisive break, so that Semitic orthographic principles have little influence on European scripts. In the next section we shall look at a case – the Indian family of scripts – where the special features of Semitic orthography have continued to exert noticeable influence on the way a group of languages are written, despite the fact that as spoken languages that group has nothing in common with Semitic languages.[13]

The origins of Indian alphabetic writing are largely lost, but it is fairly clear that Indians borrowed their earliest alphabet from speakers of Aramaic

(Diringer 1968: 262; Salomon 1996: 378). Aramaic is a Northwest Semitic language closely related to Hebrew, which was a *lingua franca* over an extensive tract of southwest Asia from early in the −1st millennium up to the +7c (it was Christ's native language, and is still spoken today).[14] The Indian borrowing of the Aramaic version of the Semitic alphabet occurred not later than the −3c. Many local variants developed out of that first Indian alphabetic script in different parts of India and neighbouring countries. The most important of these today is the Devanagari script, which first emerged in the +7c and +8c, and is used nowadays to write the literary language Sanskrit and colloquial modern languages including Hindi, Nepali, Marathi, and many smaller languages. All the languages named belong to the same Indo-European family as English. In the 21c Devanagari is one of the world's most heavily used writing systems.[15]

The shapes of Devanagari letters have changed so much from those of their Semitic ancestors that no relationship is now visible. (Indian languages have a very different range of consonants from Semitic languages, and it is quite likely that some of the Indian letters were new inventions, but when the earliest Indian ancestor of Devanagari script is compared to early Semitic alphabets there are enough coincidences to make the relationship clear.) A common feature of most Devanagari letters is a horizontal line at their head. When we Europeans use a ruled guideline to keep our writing even, we treat it as a baseline and write our letters above it, but Devanagari writers hang letters down from a top line. (The direction of writing is left to right.) It seems that Indian writing implements produced serifs at the heads of letters which came to be seen as essential parts of the letterforms and were enlarged into fuller horizontals; in Devanagari script most words are headed by a continuous horizontal, though a few letters involve breaks in the line.

That is a matter of outward appearance; for our purposes it is more worthwhile to look at how a vowel-less script was adapted to languages in which vowels are as significant as in English. We shall use Sanskrit to exemplify the languages which Devanagari is used to write. (To use a modern language such as Hindi would introduce extra complications.)

The Sanskrit vowel system can be treated in terms of three vowel qualities, two diphthongs, and a syllabic [ṛ], all of which can be distinctively long or short (I shall mark long vowels with a macron and leave short vowels unmarked):[16]

a	i	u	ai	au	ṛ
ā	ī	ū	āi	āu	ṝ

As in Hebrew script, where a consonant symbol normally stands for a consonant + vowel combination, in Devanagari a consonant letter without additional marks represents a CV syllable, but in the Devanagari case the implied vowel is always /a/ (which is the most frequent vowel phoneme). Thus the letter प, which shares a common ancestry with Hebrew pē and the Roman letter P, represents the syllable /pa/. Other vowels are indicated by additional subsidiary marks (which might be compared to the pointings of Masoretic Hebrew, though they were an independent invention). Long /ā/ is shown by a vertical added to the right of a consonant letter. The vowels /i ī/ are indicated by a vertical linked at the top to the consonant, to its left for short /i/ and to its right for long /ī/. Short and long /u/ are shown as curls in opposite directions below the consonant letter. Diphthongs are marked by "plumes" rising from the top line, springing from the consonant letter itself for diphthongs in /–i/ and from a right-hand vertical for those in /–u/; single versus double plumes represent the length contrast. The syllabic /ṛ/ is shown as a reversed cedilla mark below the consonant letter, and again this is doubled to indicate long /ṝ/. Each of these vowel signs overrides the /a/ which is inherent in an unadorned consonant symbol. Thus we find the following /pV/ syllable writings:

pa	pā	प	पा
pi	pī	पि	पी
pu	pū	पु	पू
pai	pāi	पे	पै
pau	pāu	पो	पौ
pṛ	pṝ	पृ	पॄ

There remain cases where a consonant is not followed by any vowel, at the end of a word. In Hebrew script these are written as simple consonant letters, which exceptionally do not stand for whole syllables. There is no ambiguity, because a word-final vowel is always spelled explicitly with a *mater lectionis*. Devanagari orthography does not use *matres*; instead, it uses a vowel-cancelling symbol, a diagonal below the consonant letter, to show that the letter represents not /Ca/ but /C/ alone:

प	pa	प्	p

(In transliterating, I shall represent the vowel-cancelling symbol as < V̸ >.)

Another phonological difference between Semitic and Indo-European languages is that the latter contain true consonant clusters. We have seen that in a language like Hebrew, the vowels of a root vary between fuller and more reduced versions depending on the inflexional or derivational form in which the root appears, comparable to the English alternation between e.g. *metre* and *metric*. When two consonants are immediately adjacent in a Hebrew root, that is seen as a case of the vowel which is "underlyingly" there being reduced all the way to zero; even if a word has a consonant cluster in all inflected forms, one can usually find a related word that has a vowel breaking up the cluster, e.g. /miʃpāħā/ "family", with inflected forms /miʃpaħat miʃpāħōt miʃpəħōt/, is related to /ʃiphā/, roughly speaking "au pair girl". So, phonologically if not phonetically, Hebrew is essentially a CVCV... language, and a single consonant letter normally stands for a whole syllable. Indo-European languages are not like that. In the English word *strong*, for instance, /str-/ is a continuous sequence at any phonological level – there is no sense in which it can be seen as "underlyingly" /sVtVr-/ or the like. Sanskrit is the same.

The result of adapting a script in which letters stood for whole syllables to languages containing consonant clusters was that, in Devanagari, consonant clusters are indicated by something akin to single letters. Usually, letters for consonant clusters are formed by ligaturing together the distinctive elements of the individual consonant letters. Thus प is < p > and य is < j >; < pj > is प्य. Or, द < d > + व < v > give द्व < dv >. For clusters in which one of the consonants is /r/, the /r/ is reduced to a small mark attached to the other consonant letter: र्प < rp >, प्र < pr >. In some cases, the consonant-cluster letter has a shape of its own, not obviously derived by combining the simple consonant letters. For example:

त < t > + र < r > = त्र < tr >
क < k > + ष < ṣ > = क्ष < kṣ >

Consonant sequences are written as single letters irrespective of whether the successive consonants belong to the same syllable. In English a word like *sandpit* would be seen as a syllable ending in a cluster /-nd/ followed by a syllable beginning with /p-/. But if English were written in Devanagari, /ndp/ would be written with a single ligatured letter; from left to right (remembering that /a/ is not written and /i/ is written to the left of its vowel) the graphs for *sandpit* would be < s-i-ndp-t-् >.

One sound which a phonographic script really must indicate is the *first* sound of any word; initial sounds are so psychologically salient that a script which omitted them might be barely usable. This creates no special problem for writing Semitic languages in a vowel-less alphabet, since every Semitic word begins with a consonant, if only a glottal stop. But Sanskrit has plenty of vowel-initial words.[17] As described so far, Devanagari offers no way of writing initial vowels. But in fact it has a set of letters, comparable in size and shape to consonant letters, which are used to write vowels exclusively at the beginnings of words:

a	ā	अ	आ
i	ī	इ	ई
u	ū	उ	ऊ
ai	āi	ए	ऐ
au	āu	ओ	औ
r̩	r̩̄	ऋ	ॠ

The letters for long vowels and diphthongs are derived from the letters for their short counterparts, but the symbol for a given initial short vowel in many cases has no visible relationship with the subsidiary symbol for that same vowel when it follows a consonant or consonant-cluster.

Once Indian scribes had invented letters for vowels, it might seem strange to us that they would not go on to use those letters for vowels wherever the vowels occurred – in which case they could have abandoned the complex system of ligatured letters for consonant clusters and diacritic marks for following vowels.[18] But they did not do that. Presumably, the precedent of Semitic script, in which, to a close approximation, a letter stands for a syllable, held too much authority for that step to seem natural. And what seems convenient or inconvenient to us is heavily coloured by the particular technology we use. When all writing was handwriting, there was no great difficulty about using a range of ligatured forms, though working at a 20c typewriter they must have been much more problematic. Mediaeval scribes in Europe used many ligatures and diacritics to represent combinations of Roman letters, which were abandoned after printing came in.

As an example of Devanagari script, here is a line of Sanskrit from the *Bhagavadgītā* (quoted by Bright 1996: 389); it describes the human soul, and runs in English “Weapons do not cut it, fire does not burn it”:

नैनं छिन्दन्ति शस्त्राणि नैनं दहति पावकः
n-āi-n-~ i-c^h-nd-i-nt ʃ-str-ā-i-ɳ n-āi-n-~ d-ɦ-i-t p-ā-v-k-h
nāinã c^{h}indanti ʃastrāɳi nāinã daɦati pāvakah

The first line of transcription shows the values of the Devanagari letters in left-to-right sequence, with hyphens to indicate which IPA symbols jointly correspond to one “letter”: e.g. /str/ in the third word is written as a ligature of स < s > with the unitary symbol for < tr > discussed above. Again, remember that short /i/ is written to the left of the consonant it follows; the second word begins with the subsidiary form for short /i/, so < i-c^h > is pronounced /c^{h}i-/ (if the word-initial vowel letter इ had instead appeared, the pronunciation would be /ic^{h}a-/). My symbol /~/ represents the dot over the end of the first word, which indicates vowel nasalization; the colon-shaped mark at the end stands for /h/, which never occurs before a vowel and hence does not require the < ् > mark to suppress an implied /a/. The second line of transcription shows the actual Sanskrit pronunciation.

* * *

Now we have looked at how the original all-consonant alphabet worked, a further question is where it came from. How come that the world's first alphabet emerged in Palestine rather than anywhere else?

The homeland of the Semitic alphabet occupied an intermediate location within the so-called "Fertile Crescent", between Mesopotamia in the east and Egypt in the west. Both of those latter areas had early, non-alphabetic writing systems: Cuneiform in Mesopotamia, and in Egypt the Hieroglyphic script (on which see e.g. Davies 1990). It has been supposed for a long time that the impetus to create the alphabet, including at least the idea of writing, must have stemmed from exposure to one or other of those scripts (at times the use of Cuneiform spread as far west as modern Syria, and of Hieroglyphics as far north as modern Lebanon; Man 2009: 176). Until recently there was no decisive ground for picking one of the two candidates, but new discoveries seem to have definitively resolved the question.

Cuneiform and Hieroglyphic scripts are apparently unrelated, and superficially they look quite different. Cuneiform script, although originally based on (rather crude) pictures, was reduced at an early stage to abstract arrangements of linear marks, whereas Egyptian hieroglyphs retained their pictorial quality, and inscriptions were often executed with great graphic detail in many colours. (Cursive variants of the hieroglyphs, which lost their pictorial quality, were also developed, but because these were written with pen and ink rather than pressed into clay tablets they look nothing like cuneiform writing.)

As systems, though, Cuneiform and Hieroglyphic scripts were not so very different; both were mixtures of logography and phonography. As we have seen, Cuneiform graphs functioning phonographically stood for syllables, CV or CVC. In the Egyptian script, vowels were largely ignored, and phonographic symbols represented sequences of three, two, or one consonant(s). (The Egyptian language, now long extinct, was distantly related to the Semitic group of languages, and hence had similar reasons for not writing vowels. Because the Hieroglyphic scribal tradition never developed any equivalent to the Hebrew pointing system, we do not today know much about the vowels of Egyptian words.)

As a brief example, consider the hieroglyph array:

This inscription corresponds to the following logographic and phonographic values, here arranged on the page to reflect the arrangement of the hieroglyphs:

s HOUSE
sɟ m xr w SPEAK m
MAN LOGO

which represents the following Egyptian wording (of course the words contained vowels as well as consonants, but we do not know what the vowels were):

/ sɟm s xrw m pr /

This translates into English word for word as:

hear man voice in house

and idiomatically as:

the man hears the voice in the house

The logographic signs MAN and SPEAK (the latter showing a man pointing to his mouth) are in this context being used as "determinatives": they have no pronunciation of their own, but SPEAK, for example, shows that, out of various words containing the consonants /xrw/ (or just /w/ – the script did not indicate word boundaries), the word intended here (namely "voice") was one which had something to do with speaking. The vertical line below the HOUSE graph shows that that graph is being used logographically, that is it stands in this context for the word /pr/ "house", rather than for a consonant sequence /pr/ within some other word.

Since the hieroglyphic script of Egypt included graphs for single consonants (though these were a minority among the full range of signs), an obvious possibility would be that people who had experience of Hieroglyphic devised a simpler writing system for themselves by using exclusively that principle, without any logograms or multi-phoneme phonograms. It now seems likely that this is indeed what happened, since the discovery in the 1990s of two inscriptions on rock in the Western Desert of Egypt, tentatively dated to early in the –2nd millennium (Darnell *et al.* 2005). These inscriptions appear to be alphabetic, and most individual graphs included in them are recognizably ancestral to early forms of Semitic letters, while at the same time they have clear links with Hieroglyphic forms.

The discoverers suggest that the inscriptions could represent a script created by Semitic-speaking immigrants in Egypt (there are known to have been many of these), who grossly simplified the Hieroglyphic system in order to adapt it to their own language, and who then took this simple script with them when some of them returned to their Palestinian homeland.[19]

It has long been recognized that there are similarities between early forms of a few of the Semitic letters and some of the Egyptian phonograms (though where the forms are similar they stand for different sounds in the respective scripts). For instance, the Hieroglyphic sign 𓈖, representing the rippled appearance of water, stood for /n/, the first sound of the Egyptian word for "water"; the Semitic letter < m > appears to be an abbreviated version of that graph, used by the Semites for /m/ because their own word for "water" began with that sound. The Semites wrote /n/ with the graph nūn, which means "fish" but does not look much like a fish; however Gelb (1952: 140) pointed out that in one Semitic language, Ethiopic, the name of the letter is /naħāʃ /, "snake". The letter shape is quite similar to the conventional Hieroglyphic representation of a snake, 𓆓 (which stood in Egyptian for a sibilant consonant); it is easy to imagine that the Semites could have borrowed the graph shape and called it /naħāʃ/, using it for /n/, and later rechristened it nūn by analogy with the CVC shape of the preceding letter name mēm, rather as the Americans have rechristened the Roman letter Z as "zee" by analogy with the names of B, C, etc. (In Arabic most letters have been rechristened in a similar fashion.) Again, the name of the Hebrew letter bēt is a form of the word for "house" but the early shape of the letter (see Figure 16) does not obviously look like a house; however, it is not hard to see it as a hasty distortion of the Hieroglyphic logogram for /pr/ (see above), which certainly was intended as a schematic picture of a house.

One might wonder how plausible it is that a community acquainted with an established form of phonographic writing should have created a wholly new set of graph/sound correspondences – would it not have been simpler just to take those Hieroglyphic graphs which could be used to write Semitic speech and use them with their values unchanged? As we shall see, when the Greeks borrowed writing from the Semites this is what happened. But it is rash to project our own sophisticated ideas about the conventionality of symbols into the minds of men at the dawn of civilization. It seems very possible that when the Semites first encountered writing they saw the acrophonic principle as part of its essence: writing might at first have *meant* drawing things to symbolize their initial sounds, so that a picture of water could represent no sound other than /m/ for people who called water /majim/. As already mentioned, Egyptian hieroglyphs were very obviously pictures (whereas, when Greeks later borrowed the Semitic alphabet, the letters were only abstract shapes).

Even if it is true that the inspiration for the Semitic alphabet came from Egypt, incidentally, that does not necessarily imply that Mesopotamian writing played no role whatever in its ultimate ancestry. It is often suggested that the Egyptians themselves may have borrowed the *idea* of writing from the Sumerians when creating their hieroglyphic script. They could hardly have borrowed much more than the bare idea – although both systems began (and the Egyptian system continued) as pictorial symbols, the pictures were largely of different objects. Whether it is plausible that the one script influenced the creation of the other even in this limited sense very much depends on dates, and although at one time there was a consensus that Sumerian writing went back a little further than Hieroglyphic, scholars these days hold conflicting views about that (Baines 2004: 154.) When new discoveries by Egyptologists some years ago seemed to push the beginnings of Egyptian writing back before the earliest Sumerian script, one Mesopotamianist, Christopher Walker, commented that the two sides would end up "leap-frog[ging] each other. If they think they have evidence of a fully developed script at that point, we would start looking for earlier stages" (quoted in Alberge 1998).

Whether or not Egyptian writing was an entirely original invention, though, alphabetic writing probably did begin in Egypt.

Notes

1. There are differences of grammar and vocabulary also, but these are largely irrelevant to a consideration of how the orthography works. Some individual words cited as examples in what follows are first attested in post-Biblical times.
2. Evidence from the site of Ugarit, near modern Latakia on the coast of Syria (see e.g. O'Connor 1996: 92), shows that one very early version of the Semitic alphabet contained additional letters for proto-Semitic consonants which were not needed for Hebrew because they had merged with other phonemes. It is not known whether the longer alphabet was original or whether the extra letters were added to what began as a shorter alphabet (Goldenberg 2013: 33).
3. My Hebrew transcriptions ignore stress placement unless it is directly relevant to the point under discussion, as it is here.
4. Some writers suggest that gīmel was a picture of a "throwing stick" (a kind of boomerang); but it is not clear whether this hypothesis is founded on positive evidence or is simply a guess based on the angular shape.

5. Gelb argued that the history of all scripts involves a progression from logographic through syllabic to segmental, and that it is "unthinkable" that the middle stage could be skipped. Yet he acknowledged that most Egyptologists thought it.
6. Readers who find it surprising that a real-life language could function in this way might like to look at a plausible account of the likely origin of the Semitic inflexion system by Guy Deutscher (2005: 171–206).
7. It is debatable which word-final < h > letters corresponded to actually pronounced /h/ phonemes (Lambdin 1971: xxv).
8. Likewise, James Barr remarked (1976: 81–2) that a Hebrew equivalent of a nonsense text such as Lewis Carroll's "'Twas brillig, and the slithy toves ..." would have to be pointed. (Of course this is itself a poem, but the same thing would apply equally to a nonsense text in prose form.) An English reader encountering a word like < brillig > or < slithy > knows quite certainly that it is not English, but a Hebrew reader faced with unpointed transcriptions of Hebrew nonsense-words would feel puzzled and unsure of what was being written.
9. In the noun /k'ōp/ "monkey", which gave the letter < k' > its name, the /ō/ vowel is inherent.
10. "Focus" is used loosely here. What is relevant is not simply whether the lens is accommodated to focus letters on the retina but whether given letters are brought within the two-degree portion of the whole visual field that focuses on the very sensitive retinal area called the fovea. See e.g. Rayner *et al.* (2012: 9–10).
11. On the analogous problems which arise for Arabic readers, see e.g. Mahmoud (1979).
12. I have been assuming throughout this chapter (as many others do) that the "vowel-less" nature of the Semitic alphabet is causally related to the special role of vowels in spoken Semitic languages. One distinguished Semitic expert, Guy Deutscher, tells me that he disagrees, and sees the nature of the Semitic alphabet as a mere historical accident deriving from the circumstances in which it was first devised (on which more below). Against this, one might argue that it would be a strange coincidence for languages in which vowels play an unusually limited role to just happen to use an alphabet with no vowel letters, and one might wonder why, in that case, full-scale vowel writing never developed over thousands of years. But a possible answer to that last point would allude to the sacred status of the Hebrew Old Testament and Koran, creating a reluctance to tamper with their ancient orthographies.
13. The actual letter shapes of European alphabets have changed less than Indian letter shapes from the common ancestral Semitic forms, but the change in the way letters are used is greater in the case of European scripts.
14. The Hebrew alphabet itself descends from the Aramaic version of the parent Phoenician alphabet. It was adopted by the Jews in about the –2c,

replacing the letter shapes which they had previously inherited from Phoenician script independently of Aramaic writing.

15. The etymology of the name Devanagari is disputed, and for our purposes the issue is too peripheral to enter into.
16. In the historical period, /ai au/ had become /e o/ and /a/ had become /ə/, but the logic of the script is rather clearer if discussed in terms of the phonology as it was before the operation of these sound changes. Also, I ignore a rare syllabic lateral phoneme, /l̥ /.
17. One might be tempted to think that "vowel initial" and "glottal stop + vowel initial" are merely alternative ways of perceiving the same phonetic realities – who is to say what state an English-speaker's glottis is in immediately before he begins speaking? But there is more to it than that. In languages where a word ending in a vowel can be followed by a word beginning with a vowel, the adjacent vowels will often be run together or elided – this happens a great deal in Sanskrit (e.g. /sā uvāca/ "she said" > [sōvāca], /maha ātman/ "great souled" > [mahātman]). In Hebrew, initial glottal stops prevent neighbouring vowels from coalescing in this way.
18. It is not clear historically how the vowel letters were devised, or whether the full letters or the diacritic marks came first.
19. Orly Goldwasser (2010) argues for an essentially similar account of the birth of the alphabet, but places the site of origin at Serabit el-Khadem in the southern Sinai. See BAS Staff (2012) for discussion of controversy surrounding this account.

6 European alphabetic writing

We usually think of European languages as using different alphabets – our own Roman alphabet, the Greek alphabet, the Cyrillic alphabet used for Russian and Bulgarian – but, in reality, these are best thought of as variants of one system. Where to draw the line between "different scripts" is as problematic as deciding when spoken language varieties should count as separate languages rather than dialects of one language. In the alphabet case, what unites all European alphabets and sets them apart from their Semitic cousin-scripts is that, in Greek, Roman, and Cyrillic script, vowel sounds have the same status as consonant sounds, being assigned letters of their own. This important step was taken once, by Greeks, and all modern European writing embodies it. For some commentators, its significance is tremendous. Eric Havelock (1986: 10) held that it "chang[ed] the character of the Greek consciousness ... and in fact could be held responsible for creating the character of a modern consciousness which is becoming worldwide".

* * *

In case it sounds too glib to suggest that European alphabets are just "variants of one system", consider some reasons for seeing them that way. We think of the Greek alphabet as separate from ours, but more than half of the capital letters are common to both, and several others can be seen as minor variants of shape – D is a fairly straightforward distortion of Δ, Greek delta. The lower-case letters diverge more; lower-case letterforms represent the shapes that arise through hasty cursive writing, and these were different for the ancient Greeks and ourselves because, evidently, even when writing careful capitals the Greeks went about it differently. Personal handwriting techniques vary, but most modern Europeans are happy to raise their pen in the middle of forming a letter if that permits a sequence of mainly downward or rightward strokes: thus we begin a B at the top left and make the vertical first, before returning to that corner to make the two bowls. The Greeks evidently set more store by forming each letter with one continuous pen stroke; they must have begun a B at the bottom left corner and written the vertical upwards, since only that sequence explains how B "decayed" into cursive β, lower-case beta. Likewise, A can be written continuously if one end of the crossbar is allowed to droop and meet the left-hand oblique at its foot, A – Greeks often used that form as a capital, and it explains why lower-case alpha is α. But differences in how people form the same shapes are a meagre basis for thinking of scripts as different.

True, Greek and Roman alphabets each have some letters with no equivalent in the other. But Scandinavian languages use several letters not used in English (e.g. ø and æ in Norwegian, þ and ð in Icelandic) yet we do not normally think of Scandinavians as using "different scripts". Indeed, judgements of "same versus different script" are not even always symmetrical. When English is written in mediaeval black-letter (**Olde Curiosity Shoppe**), or when German was written in the essentially similar *Fraktur*, we English-speakers think of these as a quaintly shaped variant of our own script. But, for prewar Germans, they were two separate scripts, so that if a foreign phrase or an algebraic equation appeared within a passage of German printed in *Fraktur*, the non-German elements were set in roman. See Figure 19, an extract from a novel of 1892. Marcell is chaffing Corinna for some rather fierce remarks, when an English visitor breaks in in a mixture of schoolboy German and English which accordingly is set in alternating *Fraktur* and roman.[1] If Germans treated their script and ours as two separate scripts, while we regarded them as varieties of one script, it is hard to agree that this is a question with a right answer. From the point of view of scientific linguistics, what matters is the system underlying the signs, rather than their outward appearance, and relative to the diversity of the world's writing systems all European alphabets embody essentially the same system.

* * *

Marcell drohte halb ernst-, halb scherzhaft mit dem Finger zu Corinna hinüber und sagte: „Cousine, vergiß nicht, daß der Repräsentant einer andern Nation dir zur Seite sitzt und daß du die Pflicht hast, einigermaßen für deutsche Weiblichkeit einzutreten."

„O, no, no," sagte Nelson: „Nichts Weiblichkeit; always quick and clever …, das is was wir lieben an deutsche Frauen. Nichts Weiblichkeit. Fräulein Corinna is quite in the right way."

„Da hast du's, Marcell. Mr. Nelson, für den du so sorg-

Figure 19

After the collapse of Mycenaean civilization in the −13c the Greeks lost the art of writing for centuries. In the Classical period, when they were writing alphabetically, the Greeks were unaware that some of their ancestors had once used a different, syllabic form of writing. Greek tradition dated the adoption of the alphabet to the First Olympiad (i.e. −776). The archaeological evidence is reasonably compatible with this general date, and it is supported by L.H. Jeffery (1990: 21, 425–7), James Whitley (2001: 130–31), and Benjamin Sass (2005).

The Greek alphabet derives from some version of the Semitic alphabet. Almost certainly the version encountered by Greeks was that used by the Phoenicians, who were the one Semitic nation which travelled and traded overseas; the Greeks are known to have called their alphabet "Phoenician letters".[2]

It is generally agreed that the alphabet must have been transmitted to the Greeks just once, rather than being borrowed independently by Greeks in contact with Semites on different occasions; Barry Powell (1991: 10–11) holds that it is "beyond doubt" that "the [Greek] alphabet was created by a single man at a single time". After the Greeks acquired the alphabet, many local variations evolved in various parts of the Greek-speaking world, differing in shapes and Greek values of some Semitic letters and in a number of supplementary letters invented by the Greeks themselves. These locally varying versions of the Greek alphabet are classified into a "Western" and an "Eastern" group. After the early diversification, there followed a period of convergence, during which districts that used other alphabet versions gradually discarded them in favour of the Ionic version, one of the "Eastern" group, and this became standard throughout Greece by about −350. This is essentially the classical Greek alphabet that we know today.

Most Greek consonant letters derive their values from the Semitic ancestor-script in a straightforward way. Some letters were used for slightly different consonant sounds because Greek lacked a sound precisely like the Semitic sound. Take the Semitic letters for ejective stops: Greek had no ejectives. The letter t'ēt for /t'/ was used by the Greeks, in the form Θ, for a different, aspirated rather than ejective phoneme /tʰ/. One might have expected that the Greek letter Ϙ, formed from qōp, would have stood analogously for Greek /kʰ/; instead it was used to mark a purely allophonic difference in Greek. As in many other languages, /k/ in Greek varied in its exact place of articulation depending on the following vowel, and the Greeks wrote Ϙ for the relatively back allophone of /k/ found before back vowels, keeping K (from kāp) for the allophones of /k/ occurring before central and front vowels. (Since we do not know what precise pronunciation < t' k' > had in the Semitic language encountered by the Greeks, at the time they encountered it, we cannot know why the two letters were used in these different ways.) After the –6c the logic of the phonemic principle asserted itself so that back allophones of /k/ were also written with K, and the letter Ϙ, called by the Greeks "koppa", did not survive into the Classical period.

The development that was really significant and novel was the Greek use of six Semitic letters, < ʔ h w ħ j ʕ >, to represent vowels. Let me defer for a few pages an exposition of the Greek vowel system, and say simply that the Semitic letters were used roughly as follows: ʔālep for Greek /a/, hē for /e/, wāw became two letters of slightly different shapes < F Y > standing respectively for /w/ and /u/, ħēt was used either for /h/ or for an /e/-like vowel, jōd for /i/, and ʕajin for /o/.

Of these six Semitic letters, only wāw stood for a sound, /w/, which also existed as a phoneme in –8c Greek, and one of the two Greek letters developed from wāw retained that value. (In the later evolution of spoken Greek, the phoneme /w/ dropped out, so that the letter F, like Ϙ, became obsolete in the Classical Greek alphabet.) The pharyngeal sounds [ħ ʕ] and the glottal stop [ʔ] did not occur at all in Greek, and [h j], though they did occur, had a marginal, scarcely phonemic status.

On the other hand, distinctions between vowels were more crucial in Greek than in Semitic languages. Greek is a European language: it uses vowel distinctions heavily for lexical contrasts, and only to a minor extent for grammatical purposes. Thus in Greek script an indication of vowels is important for communication, and also does not lead to the confusion that could be caused by a vocalized script for a Semitic language, in which the written shape of a root would vary widely depending on grammatical inflexion. Furthermore, Greek words often begin with vowels. And, while sequences of two or more vowels were almost unknown in Semitic languages, in Greek they are normal: e.g. /paideuousi/ "they teach". Indeed, Greek words can consist entirely of vowels, whether short common words like /ǣ/ "or", /ou/ "not", or longer words such as /aiaia/, the name of the mythical island where Odysseus met the enchantress Circe.[3]

All these are reasons why it was desirable for Greek to be written with vowel letters, if it was going to be written in a segmental script at all. But there remains a question about how the redundant Semitic letters were adapted to this purpose. Some have supposed that this was the result of a conscious plan by a clever Greek scribe. I am sceptical. It seems easier to imagine the reinterpretation of the letters as having happened automatically when speakers of a language with a non-Semitic phonological system learned the letter names and the acrophonic principle (cf. Jeffery 1990: 22).

In general, the Greek names of the letters are simply the Semitic names modified to make them pronounceable in Greek: thus kāp became Greek kappa, since Greek words cannot end in /p/. (I shall quote Greek letter names in their ordinary English spelling rather than a scientific transliteration.) In Greek the letter names are meaningless, but the relationship between names and letter-values is retained: K is called kappa, and its value is /k/, the first sound of kappa. Any teacher of phonetics knows how hard people find it to hear a sound that is not used in their own language. One can readily imagine the following scenario. A Greek sees a Phoenician using a system of written marks and asks for an explanation. The Phoenician (who probably called the first letter /ʔalp/ – the /e/ of Hebrew "ʔālep" is epenthetic) begins, "This mark is called ʔalp – no, not 'alp' – ʔalp, ʔalp, can't you hear, ʔʔʔalp!", while the bewildered Greek perceives only the [alp], and ends up calling the letter "alp^{h}-a" *and using it for* /a/, since by the acrophonic principle that will now seem to him to be its proper value. This would explain the Greek use of Semitic < ʔ h ħ ʕ > as vowel letters without the need to attribute any special linguistic sophistication to the first Greek user of the alphabet, if we make the plausible assumption that the vowels in the Phoenician names of those letters were something like the Greek vowels for which the letters came to be used. And the phonetic similarity between the vowel /i/ and the approximant /j/ is such that, again, the adaptation of jōd would seem to have required no special act of intelligence.

The only one of the letters in question for which this account is known to be oversimplified is ħēt: in this case it seems that the Greeks identified the Semitic /ħ/ with the /h/ which is one of the alternative ways of beginning a Greek word whose first phoneme is a vowel (cf. p. 64), and the reinterpretation of ħēt as a vowel letter happened not when it was transmitted from Semites to Greeks but, later, when it was transmitted from one group of Greeks to another whose dialect lacked [h]. In the classical Greek alphabet, H from ħēt was used for a vowel akin to /e/; but the fact that other Greeks had used this letter for [h] was reflected in the diacritics classically used to mark the word-initial [h] versus zero contrast. The so-called "rough and smooth breathing" marks, as in < ἁ > /ha/ versus < ἀ > /a/, derive graphically from ⊢ and ⊣, i.e. two halves of H. (The early Greek use of H for [h] also explains this use by the Romans, for whom /h/ was fully phonemic.)

An aspect of the original Greek use of vowel letters which does suggest conscious thought is the creation of two letters from the one Semitic letter wāw, in order to distinguish the Greek vowel /u/ from the consonant /w/. The vowel letter derived from wāw, being an extra letter, was added at the end of the alphabet.

Later, different Greek communities created further supplementary letters, always adding them to the end of the current alphabetic order. Ignoring some which did not survive into the classical Greek alphabet, the letter Φ was invented for /pʰ/; X was used in the Western group of alphabets for /ks/ and in the Eastern group for /kʰ/; Ψ was used in the Western group for /kʰ/ and in the Eastern group for /ps/; and Ω, an opened-out O, was created to differentiate long, open /ɔ̄/ from short, close /ŏ/ – hence the names o-mega, o-micron, "big O", "little O", for Ω and O. Since the Ionic alphabet belonged to the Eastern group, the letters X, Ψ had their Eastern values in the eventual standard Greek alphabet.

There is an odd situation with respect to the sibilant letters. As we know, the Semitic alphabet had four sibilant letters: zajin, sāmek, s'ādē, and ʃīn. In Hebrew the last of these stood for two different phonemes, and it is clear that Proto-Semitic had five sibilants (though we do not know whether that was true for Phoenician). The early Greek alphabet had four letters, Z Ξ M Σ, whose shapes are derived from those four Semitic letters respectively and which occurred in the same places in the alphabetic sequence. But their names somehow got swapped about: their Greek names zeta, xi, san, sigma seem to derive respectively from s'ādē, ʃīn, zajin, sāmek.

Greek had only two sibilant phonemes, /s/ and a phoneme which in modern Greek is pronounced [z], but at the time of adoption of the alphabet may have been an affricate [dz] (cf. p. 64 above), which is how I shall transcribe it. This /dz/ was represented by Z. Ξ was used for /ks/ in Ionic and some other local alphabets, but it was ignored in the alphabets which used X for /ks/. M from Semitic s'ādē and Σ from Semitic ʃīn, in Greek named san and sigma respectively, seem to have been used interchangeably for /s/; as time went on some local alphabets used only san, others only sigma. In consequence, san did not survive into the classical Greek alphabet, and that allowed the Greek version of Semitic mēm, initially written with five strokes, to lose one of them and take on a shape which coincided with that of the obsolete san.

Some scholars see the confusion of names as clear evidence that transmission of the Semitic alphabet to the Greeks was an informal initiative by one individual, perhaps a Greek trader who tried to learn the alphabet and pass it on to some of his countrymen as a sideline to his real business. Such a man, faced with a set of letters for four or five shades of sound with no equivalents in his own speech, might well muddle them in his mind. If some official group had been charged with the task of importing this useful technology from the East, would one not expect them to treat the alphabet more systematically?

Figure 20 compares the original Semitic alphabet with the letterforms, letter-values, and letter names of the classical version of the Greek alphabet, as used in Athens after −402. (Items within brackets were obsolete by that time.)

* * *

𐤀	ʔālep	ʔ	Α	alpha	ă, ā
𐤁	bēt	b	Β	beta	b
𐤂	gīmel	g	Γ	gamma	g
𐤃	dālet	d	Δ	delta	d
𐤄	hē	h	Ε	epsilon	ĕ
𐤅	wāw	w	Ϝ	wau	w
𐤆	zajin	z	Ζ	zeta	dz
𐤇	ħēt	ħ	Η	eta	ǣ
𐤈	t’ēt	t’	Θ	theta	t^h
𐤉	jōd	j	Ι	iota	ĭ, ī
𐤊	kāp	k	Κ	kappa	k
𐤋	lāmed	l	Λ	lamda	l
𐤌	mēm	m	Μ	mu	m
𐤍	nūn	n	Ν	nu	n
𐤎	sāmek	s	Ξ	xi	ks
𐤏	ʕajin	ʕ	Ο	omicron	ŏ
𐤐	pē	p	Π	pi	p
𐤑	s’ādē	s’	Ϻ	san	s
𐤒	k’ōp	k’	Ϙ	koppa	k
𐤓	rēʃ	r	Ρ	rho	r
𐤔	šīn	ʃ, ś	Σ	sigma	s
𐤕	tāw	t	Τ	tau	t
			Υ	upsilon	(ŭ, ū >) ȳ̆, ȳ
			Φ	phi	p^h
			Χ	chi	k^h
			Ψ	psi	ps
			Ω	omega	ō

Figure 20

The Greeks naturally followed Semitic practice by writing from right to left, but from an early period – possibly from their first use of the alphabet – they usually wrote multi-line inscriptions not all right-to-left (as the Semites did and do), but in so-called *boustrophedon* ("ox-turning") style, alternately right-to-left and left-to-right in successive lines as furrows are ploughed, so that there were no big jumps between the end of one line and beginning of the next. This gradually gave way to the system we use today of consistent left-to-right writing, which was standard by the Classical period.

This gradual evolution from R-to-L to L-to-R writing might sound an odd thing to happen. But, everywhere in the world, the right is seen as the "good, important" side – a king's guest of honour will sit at his right hand; so, at the very beginning of writing, it may have been natural to start making marks on that side. Once writing lengthy documents became routine, for the right-handed majority the L-to-R direction is more practical, since the hand does not cover what has just been written. The same development, from R-to-L through a *boustrophedon* stage to eventual L-to-R writing, happened independently in the early history of the Indian alphabet whose modern descendants include Devanagari.

In *boustrophedon* writing the shapes of the individual letters were reversed with the writing direction, so the same side always faced forwards. Consequently, when the L-to-R direction became standard, the final letter shapes were the reverse of those inherited from Semitic script. (In Figure 20, compare e.g. B E N with their Semitic counterparts.)

* * *

The Greek adoption of the alphabet was a unique episode, not only because of the novelty of representing vowels as well as consonants by independent symbols, but also because it was a striking exception to Marcel Cohen's generalization (p. 42 above) about early writing being used predominantly for utilitarian purposes. Linear B script seems to have been used exclusively for administrative purposes, but "there are no early Greek [alphabetic] inscriptions which are, by any stretch of the imagination, administrative"; rather, from an early stage "Greek literacy became an integral part of Greek art, culture and life" (Whitley 2001: 131, 133). Early Greek alphabetic literacy seems to have been so much geared to humane rather than official purposes as to lead Barry Powell (1991) to claim that the motivation for adopting the alphabet may actually have been to record the Homeric epics, Europe's first literature. That might sound implausible, but Powell makes a surprisingly convincing case.

Furthermore, while the use of other early scripts was often limited to narrow specialist groups, in Greece alphabetic literacy seems to have spread rather widely. Henri-Irénée Marrou (1965: 83) claimed that the institution of ostracism which operated in Athens throughout the –5c implies that, by the beginning of that century at the latest, the average Athenian citizen must have been literate. Debate about this has continued, but the weight of scholarly opinion seems to side with Marrou (see Burns 1981 and Missiou 2011 against Havelock 1977: 382–4). As Anna Missiou sees it, widespread literacy was a concomitant of Athenian democracy: "it was not simply that some or many Athenians could write: they were repeatedly asked or required to write. ... Popular participation motivated the ordinary citizens to learn to read and write" (Missiou 2011: 148–9).

* * *

The Greek alphabet was not a perfect, complete reflection of the phonemic system of spoken Greek. It came fairly close to that ideal, though, and the respects in which it deviated are easy to understand.

To begin by disposing briefly of an oddity which is not so much a shortcoming in the system as an unnecessary luxury: it is natural to wonder why the alphabet should have included special graphemes for /ks ps/, which phonetically speaking are clusters of distinct consonants (they are not like affricates such as /ts/, which are phonetically single sounds). The answer seems to be that /ks ps/ were the only consonant clusters that could occur at the end of a syllable in Greek, and that led the Greeks to perceive these clusters as belonging together more tightly than other consonant groupings, and hence as deserving letters of their own.

Two consonant phonemes had alternative allophones: /r/ was voiceless [r̥] initially and in certain other positions, voiced elsewhere, and /s/ was voiced [z] before voiced consonants, voiceless elsewhere (Allen 1968: 39–41, 43–4). In each case a single grapheme, Ρ and Σ, covered both members of the phoneme.

The vowel system deserves fuller examination. Following Allen (1968: ch. 2) we can reconstruct as follows the pure vowel phoneme system of Attic Greek (that is, the dialect of the Athens area, which eventually became the spoken standard for all Greeks):[4]

long	short
ī ȳ ū	ĭ y̆
ē	
	ɛ̆ ŏ
ǣ ɔ̄	
ā	ă

These phonemes were represented by Greek letters as follows:

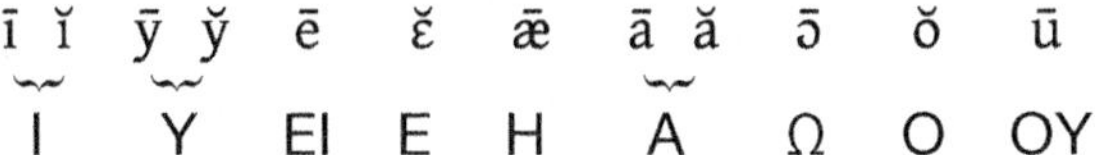

A sound change shortly before or during the Classical period had fronted [ū ŭ] to [ȳ y̆], so the letter Y automatically came to stand for these fronted sounds. The phoneme /ē/ resulted from the merging of an earlier contrast between /ē/ and the diphthong /ei/; while these sounds still contrasted, the pure vowel was written, like its short counterpart, with E, but after the merger the digraph EI (which had been phonetically appropriate for the diphthong) was used for all cases of the /ē/ phoneme. Likewise, /ū/ was the outcome of a merger between earlier /ō/ and /ou/; while these contrasted, long and short /o/ were both written O, but after the merger the digraph OY which had been phonetically appropriate for /ou/ was used for all cases of /ū/.

(After the mergers just mentioned, there remained various diphthongs in [-i -u], and these were written with -I -Y; the letter Y retained the value [u] for writing diphthongs after it had shifted to the value [y] as a pure vowel.)

Vowel length was contrastive, e.g. /dănŏs/ "a debt" contrasted with /dānŏs/ "parched". But the script distinguished only vowel quality, not quantity. Long and short versions of /a i y/ were written alike. Separate writings were used for those long and short vowels which were intermediate between fully open and fully close, but a pair such as /ɔ̄ ŏ/ differed in quality as well as in quantity. (As in Chapter 4, I shall normally omit short-vowel marks in Greek examples cited below.)

Greek also had a quantity contrast in consonants, as in /or̄os/ "rump" versus /or̆os/ "mountain". In the early days of Greek writing, long and short consonants were not distinguished, but by –500 Attic writing distinguished long consonants by writing them double. Doubtless that is why, to this day, orthographies which mark quantity in consonants commonly use single versus double consonant letters, whereas for many languages long vowels are indicated by adding a diacritic to a single vowel symbol.

The alphabet had no symbol for the velar nasal [ŋ] and represented it by Γ, i.e. < g >. The distribution of [ŋ] was extremely limited (it occurred only before nasals and /g/), and it came close to being an allophone of /g/, so this treatment was reasonable even though, according to Allen (1968: 36–7), [ŋ] must be assigned separate phoneme status because of a few contrasts such as [εŋgεnǣs] "innate" versus [εggonos] "offspring".

These words are derived by adding the prefixes /εn-/ "in" and /εk-/ "out of", respectively, to stems beginning with /g-/, to which the prefix consonants assimilate. They were commonly distinguished in spelling by writing the former < εgg... > but the latter, in line with its derivation, < εkg... >.

This is a case where the aim of avoiding ambiguity leads to "deep" rather than "surface" orthography being used at an earlier period than was normal for Greek. Allen points out that [εg-] from underlying [εk-] was spelled < εg > before < b d > (where no possibility of interpreting < g > as [ŋ] arises) until the –1c. And in general, when assimilation rules or other phonological processes lead to differences between deep and surface phonological forms, Greek orthography tended more often than modern English orthography to reflect the surface facts and ignore morphological structure. Consider, for instance, the fact that the preposition /syn/ "with" regularly assimilated its /n/ to following consonants in compound words such as /syl-logos/ "a gathering", /sym-ptɔ̄sis/ "a coincidence", and the assimilated segments were written < l >, < m >, etc. rather than, in accordance with derivation, < n > – as if we were to spell the English word *input* as **imput*, which is how we say it. Or consider the spelling of the consonant clusters that occur regularly in various forms of the perfect passive of a root like /prāg-/ "do":

1st person sing.	pε-prāŋ-mai
2nd person sing.	pε-prāk-sai
3rd person sing.	pε-prāk-tai
2nd person pl.	pε-prāk^h-t^hε

Each of the clusters /ŋm ks kt $k^h t^h$/ straddles the boundary between root and suffix; they are spelled respectively ΓΜ, Ξ, ΚΤ, ΧΘ. This is as if the English words *optic, optics, optician, opticist* were to be spelled < optik, optix, optishan, optisist >.

The final respect in which classical Greek orthography is less than fully complete has to do with so-called "accent". Ancient Greek had a stress system, meaning that one mora in each word was given special prominence; and, as in English, the position of stress was not fixed but varied from word to word. A "mora" is a vowel unit such that short vowels consist of one mora and long vowels consist of two; a long-vowel syllable could take stress either on its first or its second mora.[5] Stress was sometimes contrastive, with minimal pairs such as /tómos/ "a cut" versus /tomós/ "cutting, sharp", or /lýysai/ "to have released" versus /lyýsai/ "he would have released" (I represent long /ȳ/ as /yy/ here to show the position of stress). But contrastive use of stress relates almost wholly to grammar (lexical contrasts, such as /pʰɔɔ́s/ "man" versus /pʰɔ́ɔs/ "light", are very rare), and even in the grammatical domain minimal pairs differing only in position of stress are few. So it is not surprising that classical Greek orthography ignored stress.

As in the case of Hebrew script, the Greeks too in due course supplemented the orthography described here with diacritic marks indicating many of the aspects of pronunciation ignored by their alphabet, such as stress and the allophonic distinction between voiced and voiceless /r/. But the period when this "Byzantine" diacritic system came into use seems to have roughly coincided with the period when many of the contrasts marked by that system were ceasing to be part of the spoken language. As in the case of Masoretic pointing of Hebrew, the diacritics were more about preserving detailed knowledge of a canonical but obsolete language than a phonographic orthography in the ordinary sense.

* * *

Segmental script, for Western readers, is the most familiar kind of writing, and it is illustrated by classical Greek orthography about as well as it could be by any example. But, since the writing system we ourselves use descends from the one we have been examining, in the remainder of this chapter it will be worth looking briefly at how the Roman alphabet acquired its present form. (There are many good books nowadays written for non-experts which give much more detail on the history of our alphabet than I can give here; see e.g. Man 2009.)

The Romans acquired the art of writing about a century after the foundation of the city of Rome in −753. In the −7c Rome was still a small place, and the dominant culture in that part of Italy was Etruria, to the north of Rome. (Later, as Rome's strength grew, it gradually absorbed the Etruscans until by −200 Etruria no longer existed as a political entity.) The Etruscans spoke a non-Indo-European language about which only a little is now known, and they had borrowed a Western version of the Greek alphabet, with H standing for /h/ rather than for a vowel, and X standing for /ks/ rather than /kʰ/ (on Etruscan, see Bonfante 1990).

One fact that is known about the linguistic structure of Etruscan is that voice was non-contrastive in stops: the sounds [b d g] either did not occur or, if they did, they were allophonic variants of [p t k]. This meant that the Etruscans had no use for the Greek graphemic contrasts between Π B, T Δ, K Γ, and in due course the letters B and Δ were given up.

When the Romans encountered Etruscan writing, these letters were still included in their alphabet, so the Romans were able to use them for the voice contrast which exists in Latin as it does in Greek. (When people first encounter writing, they are often slow and cautious about discarding elements of the system which serve no purpose with respect to their own language.) However, in the case of the velar letters the Etruscans had already rationalized the system they had taken over from the Greeks. We have seen that early Greek writing used the letters K Ϙ for different allophones of the /k/ phoneme. The Etruscans took this logic further: since they did not need Γ to stand for a separate voiced consonant, they used it too for an allophonic variant: they wrote Ϙ for the back allophone of /k/ found before /u/, K for the neutral allophone found before /a/, and Γ – the shape of which evolved into C – for the front variant of /k/ found before /i e/. (Etruscan had only these four vowels.)

When the Romans first borrowed the alphabet, they took over this method of using C, K, and Q (i.e. Ϙ), but they soon abandoned K as redundant, and they came to reserve Q not for the ordinary /k/ before /u/ but rather for the "labiovelar" phoneme /k^w/ which occurred in Latin as it did in early Greek (p. 64), and which the Romans wrote QV – so that e.g. /k^wī/ "who" contrasted in writing with /kuī/ "to whom" as QVI, CVI. The Romans had no knowledge of the fact that C had once been reserved for /g/, so they used C for both of their phonemes /k g/.

Another letter which the Romans inherited via the Etruscans but had no use for was Z for /dz/; Latin had no /dz/-like sound. In the –3c the freedman Spurius Carvilius Ruga (the first Roman to open a fee-paying school) remedied the lack of graphic differentiation between /k g/ by adding a stroke to C to make a new letter G for /g/, and he inserted this new letter in the place in the alphabet that had been vacated by the useless Z.[6] Evidently the alphabetic order was felt to be such a concrete thing that a new letter could be added in the middle only if a "space" was created by dropping an old letter.

At this point, the Romans had a 21-letter alphabet: A B C D E F G H I (K) L M N O P Q R S T V X. All vowel letters covered both long and short vowels (which contrasted in Latin), and the letters I V were used for semivowels /j w/ as well as for vowels /i u/. (Greek F for /w/ had been adapted by the Etruscans to write /f/, a sound lacking in Greek – the Etruscans heard /f/ as like a voiceless /w/ and wrote it FH or simply F, and the Romans followed them, never using F for their own /w/ phoneme.) K was used only in a few words which retained an archaic orthography. The phonemes /k^w g^w/ were written QV, GV, and X was used for the cluster /ks/. Otherwise the alphabet was almost perfectly phonemic (Allen 1965).

One discontinuity with earlier versions of the alphabet, for which the Etruscans were responsible, related to the names of the letters. We saw that the Greeks took over most of the Semitic names. The Etruscans simplified things, rather like an English child who spells out *cat* as "ker-a-ter". Vowel letters were named by their own sound; most consonant letters were named by adding the most neutral Etruscan vowel, /e/, to give names such as /pe te/ for P, T. Because of the special usage of C K Q these had to be named /ke ka ku/. Continuant consonants were named simply by pronouncing the consonant without a vowel: L was "lll", S was "sss", and so on; and these names were eventually turned into respectable words by prefixing a vowel, /el es/ as opposed to /pe te/. (X was /eks/ rather than /kse/ because in Latin – and Etruscan? – unlike Greek, initial /ks-/ was phonologically impossible.) With two exceptions discussed below, the resulting 21 letter names are the direct ancestors of our English names, having undergone the regular sound changes of late Latin and English which caused e.g. Latin /ge/ for G to become our /dʒi/ just as /geniāl-em/ became our /dʒinɪəl/, *genial.*

In the –2c Rome conquered the Greek world, and the sophisticated culture of the Greeks, and with it the Greek language, proceeded massively to infiltrate Roman life (indeed, this process had begun well before Roman political hegemony over Greece). Many Greek words were borrowed into Latin, so the Romans needed to write two Greek sounds that Latin lacked: /y/, and /z/ from earlier Greek /dz/. The Romans had inherited Greek upsilon, via the Etruscans, in the form V, but for the Romans this still stood for its original Greek value /u/; so they formed a new letter Y for the /y/ vowel, imitating what had become the standard Greek shape for upsilon. Similarly, the Greek Z was copied into the end of the Roman alphabet. Hence our name *zed*, from Greek *zeta*, and the German *Ypsilon* or French *y-grec* for Y. (It is not known how we got the English name /wai/.)

* * *

The alphabet we know today was now almost complete. Before going on to discuss the final additions to it, we should briefly mention the third important modern European script, the Cyrillic alphabet used for Russian and some other Slavonic languages.

The Cyrillic alphabet was devised as a result of the Byzantine mission to the Slavs led by the brother-saints Cyril and Methodius in the +860s – Slavonic languages had not been written earlier. The history of Slavonic literacy is rather complicated, with the alphabet we know as Cyrillic being only one of two very different scripts devised about that time; the other, "Glagolitic", is long obsolete. It is probable that Cyrillic came after Glagolitic and was created by disciples of Cyril rather than by the saint himself (Cubberley 1996).

Since the missionaries and the culture from which they emerged were Greek, the Cyrillic alphabet is naturally based mainly on Greek (even if some of the letters in their modern printed form seem lightly disguised, e.g. Д is the Cyrillic reflex of Greek Δ for /d/). Graphs for non-Greek sounds were borrowed from other scripts, for instance /ʃ/ is Cyrillic Ш, from Hebrew ש.

* * *

Returning to the Roman alphabet: developments after the Classical age were a consequence of phonological developments in Latin and its descendant ("Romance") languages.

The sound /h/ dropped out of the Romance languages, which caused a problem for the name of H (which, as a grapheme, was retained). What seems to have happened is that, so long as early Romance speakers retained some ability to make an [h]-like sound, they made increasingly desperate attempts to utter a name including such a noise: [ahha] passed into [axxa] and finally ended in the pronounceable if not very appropriate name [akka]. Just as Latin *vacca*(*m*) "cow" gave Norman French /vatʃe/ and modern French /vaʃ/ *vache*, so /akka/ gave Norman /atʃe/, which by the sound-laws of Middle and Modern English yielded our name /eitʃ/, while simultaneously developing into Modern French /aʃ/.

The Latin approximants /j w/ developed into obstruents in the modern Romance languages: Latin /jūdikem/ "judge", /wītam/ "life" are Italian /dʒuditʃe/, /vita/, French /ʒyʒ/, /vi/. The double use of V for /u v/ was inconvenient for speakers of Germanic languages, which had a /w/ phoneme distinct from /v/, so in the 11c they began to indicate /w/ by writing V double; in due course VV, "double /u/", came to be seen and written as an independent letter W. In the 16c, speakers of Romance languages also found it awkward to use the same letters I V both for vowels /i u/ and for consonants that were now very different. The letterforms < I i > had swash allographs (cf. the mediaeval practice of writing e.g. 13 as xiij), and these were elevated to the status of a separate letter < J j >, whose English name /dʒei/ was perhaps formed by analogy with the adjacent K to avoid homonymy with the name of G. Likewise, the cursive, minuscule form of capital V was < u >, so this was used to form a new capital letter U while the shape of V gave a new minuscule < v >, splitting V into two letters. (It is noteworthy that no fewer than five of our 26 letters, F, U, V, W, and Y, all descend ultimately from the same ancestral Semitic letter, wāw.)

* * *

Once J, U, and W were distinct letters, our "twenty-six soldiers of lead" were all present and correct, and ready to "conquer the world".[7]

Notes

1. "Marcell wagged his finger half seriously, half jokingly at Corinna and said 'Cousin, don't forget you have the representative of another nation sitting next to you, and you have a certain duty to champion German womanliness.' / 'Oh no, no', said Nelson: 'Not womanliness; always quick and clever ... that's what we love about German women. Not womanliness. Miss Corinna is quite in the right way.' / 'There you are, Marcell ...'"
2. Benjamin Sass (2005: 146) suggests that the Greeks may have received the alphabet not directly from Semitic speakers but via the Phrygians, speakers of an Indo-European language in an area of what is now Turkey. (The famous King Midas was a Phrygian.) However, it is not clear whether there is any positive evidence against direct transmission between Semites and Greeks, and the "Phoenician letters" phrase might be hard to explain if the Greeks got the alphabet from fellow Indo-Europeans.
3. I am writing in the present tense, but the Greek I am describing is Ancient Greek. Modern Greek remains remarkably similar, considering the immense length of time that separates the two, but there are considerable differences in phonology and some vocabulary differences. The word for "or" is pronounced /i/ rather than /ǣ/ in Modern Greek, and "not" is expressed by a different word, /ðen/.
4. My choice of phonetic symbols differs from Allen's in certain respects.
5. I ignore a special issue relating to certain diphthongs, discussed by Allen (1968: 114 n. 2) and Sommerstein (1973: 125).
6. Some scholars attribute the invention of G to Appius Claudius Caecus (late -4c) rather than to Ruga.
7. The saying "Give me 26 lead soldiers and I will conquer the world" is often, mistakenly, attributed to Benjamin Franklin (Mosley 1993). For 21c readers it should be explained that the pieces of type used for letterpress printing were made of a lead alloy.

7 Influences on graph-shape evolution

We have seen that the outward form of a script is liable to change hugely, even if in terms of its inner logic it remains essentially the "same script". The Roman alphabet has been no exception. Figure 21 illustrates some of the diverse styles of forming its letters which developed at different times and places, before printing arrived to introduce a degree of fixity in writing styles.

In its Greek version, alphabetic writing was characteristically "mono-line" – that is, without variation of thick and thin among strokes written

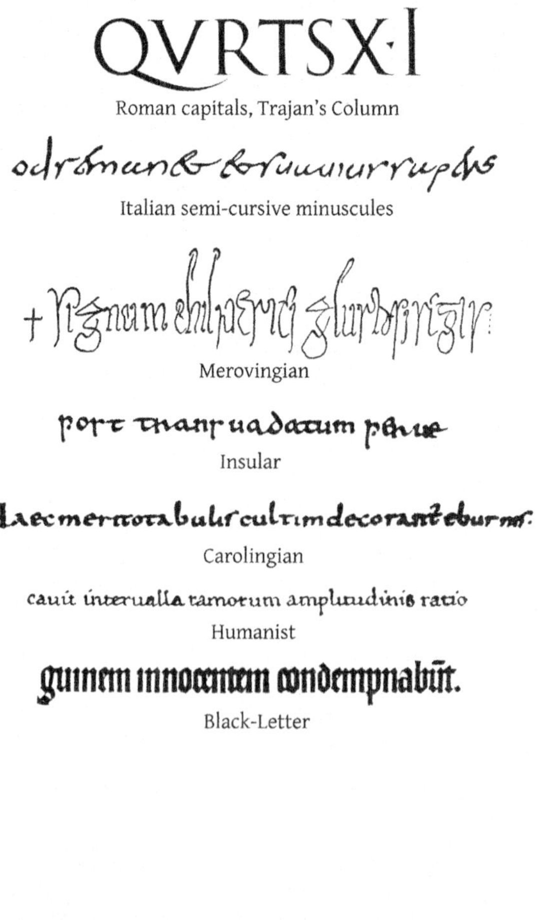

QVRTSX·I

Roman capitals, Trajan's Column

Italian semi-cursive minuscules

Merovingian

Insular

Carolingian

Humanist

Black-Letter

Figure 21

in different directions – and devoid of serifs, the little lateral flicks at the ends of strokes which occur in most styles of present-day printing and which give a typeface much of its "character". Serifs were not entirely unknown to the Greeks. The earliest known inscription including rudimentary serifs is on a temple at Priene, then in Greek Ionia (now western Turkey), recording its dedication by Alexander the Great in −334 shortly before he set out to conquer the world. But the monumental inscriptions of Imperial Rome were more consistent in including serifs, and in a more pronounced form. Including serifs makes it easier for a stone-carver to finish off the ends of unconnected lines neatly, but serifs are also held to make an important contribution to both the beauty and the legibility of lettering. Also, rather than being monoline, Roman capitals had light, oblique stress – that is, the line of a letter such as O varied smoothly in width, being narrower at the eleven o'clock and five o'clock positions, and widest at the points 90° from these. In this respect the men who chiselled lettering on stone were influenced by the variation of line that occurs naturally when letters are written in ink with a broad nib. The inscription on Trajan's Column (+214) is often cited as an example of monumental Roman lettering at its finest.

In handwriting, and even for less formal public inscriptions, various less authoritative, more cursive styles of lettering evolved. The term "cursive" may be misunderstood; so far as is known, even in the most informal styles of writing each letter was formed separately. But the outlines of individual letters were simplified in various ways, and most letters could be produced by a single stroke of the pen; and, significantly, a "minuscule" hand developed in which letters differed in height, some having ascenders and others descenders.

After the break-up of the Roman Empire, divergent "national hands" developed: Italian semi-cursive minuscules, the spidery Merovingian script of France, the rounded and heavily serifed "Insular" or Anglo-Irish hand, and others. About +800 the Carolingian hand was developed in the empire led by Charlemagne, in association with the reform of education which he sponsored. Over the next few centuries Carolingian script spread throughout Europe, replacing local hands almost everywhere.

The graphic unity created by the success of Carolingian script began to break up again in the 12c. By the 15c two important rival styles of writing had developed out of the Carolingian hand. "Humanist" script was an attempt to reconstruct the handwriting of Classical Rome, but in practice remained relatively close to the Carolingian original: it was the script of secular learning and the study of pagan antiquity, thus primarily of northern Italy (and eventually of the Renascence); while black-letter, or "gothic", became the script of France and of Christian rather than pagan Europe.[1] Humanist letters were rounded, wide, and written with a fine pen; gothic letters were written with a broad pen held at a sharp angle to the horizontal, were narrow, and contained few curves – in many gothic alphabets an < o >, for instance, was a wholly curve-free, tall, narrow hexagon.[2]

Many different factors have contributed to changes in the form of scripts, including our alphabet. We shall examine three of these factors in turn: *writing materials*; *ideology*; and the need for *distinctiveness*.

* * *

Choice of writing materials – what kind of surface is marked, and what instruments are used to mark it – is a central factor in determining what a script looks like. We saw in Chapter 3 that the distinctive appearance of Cuneiform script was a direct consequence of the fact that the most readily available writing surface was clay, which accepts impressed marks easily but does not lend itself to the drawing of lines and curves.

For an example closer to home, consider runic script.

The runic alphabet was devised early in the Christian era. (The earliest examples we have are from about the late +2c, but the system was well enough developed to suggest a century or so of previous evolution.) Runes were used by the Germanic-speaking tribes neighbouring the Roman Empire to the north (Scandinavia) and east (central and eastern Europe), and who moved into areas such as what is now England after Roman rule weakened and eventually collapsed.

As an example, Figure 22 shows the opening lines of the famous Old English epic *Beowulf*, written in Anglo-Saxon runes.[3] (There was some variation in rune alphabets between different Germanic-speaking territories.)

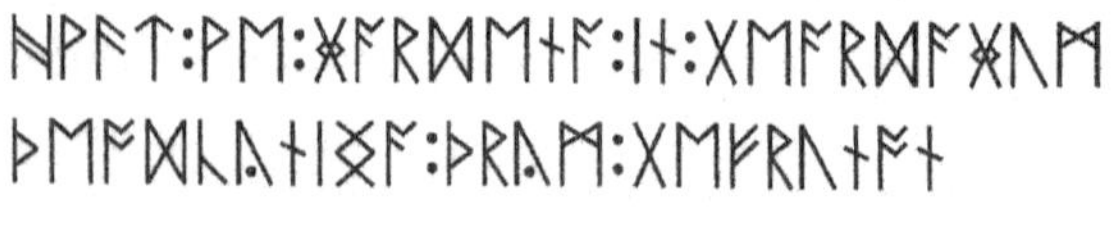

ᚻᚹᚫᛏ:ᚹᛖ:ᚸᚪᚱᛞᛖᚾᚪ:ᛁᚾ:ᚷᛖᚪᚱᛞᚪᚸᚢᛗ
ᚦᛖᚩᛞᚳᚣᚾᛁᛝᚪ:ᚦᚱᚣᛗ:ᚷᛖᚠᚱᚢᚾᚩᚾ

Hwæt wē Gār-Dena in geār-dagum
þēod-cyninga þrym gefrūnon

"We have heard of the might in days of yore of the Spear-Danes, kings of the people"

Figure 22

(The letter < þ > in the Roman version of the lines, standing for the sound /θ/ – compare the first letter of the second line in the two versions – was borrowed from the runic into the Roman alphabet to write Old English, since the Roman alphabet had no letter for that sound.)

Clearly, many rune shapes are related to Roman letterforms. In the first word, *hwæt* (which is an introductory, throat-clearing exclamation – "Now then!"), ᚻ for H and ᛏ for T are recognizable, though ᚹ for W or ᚫ for the Old English front /æ/ vowel are not. (Some scholars have suggested that runes may have originally been inspired by the Greek rather than Roman alphabet, though that would not help to explain these two discrepancies. Geographically this suggestion is quite feasible: there were Germanic-speakers living adjacent to the eastern, Greek-speaking half of the Roman Empire.) But the runes had their own distinctive appearance, unlike any style of Roman or Greek alphabets.

This distinctive look must surely bear some of the responsibility for the extraordinary way in which runes have been taken in recent times to have a special relationship with paganism, witchcraft, and magic. There can surely be no other script in world history about which so much nonsense has been written.

It is of course true that the first users of runes were pagans, since the Germanic-speaking tribes had not yet been converted. Because Christian missionaries came from Rome, they naturally used the Roman alphabet. But it is not true that the Christian Church, when it arrived, saw runes as intrinsically pagan or objectionable. Gravestones often combined a Christian cross with the name of the deceased in runes, which the Church would have forbidden if it had been hostile to the script. The names of Christ and the evangelists are written in runes on the coffin of no less zealous a missionary than St Cuthbert, bishop of Lindisfarne. In Scandinavia the use of runes continued into the early modern period, long after that region had been converted.

As for magic, it is true that surviving pre-Christian inscriptions in Germanic-speaking Europe include a few magic charms, which were written in runes because that was the only script the writers knew. But there just is no evidence that the runic letters themselves were seen as having "magical power" or were used for fortune-telling. Present-day misunderstandings are incisively described by Raymond Page, until his death in 2012 the foremost expert on English runes:

> occult bookshops can usually be expected to have a shelf or two of books on runes. They have no scholarly value, and serve only to document that fascination with fantasy, that flight from reason that is such a sad feature of the modern world. (Page 1995: 315)

The true explanation for the distinctive appearance of runic writing is much more prosaic. The inhabitants of Mesopotamia converted pictorial graphs to collections of wedges because the material they had to write on was clay. What Germanic-speaking tribesmen had in abundance was trees, and they wrote by using a knife to carve marks on wood. (The runic inscriptions which have come down to us are mostly on stone, but that is merely because stone lasts while wood rots or crumbles.) To quote Page again:

> Most Germanic men would carry a knife at their belt. A stick of wood could be picked up anywhere. What more easy than to shave a stick so that it had two or more flat sides, and on each side to cut the letters of a message? ... When you had finished with the message, the stick could serve as kindling. (Page 1987: 6–8)

(Page compares this favourably with Christian writing technology, which involved manufacturing parchment, ink, and quills.) Knife-cuts are straight lines; and a shaved stick has a grain running in the direction of writing, so cuts in that direction will fail to show up clearly against the grain (they might even split the stick). Runes had to consist of straight lines in directions other than horizontal. That is why, for instance, a runic T is written as ↑. To a modern romantic, the angularity of the runes might have a "witchy" look, but that was really quite irrelevant. The distinctive appearance of the runic alphabet, like that of cuneiform script, is a simple physical consequence of the writing materials used.

The link between early Germanic writing and wood is reflected in the fact that the words "book" and "beech" seem to share a common root in Germanic languages – in German they are closer, *Buch* and *Buche*. Perhaps the fine grain of beechwood made it specially suitable as a writing surface. "Book", *Buch*, must originally have meant (indeed, we know it did mean) something far smaller-scale than what the words mean today, because the downside of wood-carving as a writing technique is that it is too laborious for long documents. "Books" in the modern sense, and other lengthy documents, were where the Christian technique of writing with pen and ink on parchment came into its own. Since the bringers of this technology happened to be users of the Roman alphabet, it was inevitable that this eventually displaced runes.

* * *

Carving in wood forced runes to use straight lines. As a contrast, consider the scripts of southern India and adjacent areas of southeast Asia. In terms of ancestry, these scripts are closely related to the Devanagari alphabet, which we examined in Chapter 5. But when writing came to southern India and countries to its east, it was commonly executed with a pointed instrument on palm leaves. Leaves have veins running in various directions, so straight lines in any orientation would be liable to coincide with a vein and split the leaf. As a consequence, letter shapes were adapted to make them as curvy as possible.

Figure 23 displays the Burmese alphabet (consonants only – as in Devanagari, vowels are usually indicated by small marks above or below the consonant letters). The letters consist almost wholly of circles and sections of circles.

A few letters do include long straight lines. Part, at least, of the explanation for this is that some of the letters in question are used for sounds which occur in foreign loan words in Burmese. For instance, /ogut/ "August" is written ဩဂုတ် – with an initial letter representing /o/ not preceded by glottal stop, as it normally would be in a native Burmese word. Perhaps, by the period when Burmese needed to write foreign words, writing surfaces less fragile than palm leaves had become available.

* * *

Changes in writing materials enforce changes on graph shapes. One might imagine that, as between alternative styles which can all be easily produced with the materials in use in a given community, preferences for one style or another would be merely a matter of aesthetic taste. But human societies are very given to investing superficial differences in any area of life with political or ideological significance. Writing styles are no exception.

We have already seen hints of this, in the contrasting associations of humanist and gothic hands in early modern Europe. The history of the Roman alphabet offers many other examples. Stanley Morison (1972:

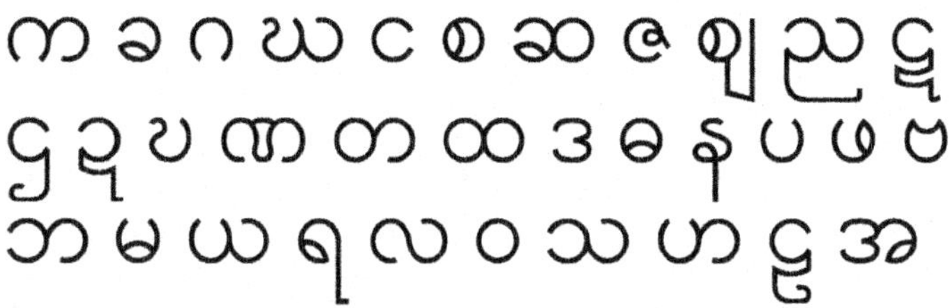

Figure 23

57ff.) describes how the conversion of the Roman Empire to Christianity in the +4c was felt to require a break with the lettering styles used in pagan writings, so the script called Uncial was developed out of cursive Roman writing, with the result that letters with ascenders and descenders (like modern d or p) appeared for the first time in formal documents. After Eastern and Western churches grew apart, alternating periods of hostility and attempted rapprochement were reflected in styles of Roman lettering that respectively magnified or minimized the differences from the Greek alphabet.

As a case study from closer to our own time, consider the history of Irish script (for details see Lynam 1924; McGuinne 1992). Until recently, Irish Gaelic, the first official language of the Irish Republic, was standardly written in a script that looks very different from roman. Figure 24 displays a paragraph from a short story by Pádraic Pearse, poet and leader of the 1916 Easter Rising, in Irish script and transliterated into roman (the passage describes a boy on a spring evening waiting for the swallows to return from the south).

This style of lettering is essentially the "Insular" or "Anglo-Irish" hand, which was used for English too before the 11c Norman Conquest led to its replacement by Carolingian script in England. The style is called "Insular" because it was used throughout the British Isles, but it was first created in Ireland, when England was too sunk in Dark Age barbarism to be capable of such a development. The earliest extant example is a manuscript of the 6c. Stanley Morison (1972: 152ff.) suggests that the script may have been created by St Columba, or even St Patrick in person, though these suggestions seem highly speculative.[4]

As a distinctive printed typeface rather than handwriting style, these letters were first turned into an icon of Irishness by Elizabeth I (reigned

Ṫáinig tráṫnóna aoiḃinn i ndeireaḋ an Aibreáin. Ḃí an t-aer glan fionnuar tar éis múir báistí. Ḃí solas iontaċ sa doṁan ṫiar. Ḃí séis ċeoil ag na héanlaiṫ sa gcoill. Ḃí duan dá ċanaḋ ag na tonntraċaiḃ ar an tráiġ. Aċ ḃí uaigneas ar ċroí an ṁalraiġ agus é ag fanaċt leis na fáinleogaiḃ.

Tháinig tráthnóna aoibhinn i ndeireadh an Aibreáin. Bhí an t-aer glan fionnuar tar éis múir báistí. Bhí solas iontach sa domhan thiar. Bhí séis cheoil ag na héanlaith sa gcoill. Bhí duan dá chanadh ag na tonntrachaibh ar an tráigh. Ach bhí uaigneas ar chroí an mhalraigh agus é ag fanacht leis na fáinleogaibh.

Figure 24

1558–1603). Printing came late to the Gaelic language which was then the common speech of much of Ireland and the Scottish Highlands. It happened that the first book printed in Gaelic, in Edinburgh in 1567, was a translation of a Calvinist prayer book compiled by John Knox, set in roman type. For Elizabeth, while Ireland was one of her own dominions Scotland was a foreign country, and one which embraced a radical form of reformed Christianity; its doctrine may have felt threatening to Elizabeth's realm, with its mildly reformed state Church, in much the way that the communism of the Soviet Union and Cuba was perceived as a threat by Western countries in the Cold War years. (Knox's preface referred explicitly to "we the Gael of Scotland and Ireland".)

Elizabeth was an able linguist who enjoyed using foreign languages as a tool of diplomacy. Accordingly, she paid for a typeface to be cut in the style usual in Irish manuscripts, in the hope that religious writings in a format the Irish could identify as their own might help to foster allegiance to her Church. The new type was first used for an Anglican catechism of 1571.

It didn't work. The Irish continued to reject not just radical but all reformed religion, staying loyal to the Pope. And Irish monks exiled on the Continent were inspired by Elizabeth's initiative to use Irish type to print Catholic literature for circulation in Ireland. Irish script became emblematic of Irish nationalism, as opposed not to Scottish Presbyterianism but to English rule. The population grew hostile to the idea of printing Irish in roman. One early 19c prison warden observed that when he gave his prisoners an Irish New Testament set in roman, they made him promise to swap it for one in Irish type when available.

As Irish separatism became a serious political movement later in the 19c, nationalists "used the language and the letterforms to justify their claims for independence. Newspapers were the main source of propaganda at this time and it can be argued that ... Irish nationalism was very much a conspiracy of printers" (Staunton 2005). Irish script started popping up in unexpected places like the side of delivery vans; "[s]cript became a form of resistance to British rule" (Staunton and Decottignies 2010). In the 20c only a few Irish people could master the Gaelic language, but all could recognize the distinctive script.

Irish script does have a practical advantage for writing the Irish language. Gaelic has a phonological process which modifies consonants in certain grammatical environments, for instance /m/ becomes /v/. Irish script represents this modification by a simple dot over the affected consonant letter, so the essential appearance of the root is not altered. In roman script, some consonant letters, such as t and f, have no convenient place for a dot. There were experiments with cutting special roman fonts in which the problematic letters were replaced by versions without ascenders, but these did not find acceptance, and the standard way to print Irish in roman type replaces a dotted consonant with a combination of consonant + < h >. The visual effect of this can be unfortunate; when a word like ṁoḋṁaꞃaċ, "polite (fem.)", has to be spelled *mhodhmharach* it can feel as though the language is all h's. But from a practical point of view this might seem a minor point, set against the difficulties of providing special fonts of type for a small market, and teaching children two alphabets. Nevertheless, so long as Irish independence remained a contentious issue, there was little interest in switching to roman.

Once the country became a republic wholly independent of Britain in 1949, though, the heat went out of the issue. When the Irish government changed the language over to roman script in the early 1960s, one senator grumbled about "all these h's cluttering up the words", but there was no real opposition.

* * *

In Ireland, while national feeling was a live issue, it trumped considerations of economics or efficiency. But in general, when such factors pull in different directions, there is no predicting how the tension will be resolved. Consider the case of German *Fraktur*, which was the standard script in German-speaking Europe (a far larger market than that for Irish Gaelic) until the Second World War. The English-speaking world has not used gothic faces seriously much after the Middle Ages, and when the somewhat gloomy associations of that period are combined with strongly negative reactions to the history of Germany in the first half of the 20c, it is inevitable that many Britons and Americans think of *Fraktur* as a grim kind of writing. But for the Germans it was quite otherwise. Roman type (called in German *Antiqua*) was seen as embodying the austerely intellectual spirit of classical antiquity; *Fraktur* by contrast was the "touchy-feely" kind of writing that spelled family, home, Nature, and romance. Figure 25 comes from a souvenir booklet circulated to clients by a German press at Christmas 1918. The contrasting female figures, standing for the respective scripts, are addressed in verses which call *Antiqua* the "awesome herald of the Classical spirit ... how can we fail to revere you?", while *Fraktur* calls to mind "the blackbird's distant evening call, the dainty trembling of meadow grasses"; *Fraktur* is the "loveliest, most German script". While intellectuals who saw themselves as citizens of a worldwide republic of letters often favoured roman, nationalist Germans were commonly enthusiasts for *Fraktur*; Bismarck in the 19c commented "I don't read books on German topics set in roman type".[5]

Figure 25

Yet it was in 1941, when nationalism was at the top of the German agenda, that the arch-nationalist Adolf Hitler ordered the country to switch over to roman; and this it did.

* * *

Writing materials, and political associations, are powerful external factors influencing the evolution of graph shapes. Internally, though, the chief imperative would seem to be distinctiveness. To be usable, a letter just needs to be visibly different from other letters. Ferdinand de Saussure told us that "in language there are only differences without positive terms" (Saussure [1915] 1966: 120; emphasis in original removed). Saussure is commonly taken to have been referring to spoken language, but his immediately preceding example in fact related to writing: "The value of letters is purely negative and differential. The same person can write *t*, for instance, in different ways ... The only requirement is that the sign for *t* not be confused in his script with the signs used for *l*, *d*, etc."

The truth, even with respect to spoken language, is more complicated. Following Saussure, many linguists have believed that sound changes are governed by a measure which André Martinet (1955) called *rendement fonctionel* (usually translated as "functional yield" or "functional load"): a merger between two phonemes is less likely if that particular contrast keeps many pairs of words distinct. But Robert King (1967) tested this idea and concluded that "functional load, if it is a factor in sound change at all, is one of the least important". Despite King, numerous other linguists have continued to assert that functional load *is* important, but I have looked at recent attempts to resurrect the idea and offered evidence that it cannot be right (Sampson 2013, 2015). It just is not true in general that spoken languages avoid sound changes that make words confusable.

And whatever the facts may be about spoken language, in written language it does not seem that the need for distinctiveness is so universal a constraint on script evolution as Saussure's remark (and indeed common sense) might suggest.

When all writing was handwriting, it was subject to two opposite pressures: the need for clarity and for the appearance of authority called for letters or other graphic elements to be formed carefully and distinctively, while the urge to economize effort and time pushed scribes towards hasty cursive writing in which graphs would tend to lose some of their distinctiveness. These contrary pressures seem universal, so one might expect them to be resolved in roughly similar ways in all scripts, with letter shapes retaining a high degree of distinctiveness in formal inscriptions while ephemeral and informal notes were more cursive. In reality, scripts differ greatly in the way they have resolved these pressures.

Compare the different fates of the original Semitic alphabet in its Middle Eastern homeland, and in Europe.

Take the letter O, for example: we have seen that its ancestral form (which stood for the consonant /ʕ/) began as a circle depicting an eye. European scripts have never lost touch with that original shape. Someone jotting a hasty note in English might form a small o carelessly so that the circle fails to meet at the top, but in careful writing a small or capital O remains a circle; likewise in the sister Greek and Cyrillic alphabets. In the Middle East, on the other hand, letters were written *only* cursively. The circle was evidently formed as two semicircles meeting at top and bottom, but the two strokes were allowed to splay apart at the top and meet inexactly at the bottom (as would be natural in hasty writing), so that in Hebrew script the letterform ע became the only allowable shape for the letter ʕajin. In a formal document it may be made beautiful with serifs and contrast of line, ע, but it remains essentially a carelessly written circle. And what is true of this letter is true of the alphabet generally. In Europe some of the original forms have been simplified in minor ways, for instance the multiple crossbars of the original ħēt have been reduced to one in the letter H, but without much affecting the distinctiveness of the letters. In Hebrew script cursiveness has gone much further, so that distinctiveness is often affected. Many groups of Hebrew letters are strikingly similar in shape:

רדך החת גנכב יון סם

It is true that in Roman script the minuscules (lower-case letters) have departed much further than the capitals from the original letterforms. But that has not led to reduced distinctiveness. If anything, the reverse: it is the minuscules which contain ascenders (in letters such as b f k t), together with the dots of i j, and descenders (as in g p y), which make for greater recognizability. That is why highway authorities who produce road signs that have to be read at speed have abandoned all-capital lettering, normal in Britain until the 1960s. In the Hebrew alphabet, if we leave aside the special word-final allographs, only one letter, lāmed, has an ascender, and one letter, k'ōp, has a descender. Most of the word-final allographs have descenders, but that gives little help in recognizing words. If in rapid reading one sees a descender, it tells one in effect "Unless I am part of a < k' > you are at the end of a word" – but that latter information is signalled anyway by the salient feature of blank space.

We must not exaggerate here. It used to be believed that overall word-shapes played an important role in the reading process, so that initial reading programmes for English were advised to avoid words like *run, now, cream* whose shape is not distinctive. If that were right, Hebrew script would be highly inefficient. However, we now know (Paap *et al.* 1984) that the overall *shapes* of words, that is the envelopes containing the written marks, as opposed to the letter-sequences contained in them, are not very important for word recognition. Individual letters certainly do need to be recognized, though, and ascenders and descenders are important for that (Beech and Mayall 2005).

If it seems surprising to European readers that distinctiveness has been assigned such low priority in the evolution of Hebrew script, its Arabic sister script is even more surprising: loss of distinctiveness proceeded so far that various letters became identical. In the history of Arabic writing, < z > merged with < r >, < p > with < k' >, < g > with < ħ >, and < n t b j ʔ > all fell together in shape except that < n >, < j >, and < ʔ > have distinctive word-final allographs. (I identify the letters by reference to their original values; some of the phonemes have acquired different pronunciations in Arabic, but that is beside the point here.) The degree of confusion created was such that in the 8c a system of dots had to be introduced in writing Arabic to differentiate identical letter shapes. In modern Arabic script the visual difference between < n t b j ʔ > has nothing to do with differences between the original shapes of the letters, and rests purely on the fact that they are written with respectively one dot above, two dots above, one dot below, two dots below, and a small mark like a reversed 2 above (see Figure 26).

Figure 26

(The diacritic dots which distinguish Arabic consonant letters are separate from the pointing system for specifying vowels, which is also available in Arabic script but, as in Hebrew script, is not normally used.)

When the dots are written (as they invariably now are), they make the letters of Arabic distinctive enough. However, someone impressed by Saussure's remark quoted above might have expected that cultural evolution could never have allowed a system of signs to reach the point where a remedy as *ad hoc* as the dot system was needed. (And, if any script were to suffer this fate, one would not have expected it to be a script that already contained as little redundancy as vowel-less Semitic script.)

The point is strengthened by the fact that the system of special word-final allographs is taken further in Arabic than in Hebrew script. A feature of Arabic script is that all writing is "joined-up writing": there is no style of writing in which the letters of a word are separate, even printed Arabic imitates the continuous, flowing motions of handwriting. (This sinuous quality is largely responsible for the great beauty of Arabic script, which has probably been a powerful factor determining its development in practice.) Users of the Roman alphabet tend to see handwritten forms as imperfect "performance" deviations from the underlying "ideal" printed forms. Perhaps because Arabic script does not suggest such a point of view, it has gone further than most scripts in developing diverse allographic variants of letters. About two-thirds of the letters of the Arabic alphabet have special word-final forms, and the difference between these forms and the corresponding non-final allographs is greater than in Hebrew script, and much greater than the differences between many contrasting pairs of Arabic graphemes: see Figure 27 for examples. The consequence is that, perhaps even more than in the Hebrew case, much of what is visually salient in a page of written Arabic is linguistically non-significant. It merely marks the ends of words which are marked more obviously by blank spaces.

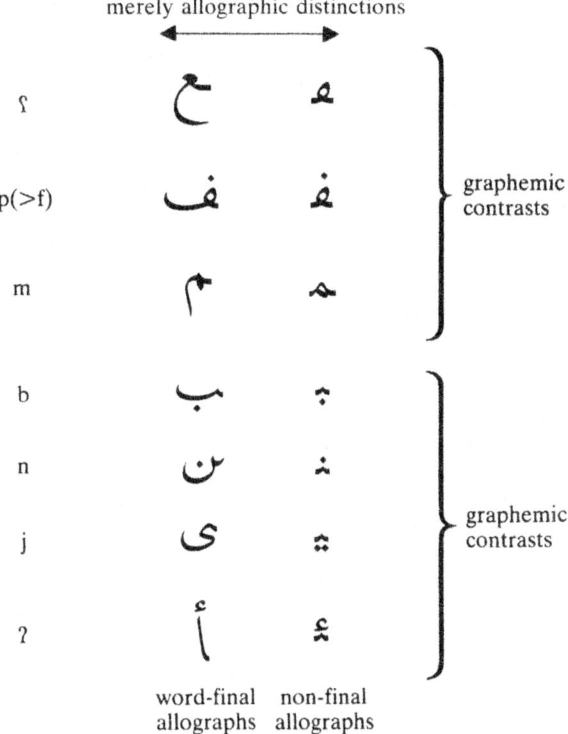

Figure 27

The "joined-up" nature of Arabic script does mean that it can be written rapidly, like a system of shorthand. Even that virtue is lacking in Hebrew script, however. There are conventional handwritten letter shapes which diverge from the shapes used in printing, just as a handwritten roman *a* differs from a printed < a >. But these handwritten forms are normally written separately; there is no system of writing long letter-sequences with a continuous motion of the pen. The English word *alphabet*, containing eight letters, is commonly handwritten with only one lifting of the pen between beginning and end (to make the cross-stroke of the t). Its Hebrew equivalent /ʔālepbēt/ is written with six letters < ʔlpbjt >, but its handwritten form would standardly involve seven separate pen-strokes:

alphabet	אלפבית
alphabet	אלפבית

We saw on pp. 92–3 that Hebrew script expresses a given quantum of meaning in fewer letters than English writing uses, so that each individual letter tends to "count for more" than an individual letter in English. That kind of redundancy in Hebrew script could simply mean that it offered a way to pack information densely into a given area of paper, if the individual letter shapes were distinctive. Readers of Hebrew might be forced to sample a higher proportion of the graphemes in a text than readers of English (we know they do – Pollatsek *et al.* 1981: 178), but that does not imply more samplings to recover a like amount of meaning, which is what matters from the point of view of reading efficiency. But when the 22 letters of the Hebrew alphabet are as non-distinctive as we have seen above, relative to the 52 capitals and minuscules of the Roman alphabet (Hebrew, and Arabic, have no upper/lower-case contrast), it seems fair to describe traditional standard Hebrew script as relatively inefficient.

I have seen no explanation in the literature for why the need to retain distinctiveness should have been given less priority in the Middle East than in Europe. Undoubtedly a script in which too many graph shapes became indistinguishable would end up unusable, but it seems that the need to keep graphemes distinct is not always a leading factor influencing script evolution.

This property of Semitic scripts is particularly surprising because it seems to contradict findings by Mark Changizi *et al.* (2006) about biological constraints on symbol systems. Changizi *et al.* examined statistics on the topological configurations found in about a hundred different writing systems, as well as numerous symbol systems such as those of musical notation and of weather maps, etc., and many commercial logos. (By "topological configurations" they refer to presence of angles, T-junctions, crosses, etc. independently of size or orientation; for instance, a Roman L is a different shape from a Greek gamma, Γ, but topologically they are not distinct.) They find remarkable similarities among the statistical distributions for these different systems, which coincide closely with statistics of configurations found in natural scenes, but differ from the distributions found in randomly generated arrays of lines and, interestingly, from those found in shorthand systems. Changizi *et al.* conclude that our symbol systems have developed to be visually distinctive, by containing the configurations our ancestors evolved to recognize in Nature, at the expense of motor simplicity (ease of production) – shorthands are exceptional because for them easy, rapid writing is an overriding requirement. Yet the history of Semitic scripts seems to imply that, in their case, motor simplicity has been given priority. (Arabic and Hebrew were two of the many scripts used in Changizi *et al.*'s research, but they are not individually discussed – if their topological statistics are exceptional, this may have been hidden by the fact that statistics were extracted from all phonographic scripts collectively.)

Research half a century ago (Gray 1956: 59) suggested that readers of Hebrew and Arabic make rather longer eye-fixations than readers of European languages. The evidence was far from conclusive, but for what it is worth the result conforms to what would be expected on the basis of this discussion. Each sampling of a text has to be more thorough, and therefore takes longer, if the graphemes have few distinctive elements buried amid a mass of non-distinctive visual material.

* * *

Finally in this chapter, we shall look at the main developments that have affected the Roman alphabet since printing was introduced to Europe.

The first important developments were structural. Morison (1972: 112) traces the beginnings of the convention that "capital" and "minuscule" letters are co-ordinate partners within a single style of writing (rather than alternative styles) to practice in the scriptorium of Luxeuil Abbey in eastern France in about the 7c or 8c. But this system was not fully formalized until 15c Italian typefounders designed fonts which combined an upper case modelled on monumental capitals with a lower case imitating minuscule handwriting. Thus, in roman type, most letters differ quite markedly in shape as well as size between upper and lower case: compare < A a >, < D d >, < E e >, etc. Alphabets which share this feature today, such as the modern version of the Greek alphabet, do so because they borrowed the idea from roman type; and other alphabets (e.g. Cyrillic, which was created on the basis of the Greek alphabet of the +9c) lack the feature. In modern Russian typography most lower-case letters are merely smaller versions of the capitals.

A further structural development was the co-ordination of italic and roman fonts. "Italic" type began life in 1501 as a different style of type, modelled on Italian handwriting which was relatively cursive. One book would be printed in roman, another in italic. At first the difference referred only to lower-case letters, since capitals were by definition formal while italics were by definition cursive. Fairly soon, however, printers began to cut sloping capitals to match the slope in italic minuscules. Not until the mid 16c, in Paris, were roman and italic treated as "fellow halves of a single design" (Morison 1973: 70), to be mixed in a single text with italic reserved for purposes such as emphasis and differentiation. Non-Roman alphabets have no parallel graphic distinction: a word to be emphasized in a German text printed in *Fraktur*, or in a Hebrew text, is set with spaces between the letters – a less salient distinction.

* * *

Once italic and roman had been co-ordinated, roman type as a symbolic system had become what it is today. It remains to consider the various letterforms which have instantiated the system.

The first printers, naturally enough, imitated the styles of lettering current in handwriting. In the early years of printing, gothic type was much commoner than roman; but in Britain gothic was given up for all but marginal uses in the 17c, and we shall not consider it further. What is relevant for practical purposes today are the varieties of letterforms that have evolved within roman script.

This is an area where the average reader today is far better informed than the readers of my first edition in the 1980s. Thirty years ago, non-experts were scarcely aware of the concept of a "font", and certainly were unlikely to be able to name any fonts. Thanks to the spread of computer word-processing, choosing a font for a document is a routine activity today, and everyone knows the names of a number of fonts.

What one does not learn, by selecting individual fonts from a list offered by one's computer, is how ranges of fonts group together as examples of general styles of typeface, and how those styles resemble and contrast with one another. There were a huge number of individual typefaces even before the arrival of type-design software made it far easier to create new ones: one 2013 estimate suggests about 7,000 faces in the 1970s, and perhaps as many as 200,000 today (*Economist* 2013: 115). But, provided we limit our attention to "book faces" – typefaces designed for printing continuous text, as opposed to "display faces" used for printing short stretches of wording on posters, in headings, and the like – then the mass of individual faces can be classified into a small set of families. (The distinction between book and display faces is not hard-and-fast; but display faces are very diverse indeed, and many of them would be quite unacceptable, used for printing whole paragraphs.)

Roman book-faces can be classified into three main families: in chronological order of emergence, these are "Old Style", "Modern", and "Sans-Serif".[6] Figure 28 displays specimens which exemplify these families.

Tre, Pol, and Pen are the Cornish men

An Old Style face: Goudy Old Style

Tre, Pol, and Pen are the Cornish men

A Transitional face: Baskerville

Tre, Pol, and Pen are the Cornish men

A Modern face: Didot

Tre, Pol, and Pen are the Cornish men

A Sans face: Helvetica

Figure 28

Old Style faces (many of which are in fact new, such as Stanley Morison's Times New Roman of 1931) are relatively close to the original shape of roman type. An Old Style face has fairly light, oblique stress; serifs are bracketed, and those at the upper end of verticals are oblique. Apart from Times, just mentioned, some Old Style faces in common current use are Imprint (1912), Bembo (1495), and Garamond (1621). (Here and below, dates quoted are for the earliest type of which the contemporary type named is identifiably a rendering. Thus, the type produced by the Monotype Corporation in 1929 and named by it "Bembo" is not identical to the type which the 15c printer Aldus Manutius cut and used to print Pietro Bembo's *De Aetna*, but the former is consciously a 20c "interpretation" of the latter.)

"Modern" faces are a product of the spirit of rationalism which swept through French culture in the 18c. The first type of the class now called Modern, the so-called *romain du roi*, was produced by a committee of the Académie des Sciences charged by Louis XIV in 1692 with the task of creating new types for the Imprimerie Royale; these were eventually completed in 1745. The committee approached its task in a highly theoretical way, planning at one stage to define each letter shape on a grid divided into 2304 squares like the pixels of a computer graphic display.

Old Style letters have oblique, bracketed serifs, because that is how serifs are naturally formed when letters are handwritten. The Académie des Sciences found it irrational to let the mechanics of penmanship dictate the design of printing type; in Modern faces, serifs are horizontal (i.e. at right angles to the line they terminate), and usually unbracketed. Typecasting techniques of the 15c did not allow very thin lines, since they would break in use. Modern type exploited superior 18c technology by introducing extreme stress contrast, with hairline serifs and upstrokes and thick downstrokes; and, since the obliqueness of Old Style stress was another hangover from the natural way of holding a pen, in Modern faces the stress was made vertical (i.e. the thinnest parts of an O are at the twelve and six o'clock positions).

Modern type became increasingly popular throughout Europe during the 18c and early 19c. It was resisted for some time in Britain: in the later 18c British typographers created "Transitional" faces having a more vertical and somewhat heavier stress than Old Style but retaining oblique, bracketed serifs. Such faces include the beautiful Baskerville (1757) and Bell (1788). But by the early 19c the tide of fashion overwhelmed this country too, and throughout that century most printing was in Modern type. Many Modern fonts, such as Bodoni (*c*.1767), Didot (*c*.1784), or Walbaum (*c*.1805), are relatively narrow-bodied, and have ascenders and descenders that are short relative to x-height: both of these features make them economical of paper. (Bodoni and Didot are rarely now used as book faces in Britain, and the Monotype Bodoni which is used for some purposes is much less "extreme" aesthetically than the 18c original; but Bodoni and Didot closer to the original are common in France.) In the 20c, Monotype created a new series of Modern fonts, less extreme than the original Moderns, which are still widely used for technical printing, particularly in America.

The initial success of Modern type was a matter of pure fashion. Interestingly, the professionals tended to oppose it in France, as well as in Britain. Updike (1922, vol. 1: 243) quotes the younger Fournier (designer of a fine Transitional face, *c*.1740) as remarking "Must there be so many squares to make an O that is round". As printers began to revert to Old Style in the later 19c and early 20c, though, Modern came to be seen as a practical type suitable for serious, scientific writing, while Old Style was seen as more appropriate for literary texts.

However, it is natural to feel that the chief practical virtue of any type is legibility. The objections repeatedly voiced against Modern type were not merely that it appeared mechanical and ugly but also that it was hard to read. Already in 1800 one *citoyen* Sobry complained in Paris that whereas Old Style emphasized the parts of letters which differentiated them from one another, Modern with its heavy vertical stress emphasized the parts that are common – in this respect Modern type is somewhat reminiscent of gothic.[7]

Since the great revival of fine typography which occurred in Britain in the early 20c, Modern has been relatively little used here; the role of "default" face, which once belonged to Monotype Modern, seems to have passed to Times. The connotations of the styles have changed to the point that Modern type is now associated with a Victorian "period" atmosphere (two editions of John Betjeman's poetry on my shelves are set respectively in Monotype Modern and in Walbaum). Routine use of Modern fonts lingered later in the USA and France.

* * *

Rationalism in typography has manifested itself anew in the past hundred years, however, in the promotion of Sans-Serif types. Sans-Serif letters, as the name implies, have no serifs; they are usually monoline – although some Sans faces, such as Optima (1958), have slight stress – and they tend to simplify letter-outlines into assemblages of a few geometrical elements. The most widely used Sans faces are Helvetica and Univers (both 1957).

Sans faces were originally developed in the 19c as display faces; lower-case Sans are not known to have existed before 1850 (A.F. Johnson 1966: 159). Although necessarily austere, Sans type used for display purposes can have great beauty: outstanding in this respect is Edward Johnston's Railway Type (1916), used throughout the London underground and bus system for the lettering of notices, destination-boards, and the like.

Between the wars, however, as part of the general movement in the arts associated with the "Bauhaus", German and Swiss typographers began to elevate Sans to the role of a book face. Sans type, stripped of all unnecessary frills, was advocated as the proper lettering for modern Man, liberated by Freud from his complexes. Morison (1972: 336) suggests that Sans was seen as a democratic, anti-élitist style.

In Britain Sans has not been widely used as a book face, but in the late 20c it was used to some extent in works discussing urgent "current affairs" issues, where it is important to convince the reader of the up-to-date, radical outlook of the writer. Impressionistically, in the 21c this fashion seems to be waning. One wonders whether it was not always counter-productive. I am fairly sure that the chief subliminal effect of Sans text in my own case is to reduce the perceived authority of the printed word.

Subjectively, the legibility problem already discussed in connexion with Modern Face appears to be acuter in the case of Sans. I feel that I have to work harder to speed-read a document printed in Sans type (and others have told me they feel the same). But of course much depends on what one is used to. In the early modern period when gothic printing was still the norm, people complained that roman was hard to read – incredible as that may seem today.

Particularly open to question is the practice, currently widespread in British primary schools, of using Sans for children's initial reading books. The rationale seems to be that the letters *read* by children should be as close as possible in outline to those they are learning to *write* (cf. Watts and Nisbet 1974: 33). Obviously children writing with modern instruments will not be producing serifs, and they will not be making outlines like the traditional printed shapes of a or g, so the faces in their reading-books incorporate forms such as < ɑ g >. The effect, however, is to produce print with minimal distinctiveness of letter shapes; it is somewhat reminiscent in that respect of Hebrew script. A page of a contemporary children's basic reading-book is a sea of circles, arcs, and straight lines – "balls and sticks" – unrelieved by stress contrast or quirkiness of individual letters. Children often confuse left and right; < b d >, < p q > in these faces are formed symmetrically, which must surely aggravate that tendency (cf. Downing and Leong 1982: 56; Treiman and Kessler 2014: 191), whereas in a serifed face such letter-pairs are not symmetrical.

Around the millennium, Sans type for documentation intended for adults was promoted by organizations like the Royal National Institute for the Blind, which represents the interests of blind people; the RNIB claimed that Sans is more easily read by people with limited vision. Many public-sector organizations fell into line and switched to Sans faces in all their documentation. But no hard evidence was cited. More recently the RNIB has backtracked; its website currently suggests "you can use either type of font [sans or serifed], as long as the typeface is clear and the characters are distinct".

Where Sans has an unquestionable advantage is on the Web. The low-resolution nature of the Web, where the same page has to be rendered on the unpredictably different pixel rasters of various users' monitors, means that small details such as serifs are distorted; it is easier for a Sans face to look clear and attractive. That is not to say that it is impossible to design a serifed face that works well in web pages. Over the years 1996 to 2002 Microsoft sponsored the design of what was intended as a standard "Core" pack of fonts for Web use; one of these, Georgia, is an adapted version of Times, but with wider and blunter serifs, wider letter bodies, and greater x-height – all features intended to compensate for the limitations of the

Web. Georgia is a success. But it is noticeable that almost all the other Core fonts (e.g. Arial, Trebuchet, Verdana) are Sans.

Faces designed for the Web tend not only to be Sans faces but rather bland, because strong character in a typeface, even a Sans face, usually derives from properties that cannot be preserved reliably on the Web. What is beginning to worry some people who care about design matters is that as documentation is increasingly made available online, and organizations aim to maintain consistent brand images on- and offline, the limitations of Web typography may be leading to impoverishment of letter design in the physical world. There was an outcry in 2009 when the home-furnishing company Ikea (often seen as an admirably design-conscious organization) switched from a proprietary variety of Futura to Verdana in its global branding. Futura and Verdana are both Sans faces, but Futura (created in 1927 by the German Paul Renner, later an active opponent of Nazism) is a typeface of great distinction. Verdana is seen by some as epitomizing the lowest-common-denominator approach imposed by the Web. *Time* magazine quoted an Australian typographer, Carolyn Fraser, as responding to the Ikea furore with the remark that Verdana is "dumbed down and overused. It's a bit like using Lego to build a skyscraper" (Abend 2009).

* * *

By this point, readers may be feeling that typography has been discussed too subjectively. Aesthetic considerations are all very well, but surely scientific methods should have a leading role in determining which styles of print are to be preferred?

There has by now been a fair amount of empirical research on typeface readability (for summaries see Lupton 2003; Poole 2008; Assitt 2009). But the conclusions are very inconclusive. No type style comes out as unambiguously more usable than others. As Ellen Lupton puts it, "In its drive to uncover fixed standards, the research has affirmed, instead, human tolerance for typographic variation and the elasticity of the typographic system" (Lupton 2003). Historically, typographers have selected among printing styles using aesthetic and intuitive judgements rather than scientific principles. The research seems to be telling us that this is the best way to do it.

Considering the large part played in our lives nowadays by the printed word, it may be welcome news that no better guide than beauty is available.

Notes

1. Stanley Morison (1972: 235) notes the irony that gothic lettering is nowadays associated particularly with Germany, whereas in its origin it was seen as "un-Germanic – or even anti-Germanic", having been created at a period when France was asserting its independence from the German-dominated Holy Roman Empire founded by Charlemagne.
2. Terms such as "gothic", "roman", and "humanist" are written with lowercase letters when they refer to varieties of the Roman alphabet.
3. I do not mean to imply that *Beowulf* was originally written in runes. We do not know how it was first written down; the only surviving manuscript dates from long after the poem's composition, and it is in Roman script, with just an occasional rune for special purposes. The extant runic inscriptions are mostly brief memorials to the dead and the like; I use *Beowulf* to offer a text of wider interest.
4. Rosamund McKittrick (1983: 158) does not hesitate to dismiss as "utter nonsense" Morison's similar suggestion that Charlemagne's "minister of education", the Englishman Alcuin, was personally responsible for the later creation of Carolingian minuscule, so we are entitled to be cautious about his remarks concerning SS Columba and Patrick.
5. Quoted (without source reference) on p. 324 of *Archiv für Buchgewerbe und Gebrauchsgraphik* vol. 71 no. 6 (1934), a special issue on "Fraktur: die deutsche Schrift"; my translation.
6. There has been an attempt to replace the somewhat vague and variable terms for type styles with artificial, internationally agreed names: Old Face becomes "Garalde", Modern Face "Didone", and Sans Serif "Lineale". In my experience the new names are rarely used, and I shall ignore them.
7. The assumption that, other things being equal, a more legible typeface is a better typeface has been challenged by the psychologist Daniel Oppenheimer, who finds experimentally that subjects reading factual prose remember the content better if the print is less than maximally legible (see Diemand-Yauman *et al.* 2011). Presumably this is because the subjects have to read slower and hence have more time to absorb the material.

8 A featural system: Korean Hangul

Korea is a fairly small and very distant country, but for the linguist it has great significance. It was in Korea, in the 13c, that the Chinese invention of printing from movable type was first seriously exploited; and in the 15c a Korean created a wholly original and quite remarkable phonographic script, nowadays called Hangul, which has been called "perhaps the most scientific system of writing in general use in any country" (Reischauer 1960: 435), or more simply "the world's best alphabet" (Vos 1964: 31).[1]

* * *

Any discussion of writing in Korea must begin by considering the relationship between the cultures of Korea and China.

China was the first civilization to emerge in East Asia. Accordingly, when neighbouring nations such as the Koreans, the Japanese, and the Vietnamese began their own climb from barbarism towards civilization, they looked towards China as the ancient fount of culture, and often borrowed its institutions and inventions rather than creating their own from scratch. There is a sort of parallel in Europe: since the Renascence, European nations have looked towards Classical Greece and Rome for sources of everything from theories of political life to words for new ideas such as *helicopter* or *audiovisual*. But the analogy is weak; China loomed larger on the mental horizon of its satellite nations than the Classical Mediterranean civilizations did in the minds of post-mediaeval Europeans. In the European case, the Classical civilizations had died before the new one was born. Furthermore, the two Classical European civilizations were very different from one another, and Christianity provided a rival, Asiatic source of cultural authority which was in some ways at odds with the Classical heritage.

In East Asia it was different. Chinese civilization has grown more or less continuously, in population, geographical spread, and cultural complexity, from its beginnings to the present. Modern China is both the most populous state in the world and possessor of the oldest living civilization. Furthermore, it was a characteristic of Chinese culture from an early stage to be monolithic and unwilling to recognize any value in cultural diversity. And for a peripheral East Asian nation such as Korea there was no other external source of culture; everything came from China. Even the few institutions, such as Buddhism, which the Chinese themselves borrowed from elsewhere came to the Koreans only after being thoroughly digested and reshaped by the Chinese.

Politically, the satellite nations contracted diverse relationships with China at different periods; but culturally China was always the sun round which they revolved as minor planets. And this was true most of all for Korea. During much of Korea's history, the aim of Korean education was quite explicitly to make Korea a *Sohwa*, a "Small China". In some ways Korea became a better realization of Confucian Chinese cultural norms than China itself ever was. One consequence of this cultural dependence on China was that the Korean language was not much written until recently.

As a spoken language, Korean is quite different from Chinese. It belongs to a different language family, the Altaic family; within this family, Korean is related relatively closely to the Tungusic languages such as Manchu, more distantly to Mongolian, and more distantly still to Turkish and to less well-known languages such as Chuvash.[2] Not only is Korean genetically unrelated to Chinese, but the two languages are different in type. Chinese is an "isolating" language whose words consist of one or more invariant monosyllabic roots; Korean is an "agglutinating" language with polysyllabic roots which take a fairly complex range of grammatical suffixes. Word order is different: for instance, Chinese places verb before object and preposition before noun as in English, while Korean puts the verb at the end of the clause and uses "postpositions" rather than prepositions. Korean is much more different from Chinese than one European language is from another. Nevertheless, until the 20c the normal medium of written communication in Korea was the Chinese language. To be educated meant to study Chinese language and literature. Until recently a Korean scholar would have been less likely to write in Korean than a mediaeval European would be to write in his native language rather than Latin.

Naturally, the Korean language borrowed vocabulary from Chinese on a massive scale, adapting Chinese roots to Korean pronunciation; in modern spoken Korean, the grammar is purely Korean and the commonest words are formed from native Korean roots, but the majority of items listed in a dictionary are "Sino-Korean" (i.e. Chinese words in Korean pronunciation). The relationship between the languages is such that *any* Chinese word automatically counts in its conventional Sino-Korean form as a word of Korean. If an English-speaker coins a neologism from a Latin or Greek root then he normally feels obliged to explain and justify his coinage briefly, but Chinese words are used freely in Korean without any such "naturalization ceremony". Sino-Korean vocabulary is by no means restricted to learned usage, as Classical-derived vocabulary tends to be in English. For instance, almost all Korean personal and place names are Chinese rather than Native Korean; and there are many grammatical environments where Sino-Korean rather than Native Korean number words have to be used.

The prestige of the Chinese language in Korea was so great that Korean was little used as a written language before the 1880s. After they conquered Korea in 1910 the Japanese encouraged the use of their own written language. Thus only since the Second World War has Korean been a standard national written language in general use for even as long as a generation.

But that does not mean that Korean was not written at all until the late 19c. As early as +600 or thereabouts the Koreans were beginning to adapt Chinese script to write their own language, and throughout subsequent Korean history the native language was used in certain kinds of writing, though normally relatively low-status, "unofficial" writing (largely poems and novels).

Chinese script, as we shall see in Chapter 9, is logographic, and consequently not easy to adapt in order to transcribe a non-Chinese language. Several relatively cumbersome methods were used to solve this problem. We shall not examine these in detail, because they are very similar to the methods the Japanese still use to solve the same problem for their language – these will be examined at length in Chapter 11. (It is no coincidence that Koreans and Japanese used the same devices in order to write non-Chinese languages in Chinese script: the Japanese originally borrowed Chinese culture from Korea rather than directly from China, and Koreans taught the Japanese how to write.) In Korea these clumsy systems were eventually made largely obsolete by the creation of the far simpler Hangul script, the logic of which owes nothing to China.

* * *

The Hangul script was created by King Sejong (reigned 1418–50), who assembled a group of scholars for the task in a "Bureau of Standard Sounds". (It is often supposed that Sejong's role in the creation of the script was purely managerial. However, Lee Ki-moon, the leading authority on the history of Korean, suggests (1977a: 61) that Korean tradition may be correct in asserting that the King invented the script personally. I shall write as if that were so, simply for ease of exposition.) The script was promulgated in 1446 in a book entitled *Hunmin Jeong-eum*, "The Standard Sounds for the Instruction of the People" (translated in Zachert 1980). This title was also the official name for the script, though various other names have been used; for much of its history it was commonly called *eonmun*, "vernacular writing". The educated classes tended to see the script as a trivialization of the serious and difficult task of writing in Chinese, and when the name Hangul was coined early in the 20c this may have been in part intended to upgrade its status: the name literally just means "Korean script", but *han* in archaic Korean also meant "great", so the name can be understood as "great script".

The script is reckoned by the Koreans as containing 28 "letters" in its original form; four of the 28 are now obsolete. But, unlike Roman letters, those of Hangul have internal structure correlated with the phonetic feature composition of the phonemes. In this respect Hangul is very like Pitman's shorthand (p. 34), and quite unlike any other script used as the ordinary writing system of a society.

The Korean analysis of the script into 28 (now 24) letters is not the most enlightening way of presenting it to the newcomer, since some combinations of these letters are better treated as separate graphic units. In what follows I begin by discussing the subset of the original system which is still in use, arranged so as to display its linguistic logic rather than in accordance with Korean tradition.

Before presenting the alphabet, I should make some preliminary remarks about Korean phonology. In Korean, voice is not a contrastive feature. The primary distinction of manner among Korean obstruent consonants (stops, fricatives, affricates) is the distinction of "tense" versus "lax" (or "fortis" versus "lenis"); a "tense" consonant involves greater muscle-tension and higher air-pressure than its lax equivalent (Kim 1965). At most places of articulation Korean has two tense obstruents and one lax obstruent, the tense obstruents being respectively unaspirated (i.e. voice onset is simultaneous with release of the consonant-closure) and heavily aspirated (it follows from the definition of "tense" that if a tense stop is aspirated the aspiration will be heavy, because the air-pressure is high). Taking bilabial as a typical place of articulation, I shall symbolize the three phonemes as /p*/ (tense unaspirated), /p^h/ (tense aspirated), and /b/ (lax). The lax obstruents each have several different allophones in complementary distribution, being voiced in some positions and voiceless in others. My transcriptions will ignore these allophonic differences, as does the Hangul script (which in this respect is phonemic rather than phonetic).[3]

The Hangul symbols for simple phonemes are shown in Figure 29. The major graphic distinction is between vowels and consonants: vowels are based on long horizontal or vertical lines with the addition of small distinguishing marks, consonants are represented by more compact, two-dimensional signs.

Consonants

	bilabial	apical	sibilant	velar	laryngeal
lax continuant	ㅁ m	ㄴ n	ㅅ s		ㅇ q (see p. 148)
lax stop	ㅂ b	ㄷ d	ㅈ dʒ	ㄱ g	
tense aspirated stop	ㅍ pʰ	ㅌ tʰ	ㅊ tʃʰ	ㅋ kʰ	ㅎ h
tense continuant			ㅆ s*		
tense unaspirated stop	ㅃ p*	ㄸ t*	ㅉ tʃ*	ㄲ k*	
liquid		ㄹ l			

Vowels

	front		back	
	spread	rounded	spread	rounded
close	i ㅣ		ɯ ㅡ	u ㅜ
mid	e ㅔ	ø ㅚ	ɤ ㅓ	o ㅗ
open	æ ㅐ		a ㅏ	

Figure 29

The consonants are divided into five families corresponding approximately to what a Western phonetician would call "places of articulation". From a strictly phonetic point of view it may seem odd to separate off the "sibilants" as a separate column, since these fricatives and affricates are made at or near the same place of articulation as the apical stops in the second column. Phonologically, however, this makes good sense for a language such as Korean, which has consonants involving friction only in one area of the mouth – Korean has no [f] or [x], for instance. In that area, Korean distinguishes much the same "manners of articulation" as at any of the stop positions, so the sibilants are appropriately treated as a separate sound-family. In the "Middle Korean" of the 15c it is likely that the affricates were pronounced dentally, [ts dz] rather than present-day [tʃ dʒ] (Lee 1977a: 108), making it all the clearer that the phonemes of this column form a single family.

Taking the lax rows as basic, we find that the five consonant-families are represented by (highly stylized) pictures of the articulations involved. Thus, the symbols for /n/ or /d/ show the tongue-tip raised to touch the front of the palate, while the symbol for /g/ (particularly when it is written like a 7 rather than a right-angle) suggests the back of the tongue touching the rear of the palate – Sejong evidently visualized the speaker as facing left. It may be less easy to see the /m/ symbol as portraying the lips, but it is relevant that this sign is identical to the Chinese graph for "mouth", which was originally a picture of a mouth. The /s/ sign was originally an inverted V representing a tooth,[4] and the two columns which I have labelled "sibilants" versus "apicals" are called in *Hunmin Jeong-eum* "tooth sounds" and "tongue sounds".

Lastly, the circle on which the "laryngeal" graphs are based represents the throat in cross-section. I call this column "laryngeal" because the original version of Hangul contained a range of symbols based on circles for sounds occurring in Chinese loanwords, most of which could be classified phonetically as laryngeal. Differences between the sound patterns of Chinese and Korean mean that today only two of those symbols are in use: one for /h/, and another (which I transcribe arbitrarily as < q >) that at the beginning of a syllable represents zero initial consonant (a syllable beginning with a vowel must have a < q > in Hangul), but at the end of a syllable represents /ŋ/ (a consonant which in Korean, as in English, occurs only syllable-finally). Originally the symbol for /ŋ/ was distinct, having a vertical stalk above the circle. But because it always appeared below the other letters of a syllable, the stalk was squeezed down until the two letters became identical.

Until recently it was controversial whether the forms of the Hangul graphs were in fact motivated as I have described, rather than being mere arbitrary shapes, some of which happened accidentally to look appropriate in terms of articulatory phonetics. This question was resolved in 1940 with the discovery of a longer original version of the *Hunmin Jeong-eum* which included a section explaining the logic of the forms in the terms I have given. In this respect, then, Hangul is even more phonetically systematic than Pitman's shorthand (in which the correlation between phonetic and graphic features is entirely arbitrary).

Stop as opposed to continuant articulation is shown by adding a horizontal line at the top of the symbol. Perhaps because the /m/ graph is already well-supplied with horizontals, an exceptional solution is adopted in the bilabial column and /b/ is symbolized by what was historically the earlier form of the square Chinese "mouth" graph. Tense aspirate articulation is shown by doubling the horizontal line, though again an exception is made in the bilabial column and a special symbol is provided for /pʰ/. Tense unaspirated articulation is shown by doubling the whole lax symbol. (One of the respects in which my presentation of the Hangul system differs from the traditional analysis is that the Koreans do not count the tense unaspirated symbols as separate letters – they are regarded as pairs of the lax letters.) The unique liquid phoneme is shown by adding an angular mark to the basic apical symbol.

Let us turn now to the vowels. Here the Hangul system provides six basic vowel graphs, those for the back vowels and for the vowel /i/. Each is based on a horizontal or vertical line, to which in four cases is added a distinguishing mark – originally a circular dot close to the line, now turned into a second short line at right angles to the base-line. Originally there was a seventh basic vowel, written with a simple dot, standing for a vowel /ʌ/ which no longer occurs in speech.

The front vowels other than /i/ are written by adding the graphs for the corresponding back vowels to the < i > symbol. (The Koreans do not count the combinations as separate letters, but as pairs of basic vowel letters.) We might say that the vertical stroke is not so much a symbol for the phoneme /i/ as for the feature of front vowel-quality in general: with a back-vowel symbol it represents the front counterpart to that vowel, in isolation it represents the frontest of all vowels, namely /i/. The front vowels other than /i/ were not originally assigned separate graphemes because, when Hangul was created, they were diphthongs: /e æ/ derived from /ɤi ai/ in the late 18c, /ø/ from /oi/ more recently.[5]

The graphic relationship between front and back vowels is plain. One might suppose, though, that there is little logic in the choice of symbols to represent the six "basic" vowels (seven including the obsolete /ʌ/). However, the symbols reflect a system of a surprising kind.

Like other Altaic languages, Korean is a "vowel-harmony" language. This means that most of its vowels fall into one of two classes, such that all the vowels of a given word are drawn from one class or the other but not from both. If a root has vowels from class A, then a grammatical suffix will contain a class A vowel; with a root containing class B vowels, the same grammatical suffix will show the corresponding vowel from class B (the vowels in the two classes pair off with one another). In most Altaic languages this system is very salient and well-defined. It happens that modern Korean has lost all but a few traces of vowel-harmony (a fact which may be connected with the massive borrowing of Chinese words into Korean; two-syllable Chinese compounds contain all kinds of vowel-combinations violating Korean harmony rules, and must therefore have made those rules hard to maintain). However, the Middle Korean spoken in the 15c still possessed vowel-harmony. The vowels /ɯ u ɤ/ formed one class, whose members paired off respectively with /ʌ o a/ in the other class; /i/ was a "neutral" vowel which could occur with vowels of either class. Thus, for example, the topic-marking suffix was /-ɯn/ after roots containing vowels of the first class, /-ʌn/ after roots containing vowels of the second class, and /-ɯn/ or /-ʌn/ interchangeably after roots containing /i/:

bom + ʌn	"as for spring"
sjɤm + ɯn	"as for the island"
dʒib + ʌn dʒib + ɯn	"as for the house"

Sejong associated the relatively close and relatively open vowel-classes with the Chinese philosophical terms *yin* and *yang*, representing the female and male principles respectively and correlated with the first two elements of the mystical trinity Earth, Heaven, and Man. The vowel /i/, being phonologically neutral, was associated with Man, who mediates between the *yang* of Heaven and the *yin* of Earth. Of the shapes used to make up the vowel symbols, the dot stands for Heaven, which is round; the horizontal stands for Earth, which is flat; and the vertical stands for Man, who is upright. Sejong further postulated that a symbol containing a dot over or "outside" (to the right of) a line was to be classed as *yang*, a symbol with a dot under or "inside" (to the left of) a line was *yin*. This gives the system shown in Figure 30, in which the vowels pair off just as required by the vowel-harmony rules.[6]

Hangul also has a number of diphthong symbols, as shown in Figure 31. For diphthongs in /j-/, the rule is: double the distinguishing dot of the basic vowel-symbol (and, in the case of /j-/ preceding a front vowel, add

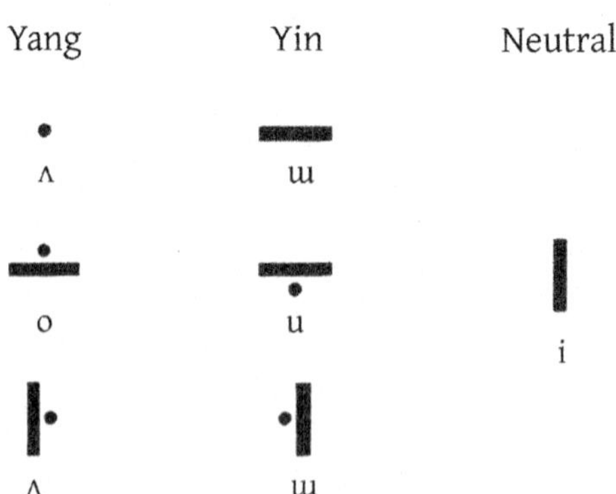

Figure 30

		ㅠ	ㅟ		ㅢ
		ju	wi		ɯi
ㅖ	ㅕ	ㅛ	ㅞ	ㅝ	
je	jɤ	jo	we	wɤ	
ㅒ	ㅑ		ㅙ	ㅘ	
jæ	ja		wæ	wa	

Figure 31

the corresponding diphthong with a back vowel to the frontness-marking vertical stroke). This rule which indicates a /j-/ diphthong by doubling the dot could not be used to indicate diphthong /ji/, /jɯ/ (since < i ɯ > have no dots to double), but that does not matter because Korean has no such diphthongs.

Diphthongs in /w-/, like front vowels, are indicated by combinations of phoneme-symbols. Indeed, one noteworthy point is that Hangul fails to make a graphic distinction between pure vowels and diphthongs: in particular, by the logic of the system the /wi/ graph might equally well be pronounced [y] (a fronted /u/). At first blush this looks like a defect in the script, but it is not. Korean actually has free variation between [wi] and [y] – and also between [we] and [ø], and between [wæ] and [œ] (Kim 1968: 517) – so it is quite appropriate for the script not to mark the pure-vowel/diphthong distinction. (Hangul does provide alternative writings for [we] and [ø]; but in this case, unlike the other two pairs, there is an etymological basis for the distinction and it is still maintained by some speakers, although it is merged for most.) Before the close and mid vowels /i e ɤ/, the semivowel /w/ is written with a miniature < u >, before the open vowels /æ a/, /w/ is written with a miniature < o >, thus preserving the vowel-harmony principle. The diphthong /ɯi/ has a marginal status in Korean, but when it occurs it is written as shown at the right of Figure 31.

The only phonemic contrast among vowels not indicated in the Hangul system is that between long and short vowels (which my transcriptions also ignore). There are various possible explanations for this. Although length remains contrastive today in most Korean dialects, including the standard dialect of Seoul, this contrast seems to be one of low functional yield (Martin 1951: §1.32). And we have already seen that contrasts of phonological length (and perhaps suprasegmental contrasts in general) seem to be less noticeable than segmental contrasts to speakers of languages which include them. (Length is not always ignored, of course; e.g. Czech orthography marks it consistently.)

Rather than being written in a linear sequence like letters of European alphabets, Hangul symbols are written grouped into syllables; some examples are shown in Figure 32. The reason for syllable grouping is historical, having to do with Koreans' familiarity with Chinese script: a syllable-sized grouping of Hangul symbols looks somewhat like a Chinese graph, having roughly comparable visual complexity, and since each Chinese graph is pronounced as one syllable, it seemed appropriate for Hangul writing to be organized into that size of unit. Whatever the historical cause of the system, it might be argued that by using a small number of basic graphic units and arranging them into syllable-sized perceptual groups Hangul succeeds in reconciling two contradictory desiderata for a writing system: the fewness of the basic graphic elements makes Hangul easy to learn, while the large size of the perceptually salient units makes it efficient to read.[7]

The placement of elements within a syllable grouping is fixed, but syllables can be written one after another in different directions. Traditionally the Chinese system of vertical downward columns was used, but this has nowadays been replaced by the European system of left-to-right horizontal rows.

* * *

	transliteration	*pronunciation*	
바 다	ba-da	/bada/	sea
나 무	na-mu	/namu/	tree
하 늘	ha-nɯl	/hanɯl/	sky
바 람	ba-lam	/balam/	wind
부 엌	bu-qɤk^{h}	/buɤg/	kitchen
빨 강	p*al-gaq	/p*algaŋ/	red
서 울	sɤ-qul	/sɤul/	Seoul (S. Korean capital)
평 양	p^{h}jɤq-qjaq	/p^{h}jɤŋjaŋ/	Pyeongyang (N. Korean capital)

Figure 32

제 7 장 자질적 체계: 한국의 한글

한국은 상당히 작고 또 아주 먼 나라다. 그러나 한국은 두 가지 점에서 언어학자에게는 아주 중요한 나라다. 가동성(可動性) 활자에 의한 중국의 인쇄술 발명이 처음으로 진지하게 개척된 것은 13세기에 한국에서였다. 그리고 15세기에 한 한국인이 그의 국민이 사용하도록 오늘날 한글이라 부르는 전적으로 독창적이고 아주 훌륭한 음성표기의 글자체를 창조했는데, 이것은 '어떤 나라에서고 일반적으로 사용되는 아마 가장 과학적인 문자체계'이며 (Reischauer 1960, p. 435), 또는 더 간단히는 '세계 최상의 알파벳'(Vos 1964, p. 31)으로 묘사되어 왔다.

한국에서의 문자에 관한 어떤 논의도 한국과 중국의 문화 사이의 관계를 고려함으로써 시작되어야 한다.

Figure 33

As an example of running Hangul text, Figure 33 displays the opening of this chapter in the Korean edition of the present book, published in 1999. (In that edition it was Chapter 7.) In scholarly material like this, foreign names are commonly quoted in the Roman alphabet (cf. "Reischauer", "Vos"), though in more general kinds of text they will be transliterated into Hangul; better-known foreign names are likely to be Koreanized in any genre of writing. (I datelined the preface to my first edition with the name of the village where I then lived – Ingleton, Yorkshire; in the Korean edition, "Ingleton" is given in Roman but "Yorkshire" is written in Hangul, as < qjo-qo-kʰɯ dʒu >, "York province".)

Apart from literature citations in Roman, Figure 33 contains one word in a third script: the English word *movable* is translated in the second line as the Sino-Korean /gadoŋsɤŋ/, and after this word has been spelled out in Hangul it is shown in Chinese script in brackets: 可動性. Traditionally, Korean writing made heavier use than this of Chinese script. We have seen that much Korean vocabulary is borrowed from Chinese, and until recently it was usual to write all Chinese roots using Chinese graphs (alone, rather than added in brackets), with Hangul used only for Native Korean roots, together with grammar words and derivational and inflexional affixes. Despite the complexity this created, there was a good practical reason for it. We shall see in Chapter 9 that the Chinese language has a remarkably high incidence of homophones. Chinese script is logographic, so homophones cannot be confused when written in Chinese, but in phonographic Hangul they become indistinguishable. Wikipedia[8] quotes the example of Hangul 수도 /sudo/, which represents any of seven different Sino-Korean terms, each of which looks entirely distinct in Chinese script; meanings are "spiritual discipline", "prisoner", "city of water (e.g. Venice or Hong Kong)", "paddy rice", "drain", "tunnel", "capital city". I do not know what alternative meaning the phoneme-string /gadoŋsɤŋ/ in Figure 33 might have, but evidently my translator saw it as potentially unclear.

The Korean term for a Chinese graph is *hanja*. The contrast between this and the name *Hangul* for the phonographic script is itself a striking illustration of the homophony problem. The *han* of *hanja* means "Chinese" while the *han* of *Hangul* means "Korean". Both forms are Korean versions of Chinese roots that, in Chinese, are written and pronounced differently, but in Korean speech, and in Hangul, only context distinguishes them.

Since 1949, North Korea has used exclusively Hangul (there called "Joseon-geul").[9] But the homophony problem arises only with Chinese loans, and the North Koreans have also to a considerable extent purged these from their version of the Korean language. Furthermore the Orwellian poverty of North Korean intellectual life probably reduces confusion from the remaining Sino-Korean terms; if you know what opinions everyone must express in public, potential ambiguities will often resolve themselves. Even so, Hannas (1997: 221) quotes the then North Korean leader Kim Il-song as complaining in 1970 that Hangul-only script was bringing about a situation in which "the people were unable to understand Korean concept words, and ... their mental abilities were declining". North Korean children are now taught Chinese graphs to help them grasp the ideas underlying ambiguous Hangul renderings of roots.

South Korea, too, has toyed with replacing Korean vocabulary wholesale by neologisms formed from Native Korean roots – as if we were to give up Classically-derived words such as *reverse, hypothetical* in favour of native English calques like *againturn, undersettish*. In the 1960s a five-volume dictionary of proposed replacement words was issued (Hannas 1997: 65). But in practice South Koreans have not switched to using the Native Korean vocabulary.

Despite that, in recent decades South Korea too has been greatly reducing its use of Chinese script. Thus, comparing two books on Korean linguistic topics, one written by the leading Koreanist Lee Ki-moon in 1977 (Lee 1977b), the other by Van Jae Weon in 2002 (Van 2002), I find 86 terms written in Chinese in the opening page of the former but only six in the opening page of the latter. (Also, the title page and cover are entirely in Chinese script in the 1977 book, entirely in Hangul in the 2002 book.) Since about the 1990s, mass-circulation books and newspapers have used little Chinese script, though it continues to be used fairly heavily in documents where precision is important, such as legal writing and scholarly monographs.[10] Using only Hangul undoubtedly makes learning to read and write far easier. But one wonders what the social cost of the resulting orthographic ambiguity will be in practice.

Lee and Ramsey (2011: 289) note that, in the new millennium, "Chinese characters have undergone a mild resurgence in popularity, with mixed script proponents continuing to advocate the importance of Chinese-character education. But the possibility that Korea will ever see a return to mixed-script publishing seems remote."

South Korea has been an outstandingly successful country in recent years; that success has been most noticeable in the sphere of modern technology. The Korean language has been borrowing its technology vocabulary not from Chinese but from English (*internet* is /in-t^{h}a-ned/, *blog* is /bɯl-lo-gɯ/, *computer* is /k^{h}am-p^{h}ju-t^{h}a/ or just /p^{h}i-s*i/, i.e. "PC"); no special problem about homophony arises when these are written in Hangul. Apart from proper names, the intellectual domains where Chinese-derived vocabulary is specially crucial, so that Hangul-only writing is most likely to lead to unclarity, are older-established ones such as history, politics, philosophy, or literature. I am not aware of Korean achievements in these humanistic domains comparable to the strides they have been making in technology – though that could merely reflect my limited knowledge of things Korean.

* * *

Even more interesting than the structure of the Hangul graphemes, from the point of view of Western linguistic thought, is the history of the changing orthographic conventions that have governed the use of Hangul with respect to the distinction between "deep" and "shallow" approaches to writing.

When a spoken language contains rule-governed morphophonemic alternations, we have seen that one way of defining the range of possibilities is to posit phonological rules which apply so as to derive the pronunciation of morphemes in particular environments from single, invariant "underlying forms". Such rules tend to reflect the history of the language to which they apply. Consider, for instance, the morphophonemic variation in English between [ai] and [ɪ] in pairs of words such as *line, linear*, or *unite, unity*. We know that the same vowel letter < i > is used because, when English was first written and long afterwards, the vowels were phonetically the same – [i] – but a large-scale sound change which occurred in English in the early modern period caused the pure vowel [i] to turn into the diphthong [ai] in certain environments. What happened to [i] was one case of a sound shift, the "Great Vowel Shift", which applied to a range of English vowels: the vowel alternation in *metre* versus *metric*, discussed on p. 82, is another consequence of the same sound law.

Because efficient morphophonemic rules tend to coincide with historical sound changes, a "shallow" phonographic script which remains fixed over a long period while the spoken language changes will often end up as a "deep" script through simple inertia, as it were. English orthography is far from being a surface phonographic script, and it reflects many aspects of the mediaeval or early modern period of the language which are no longer heard in its present-day standard form; most linguists take it that this is purely a consequence of orthographic conservatism.

However, there is a school of linguists, the generative phonologists, who have claimed that morphophonemic rules have current psychological validity: speakers store their vocabulary in their minds in terms of invariant "underlying" root-shapes, and apply morphophonemic rules in order to derive the appropriate pronunciations of the roots in context when they speak. This theory was classically advanced in the book *The Sound Pattern of English* (Chomsky and Halle 1968), and for many years it was the consensus theory. The fact that traditional orthographic systems such as that of English seem to represent the underlying forms of morphemes rather than their (often strikingly different) surface pronunciations is one category of evidence sometimes cited in favour of generative phonology; it is suggested that speakers are able to use such orthographies conveniently because the spellings of words correspond to the forms stored in a speaker's mental lexicon. From this point of view, a reformed English orthography which corresponded more closely to the surface phonetic facts of the modern language might actually be *less* convenient for its users. According to *The Sound Pattern of English* (Chomsky and Halle 1968: 49), "conventional [English] orthography is ... a near optimal system for the lexical representation of English words". *The Sound Pattern of English* was written a long time ago, and generative phonology has lost some of its allure in recent decades (Goldsmith and Laks 2012), yet still today linguists' discussions about ideal orthographies "seem to be locked into phonological theories that predate the 1970s" (Snider 2014: 27).

The Sound Pattern of English went so far as to claim that the mental representations of some English roots contain sounds that never occur in *any* English surface forms. For instance, it argued that the root of *right, righteous* must contain an underlying velar fricative | x | which is foreign to the surface phonology of English, though it is recorded by the < gh > of the conventional spelling (which is, in this respect, very "deep"). We know, of course, that the sound [x] was pronounced in words such as *right* in Middle English, and that these words were originally written with < gh > for that reason. But *The Sound Pattern of English* argued that the presence of a latent | x | in these words can be established purely on the evidence of synchronic alternations in the present-day language, implying that the velar fricative continues to be a psychological – although not a phonetic – reality in < gh > words. (The argument for underlying | x | is complex; it has to do with facts such as the presence of an /ai ~ ɪ/ alternation in *expedite ~ expeditious* versus the absence of a similar alternation in *right ~ righteous.*) From the viewpoint of the generative phonologists, the change from Middle to Modern English phonology has not been the loss of a phoneme /x/, but the addition of a new phonological rule which prevents that phoneme surviving from underlying into surface forms.

It should be of particular interest, then, if we can find standard orthographies which are relatively "deep" and where we can demonstrate that this is *not* simply the result of inertia or conservatism in face of historical sound changes.

We have already seen hints, in the discussion of Greek spelling (p. 114), that a phonographic script may evolve in ways that make it "deeper" independently of any historical development in the associated spoken language. In the case of Korean script such an evolution is very striking.

Korean is rich in morphophonemic alternations, so that underlying phonological forms of words are often very different from their actually pronounced surface forms. Consider for instance the name of the Yalu River, which divides North Korea from China. ("Yalu" is its Chinese pronunciation; it translates as "duck green".) The surface form of its Korean name is /amnok*aŋ/. But this form derives, regularly, from an underlying form | ab+log+gaŋ | (where the first two syllables correspond to Mandarin "Yalu" and the third means "river"). In Korean, sequences of homorganic stops coalesce into single tense stops, so | gg | becomes /k*/. When not following a vowel, /l/ becomes /n/, so the first consonant of "green" changes accordingly. Stops become nasals before a nasal, so /bn/ becomes /mn/ – notice that the rule changing /l/ to /n/ has to apply before this rule, because the former rule "feeds" the latter. Only one of the five consonants in the underlying form appears unchanged in the surface form, though each of those underlying consonants is established by appearing in surface forms of the same morphemes in other environments – thus "green" is /log/ at the surface when it happens to follow a vowel and is not in turn followed by a velar stop.

Korean also has allophonic alternations. No version of Hangul writing has ever taken any notice of these subphonemic differences (despite the fact that to non-Korean ears the differences can be large). It is difficult to know whether the subphonemic alternations already existed in the 15c, but there has never been more than one Hangul grapheme to cover sound-families such as [l] and [ɾ] (which are in complementary distribution as members of one Korean phoneme), or [b], [p], and other realizations of the /b/ phoneme. This is not surprising: the orthographies of European languages behave similarly. Our own script is incapable of showing any distinction between plain [l] and velarized [lᵚ], or between aspirated and unaspirated voiceless stops.

On the other hand, with respect to morphophonemic rules, which involve alternations between contrasting phonemes rather than between allophones of single phonemes, the orthographic conventions of Hangul have changed greatly.

It seems likely that Sejong intended his script to be used as a "shallow" system. For instance, the language has rules which cause tense consonants to become lax and sibilants to become stops in syllable-final position, and a passage in the *Hunmin Jeong-eum* comments:

> < bʌis-godʒ > is "pear blossom", < Øjɤz-Øɯi-gatʃʰ > is "fox fur";
> but, since the letter < s > can equally well be used in such cases,
> only < s > should be used.

That is, since the four final underlying consonants | s dʒ z tʃʰ | in the words quoted all fall together at the surface (as /d/), they may as well be written alike.[11] (Syllable-final /d/ is written < s > rather than < d >, because underlying | s | is far commoner in final position than underlying | d |. This logic applies even to modern borrowings from English, where the Korean morphophonemic rules are irrelevant: the *net* of *internet* is pronounced /ned/, but written < nes >.)

Indeed, *Hunmin Jeong-eum* even included instructions for transcribing sounds that occurred only in non-standard dialects or children's speech, suggesting that users of Hangul were expected to hug the phonetic ground quite closely. Lee Ki-moon (1977a: 137, 140) confirms that 15c and 16c orthographic usage in general followed this lead, though with sporadic exceptions. Spelling reflected the surface results of applying phonological rules, so that a given root would appear now in one orthographic form, now in another. Rules (which I shall not spell out here) mean that, for instance, underlying | gabs | "price" with respective case suffixes | i | and | do | become /gabsi/ but /gabdo/; | gip^{h} | "deep" with conjugation-suffixes | ɯni | and | go | become /gip^{h}ɯni/ but /gibgo/; and the spellings were < gab-si >, < gab-do >, < gi-p^{h}ɯ-ni >, < gib-go >. We have seen that Hangul "letters" are grouped into syllables; one consequence of the choice of the "surface" approach to writing was that orthographic syllable-boundaries (indicated by hyphens in my transcriptions) represented phonetic rather than morphemic divisions – in < gab-si > the < s > is part of the root, but it was written as if it were part of the suffix when the suffix begins with a vowel.

After the 16c, however, Hangul orthographic conventions broke down. In the 1590s the Japanese ruler Hideyoshi invaded Korea as a preliminary to an (ultimately unsuccessful) attempt to conquer China. This invasion had a destructive effect on Korean society from which the country did not fully recover for centuries, and one consequence was that it became much harder to maintain nationwide written norms – particularly as the circle of users of Hangul script was widening. The 17c and subsequent centuries brought successive changes to the spoken Korean language, many of which required some adaptation of previous spelling conventions; in practice the result was deepening orthographic confusion. The matter was taken in hand only in the early 20c, when the rise of Korean nationalism led to a raising of the status of Hangul script and the foundation in 1921 of a Korean Language Research Society to examine such questions.

At present there are minor differences in spelling conventions between North and South Korea (see Martin 1968), but in the main both half-nations now follow the rules laid down in a 1933 *Guide for the Unification of Korean Spelling*. The philosophy behind these rules derives from the ideas of Ju Si-gyeong (1876–1914), the father of modern Korean linguistics (it was Ju, incidentally, who coined the name Hangul). That philosophy is precisely opposite to the orthographic principles of the 15c.

Ju Si-gyeong's ideas about language were strikingly reminiscent of recent generative linguistics theories (Lee 1981). While drawing a strict distinction between synchronic and diachronic analysis, Ju believed that linguistic forms were to be treated as possessing two levels of structure both grammatically and phonologically. Grammatically, the surface structure of a sentence conceals a "hidden meaning" (generative linguists would say "deep structure"); and, phonologically, the "temporary form" which a root displays in a given morphological environment will often differ from its fixed "original form". Orthography should reflect the "original form" of roots, ignoring the consequences of the various phonological rules that affect them.

This principle has been applied consistently to modern Korean orthography so that, now, alternations between variant pronunciations of a given root are ignored in writing unless they are irregular, i.e. not predictable by general phonological rules. Orthography is "deep" rather than "shallow". A pair of forms such as /gabdo/, /gabsi/ (see above) will now be written not as < gab-do >, < gab-si > but as < gabs-do >, < gabs-qi >; the root has a consistent written form, because the underlying | s | is written even where it is eliminated in speech. Orthographic syllable-division is now morphological rather than phonetic: the /s/ of /gabsi/ belongs phonetically to the following syllable, but semantically it is part of the root and it is written as such. In some cases the spelling of a word will be very different indeed from its pronunciation: /amnok*aŋ/ "Yalu River" is written < qab-log-gaq >.

On the other hand, the alternation between /d/ and /l/ found in cases such as | dɯd̲+da | "hears" (which by the tensing rule becomes surface /dɯt*a/) versus | dɯl̲+ɤs*+da | "heard" (surface /dɯlɤt*a/) is irregular, like the /f ~ v/ alternation in English *wife ~ wives*, *half ~ halves*; other English roots in /-f/, such as *reef*, *laugh*, do not change the /f/ to /v/, and likewise many other Korean roots in | -d | do not have allomorphs in | -l |. So these Korean forms are spelled < dɯd-da >, < dɯl-qɤs*-da >.

The 1933 orthographic system represented a decision to write synchronic underlying pronunciations; it was not an archaizing decision to write obsolete surface pronunciations, as (to some extent) we do in English script. Often these two principles would yield similar spellings, but sometimes their results differ, and in such cases modern Korean orthography is deliberately un-archaic. For instance, after the invention of Hangul the phoneme /ʌ/ disappeared from the spoken language by merging with other vowels. This meant that the sign < ʌ > no longer represented a distinct phoneme, but it was still used distinctively in writing (just as we distinguish between the vowels of *meat*, *seal*, *mead* and *meet*, *wheel*, *seek* in writing despite the fact that the spoken vowels in the two sets of words have been identical since the late 17c). Before 1933 a word like /salam/, "person", from Middle Korean /salʌm/, was still written < sa-lʌm >. An archaizing orthography would retain such spellings; but, since the mergers between /ʌ/ and other vowels left behind no synchronic alternations in the spoken language, there is no ground for positing a synchronic underlying | ʌ | in modern Korean and accordingly the 1933 reform abolished the < ʌ > grapheme – /salam/ is now written < sa-lam >.

In 1949 a further orthographic reform was promulgated in North Korea (Xolodović 1958) which would have moved Korean orthography even further in the direction of the abstract, "deep" approach. We saw that certain Korean morphophonemic alternations are irregular: for example, there are roots like "hear" which have allomorphs in /-d/ alternating with allomorphs in /-l/, but the majority of Korean roots ending in either of these phonemes do not exhibit such alternations. One can always turn an irregular alternation such as this into a regular one, by postulating that at the underlying level the root contains some third phoneme, different from both of the phonemes entering into the alternation, but which is always changed into one or the other of these by rules designed for the purpose. In English, for instance, we could make the *wife/wives* type of alternation regular by treating a root such as *wife* as, say, underlying | waiɸ | rather than | waif | (whereas *reef* would be | rif |) and positing rules by which bilabial | ɸ | (but not labiodental | f |) becomes voiced before voiced sounds, and subsequently bilabial sounds become labiodental. This, in essence, is how *The Sound Pattern of English* argued for an | x | in modern English. The 1949 Korean reform used this approach not as a technical device of academic linguistic analysis but as a route towards an improved everyday orthography for Korean.

Six sounds were defined as occurring in Korean underlying forms (though they are never actually pronounced in Korean); graphemes were created to represent them (in some cases obsolete Hangul graphemes were revived, in other cases the shapes were new), and in each case phonological rules governing the behaviour of the novel underlying phoneme were defined in such a way as to capture some class of common but irregular morphophonemic alternations. Thus, the behaviour of roots like "hear" was handled by reviving the obsolete grapheme < z >, and specifying that the consonant | z | becomes /l/ between vowels and /d/ before most consonants (the rules had to be a little more complex than this to handle certain other alternation phenomena not discussed here). This allows us to spell /dɯt*a/ "hears", /dulɤt*a/ "heard" as < dɯz-da >, < dɯz-qɤs*-da >; and now the root "hear" is regular and obeys the principle of constancy of graphic shape.

Again, it should be stressed that there is no intention here of making contemporary orthography reflect history. In the case quoted, the new grapheme < z > is a revival of a grapheme which occurred in the original Hangul system and stood for a consonant that may well have been a voiced apical fricative [z]. But the historical /z/ never turned into /l/ between vowels, and it did not historically occur in the root "hear". When the historical /z/ ceased in the 16c to be part of the living language, it simply dropped (i.e. merged with zero). The | z | of the 1949 reform was a purely theoretical, synchronic construct.

The 1949 spelling reform was abandoned after a few years. But the fact that such a scheme can be seriously considered demonstrates how far some Korean linguists have been from accepting the axiom which often passes in Europe for common sense, that the best practical orthography is one that assigns graphemes one-for-one to the phonemes of the spoken language. The orthography actually used in modern Korea, let alone the 1949 alternative, are closer in spirit to the generative phonologists' views about ideal orthographies.

At the same time, it is not clear that the history of Hangul spelling conventions supports the generative phonologists' psychological theories about how speakers store their vocabulary in their memory. If they were right about this, it ought to follow that "deep" orthography will be relatively natural, so that a society which acquires the use of a phonographic script will begin by writing underlying forms. A move towards shallow writing would come, if at all, only as speakers with increasing phonetic sophistication gradually learn to perceive consciously the effects of the phonological rules which they apply unconsciously to their stored forms when they speak. But the historical movement, in the case of both Greek and Korean orthographies, was the reverse of this. Spelling began with a surface approach and became gradually deeper – even setting aside the cases of "inertial deepening" resulting from failure of the orthography to adapt to historical sound changes.[12] (I have discussed the move from shallow to deep Hangul spelling as if it were a sudden switch brought about by Ju Si-gyeong single-handed, but Lee Ki-moon (e.g. 1977a: 234–5) suggests that movements in that direction had been occurring in previous centuries.)

* * *

From a scientific point of view, Hangul is certainly a remarkable achievement. In terms of practical everyday use, though, one can be sceptical about Frits Vos's claim (Vos 1964: 31) that it is the best alphabet in the world.

The special characteristic of Hangul is that it is based on phonetic features rather than on segments as unanalysed wholes. In Korean, as in any language, a largish number of segmental phonemes are built up by combining a smaller number of features in different ways, so a featural script should have the virtue of fewness of graphic units to be learned. One might claim that theoretically Hangul comprises just fifteen distinctive graphic elements: the five outlines for places of articulation, four manner-of-articulation modifications, outlines for the three *yang* vowels and < i > together with the principle for converting *yang* into *yin* outlines, and the principle for depicting diphthongs in /j-/. Admittedly there are complications such as the irregular outlines of bilabial stops; but, even so, there will still be many fewer Hangul graphic elements than there are segmental phonemes in Korean (thirty, including /j w/ but ignoring vowel-length contrasts).

However, it is not at all clear that a script involving fifteen graphemes is in practice much easier to learn than one of thirty graphemes, particularly when the small inventory is achieved at the cost of requiring the learner to analyse sound-segments into features. It could be argued that memorizing the shape of graphemes is only a trivial part of the whole task of learning a phonographic script, so that size of grapheme inventory would not be a sensitive script-design factor. Indeed, one may doubt whether Koreans do commonly learn or perceive their script in terms of the featural principle that was used to construct it. We saw in Chapter 2 that Pitman's shorthand is based on the same principle, but I believe shorthand-typists have commonly learned the outlines for the various phonemes as unanalysed units, paying little or no attention to the logic behind the outlines – it is only people who have studied phonetics who classify consonants as "voiced" versus "unvoiced", for instance. Similarly, Koreans regard Hangul < n >, < d >, < t^h >, etc. as separate individual "letters" rather than as partly identical graphic composites.

Furthermore, while the fewness of Hangul graphic elements conceivably offers an advantage for learnability, it carries an offsetting disadvantage for readability. From the reader's point of view, distinctiveness in the written shape of linguistic forms is desirable. The fact that Hangul uses so few graphemes means that there is little for the eye to fasten on in a page of Korean writing; everything is composed of the same few simple geometrical shapes repeated over and over again. Because Korean phonology allows little variety of syllable-structure (almost all written syllables will be of CVC or CV structure), the syllables which are the visually salient elements of the script are not really very diverse in visual outline.[13]

Now that South Korea has become one of the most economically successful countries in the world, we are beginning to hear assertions about the overall superiority of the Hangul script that sometimes verge on the chauvinistic. In 2007 a group of Korean linguistics scholars launched a movement which aims to use Hangul as a basis for creating scripts for the unwritten languages which still exist in various parts of the world (Ha 2008). Their first success was with the Cia-Cia tribe of Buton island, Indonesia, who agreed in 2009 to adopt Hangul to write their language; since

2012 a Korean-established language school on Buton has been promoting this by running classes and producing textbooks (Na 2013). One Korean academic involved in the Cia-Cia project, Lee Ho-young, hoped that this "w[ould] serve as a meaningful opportunity to show off the excellence of Hangeul overseas", to which Kim Joo-won, the initiator of the project, added that "In the long run, the spread of Hangeul will also help enhance Korea's economy" (Park 2009). In South Korea, government-approved school textbooks boasted that the tribe had officially adopted Korean script, though this statement was removed when it was realized that there was nothing "official" about the development (there could not be: the Indonesian constitution lays down that for the sake of national unity any newly devised script must use the Roman alphabet).

Official or unofficial, the Cia-Cia project seems a questionable initiative. Apart from the fact that the Cia-Cia sound system is rather different from the system which Hangul encodes, one must wonder how wise it can be to encourage any language community to move towards literacy via a script otherwise used only by one small nation thousands of miles distant from its own homeland.

How best to design scripts for unwritten languages in modern conditions, when the speakers of such languages commonly are in contact with "bigger" languages that have established orthographic traditions, is a study in its own right, related as much to social and political as to purely linguistic issues (see Cahill and Rice 2014).

* * *

But it would be churlish to end this chapter on a negative note. Whether or not it is sensible to use it for other languages, as a phonographic script for Korean Hangul is a success. Any disadvantages it may have relative to a phonemic script containing more diverse graphemes are fairly marginal. The fact that confusion can be created when Hangul is used to write Chinese loanwords is a problem that stems from the nature of the Chinese language, rather than from the nature of Hangul.

It is worth re-emphasizing what a prodigious scientific achievement Hangul represents. Not only the principle of writing phonemes in terms of their constituent features, and the outlines of the individual graphemes, but even the very principles on which Sejong analysed syllables into component sounds were entirely original. Sejong was familiar with the Chinese tradition of phonological analysis, but his decision to divide syllables into what we know as vowels and consonants represented a sharp break with that tradition.[14]

Whether or not it is ultimately the best of all possible scripts for Korean, Hangul must surely rank as one of the great intellectual achievements of Mankind.

Notes

1. The standard scheme for representing Korean in the Roman alphabet was changed by the South Korean government in the year 2000, and this chapter uses the new scheme. Following the lead of Lee and Ramsey (2011: 10), though, I shall spell the name of the Korean script as "Hangul". The correct spellings under old and new systems are "Han'gŭl" and "Han-geul" respectively, but to English-speaking readers these both look peculiar.
2. Lee and Ramsey (2011: 14–17) imply that the word "probably" should be inserted in this sentence; the family relationships of Korean are not yet entirely beyond debate.
3. One of the main differences between the pre-2000 and post-2000 romanization systems is that the former was phonetic with respect to voice while the latter is phonemic; thus the name of the large island off the south coast of Korea used to be written "Cheju" and is now written "Jeju".
4. The usual present-day graph shapes, in which for instance the left-hand stroke of < s > is slightly bowed and the right-hand stroke meets it a little below the vertex, stem from the fact that for centuries the graphs were written with brush and ink by people used to the ductus of Chinese writing. The original graphs in *Hunmin Jeong-eum* were all simple geometric forms.
5. The implication is that the previous Korean vowel system had just one front vowel phoneme /i/, alongside six back vowel phonemes. This is a very unusual system on a world scale, but Lee and Ramsey (2011: 95) confirm that that is how they believe 15c Korean worked.
6. *Hunmin Jeong-eum* introduces astrological concepts also in connexion with the consonant letters, but I do not discuss this since it is not relevant to the functioning of the script.
7. Taylor and Taylor (1983: 84–6) quote experimental evidence that grouping of "letters" into syllable-sized blocks aids recognition, and they note that Korean children are taught Hangul as a syllabary.
8. Article on "Hanja" (accessed 14 February 2014).
9. Since North Korea has not adopted the new romanization scheme used in the South since 2000, a North Korean English-language publication would write this name as "Chosŏn'gŭl".
10. Some Korean linguists are ideologically committed to a policy of minimizing the use of Chinese script. To judge by the fewness of Chinese graphs in Figure 33, it seems that my translator may have been one of these.
11. The phoneme /z/ has dropped out of the language since the 15c, and accordingly the triangular sign used for it in *Hunmin Jeong-eum* is now obsolete.
12. I know of one case where phonographic writing is claimed to have begun

"deep" and evolved towards a shallower approach, namely in Sumerian cuneiform (Civil and Biggs 1966: 14ff.); but the fact that this script was principally logographic makes it questionable whether this development offers much support to generative phonology.

13. On the other hand, it is known that the internal phonological processing which occurs during silent reading of English is sensitive to the phonetic values of letters at the distinctive-feature level rather than merely as unanalysed phonemes (Ashby *et al.* 2009), so it is possible that the transparency of feature marking in Hangul does benefit the Korean reader.
14. So remarkable an achievement was Hangul that some Western scholars have argued that it must have been developed on the basis of an earlier model. Gari Ledyard (1966), for instance, suggested that some aspects of Hangul may have been modelled on the 'Phags-pa script used at that time for Mongolian. But Ledyard argued this largely by interpreting a remark in the *Hunmin Jeong-eum* as a deliberately cryptic reference to Mongolian writing, and this seems contrived. The similarities Ledyard discerned between a few 'Phags-pa letters and Hangul graphs are distant at best. It may well be true that Sejong knew of 'Phags-pa and other phonographic scripts in use in East Asia, but those scripts were all segmental: they offer no precedent for Hangul.

9 A logographic system: Chinese writing

The alphabet, as a general system of which Hebrew, Roman, and Cyrillic scripts are three representatives, is one of two great systems of writing which between them provide the media of most of the world's written language. We turn now to the other of these, Chinese script. Until fairly recently it is likely that Chinese script was used more than all alphabetic scripts put together. It has been estimated, for instance, that up to about the end of the 18c more than half of all books ever published were written in Chinese.[1] Even today, Chinese and Chinese-derived writing comes a very respectable second to alphabetic scripts in terms of numbers of users. Most scripts which have no historical connexion with either Semitic or Chinese systems are (or were) used in quite small corners of the world.

What are historically the two major systems of writing exemplify the two main types of script: the Semitic family is phonographic, but the Chinese system is logographic. A graph of the Chinese writing system stands not for a unit of pronunciation but for a morpheme, a minimum meaningful unit of the Chinese language. Since Chinese, like English or any other language, has thousands of morphemes in its vocabulary, Chinese script includes thousands of graphs, rather than the few dozen found in a segmental, or even syllabic, phonographic script. If two morphemes are pronounced identically (which, as we shall see, is very common in Chinese), they will normally have separate graphs which may not share even a partial resemblance. Thus, one pair of Chinese homophones are the words /$ts^{h}uan^{1}$/ "parboil" and /$ts^{h}uan^{1}$/ "leap".[2] These two words are written as follows:

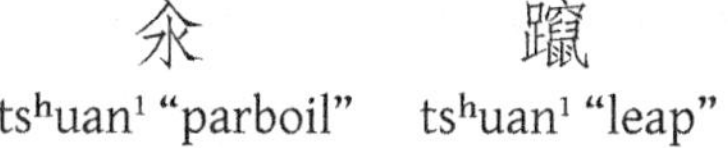

汆 躥

$ts^{h}uan^{1}$ "parboil" $ts^{h}uan^{1}$ "leap"

The two graphs are entirely different and unrelated. The European expectation that homophones, such as English *can* "be able to" and *can* "metal box", will normally be written alike, and that a special explanation is in order when homophones such as *meet* and *meat*, or *doe* and *dough*, are written differently, is alien to the Chinese method of writing. That is not to say that similarities between the shapes of Chinese graphs never correspond to similarities between the pronunciations of the words they represent; we shall see that such correspondences do play a part in the organization of Chinese writing. But although words which sound the same or similar are sometimes written with partly similar graphs, there is nothing regular about this. Very often there is no link between the graphs for words which are perfect homophones. The Western idea that from a knowledge of the pronunciation of a word one should be able to make at least a good guess at how to write it would seem strange to a Chinese who was unfamiliar with alphabetic writing, as until recently almost all Chinese were.

* * *

I have been playing somewhat fast and loose with the terms *word* and *morpheme*, because the distinction between these concepts is not nearly as clear-cut for Chinese as it is for European languages. Chinese, as a spoken language, has a number of interrelated special features which are essential to understanding how Chinese writing works.

First, Chinese is a language in which syllables are clearly demarcated. In English it is usually straightforward to *count* syllables – *river* has two, *rhododendron* four – but difficult to say where one syllable stops and the next starts. For example, does the /v/ of *river* end the first syllable or begin the second? Should the /ndr/ of *rhododendron* be split /n$dr/ or /nd$r/? This sort of thing does not happen in Chinese. Any Chinese consonant can easily and unambiguously be identified either as closing one syllable or as opening another, so that boundaries between syllables are obvious.

Second, morphemes in Chinese are co-extensive with syllables. Each morpheme is one syllable long, and there are virtually no cases such as *feather* or *elephant* where a single meaning-unit spans multiple syllables, or like the /s/ of *cats* or the /t/ of *height* where a meaning-unit corresponds to a fraction of a syllable. (There are certain relatively marginal phenomena in view of which this statement is not entirely correct, but the Chinese writing system can most easily be understood in relationship to an "idealized" account of the spoken Chinese language which ignores various exceptions to generalizations which are valid for the great majority of its structure.)

Third, Chinese is an "isolating" language. Its grammar works exclusively by stringing words together, as in English we say *I write, I will write*, rather than by modifying the pronunciation of words as in English *I write, I wrote, he writes*. This characteristic is closely related to the two already listed. Most of the inflexions of European languages derive ultimately from what were once independent suffix-morphemes which have influenced the pronunciation of the root and been influenced by it reciprocally, so that often one can no longer recognize the identity of the suffixes or separate them phonologically from the roots. Because Chinese morphemes all consist of syllables which are kept phonetically separate from one another, nothing comparable has happened in that language; individual morphemes have modified their pronunciation down the ages, but there is hardly any morphophonemic alternation, and no coalescence of roots with affixes.

Finally: although a single word in a European language will often translate into modern Chinese as a sequence of two morphemes, it is difficult to identify these unambiguously as compound words akin to English *blackbird*, *interview*, *overthrow*, because the borderline between morpheme-combinations which are and those which are not established elements of the language is vaguer for Chinese than it is for English – a user of Chinese is relatively free to group morphemes into different combinations. This fact may be partly a consequence of the different writing systems. In written English the visual unit is the word, so words are what we learn to regard as the elementary building-blocks of the language, whereas in written Chinese the visual unit is the morpheme – the script does not group pairs of graphs together spatially to show that they belong together as a compound term, all the morphemes of a sentence are written with equal spacing, so a Chinese sees the morphemes as the units which the language system supplies and thinks of the combining of morphemes as falling within the domain of individual language-use. This difference should not be exaggerated – there certainly are many cases where a compound of two morphemes is standardized with its own fixed and idiosyncratic meaning. But such cases might be compared with multi-word European idioms such as *white spirit*; in relative terms morphemes have more freedom of combination in Chinese than in European languages.

Since morphemes in Chinese are independent units of pronunciation and are the units symbolized in the writing system, and since they are relatively free to combine with one another grammatically, for Chinese there is no very clear notion of "word" as a unit larger than the morpheme. Whether it is theoretically appropriate to distinguish between two kinds of unit has been a standard debate within the linguistics of Chinese (see e.g. Lu 1960). Some linguists insist that Chinese "really does" have multi-morpheme words even though the script does not identify them. The truth is that combinations of Chinese morphemes range from absolutely fixed, like English *cran+berry* or *trans+mit*, through more or less tightly bound set phrases like *white spirit*, to free syntactic combinations like *new car*. If you want to define some cut-off in this continuum and say that morpheme-combinations which are bound more closely than the cut-off are "words" rather than "phrases", of course you can. But linguistics gives us no "right" place to establish the cut-off.

If we do choose to draw a distinction between morphemes and words in Chinese, then it is morphemes to which the graphs of Chinese script correspond; but since "word" is so much more familiar a term, and since in practice morphemes are the only word-like units whose identity is indisputable, for the sake of simplicity I shall usually talk of Chinese graphs as standing for words.

* * *

The foregoing should explain why I describe Chinese writing as logographic rather than phonographic. It is true that the units of script are co-extensive with syllables, which are phonological units; but this is an accidental consequence of the fact that in Chinese the units of meaning happen always to be one syllable long. When a given spoken Chinese syllable stands for different homophonous words, those words will normally have distinct graphs which will often share no similarities; and on the other hand a group of Chinese graphs may be very similar in shape but stand for words whose pronunciations are unrelated.

Here, though, I need to warn against an alternative error, namely that of supposing that Chinese writing is semasiographic (p. 21). This is a widespread misunderstanding, and has been so ever since Chinese writing became a subject of intellectual interest in Europe. In the 17c, European philosophers became enthusiastic about the idea of creating a universal philosophical written language that would cut through the arbitrary inconsequentialities of natural languages by symbolizing ideas directly, in some fashion related straightforwardly to their logic. Advocates of this concept often appealed to Chinese writing as an existing, if perhaps imperfect, example of such a scheme. Knowlson (1975: 25) tells us that:

> the majority of the projectors of a common writing or, later, of a character based on philosophical principles referred to the use of these [Chinese] characters as a form of common script in the East. ... De Vienne Plancy expressed his ... surprise that the Chinese characters had not been adopted throughout the world "pour le commerce des Nations, puisqu'ils signifient immédiatement les pensées." ... [Chinese writing] indicated that the only way to form a script that would be universally intelligible was ... to use characters "which are real, not nominal, expressing neither letters nor words, but things and notions."

This view of the nature of Chinese script is still widely held. It is reinforced by the common use of the term "ideogram" to refer to Chinese graphs, suggesting that they stand for ideas rather than for words.

The truth is, however, that Chinese writing comes no closer than European scripts to "signifying thoughts directly", or to expressing "things" rather than "words". Chinese script is thoroughly glottographic: it symbolizes units of a particular spoken language, namely the Chinese language, with all its quirks and illogicalities. There are various ways to demonstrate this. One concerns synonyms. Like other languages, Chinese contains sets of synonymous words. Thus, as it happens, Chinese has four words for "red": /xuŋ^2/, /tʂʰɯ^4/, /tan^1/, /tʂu^1/. So far as I know there is no distinction of meaning between these words, so a "philosophical script" which represented ideas directly and logically would presumably need only one symbol to cover all four. But, in Chinese, they are four separate words, and they are written with four distinct and unrelated graphs: 紅 赤 丹 朱.

Again, many languages contain terms comparable to English *buttercup*, which looks as though it ought to be the name of a kind of cup but is in fact a flower. In a "philosophical script" the symbol for *buttercup* would be related to symbols for flowers rather than utensils, but a morphemic script would spell *buttercup* with the *butter* graph followed by the *cup* graph. Chinese has many such terms, for instance /tʃʰiŋ^1 pʰi^2/, literally "green skin", is a term for "rogue": it is written with the ordinary graphs for /tʃʰiŋ^1/ "green" and /pʰi^2/ "skin", and the writing gives no clue that the term denotes a kind of person.

Finally, the syntax of spoken Chinese, like other languages, is often idiosyncratic and logically opaque; a philosophical language would replace illogical turns of phrase with simpler and more transparent constructions, but written Chinese reproduces on paper the grammar of the spoken language.[3] Chinese graphs stand for *words*, not directly for "things" or "ideas".

Incidentally, the fact that synonyms such as the words for "red" have different graphs in Chinese script exemplifies a major difference between Chinese and Sumerian writing – a point which is worth stressing, because in certain other respects the early histories of Chinese and Sumerian systems were similar. We saw on p. 48 that in archaic Sumerian script a picture representing a mouth stood for a range of different words from that semantic area: "mouth", "speech", "tooth", etc. That sort of thing is unknown in Chinese script. We shall see, below, that in the early stages of Chinese writing a graph coined to write one word would often be borrowed to stand for a range of other words, but such loan-uses were not based on semantic relationships.

* * *

Having examined the relationship between the units of Chinese writing and the language it is used to write, we turn now to the internal structure of the individual graphs. When a script uses only a few dozen separate graphs, the question of how the various shapes are derived is of little more than antiquarian interest; from an English-speaker's point of view the different Roman letters are just arbitrary marks. When a script contains thousands of graphs, on the other hand, their structure becomes very important: nobody could learn such a system unless the graphs were produced by combining a smaller number of distinctive elements in various ways, and the system could hardly be learned unless there were a degree of regularity in the manner in which elements are combined into wholes.

To understand the logic underlying the graphs of Chinese, we must approach the subject historically. However, it is not possible to examine the ultimate beginning of Chinese script. When we study the origins of a script, a frequent problem is that the earliest stages are hidden because inscriptions were on perishable materials that have not survived, and this very much applies in the case of Chinese writing. The earliest examples we have date from about −1200; in Chinese terms, towards the end of the Shang Dynasty. But the script of that period was already so sophisticated that it must have developed from simpler beginnings which are now lost from the record.[4]

Nevertheless, those late −2nd millennium writings show us a script which is rather different from what it later turned into (namely, the Chinese script of the present day), and which gets us far enough back that we can infer fairly clearly how the system developed.[5]

Those earliest examples of Chinese writing are known as *oracle bone inscriptions*, because of their topic. Like rulers of other pre-scientific societies, those of early China were anxious to foresee future events. One way in which they believed that could be done was by interpreting cracks in bones or turtleshells. A yes-or-no question would be formulated, and a heated metal point would be applied to a hollowed-out spot on an ox shoulderblade or turtleshell; the questioner, aided by an expert soothsayer, would deduce the answer from the resulting pattern of cracks (we do not know what features they looked for in the patterns), and then the question, and sometimes the answer also, would be written on the bone or shell, by carving or painting. Luckily for us, bones and shells are very resistant to decay.

Robert Bagley (2004) discusses an example. Translated into English it reads:

> Crack-making on day *jia shen*, Que as soothsayer.
> Will Lady Hao's childbearing be lucky?
> The king prognosticates: if it happens on a *ding* day, lucky; if on a *geng* day, vastly auspicious.
> Thirty-one days later, on day *jia yin*:
> The child was born. Not lucky. It was a girl.

The terms *jia*, *shen*, and so on refer to the way that the Chinese calendar divided time into cycles of six ten-day weeks. *Ding* and *geng* were the fourth and seventh days of the week, but *jia* was the first day; the king was evidently hoping for a male heir, so his prediction was correct. (Normally, when outcomes are recorded, the predictions did turn out to be right. Perhaps the professional soothsayers "forgot" to include the others in the archives?)

Other early Chinese writing occurs as inscriptions cast on bronze vessels used for ritual purposes. The oldest of these consist of little more than personal names, but by the –11c they were beginning to comprise extended prose passages. Between the oracle bone and early bronze inscriptions we find a rich enough vocabulary to show that this was a full-scale writing system, capable of expressing whatever scribes wanted to express.

Figure 34

From these categories of evidence, the script seems to have evolved as follows. Initially, graphs were coined by drawing pictures to represent their meanings. Figure 34 shows a few simple examples. As one might expect, there was a great deal of variation in these early graph forms; Figure 34 shows one typical example in each case. "Child" was shown as a human with head large relative to body size. "Woman" was shown kneeling to do housework (Shang dynasty China would not be regarded in the 21c as a politically correct society); the horizontal element probably stood for breasts. "Prisoner" was a man in a cell. (The words are transliterated here in terms of their modern pronunciations; the pronunciations 3000 years ago were very different, as we shall see shortly.)

Not all words written with simple pictorial graphs were words for concrete physical objects. Sometimes, pictures were used to suggest more abstract concepts, as in Figure 35. "Big" was a man with arms outstretched like a fisherman describing the one that got away. "Stand" was a man standing on the ground. "Love" was written as a woman with a child – a mother's feelings for her baby are perhaps the most obvious and reliable type of love.[6] The word /ɽuo^4/, with a range of meaning corresponding to English words such as "conform", "compliant", was shown as a warrior with dishevelled hair and hands up kneeling submissively (conforming, complying with his vanquisher). In other cases, such as "above", "below", "turn round", the graph shapes themselves were abstract.

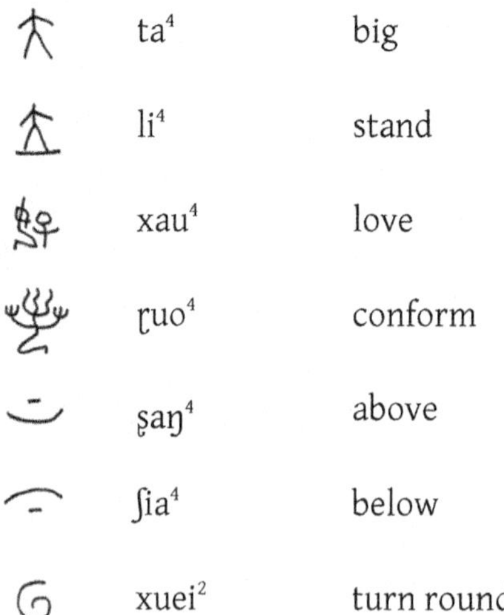

Figure 35

As one might expect of a culture which developed quite independently from European cultures, the pictorial conventions of Chinese writing are often alien to us. Consider the cases in Figure 36. While a Westerner will instinctively sketch, say, a tree as trunk and branches only, Chinese script showed entire plants including roots, as in the cases of "tree" or "wheat". Animals were typically shown with a large eye standing for the entire head: see "horse" and "deer". Brightness was indicated not by centrifugal rays but by dots or small lines in the centre of the bright object, as in "sun" and "moon".

In many cases we can recognize these early pictorial graphs only because we know what the relevant word means. Knowing the meaning of the "flute" graph in Figure 37, we can see it as an instrument sprouting out of a mouth, but it would be hard to guess at that interpretation if we had only the picture. And for many other early graph forms, even though we know what they mean, we cannot understand how the shape fitted that meaning. Why was the form shown appropriate for /pi^4/ "prince"? We know that various types of object symbolized royal authority, comparable to orb and sceptre for the Queen of England; one of these was a jade disc, so perhaps that is what the circle represented, but for the other two graphic elements your guess is as good as mine. Graphs such as those for "south", "old", "now" are entirely mysterious. Perhaps, if we lived in –2nd-millennium China, some of these pictures would be obvious to us. Since we don't, it is no surprise that many early graphs are now opaque.

* * *

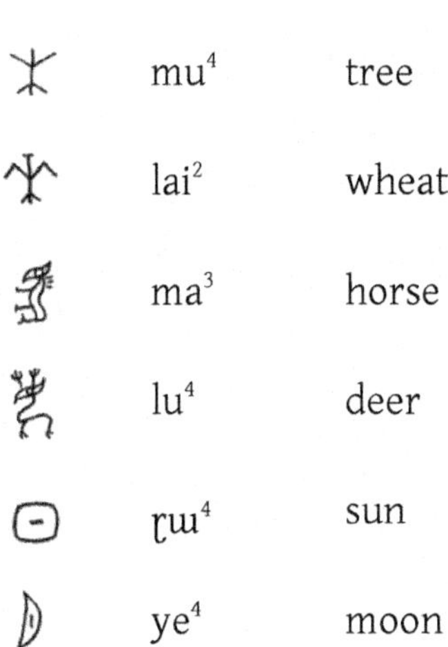

Figure 36

jen² flute
pi⁴ prince
nan² south
lau³ old
tʃin¹ now

Figure 37

Rather more than a thousand words were equipped with simple pictorial graphs in this fashion. Then the script developed, in two respects. First, various methods were used to produce graphs for all the many other words in the Chinese vocabulary. Also, the forms of the graphs changed, removing their pictorial quality.

Those two developments happened in the order given: by the period when the graphs were losing their iconic quality, coverage of the vocabulary was already more or less complete. Nevertheless, it will be convenient to consider the developments in the reverse order. The main aim of this chapter is to describe Chinese script as it exists as a heavily used living system today, so we need to move on to illustrating the system in terms of the current versions of graphs.

When graphs were inscribed with a sharp point on bone or similar materials, or modelled in wax which was then replaced by molten bronze in a clay mould, curves were as easy to draw as straight lines, so there was no constraint other than artistic convention on rendering pictures naturalistically. But as these media gave way to brush and ink, on surfaces such as bamboo or, eventually, paper, the trend was for tight curves to be replaced by straight lines or gentle curves and angles. For instance, the graph for /$k^{h}ou^{3}$/ "mouth" began as ㅂ, with the lower lip shown as a U shape – not too different from the way a Western caricaturist might show a mouth. This graph ended up as a square, 口, formed as three brush strokes: a left-hand vertical, a right-angle for the top and right-hand sides, and a bottom horizontal, written in that sequence.

The change from curves to straight lines and angles inevitably made the original pictures unrecognizable, and since the script had become a well-established institution, there was no real pressure in any case for them to remain iconic. What was needed for the purpose of efficient reading and writing was shapes that were distinctive, memorable, and easy to make – not pretty pictures. As in the Sumerian case, scribal convenience and the nature of the writing materials turned clearly motivated shapes into abstract arrangements of marks.

This change was gradual, and it is not easy to specify a time when the graphs ceased to have any iconic properties; Bagley (2004: 202) puts it at the –3c. By that time the script had long since become a mundane tool for everyday administrative and other purposes. (It was also the vehicle of great monuments of literature, but the bulk of what was being written in Chinese was much more down-to-earth in nature.) By about +200, the script had become essentially what it remains today.

Figure 38 compares early and modern forms of the graphs introduced in Figures 34–37. From now on we shall exemplify Chinese script showing the modern (i.e. post +2c) forms of the graphs.

* * *

I turn now to the various ways in which the script was extended in order to cover the many Chinese words that were not given simple pictures to represent their meanings.

In the first place, some words were written with what we might call compound pictures: two simple pictures were written together, each of which had a semantic connexion with the target word. For instance, the abstract concept /u^{3}/ "military" is written 武, which combines 戈 kɤ^{1}, a word for an ancient Chinese weapon usually translated as "dagger-axe", with 止 tʂɯ^{3} "foot": "military" was indicated as a concept having to do with weapons and also having to do with marching. (Note that 武 was not a single picture of a soldier marching with a weapon: at no stage in the history of the graph was the soldier depicted, only the weapon and the foot.) Likewise 農 is nuŋ^{2} "agriculture", combining a variant of 田 tʰien^{2} "field" with what was originally a recognizable picture of a plough, 辰 (although, as it happens, the modern Chinese word for "plough" has developed from a different picture – perhaps there were different types of plough). Again, the fact that "field" was written *above* "plough" makes it clear that this was not a single picture of a field being ploughed: "agriculture" was being identified as a word that was something to do with fields and also something to do with ploughs.[7]

Another device which Chinese scribes used was to adapt a graph that had been established for a word that happened to be relatively "picturable" in order to write other words which were pronounced the same or similarly.

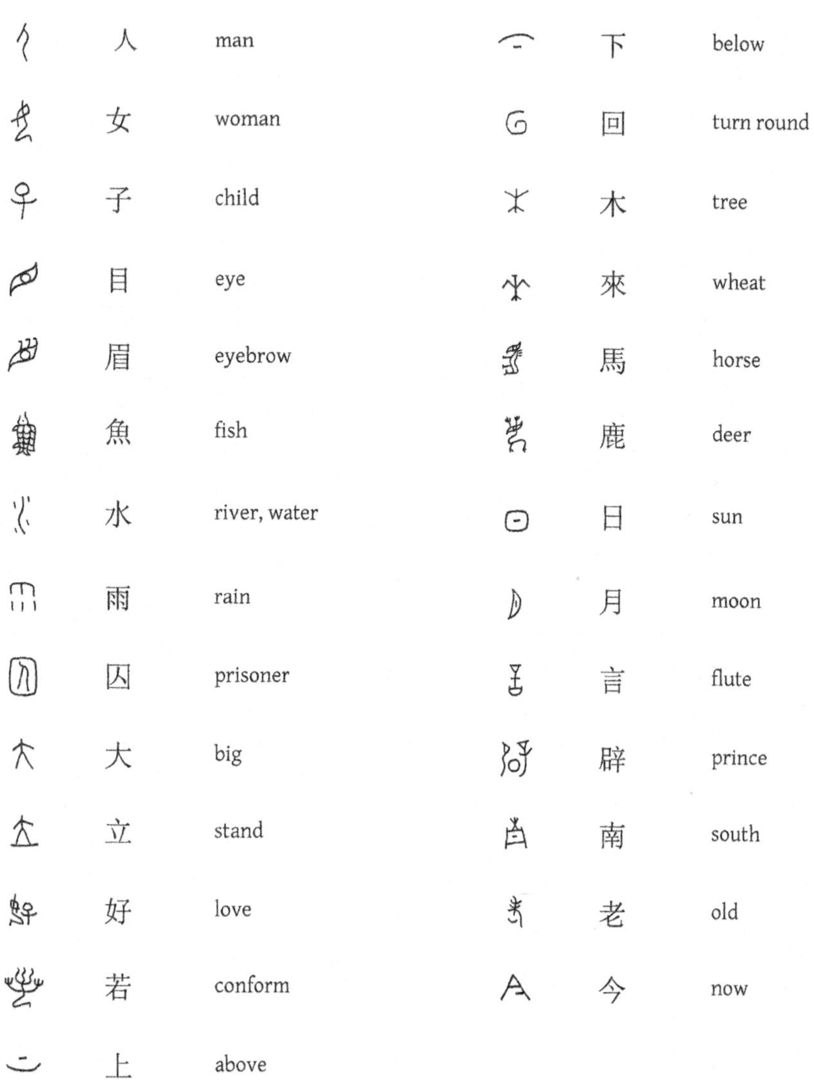

人 man
女 woman
子 child
目 eye
眉 eyebrow
魚 fish
水 river, water
雨 rain
囚 prisoner
大 big
立 stand
好 love
若 conform
上 above
下 below
回 turn round
木 tree
來 wheat
馬 horse
鹿 deer
日 sun
月 moon
言 flute
辟 prince
南 south
老 old
今 now

Figure 38

Here a complication arises in giving examples: the pronunciations of Chinese words that are relevant for these loan-uses of graphs are the pronunciations current at the period when the script was developing, which were often extremely different from the modern pronunciations of the same words. In what follows I use an asterisk to mark pronunciations in so-called "Old Chinese" (also called "Archaic Chinese", i.e. the Chinese of about −1000), as reconstructed by present-day scholars.[8]

(Starred forms have no tone numerals; Old Chinese was not yet a tone language.)

Thus 其 *kə "winnowing-basket" (originally a picture of a basket on a stand) was borrowed for *gə "his"; 兼 *kêm "to have two at once" (depicting a hand holding two arrows) was borrowed for *k^{h}êmʔ "dissatisfied"; 言, which as we saw above meant "flute" and was originally pronounced *ŋan, was borrowed for *ŋan "speak" and for *ŋjən "contented"; 辟 for "prince", also met above and originally pronounced *pek, was borrowed for all of the following words: *pek "thin-sliced", *pek "jade insignium", *bek "law", *bek "beat the breast", *bek "open", *bêk "inner coffin", *p^{h}ek "oblique", *bekh "avoid". At this early stage there was probably nothing very fixed about which graphs could be borrowed for which particular similar-sounding words; rather, scribes would simply have adapted the stock of existing graphs to their needs as best they might. The fact that the "prince" graph had many different recorded loan-uses while some simple graphs had none may imply that there were a lot of words sounding roughly like *pek with meanings for which it was hard to draw pictures – or it could be a chance property of the inscriptions that happen to have come down to us.

If no further principles for creating graphs had been adopted, the system would presumably have ended up as a syllabic phonographic system (though with the special feature that each word would have been written with just one syllabic sign, since Chinese words coincide with syllables). However, a system with this degree of ambiguity, in which most graphs could stand for any one of three, four, or even a dozen or more different words, was not satisfactory. Instead of curing the problem by inventing more simple graphs, which was probably impractical because of the abstractness of the words lacking their own graphs, an alternative solution was adopted. The various similar-sounding readings of a given simple graph were distinguished by supplementing that graph with another graph whose meaning gave a clue to the word intended. Thus this type of compound graph consisted of two parts, which we may call a *phonetic* – the basic graph, standing for a family of near-homophones and originally a picture of one of them – and a *signific*, an element showing the semantic category of the word. (Chinese "significs" are very comparable in their logic to the elements called "determinatives" in Cuneiform and Egyptian hieroglyphic scripts, though the latter were written as separate graphic units whereas the elements of a compound Chinese graph are written together as a visual whole.)

We can call graphs of this new kind *phonetic-semantic compounds*, whereas the compound pictures discussed on p. 177 are *semantic-semantic compounds*. To illustrate this type of compound graph, consider the simple graph 其 *kə "winnowing-basket", discussed above. Combined with 土 "earth", the winnowing-basket graph gives 基 *kə "foundation" – a word whose pronunciation is the same as that of "winnowing-basket" and whose meaning has something to do with "earth". (The reconstructed pronunciation of 土 is *tʰâʔ; but, since the pronunciation of a graph used as a signific is irrelevant, I shall omit this information in what follows.) The same graph with 鹿 "deer" gives 麒 *gə "unicorn"; with 示 "spirit, divine" it gives 祺 *kʰə "fortunate"; with 人 "person" it gives 倛 *kʰə "mask". (Several graphs commonly used as significs are written in special compressed or abbreviated versions of their stand-alone form; in the "mask" graph, 亻 is the combination form of 人 "person".)

Sometimes the signific system was not adequate to distinguish between words pronounced similarly: two more words which sounded like *kə "winnowing-basket" were *kə "aquatic grass" and *kʰə "beanstalk", and the best signific for both of these was the graph for "plant", 艸, with the combination form 艹: "aquatic grass" and "beanstalk" are both written 萁. Occasionally such problems were resolved by differences in the orientation of signific and phonetic: it seems that 言 "speak" was felt to be an appropriate signific for both *kə "to plan" and *kʰəh "fear", and these words are written respectively 諆 and 諅. But this is quite unusual. More commonly, differences of orientation are in free variation (*kʰə "chess" is written with the "wood" signific as either 棋 or 棊); but in the great majority of cases orientation of signific with respect to phonetic is fixed, and is commonly determined by the identity of the signific. The combination form 艹 of "plant" always appears above a phonetic, 言 "speak" almost always appears to the left of a phonetic, 鳥 "bird" almost always to the right, and so on.

This phonetic–semantic approach to creating graphs proved enormously fertile, and most present-day Chinese graphs are compounds of this type.

Indeed, the large proportion of the modern graph stock which is formed in this way, together with the fact that the phonetic principle makes this aspect of Chinese script look more "normal" to people accustomed to alphabetic writing, have repeatedly led Western scholars to claim even greater importance for the role of phonetics than it actually played in the evolution of the script. In recent years William Boltz (e.g. 1994) has been promoting a theory according to which *all* compound graphs are phonetic–semantic compounds: according to him, there are no semantic–semantic compounds at all. So far as I know, no Chinese scholar agrees with this, and that is not surprising because the theory seems clearly misguided: Boltz forces apparent semantic–semantic compounds into the phonetic–semantic category by circular reasoning, arguing that one element of the compound must originally have had a pronunciation making it suitable as a phonetic element but for which no evidence survives. In reality, so far as the limited evidence extends, it appears that the semantic–semantic principle may have been the first method used by Chinese scribes to enlarge the graph stock beyond simple pictures, with the phonetic–semantic approach resorted to later though it then became the default technique (see Sampson and Chen 2013).

Once the phonetic–signific system was established, a compound graph could itself be used as a phonetic to which further significs were added, making graphs of the structure (P/S)/S. This structure is less common than the structure P/S, but it is far from rare. For instance, the simple graph 可 *kʰâiʔ "can, be able" enters into the following P/S combinations: with "wood", 柯 *kâi "axe-handle"; with "water", 河 *gâi "Yellow River"; with "mouth", 呵 *xâi "scold"; with "big", 奇 *gai "strange"; and the last of these graphs, standing for a syllable with *a rather than *â (whatever this sound-difference actually was; see note 8, p. 191) is as a whole the phonetic in graphs for other –ai words, such as 騎 *gai "ride" (with "horse"), 寄 *kaih "lodging" (with "roof"), 綺 *kʰaih "patterned silk" (with "silk"), etc.

The elements I am calling "phonetics", and also those I am calling "significs", also occur as simple graphs: to call a graphic element a "phonetic" or a "signific" is to identify the role it is playing within a particular compound graph. A given graph may occur as a simple graph, as a phonetic in one series of compound graphs, and as a signific in another series of compound graphs. For instance, 女 *nraʔ "woman" occurs as a signific in a large number of words to do with women's life – with 古 *kâʔ "ancient" it forms 姑 *kâ "aunt", with 因 *ʔin "to rest, rely on" it forms 姻 *ʔin "relationship by marriage", with 某 *môʔ "such-and-such" it forms 媒 *mə̂ "matchmaker", and so on; but it acts as phonetic in another series – with 米 "rice" it forms 籹 *nraʔ "cakes made of rice and honey", with 口 "mouth" it forms 如 *na "to agree, resemble", with 氵 combination form of 水 "water, river" it forms 汝 *naʔ, proper name of a river. There is an asymmetry, though: almost every simple graph acts as phonetic in at least one or two compound graphs, and any given phonetic will be used in only a dozen or two dozen compound graphs at most, whereas significs are usually drawn from a class containing just a few dozen simple graphs with key meanings such as "wood", "metal", "person", "bird", "hand" (for actions), and so forth, and some of these are significs in hundreds of different compound graphs.

In the writing system which ultimately emerged, it was not always the case that the value attached to a simple graph was the word which originally motivated its design. For instance, the word written 言 and meaning "flute" became obsolete quite early in the history of Chinese, so that this graph now stands exclusively for what was originally its loan-use, "speak". Likewise the graph 來 which was originally a picture of a wheat plant is now only used for the high-frequency word /lai²/ "come".[9] In the case of 其 "winnowing-basket" the original value did not become obsolete, but the loan-use "his" was so much commoner a word that it came to be perceived as the basic value of the graph; 其 now always stands for "his", and the word "winnowing-basket" is written with the addition of the "bamboo" signific: 箕. And the case of 辟 "prince" corresponds to an unusually complex situation in the modern script: the words meaning "thin-sliced", "law", and "inner coffin" appear to have become obsolete, the "jade insignium" word is now invariably written with the "jade" signific, and the other loan-values are *optionally* written with significs ("hand" for "beat the breast", "door" for "open", and so on) but can alternatively be written with the simple graph which also still stands for "prince".

In some cases, significs were used to distinguish between diverse senses of a single polysemous word. For instance /mei²/ "eyebrow" (Old Chinese *mrəi), the word written 眉 (see Figure 34), has the extended sense "lintel" (the lintel was seen as the eyebrow of window or door), but when the word is used in this latter sense the "wood" signific is added: 楣. Probably, this was not perceived by the early scribes as a distinct principle for the use of significs. Rather, they would have been unclear about where to draw the line between polysemy and homophony. The distinction, for any language, is essentially a historical one. When a given pronunciation is used for more than one meaning, we say that we have distinct homophonous words if we know that at earlier stages the words were entirely separate, but we have a single polysemous word if the various meanings can be shown to have developed out of one original sense. Most speakers of a language have no access to its history, and hence no way of drawing this distinction. In English, the fact that different spellings are used shows that people take *mettle* and *metal* to be homophones (whereas in fact the sense of *mettle* developed as a figurative extension of that of *metal*); conversely, many English-speakers undoubtedly take *ear* (of wheat) to be the same word as *ear* (the organ of hearing), though in reality these are accidental homophones which derive from words originally pronounced differently. At the period when Chinese script was evolving, no Chinese-speakers had access to the earlier history of their language, so it may not have been obvious to them that the use of /mei²/ for both "eyebrow" and "lintel" was a case of polysemy. Where the Chinese could perceive polysemies as separate senses of a single word at the time the script was created, they used a single graph to cover all the senses even if its signific was appropriate to only one of them. And, once the script was fully evolved, by the beginning of the Christian Era, significs were not changed to reflect subsequent changes in the meanings of words.

For instance, 里 /li³/ "village" (from here on I give only modern pronunciations) with the combination form of 玉 "jade" stands for a homophone 理 /li³/, which means "to cut jade" but much more commonly has the abstract, extended meaning "to regulate", and as a further extension from that, "reason, principle". Likewise the same phonetic with 衣 "clothes" is 裏 (this particular signific, doubtless because of what it means, is commonly separated into two halves with the phonetic inserted as the meat in the sandwich); this graph stands for a word again pronounced /li³/ that originally meant "lining" (so that "clothes" was appropriate), but which now never means anything more specific than "inside", "in". Again, 雚 /kuan⁴/ "heron" with 木 "wood" makes 權 /tʃʰyan²/ "(wooden) weight on a steelyard", hence the originally-figurative extended senses "influence, authority, rights": in modern Chinese the original meaning is virtually obsolete. Nobody thinks it odd that "reason" includes a "jade" element or "authority" a "wood" element; when significs do remain appropriate, the graphs are that much easier to remember, but frequently they do not.

* * *

When the phonetic–signific system first evolved, significs were added optionally and variably; and by approaching the subject historically I may have given the reader an impression of much greater chaos and complexity than is actually present in the Chinese script as it has existed over the past two millennia. In fact the system was standardized by the beginning of the Christian Era so as to approach reasonably close to the ideal of providing one unambiguous graph for each Chinese word. There are still cases where a given graph can stand for alternative words, and where a given word can be written in different ways, but such cases are fairly rare. (For the latter kind of variability, compare the way that in English we can choose to write *gaol* or *jail*, *connexion* or *connection*.)

On the other hand, while the relationship between graphs and words comes fairly close to being one-to-one, for modern Chinese it is far more arbitrary than my discussion so far may have suggested.

I have already indicated that, because of the considerable shifts of meaning and changes in material culture that have occurred over the millennia, the significs are nowadays rather unreliable as a guide to graph meanings. Nouns denoting flora and fauna almost always do have the appropriate signific for their category ("plant", "tree", "bird", "fish", or the like); at the opposite extreme, verbs have very diverse and unpredictable significs.

In view of the system of "phonetic" elements, though, the reader might suppose that I am wrong to deny that the script is phonographic. One distinguished scholar in the field of writing systems, John DeFrancis (e.g. DeFrancis 1989), has argued at length that *all* the world's scripts are essentially phonographic, pointing to the large proportion of phonetic–semantic compounds in the Chinese graph stock as a reason not to treat this script as a counterexample. According to DeFrancis (1984: 125), Chinese script "should be considered to be basically a phonetic system".

This represents a confusion between history and current status. Linguists for the past hundred years have distinguished between *diachronic* and *synchronic* linguistics: it is one thing to describe how a language has evolved down the centuries, but a different thing to describe how it functions as a structured system at a given point in time, such as the present. The large number of phonetic–semantic compound graphs in Chinese script certainly show that phonography played a very important role in the original development of the system. While the script was acquiring its present form in the –2nd and –1st millennia, one might well have called it essentially a phonographic system, but one which was "incomplete" in that it did not mark all the phonetic contrasts in the language, and which added the system of significs as a non-phonographic device to compensate for that deficiency. It might be tempting to concede to DeFrancis that the *creation* of any script will inevitably involve a phonographic principle (though in fact the example of Blissymbolics seems to refute that). But our chief concern in this book is with scripts as synchronic systems, and Chinese script ceased many centuries ago to be phonographic in any substantial sense.

The reason is that, while the script has not changed in the past two thousand years, the spoken language has changed a great deal. We have seen that a given "phonetic" element could be used to represent each of a range of similar syllables in Old Chinese; since the Old Chinese period there have been many complex sound changes in Chinese, and very often these have had the effect of exaggerating what were once small differences of pronunciation. For example, Old Chinese had syllables beginning *kr-, *gr-, and these consonant clusters commonly appear in words whose graphs share a phonetic. After the graphs were fixed, *kr- was simplified to /k-/ and *gr- turned into /l-/, so the words no longer alliterate.[10]

As a result of these semantic and phonological developments, the relationship between words and graphs is by now largely opaque. A Chinese-speaker who learns to read and write essentially has to learn the graphs case by case; significs and phonetics will give him many hints and clues to help him remember, but the information they supply is far too patchy and unreliable to allow him to *predict* what the graph for a given spoken word will be, or even which spoken word will correspond to a graph that he encounters for the first time. From the modern speaker's point of view, the most important benefit of the phonetic–signific structure is that graphs involving many brush strokes can be seen as groupings of familiar visual units, rather than having to be remembered stroke by stroke. The original logic behind the phonetic–signific structure certainly is useful, but its value is limited.

Such psycholinguistic evidence as is available (Pollatsek *et al.* 2000; Tsai *et al.* 2004: 240–43) suggests that the process of graph-identification by fluent Chinese readers does make some use of the pronunciation cues offered by the phonetic elements, but the evidence is weak (and weaker still for the use of the semantic information offered by signific elements).

No complex real-life language system ever perfectly exemplifies an "ideal type"; we might describe modern Chinese script as logographic with a limited admixture of phonography, just as English script with its use of numerals, symbols such as the ampersand, and non-phonetic spellings such as *one*, is phonographic with an admixture of logography (an idea to which we shall return in chapter 13). But just as English script must surely be recognized as basically phonographic, so Chinese script is basically logographic. (For a more detailed rebuttal of DeFrancis's idea, see Sampson 1994.)

The best way to give readers a feeling for the extent to which the logic behind the graphs is apparent in the modern, everyday use of the language will be to analyse a sample of graphs in current use. I have chosen at random a set of ten graphs to examine. The sample was formed by sticking a pin into chance pages of the kind of dictionary which devotes a lot of space to common graphs and little space to rare ones, so that most of the ten graphs are fairly common and just one or two are rather rare. In the analysis below, "phonetic" and "signific" are abbreviated "P" and "S". All glosses quoted refer to current meanings (hence one or two discrepancies as compared with glosses given earlier for the same graphs); a slash separates alternative senses of words which are polysemous in the modern language.

1. 召 tʂau^{4} "summon". P 刀 tau^{1} "knife" + S 口 "mouth". The initial consonant of the P is not very close to that of the target word; on the other hand the compound graph itself occurs as a P in many (P/S)/S graphs (cf. p. 181) for words pronounced /tʂau/, /tʂ^{h}au/, or /ʂau/, which helps its value to be remembered.
2. 前 tʃ^{h}ien^{2} "before". This was originally a simple graph, and has lost any mnemonic value it may once have had; in its modern form it looks like a combination of 月 "moon" and 刂 combination form of "knife" below a near-unique element at the top. But the word is so frequent that the lack of transparency in the graph does not matter (just as English-speakers do not have trouble with the irregular spelling of *one*). It may even be an advantage that the overall shape is very distinctive rather than being yet another permutation of standard P and S elements.
3. 忽 xu^{1} "suddenly / careless". This was originally P 勿 u^{1} "don't" + S 心 "heart". No other words with 勿 as P begin with /x-/; "heart" (the usual signific for emotion words) is suitable for "careless" but not for "suddenly". Again a fairly frequent and distinctive graph (distinctive because "heart" as a signific usually appears in a combination form rather than written in full as here, and also because 勿 is an uncommon and visually simple P).
4. 絮 ʃy^{4} "cotton waste / to line with cotton wadding". S 糸 "silk" is predictable, but P 如 ɻu^{2} "as" is a surprising P (which is a nuisance, since the word is uncommon).
5. 關 kuan^{1} "shut". The element 門 is "door", and with some imagination one can see the rest as two hands stretching up to fix a bolt or the like. In fact etymologically the interior part of the graph was a phonetic element which is long-obsolete as an independent graph (it meant "a pair of tufts of hair on a child's head") and which occurs as P in no other compound graph. Thus the graph gives no clue now about its pronunciation, but again it is very frequent.
6. 廟 miau^{4} "temple". This looks as if it were S 广 "building" and P 朝 tʂau^{1} "morning" or tʂ^{h}au^{2} "dynasty" (this latter graph is one of the minority which represent either of two phonetically distinct words). But in that case the P would be baffling: phonetic elements are usually more reliable with respect to consonants than vowels, but there is no resemblance between the consonants here. Etymologically the graph is actually a semantic–semantic compound (a /miau^{4}/ was the building where the morning sacrifice was performed) – but not even an educated Chinese would be likely to know that, so the graph is largely opaque.

7. 抒 ʂu^1 "to strain, pour out" (this word is obsolete in the modern spoken language, but it is still listed in dictionaries as part of the literary language). S 扌 (combination form of "hand"), fairly predictable for this meaning, and P 予 y^2 "me" – a surprising phonetic, but the same graph is used as P in a few other compound graphs pronounced /ʂu/ or /tʂu/.
8. 釘 tiŋ^1 "a nail", tiŋ^4 "to nail" (for this grammatical use of tone, cf. note 6). The S 金 "metal" is wholly predictable, and P 丁 tiŋ^1 "individual" is natural (though there are other graphs that would have been equally suitable as P). An easy graph to learn, particularly since – by coincidence – the P element even happens to be shaped rather like a nail.
9. 自 tsɯ^4 "self / from". A simple graph which has to be learned as a unit; it is extremely frequent.
10. 油 jou^2 "oil". S 氵 combination form of "water"; P 由 jou^2 "cause"; quite straightforward.

A written text in Chinese consists of a sequence of graphs corresponding to the words of the sentences, with each graph written so as to fill a notional square of constant size (so that graphs containing many brush strokes are written relatively compactly), and spaced equally except where interrupted by punctuation. Since the graphs do not link to one another as the letters of a word handwritten in the Roman alphabet do, it is easy to write sequences of them in any direction. Traditionally they were normally written in vertical columns, beginning at the top right of a page (so that the front cover of a book was to the left as the book stood on a shelf) – though where space considerations made it convenient, for instance on a signboard over a doorway, it was common to write a line of graphs from right to left horizontally.

In modern times, as China has had increasing dealings with the West, vertical writing created an awkwardness for technical publications which needed to quote words or phrases from Western languages: these had to be printed sideways. Figure 39 shows an extract from an encyclopaedia published in 1938. Notice how several entries for types of plant include their Latin names arranged vertically, for instance *Osmunda regalis* var. *japonica* under the entry for 薇 *wéi*, a plant known in English as "Japanese flowering fern", and a chemical formula appears vertically within the entry for 薑黃 *jiāng huáng* "turmeric". (Note also that while the text of the entries is printed vertically, the picture captions are arranged right-to-left horizontally.) To avoid this awkwardness, over the past hundred years there has been a trend in the Chinese-speaking world towards Western-style left to right horizontal writing. As early as 1915 a newly founded

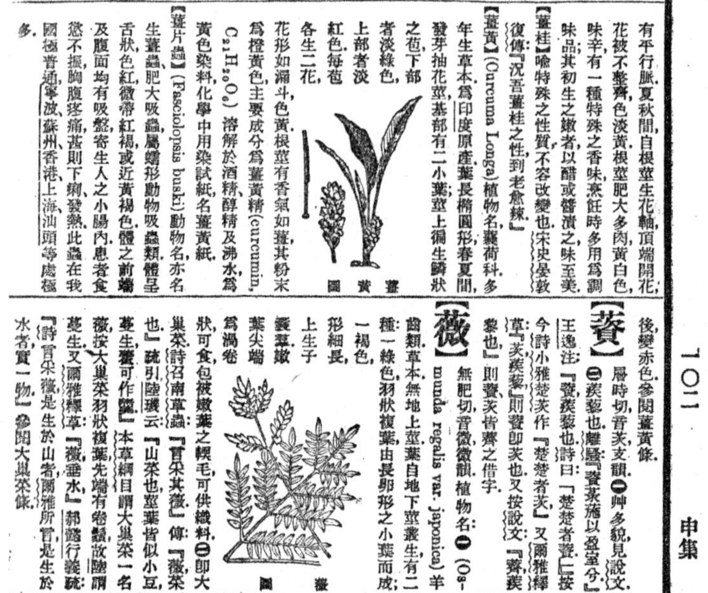

有平行脈.夏秋間,自根莖生花軸,頂端開花;花被不整齊,色淡黃.根莖肥大多肉,黃白色,味辛,有一種特殊之香味,烹飪時多用爲調味品;其初生之嫩者,以醋或醬漬之,味至美.

【薑桂】喻特殊之性質,不容改變也.宋史晏敦復傳:「況吾薑桂之性,到老愈辣.」

【薑黃】(Curcuma Longa)植物名,蘘荷科.多年生草本.爲印度原產.葉長橢圓形,春夏間,發芽抽花莖,基部有二小葉;莖上徧生鱗狀之苞,下部者淡綠色,上部者淡紅色.每苞各生二花,花形如漏斗,色黃.根莖有香氣如薑,其粉末爲橙黃色,主要成分爲薑黃精(curcumin, $C_{21}H_{20}O_6$)溶解於酒精、醇精及沸水,爲黃色染料,化學中用染試紙,名薑黃紙.

【薑片蟲】(Fasciolopsis buski)動物名,亦名生薑蟲、肥大吸蟲,屬蠕形動物吸蟲類.體呈舌狀,色紅,微帶紅褐,或近黃褐色.體之前端及腹面均有吸盤,寄生人之小腸內.患者食慾不振,胸腹疼痛,甚則下痢、發熱.此蟲在我國極普通,寧波、蘇州、香港、上海、汕頭等處極多.

後,變赤色.參閱薑黃條.

【薋】層時切,音茨,支韻.㊀艸多貌,見說文.㊁蒺藜也.離騷:「薋菉葹以盈室兮.」王逸注:「薋,蒺藜也.」詩曰:「楚楚者薋.」按:今詩小雅楚茨作「楚楚者茨.」又爾雅釋草:「茨,蒺藜.」則薋即茨也.又按說文:「薺,蒺藜也.」則薋、茨皆薺之借字.

【薇】無肥切,音微,微韻.植物名:㊀(Osmunda regalis var. japonica)羊齒類.草本.無地上莖.葉自地下莖叢生,有二種:一綠色,羽狀複葉,由長卵形之小葉而成;一褐色,形細長,上生子囊.嫩葉尖端爲渦卷狀,可食,包被嫩葉之棉毛,可供織料.㊁即大巢菜.詩召南草蟲:「言采其薇.」傳:「薇,菜也.」疏引陸璣云:「山菜也,莖葉皆似小豆,蔓生,藿可作羹.」本草綱目謂大巢菜一名薇,按大巢菜羽狀複葉,先端有卷鬚,故陸謂蔓生.又爾雅釋草:「薇,垂水.」郝懿行義疏:「詩言采薇,是生於山者;爾雅所言,是生於水者,實一物.」參閱大巢菜條.

一〇二 申集

Figure 39

magazine *Science* asked its readers' pardon for printing horizontally, in order to facilitate inclusion of equations and formulae. In the People's Republic horizontal printing has been usual since 1956; Figure 40 shows an extract from a translation of an American novel about the Watergate affair.[11] (From 2004 Taiwan mandated horizontal writing for official documents, though plenty of material continues to be written vertically.)

* * *

第十七章

夏洛特的母亲对莫利·布朗说:"我有件事非和你谈不可,莫利。你能到这儿来一趟吗?这样可能好一些,我们可以有更多的时间交谈,而且我也不必在你工作时间打搅你。"

"埃米莉,那就定个时间吧。"

"明天晚上怎么样?你能来吃晚饭吗?"

晚餐期间,莫利一面津津有味地吃着雌珍珠鸡,一面与巴林顿太太谈论塞浦路斯重新出现的问题,商讨交响乐团提出

Figure 40

Before closing this chapter, I shall briefly mention that one expert on the history of Chinese believes that, buried at the heart of the script, he has found an ancient alphabet. This idea is quite different from John DeFrancis's claim that Chinese script is essentially phonographic, which is uncontroversial provided it means just that a phonographic principle was used to devise most of the compound graphs, though that does not imply that the script is appropriately described as phonographic today.

The Canadian Edwin Pulleyblank's theory relates just to a few special Chinese graphs. I discuss the theory here not because I am convinced by it, but because it is too interesting to ignore. Pulleyblank's idea relates to a set of 22 graphs known as the "Ten Heavenly Stems" and "Twelve Earthly Branches". These go as far back in the historical record as any elements of Chinese script, but they never seem to have had meanings of their own in the ordinary sense. Their use was (and is) to form a cycle of sixty names for hours, days, months, and years. If we let digits 1, 2, 3, ... 9, 0 stand for the Stems, and letters A to L for the Branches, we can run the two cycles against one another to give pairs: 1A, 2B, 3C, ... 9I, 0J, then continuing with 1K, 2L, 3A, and so on; after sixty different pairs we will get back to 1A. This is what the Chinese do with the Stems and Branches. (When the day that Lady Hao gave birth, p. 173, was called a *jia yin* day, that meant in these terms that it was a 1C day.) Various astrological associations have accumulated round the Stems and Branches, for instance each Stem is associated with an element and each Branch with an animal; I am writing in a 1G year, a year of the Wooden Horse.

Another special feature of the Stem and Branch graphs is that many (though not all) of them began as simple geometrical shapes with no apparent pictorial quality: a cross, a shallow S-curve, an X with short crossbars across each limb, and so forth. We have seen that most graphs had a pictorial value in their original forms.

Pulleyblank's theory (Pulleyblank 1991) is that the Stems and Branches began as an alphabet. Their names never meant anything, because they were just arbitrary syllables beginning with the sound represented by the corresponding arbitrary letter shape. As Pulleyblank reconstructs the sound pattern of Old Chinese, there were just 22 consonant phonemes, and each Stem or Branch name began with a different one of these.

At one time Pulleyblank even believed that the Chinese Stems and Branches might share a common ancestry with the Semitic alphabet. Since at that period it was not yet conclusively established that the Central American systems discussed on pp. 56–8 were true writing, a link between a very early component of Chinese script and one of the scripts of the Middle East could have made it reasonable to claim that all the world's writing systems shared a single origin. By the 1980s, though, Pulleyblank gave up the idea of a relationship between the Stems and Branches and the Semitic alphabet, but he has continued to develop the theory that the Stems and Branches began as a consonantal alphabet for Chinese.

It is a fascinating idea, but I am sceptical. By tying his alphabetic hypothesis to his individual reconstruction of Old Chinese pronunciations, Pulleyblank seems to be playing a hand with too many jokers. His version of Old Chinese is very different from that of other Chinese historical linguists such as Schuessler, discussed earlier. Pulleyblank gives arguments for preferring his own reconstruction, but this is a domain where the uncertainties are so great that it might not be difficult to think of reasons justifying almost any desired sound pattern. The alphabet theory does nothing to explain the division of 22 symbols into ten and twelve. And perhaps most important: if the Stems and Branches really were an alphabet, why is there no record of them being used as such? We only ever encounter them used for calendrical purposes.

So I am not convinced. Nevertheless, there remains a question for which I have no answer: if the Stems and Branches did not begin as an alphabet, how did they begin? So far as the solid evidence extends, it would seem that the early Chinese decided to give meaningless names to a set of 22 mostly meaningless shapes and to use these abstract symbols in pairs to identify calendar units. Is it credible that an early civilization would operate in such a bloodless, algebraic fashion? If it is not, then the Stems and Branches must have had some meaningful values once, and perhaps alphabetic values are as plausible a suggestion as any.

Notes

1. So I was told when I studied Chinese as an undergraduate. John Man (2009: 74) quotes an even stronger claim, that most printed matter was in Chinese as late as 1900.
2. In my phonetic transcriptions of Chinese, superscript numerals 1 to 4 stand for the four distinctive "tones" or pitch-patterns of the language.
3. It is true that the grammar and vocabulary of written Chinese diverge from that of spoken Chinese, and before Chinese written norms were reformed early in the 20c the divergence was extreme. But Literary Chinese was no more a "logical" or "philosophical" language than modern spoken Chinese is.
4. Certain markings on recent archaeological finds, some dated as far back as the –5th millennium, have been claimed by a number of Chinese scholars to represent a prehistoric stage of Chinese writing. Others are sceptical, and in any case the meaning or purpose of these markings is too opaque

to shed light on the evolution of Chinese script as a system. (See e.g. Boltz 1999: 108.)

5. The standard catalogue of early Chinese graph forms for a Western readership is Karlgren (1957), though this is now rather out of date in view of archaeological findings of recent decades. Richard Sears's website (www.chineseetymology.org) allows one to look up an individual modern graph and view a range of early instances of it.
6. This word for "love" is obsolete in modern Chinese, and the same graph is now used for /xau^3/ "good": this is a rare case where tone variation distinguishes a pair of words sharing a common root.
7. Most popular accounts of Chinese script use as their central example of a compound picture the graph 明 for /miŋ^2/ "bright", which combines the graphs for "sun" and "moon" that we saw in Figure 36. Some readers may wonder why I did not lead with this example. The reason is that it is not in fact a valid example. The modern form of the graph is a simplification of an early form in which the left-hand element had nothing to do with "sun".
8. There is an element of circularity at this point, since graph-structure is one of the categories of evidence used to reconstruct Old Chinese. Other kinds of evidence are also available; but it must be stressed that the reconstructed forms are hypothetical – the specialist literature contains many alternative hypotheses about points of detail. The specific version of Old Chinese quoted here is Axel Schuessler's "Minimal Old Chinese" (Schuessler 2007: 121–5). The term "Minimal" is used because it is quite likely that the language had further phonetic contrasts which are now lost; where words are shown here with different starred forms, we are rather sure that they were said differently, but when starred forms are the same we are not sure that the words were perfect homophones. Note that presence versus absence of a circumflex marks a vowel distinction which is known to have existed but whose phonetic nature is not known. For an alternative take on Old Chinese, see e.g. Baxter and Sagart (2014).
9. The history of this word and graph is too complicated to enter into here; see the entry for mài$_4$ in Schuessler (2007).
10. DeFrancis (1989: 117) apparently does not accept the idea that Old Chinese phonology was much richer than that of present-day Mandarin. But to reject this is to dismiss a great deal of evidence and the combined weight of opinion of virtually every expert in the field.
11. "Chapter 17 / Charlotte's mother said to Molly Brown: 'There's something I really must talk to you about, Molly. Could you come over here some time? That might be best, we'd have more time to chat, and I oughtn't to be bothering you in your work hours.' / 'So fix a time, Emily.' / 'How about tomorrow evening? Could you come over for supper?' / At supper, Molly was relishing a guineafowl dish while discussing with Mrs Barrington the newly re-emerged Cyprus problem ..." (my re-translation).

10 Pros and cons of logography

To its users, alphabetic writing feels so inevitable and "right" that it is easy to see the Chinese type of script as unnecessarily clumsy and difficult. And many readers will know that there have been written-language reforms in China recently, which might imply that the Chinese themselves agree with this assessment. In this chapter we first look at those reforms briefly, and then move on to a general consideration of the pros and cons of Chinese-style writing.

Two separate writing reforms have been introduced under the People's Republic. First, a new romanization system (i.e. system for transcribing the sounds of Chinese in terms of the Roman alphabet), called *pinyin*, was devised and since 1979 has been accepted by Western publishers as standard, in place of different systems previously used in various Western countries. (This is why, for example, the name 毛澤東 /mau² tsɤ² tuŋ¹/ is now spelled "Mao Zedong" rather than "Mao Tsê-tung", as earlier in the English-speaking world.) Within China, *pinyin* is used for purposes such as specifying pronunciations of graphs in dictionaries, introducing young children to the activity of reading, and as a supplement to ordinary Chinese script in contexts such as road signs or slogans on posters – the pronunciation in *pinyin* is shown below the Chinese graphs for the benefit of semi-literate readers.

The most important point in the present context is that it is *not* proposed to replace traditional logographic Chinese writing with *pinyin* or any other phonographic script for general purposes. That was made clear when *pinyin* was first promulgated (Chou 1958: 17), and is an obvious implication of the other writing reform, which would serve little purpose if the logographic script were about to be swept away.

This second reform has involved changing the shapes of many of the graphs so as to reduce the number of brush-strokes. Several principles have been employed for this. Sometimes a few-stroked graph for an infrequent morpheme is used to replace a many-stroked graph for a common homophone: e.g. 里, traditionally /li³/ "village/mile", is now also used instead of 裏 for /li³/ "in". In other cases unique or near-unique components occurring within many-stroked graphs are made to stand for the whole graph: e.g. 習 "to practise" (which happens to be the surname, Xi, of the current president Xi Jinping) is now written 习. The most important principle is that various writings which were traditionally used as cursive handwritten versions of commonly recurring elements are now adopted as the standard printed forms. Thus 馬 "horse" is now 马, and the combination form of the "speak" signific has been changed from 訁 to 讠.

This reform seems misguided. It depends for its justification on the implausible judgement that the most important factor determining the efficiency of Chinese script is the number of strokes involved in the graphs. In reality an at least equally important consideration is the visual distinctiveness of the elements (a point to which we shall return), and in that respect many (though not all) of the reformed graphs are inferior to their predecessors (see e.g. Taylor and Taylor 1983: 38). The graph for "horse", and the "speak" signific, were fiddly to write in their official form, but they were very recognizable and memorable; the new versions look rather similar to a number of other graphs or graph-components. (The reformed graphs also entail disadvantages of a more technical nature having to do with dictionary look-up.) One would have thought that there was little objection to a system whereby certain complex elements had conventional quick handwritten equivalents but were printed in their full form – users of the Roman alphabet see no problem in the fact that some letters are handwritten in ways that deviate considerably from their printed shapes.

In any case, graph simplification has nothing to do with the logography versus phonography issue. The simplified graphs are as logographic as those they replace (perhaps slightly more so, since in some cases the phonetic elements are obscured; Taylor and Taylor 1983: 47).

After an initial period of enthusiasm, the Chinese authorities ceased to produce further lists of simplified graphs. Few parts of the Chinese-speaking world outside the People's Republic have accepted them; Hong Kong has retained the traditional graphs since reverting to Chinese rule in 1997. There have been calls within the People's Republic for this reform to be reversed, for instance the issue was debated heatedly at the National People's Congress in March 2009 (Chen 2009: 66), though since governments hate admitting that they have made mistakes this is unlikely to happen. This book uses the traditional graphs.

* * *

Logographic script, then, remains a fixture in the Chinese-speaking world. Is that a bad thing?

The casual remarks that English-speaking laymen make suggest that they see Chinese writing as horribly cumbersome and difficult. It is a very different system from ours, and things that are unfamiliar often seem complex for that reason alone. I have often wondered whether the common reaction is based on anything more substantial than that, because I cannot myself see that it is justified. Europeans often suppose that it would unarguably be of great advantage to the Chinese to abandon their script in favour of an alphabetic one, except that certain special features of the Chinese language unfortunately make it difficult for them to do this. We shall see in due course that there are two considerations which would create great problems for any proposal to write Chinese phonographically. But I defer discussion of these, because even if those special factors did not obtain, it is not clear to me that logographic script would be inferior to phonographic script.

If one presses the layman to be specific about why he sees Chinese writing as frighteningly complicated, one point often mentioned is its unbounded nature. People used to the 26 letters of our alphabet ask how many "letters" there are in Chinese script and are startled to be told that there is no specific answer. But this is a simple consequence of the fact that each word, roughly speaking, has its own graph: to ask how many graphs there are in the Chinese script is rather like asking how many words there are in the English language, and this is not a question with a well-defined answer. The largest Chinese dictionary, the *Kang-xi Dictionary* of 1716, includes about 40,000 graphs, but most of these either stand for thoroughly obsolete words or are obsolete variant forms of graphs for current words. Likewise, most headwords in the *Oxford English Dictionary* are unfamiliar to a contemporary speaker, even though the eight centuries of English covered by the *OED* represent less than a third of the period covered by a major Chinese dictionary.

An average literate Chinese would probably not know, and would not need to know, more than a few thousand graphs – say five or six thousand at most. (This figure may sound low as a measure of a speaker's total vocabulary; but remember that a Chinese graph represents a *morpheme*, and Chinese has never borrowed morphemes from other languages to any significant extent. A family of words such as *king*, *kingly*, *kingship*, *royal*, *royalty*, *regal*, *regalia*, *Rex*, *Basil*, *basilica* count as ten separate items in an Englishman's vocabulary, but a comparable family in Chinese would use a single root morpheme compounded with various high-frequency morphemes akin to English derivational affixes.)

Even a few thousand graphs are a lot to learn when compared to the 26 letters of the Roman alphabet. In justifying the view that Chinese script is inordinately complex, people make the point that with an alphabetic script there is essentially nothing more to learn once one knows the few simple rules for using the letters, together with the pronunciations of the various words to be written (which, as a native speaker, one has absorbed without conscious effort) – whereas for every single word that a Chinese knows he must separately learn its writing.

It is not true of English, of course, that the spellings of its words follow automatically from their pronunciations, and in fact few scripts which use the Roman alphabet are close to being perfectly "phonemic" in this sense. Nor is it really true that all our vocabulary is acquired in the effortless, unconscious fashion in which we pick up the common words in childhood; many less-common words are learned through conscious study, involving consultation of dictionaries and the like, and often we meet them first in print and then discover their pronunciation, rather than vice versa. Suppose that Chinese morphemes were written down in a phonemic script but were phonologically much more complex than they are: would the situation still seem so daunting to the Western layman? I suspect not. The phonological shape of a Chinese morpheme is in fact very simple: a single initial consonant, a vowel or diphthong with a tone, and possibly a single final consonant drawn from a very small set of alternatives. In a language containing consonant clusters and a wider range of consonants, and which allowed morphemes to be polysyllabic, each morpheme might involve almost as much to be learned, in terms of pronunciation, as Chinese morphemes involve in terms of pronunciation and writing together. Yet it seems likely that an Englishman who finds it hard to get his mind round the idea that the Chinese morpheme for "thunder" is

lei^{2} 雷

might be quite unfazed by the news that in some other language "thunder" is, say:

sprẽʃváugli (spelled as pronounced)

Admittedly, to someone unfamiliar with Chinese graphs they often look so complex in themselves that a morpheme would have to contain a very long sequence of phonemes in order to match their complexity in terms of phonology. But this is a trivial matter of what one is used to. To anyone who can read Chinese, the "thunder" graph consists of two elements, each of which is so familiar that it is difficult to see their individual strokes as separate entities.

It is not only laymen who see the Chinese type of script as problematic. The "case for the prosecution" has been made most forcefully by William

Hannas, in successive books which are far better informed than most Western discussions about the detailed facts of literacy in East Asia. In the first of these, Hannas urged that "Instead of using language to learn, East Asians are wasting their youth and resources learning about language. ... the effects of Chinese characters on literacy and learning have been uniformly negative" (Hannas 1997: 125, 152). And in the new millennium he returned to the fray with a book which argued at length that all the East Asian cultures are purely imitative rather than original (and have achieved economic successes in recent decades only through wholesale semi-legal industrial espionage against the West), and furthermore that responsibility for this sad situation rests mainly with the nature of Chinese writing. According to Hannas (2003: 5), "alphabetic literacy promotes creativity", but logographic script stifles it.

There are many levels at which one can answer this. An obvious empirical point is that, while it may have been reasonable in 2003 to predict that China's hope of achieving economic growth was doomed (Hannas 2003: chapter 2), the prediction looks pretty silly now that the Chinese economy is on course to overtake the USA before the present decade is out (*Economist* 2014). The claim in the earlier book that Chinese writing hinders literacy and learning was necessarily impressionistic, for want of objective data at the time it was made. But, since the turn of the millennium, data have become available, and they show that Hannas was quite wrong. Every three years, the Organisation for Economic Co-operation and Development has been testing fifteen-year-olds in 65 developed nations for their core educational attainments: the Programme for International Student Assessment (PISA) study.[1] Ensuring that results are comparable across differences among languages and school curricula is problematic, and some experts raise issues about individual aspects of the PISA tests, but the broad thrust of the results is so plain and consistent across the three-year intervals that few people would dispute what they are telling us. For reading, the highest-scoring countries in the tests taken in 2012 were:

1. China (Shanghai)
2. Hong Kong
3. Singapore
4. Japan

The top three use Chinese script, while Japan uses a script based on Chinese script but considerably more complicated (as we shall see in Chapter 11). Britain and the USA were far down the 2012 league table, at 23rd and 24th respectively.

The highest-scoring country using the Roman alphabet was Finland, at 6th. Finnish spelling is unusually regular in terms of letter–phoneme correspondences, very different indeed in that respect from the unpredictable spelling system of English; but in case the reader is tempted to ascribe the poor showing of Britain and the USA to the irrational orthography of the English language, consider that the country immediately below Finland in the table, at 7th, was Ireland, also English-speaking.

These differences between rankings for reading correlate strongly with rankings for the two other PISA subjects, namely maths and science (in 2012 China came top in all three tables). For those subjects the nature of the respective writing systems has little relevance. The rankings are probably heavily affected by broader cultural factors and differences among schooling regimes, for instance China is known for "tiger mothers" who push not just their children but the children's teachers; in Finland schoolteaching is a much higher-status profession than it is in Britain. The British scores might also be pulled down by the high proportion of pupils currently in British schools for whom English is not a mother tongue. On the figures, type of writing system must be irrelevant, unless logographic writing is actually giving East Asian countries an advantage – which is not out of the question.

More important than these empirical objections, Hannas simply fails in either book to explain *why* logographic writing should have such adverse consequences for intellectual creativity. Much of what he says about the conservative nature of East Asian cultures, and their encouragement of social conformity at the expense of individual initiative, is very just. But he gives no real reason to believe that these traits are caused by writing systems in particular, despite a number of fairly vague remarks such as "the decomposition of syllables into phonemes offers a model for analysis, [and] the recombination of phonemes ... facilitate[s] the exercise of synthetic operations, including those needed for creativity" (Hannas 2003: 159). If high levels of conformism in a society require special explanation, there are plenty of other candidates. Famously, Karl Wittfogel (1957) attributed the conformist tradition of China to the early need for strong social co-ordination to control the disastrous flooding to which the Yellow River is prone. Whether that is right or not, it sounds more plausible *a priori* than Hannas's idea.

What is more, Hannas defeats his own argument, by applying it to Korea as well as to China and Japan. As we saw in Chapter 8, present-day Korean script is almost wholly phonographic, yet Hannas sees Korea as suffering from the same creativity deficit as the other East Asian countries. One might imagine that he would resolve this paradox by suggesting that all-Hangul script is too new in Korea to have "unblocked" the Korean mindset already, but that is not the escape route he chooses. Instead, Hannas argues (2003: 61) that it is only *phonemic* writing which encourages mental operations of analysis and synthesis, and Hangul is syllabic rather than phonemic. But Hangul is syllabic only in the trivial sense that the signs for individual phonemes are grouped into syllables on the page. Since the ultimate elements of Hangul are phonetic features rather than whole phonemes, logically Hannas ought to predict that its use involves *more* analytic and synthetic operations than alphabetic writing. But that would wreck his thesis.

The assumption that a logographic script is more difficult to learn than a phonographic one may be not just false but meaningless, since the truth seems to be that the two kinds of script involve different, and incommensurable, *kinds* of difficulty. A logographic script requires a lot of time to commit the many graphs to memory; a phonographic script requires analytic intelligence to split words into sounds (cf. p. 28). As Ignatius Mattingly put it (1972: 144), anyone with plenty of time to spare can learn to read Chinese; if a script is phonographic, there will be "more reading successes, because the learning time is far shorter, but proportionately more failures too, because of the greater demand on linguistic awareness". Taylor and Taylor (1983: 404) discuss research by Kuo (1978) for Chinese and by Makita (1968) for Japanese showing that developmental dyslexia is extremely rare among speakers of these languages.

Logographic Chinese script may be not only easier to learn but easier to read than phonographic script once learned. We shall see in Chapter 13 that an important factor contributing to efficient reading is distinctiveness of spelling. From this point of view Chinese script – the graphs of which are composed of quite a wide variety of distinct basic elements arranged in varying spatial configurations – scores heavily over any alphabetic script in which all words are made up of reshufflings of the same two or three dozen letters in one-dimensional sequences. At an anecdotal level, literate Chinese encountering European script in the days when globalization had not yet made it a familiar sight in China were known to make comments suggesting that it produced on them the same impression of monotony and lack of distinctiveness which we might experience if faced with pages printed in the dots and dashes of Morse code (cf. Chiang 1973: 3–4; Geschwind 1973).

Hannas's condemnation of Chinese script is the latest manifestation of a longstanding tradition. Some Western commentators have regarded logographic script as inferior in ways that run deeper than alleged difficulty for learners. An extreme point of view has been expressed by the anthropologist Sir Jack Goody (see Goody and Watt 1963; Goody 1977). According to Goody and Watt, it is in the nature of logographic scripts to "reify the objects of the natural and social order", and, by so doing, to "make permanent the existing social and ideological picture"; by contrast, phonographic writing

> ... symboli[zes], not the objects of the social and natural order, but the very process of human interaction in speech: the verb is as easy to express as the noun ... Phonetic systems are therefore adapted to expressing every nuance of individual thought ... [while logographic writing records] only those items in the cultural repertoire which the literate specialists have selected for written expression; and it tends to express the collective attitude towards them. (Goody and Watt 1963: 315)

They went on to argue that the Chinese writing system militates against adoption of the standards of logic normal in "literate" societies (by which they meant societies using a phonographic script).

To anyone who respects Chinese civilization this sort of nonsense is rather offensive. It is certainly true that China was traditionally a conservative society, and arguably also one not much interested in logical issues. But the suggestion that either of these cultural traits is a consequence of logographic script is quite untenable. Chinese script provides a graph for virtually every morpheme of the language: words for ideologically crucial notions and words for banal objects, verbs as well as nouns. (The few exceptional morphemes which cannot be written down are ones occurring only in regional dialects, or slang terms which – like English *bonzer* as opposed to *stunning* – are morphemically unrelated to terms of the standard language: it is implausible to suggest that such gaps in the script had any serious effect on the evolution of Chinese culture.) There is no way that the graph for a thing expresses the collective Chinese attitude to that thing, if there is a collective attitude. Feminists might point to the number of cases where words for unpleasant character traits such as jealousy are written with the "woman" signific, and urge that this is a way in which the script expresses a negative attitude to women. But the incidence of this sort of thing is no greater than that of comparable sexist assumptions in the spoken English language; cf. *bitch* versus *dog*, for instance. As for logic: properties of Chinese *as a spoken language* may well have militated against awareness of logical considerations (the rich systems of inflexion and of particles in Ancient Greek drew attention to logical relationships within sentences, while Chinese had virtually no inflexion and a poorer system of particles);[2] but, once the spoken Chinese language is accepted as a given, I see no argument for the view that logical explicitness is affected by whether the language is written down phoneme-by-phoneme or word-by-word (Goody offers no such argument).

* * *

Certainly there are drawbacks in a logographic script such as the Chinese. However, the two drawbacks which seem to me most serious are not ones which laymen are inclined to emphasize.

One of these has to do with inputting written material into computers and similar equipment. In the days of 20c typewriters the situation was very difficult. Chinese typewriters did exist, but instead of having pieces of type fixed to a few dozen type-bars, the operator had to use a single arm to pick out separate pieces of type from large trays. The machines were extremely cumbersome, and little used. The advent of computers has improved the situation hugely. One can identify graphs either by typing *pinyin* and selecting the correct homophone on screen, or (faster but harder to learn) by specifying elements of the graph shape under a system by which any graph is uniquely identified with at most four key presses. The speeds achieved are quite comparable with European-language typists in graphs/words per minute.[3] But the effortless spontaneity attained even by non-professional Western touch-typists is probably not compatible with the need to check and correct a screen display.

This is a drawback of logographic writing, but not necessarily a very serious one. Plenty of individuals who work at alphabetic computer keyboards never learn to touch-type. And input is only one small part of all the processing activities that human language typically undergoes in a computing environment. The individuals for whom the drawback is most serious are probably creative writers, who produce free-form documents which deploy vocabulary in unpredictable ways and who would not want their flow to be hampered by their word-processing equipment. Plenty of creative writers in the West compose in longhand and only later convert their output into electronic form; in China I guess that most of them must work that way.

The other drawback of Chinese script is less obvious but perhaps more serious. This has to do with foreign words and names. In an alphabetic script like ours, there is no difficulty about writing borrowed words (*curry*, *boomerang*, *Schadenfreude*, etc.). Even names that are unpronounceable in English can be written down easily, and we can give them some conventional mispronunciation: *Tbilisi*, *Nguyen*, *Llanllwchaiarn*, etc. In Chinese script, on the other hand, each graph represents a morpheme of the Chinese language. The only way a non-Chinese word can be written is as a series of Chinese morphemes of similar pronunciation. But, since the sounds of Chinese are very different from those of European languages, the imitation usually cannot be close.

Until quite recently this limitation too was of little practical significance for the Chinese. For most of its long history, China was an area of high culture largely cut off from the outside world by geography, and the only non-Chinese peoples encountered by the Chinese were "barbarians". Even modern Western technical terminology is not normally borrowed in its original form; rather, Chinese uses morphemes of its own literary stock to coin compounds rather in the way that we use Latin and Greek roots. Koreans call a computer /kʰam-pʰju-tʰa/, but in Chinese it is 電子計算機 /tien^{4}-tsɯ^{3} tʃi^{4}-suan^{4} tʃi^{1}/ "electron calculate machine", or informally 電腦 /tien^{4} nau^{3}/ "electric brain". Uri Tadmor (2009) has studied the incidence of loanwords in languages from many language-families and all parts of the world; he finds that the proportion in Chinese is by a large margin lower than in any other language sampled.

With the tidal wave of technology that has broken over China as over everywhere else, this resistance to borrowing is just beginning to weaken somewhat: *computer* may be "electric brain", but for instance *blog* is 博客 /po^{2} kʰɤ^{4}/, morphemes chosen purely for sound rather than meaning (they literally mean "extensive guest"). But this kind of borrowing is not easy for Chinese (/po^{2} kʰɤ^{4}/ really does not sound much like /blɔg/), and so far it does not seem that English as the modern *lingua franca* is destined to have an impact on Chinese comparable to what it has had on numerous other languages. Lauren Hall-Lew (2002: 44) concluded that "the actual influence of English on the Chinese language is relatively minimal in comparison to [its influence on other languages] ... Chinese remains quite robust in the face of global English."

The words for which transliteration is unavoidable are proper names. Chinese names are composed of meaningful morphemes. Foreign names, on the other hand, are meaningless noises to the Chinese. Names of the leading foreign countries have been Sinicized, in the sense that their Chinese translations follow the pattern of Chinese place-names; thus, England is 英國 /iŋ^{1}-kuo^{2}/ "the nation of heroes", with /iŋ^{1}/ sounding like the beginning of *England*, while France is 法國 /fa^{4}-kuo^{2}/ "the nation of law"; and Westerners who live in China or have dealings with the Chinese are given Chinese names. But for the great majority of foreign names such individual treatment is impossible, and they are simply spelled out by sequences of graphs. The Chinese tend to use a limited subset of their vocabulary for transliteration purposes, and some morphemes in that subset are otherwise almost or wholly obsolete (which is useful in that it helps to show that a given graph-sequence is to be read for its phonetic value rather than its meaning – Chinese script does not normally use any device akin to capitals that would show that a sequence of graphs is meant as a proper name).[4] But these tendencies are by no means absolute.

Some examples of such transliterations, supplemented with literal morpheme-by-morpheme glosses, are the following:

迭更斯	tie^{2}-kəŋ^{1}-sɯ^{1}	"repeatedly-change-this"	Dickens
柴霍甫斯基	tʂʰai^{2}-xuo^{4}-fu^{3}-sɯ^{1}-tʃi^{1}	"firewood-suddenly-begin-this-foundation"	Tchaikovsky
比勒陀利亞	pi^{3}-lɤ^{1}-tʰuo^{2}-li^{4}-ja^{3}	"compare-compel-slope-profit-Asia"	Pretoria
里約熱內盧	li^{3}-ye^{1}-ɽɤ^{4}-nei^{4}-lu^{2}	"village-agree-hot-inner-black"	Rio de Janeiro

The results of this system are clumsy in several ways. First, the phonetic correspondence with the foreign original is usually very inexact. Also, the Chinese version of a foreign name can be as long as a whole Chinese sentence. Third, the looseness of fit between original and Chinese equivalent means that there are many possible Chinese transliterations for any given foreign name, which creates obvious practical problems. In practice the most famous foreign names are usually written in a single recognized way, but even with famous names the consistency is not perfect; two reference books on my shelves transliterate "Wordsworth" as

華滋華斯 xua^{2}-tsɯ^{1}-xua^{2}-sɯ^{1} "flowery-flavour-flowery-this"

and as

威至威士 wei^{1}-tʂɯ^{4}-wei^{1}-ʂɯ^{4} "prestige-arrive-prestige-scholar"

respectively.

This problem might be eliminated if the Chinese were happy to write non-Chinese words in Roman script in the middle of a Chinese sentence. But that is done only in technical documentation. The two scripts are felt to be so alien to one another that in general writing, such as newspapers or non-specialist books, everything must be written in Chinese graphs.[5]

* * *

However, these drawbacks of Chinese script are outweighed by advantages of the logographic system which have not been discussed yet, and which relate to special properties of the Chinese language.

One of the most characteristic features of modern Chinese (already mentioned in connexion with Korean), which seems very strange if not almost incredible to someone used to European languages, is its extremely high incidence of homophones. Each Chinese word is a single syllable, but there are few different phonologically possible syllables. That was not so when the script was invented; as reconstructed by historical linguists, Old Chinese did not have a dramatically higher incidence of homophony than the average European language – a phonographic script would probably have worked well for Old Chinese, though that happened not to be the kind of script that was devised for it. But the many sound changes which have applied since the Old Chinese period have involved massive and repeated losses of important phonological distinctions.

This means that there are now many times more words than phonologically possible syllables. The average syllable in modern Chinese will now stand for perhaps half a dozen different words of the living language (many of which will have developed widely divergent polysemies), together with a larger number of literary words which are obsolete in the spoken language but which an educated man might encounter in reading. There are scarcely any syllables in modern Chinese which represent a single word unambiguously, as is common in English (/hɪt/, /rɪp/, /deθ/, /wid/ etc. stand for one word each). There is a potential misunderstanding here: Europeans who hear about Chinese homophones often say "But they solve that problem with their tones". However, when I talk about there being few distinct syllables in Chinese, I mean syllables distinct with respect to their consonants, their vowels, *or their tone* – the tone is as much part of the pronunciation of a Chinese syllable as any other aspect of it, it is a misapprehension to think of tones as something special that were added in order to solve a problem.

Figure 41 lists the alternative values of two modern spoken Chinese syllables. In a few cases, such as "seven" and "varnish", the words were homophones already in Old Chinese (though cf. note 8, p. 191); but most of the homophony has been brought about by sound changes since the script was created. These particular syllables are more ambiguous than average, but not much more – there are plenty which are far more ambiguous yet. Thus modern spoken Chinese has immense potential for ambiguity.

The spoken language has adopted various strategies in order to overcome this problem. Some of these strategies could be imitated in writing even if the script were phonographic. For instance, very often concepts that were expressed by single words at an earlier stage are expressed by two-morpheme combinations in modern colloquial Chinese, so that each morpheme disambiguates the other. Thus /jen^{2}/ "research" is ambiguous as shown in Figure 41, and it has a near-synonym /tʃiou^1/ which also has many homophones – morphemes pronounced /tʃiou^1/ have meanings which include "gather", "pigeon", "clutch", "blame" – so in modern Chinese one says /jen^2- tʃiou^1/ for "research" rather than either morpheme alone. Various other categories of compound are also used. But one of the important factors in speech for which writing has no equivalent is the constant negotiation of meaning that occurs in a dialogue; misunderstandings that occur when people speak face-to-face are often cleared up almost unconsciously as fast as they arise.

<table>
<tr><th>graph</th><th>gloss</th><th>Old Chinese pronunciation</th><th>Modern Chinese pronunciation</th></tr>
<tr><td>欺</td><td>cheat</td><td>k^{h}ə</td><td rowspan="11">tʃ^{h}i^1</td></tr>
<tr><td>期</td><td>period</td><td>kə</td></tr>
<tr><td>崎</td><td>mountainous</td><td>k^{h}ai</td></tr>
<tr><td>溪</td><td>creek</td><td>k^{h}ê</td></tr>
<tr><td>七</td><td>seven</td><td rowspan="2">ts^{h}it</td></tr>
<tr><td>漆</td><td>varnish</td></tr>
<tr><td>沏</td><td>to mash tea</td><td>ts^{h}ît</td></tr>
<tr><td>妻</td><td>wife</td><td rowspan="2">ts^{h}əi</td></tr>
<tr><td>悽</td><td>grieved</td></tr>
<tr><td>棲</td><td>roost</td><td>sə̂i</td></tr>
<tr><td>戚</td><td>kinsman</td><td>sn̥iuk</td></tr>
<tr><td colspan="4"></td></tr>
<tr><td>研</td><td>grind, research</td><td>ŋên</td><td rowspan="15">jen^2</td></tr>
<tr><td>延</td><td>prolong</td><td rowspan="2">lan</td></tr>
<tr><td>蜒</td><td>slug</td></tr>
<tr><td>檐</td><td>eaves</td><td rowspan="2">liam</td></tr>
<tr><td>炎</td><td>flame</td></tr>
<tr><td>嚴</td><td>strict</td><td>ŋam</td></tr>
<tr><td>巖</td><td>cliff</td><td>ŋrâm</td></tr>
<tr><td>言</td><td>speak</td><td>ŋan</td></tr>
<tr><td>閻</td><td>the King of Hell</td><td>ləm</td></tr>
<tr><td>顏</td><td>face, colour</td><td>ŋrân</td></tr>
<tr><td>鹽</td><td>salt</td><td>rjam</td></tr>
<tr><td>沿</td><td>along</td><td>lon</td></tr>
<tr><td>焉</td><td>there</td><td>ʔan</td></tr>
</table>

Figure 41

The significant point is that the immense ambiguity of modern Chinese words in their spoken form is entirely eliminated in writing, where each word has its own distinctive graph – whereas, with a phonographic script, ambiguity would carry over from speech to writing. Even with the strategies of morpheme-compounding mentioned above, modern spoken Chinese does seem to be a relatively ambiguous language; when speaking to one another, Chinese will not infrequently draw a graph in the air to identify a problematic syllable. Writing tends to use a less predictable vocabulary than speech, and it can assume far less shared knowledge between speaker and hearer. It seems very doubtful whether phonographic writing could be successfully adopted as the normal script of a Chinese-speaking society.

William Hannas (1997: 87) claims that this last point is refuted by the Vietnamese language. Vietnamese, although genetically unrelated to Chinese, is typologically very similar and (as in the Korean case) most of its vocabulary consists of loans from Chinese. It used to be written in Chinese script supplemented with additional logographs for native Vietnamese morphemes, but in the 19c, under French rule, it switched to an alphabetic orthography; unlike Korean script, it makes no residual use of Chinese graphs at all. However, the phonology of Sino-Vietnamese loans reflects the pronunciation not of modern Mandarin Chinese but of an earlier stage of Chinese when many phoneme mergers had not yet taken place; as Hannas himself points out, the number of distinct syllables in Vietnamese is about five times the number in Mandarin. Consequently homophones are less problematic for Vietnamese than they would be if modern Chinese adopted alphabetic writing.

Hannas also repeatedly suggests (e.g. 2003: 173–4) that, without the logographic script, Chinese would have been forced to avoid developing so much homophony. But, although China was a more literate society than most, until recent times only a minority of the population could read and write. How could that minority have had such influence on the evolution of the spoken language?

The second special factor has to do with the Chinese "dialects", so called. I have been speaking of "modern Chinese" as if it were a single language, and what I have indicated by that term is what is known in the West as "Mandarin Chinese". There is some justice in calling Mandarin Chinese simply "Chinese": it is the speech of about two-thirds of all Chinese (with regional variation, but variation that does not prevent mutual intelligibility), and it is regarded by the present Chinese regime as the only kind of Chinese with official status. Nevertheless, many Chinese speak languages that are very different indeed from Mandarin. Since about the middle of the +1st millennium, what was originally one fairly homogeneous Chinese language has split into six or eight main varieties which have diverged so widely that they are often seen as separate languages. To give just one example of the pronunciation-differences between these divisions of Chinese: the word for "north", Mandarin /pei³/, is Cantonese /pak/, Hakka /pɛt/, Suchow /pɯʔ/, and so on. This degree of divergence runs throughout the vocabulary, and its consequences for communication are magnified because of the unusually low "margins for error" in comprehension of Chinese speech which stem from the high level of homophony.

As a result, a Pekinese could no more understand a Cantonese (without studying the latter's language) than a Londoner could understand a Berliner. Yet these different languages are spoken in a single nation which has been very civilized and politically very centralized for a long time, and which therefore needs a universal medium of communication. Again the logographic script solves this problem beautifully, since the "dialect" differences have to do mainly with divergent pronunciations of the same words, and those divergences are not reflected at all in the written graphs. Differences in vocabulary and grammar between the "dialects", while not trivial, are small enough that they can be overcome by agreeing on standards of written usage.

* * *

The homophones and the "dialects" constitute two special reasons for retaining logographic script. If these factors had happened not to be present, perhaps the logographic principle would at some point have been abandoned.

But that is far from obvious. The main point I have tried to make in this chapter is that the logographic principle for writing is by no means self-evidently inferior to the more familiar phonographic principle.

Notes

1. Because of the separate educational systems in Hong Kong and mainland China, PISA tests them separately, with mainland China represented by Shanghai.
2. Graham (1959: 110–12) argued that this aspect of Chinese has been exaggerated.
3. See the Wikipedia entry "Chinese input methods for computers" (accessed 9 March 2014).
4. For a while in the 20c, vertical lines were printed alongside graph-groups standing for proper names, wavy in the case of titles of literary works, corresponding to the Western use of capitalization and italics. Figure 39 has

several examples. But modern horizontally written Chinese has no equivalent convention. (The first line below the heading in Figure 40 does use a raised dot to separate the two graphs for *Molly* from the two graphs for *Brown.*)

5. An exception is that it is common in any kind of writing now to find Roman letters used for abbreviations such as *DNA* or *SEATO*, and in phrases like 「T恤」 "T-shirt". In these cases the letters function more like words than phonemes.

11 A mixed system: Japanese writing

Like the Koreans, the Japanese had no writing of their own when they encountered and began to absorb Chinese civilization in the +1st millennium. Like them, the Japanese made shift to adapt Chinese script to a language that was unrelated to, and typologically very different from, Chinese. (Japanese is probably related to Korean, though this is not certain and the relationship is distant if it exists.)

Unlike the Koreans, the Japanese never made a clean break to a different kind of script. Everything in modern Japanese orthography derives ultimately from Chinese writing. But, because the two languages are very different, the processes by which Chinese script was adapted to write Japanese often had to be roundabout, and the end-result is a system typologically quite different from the Chinese system. Chinese writing is to a close approximation a pure logographic script. Japanese writing is a mixed system, partly logographic and partly phonographic.

Japanese and Chinese scripts differ not only in type but in degree of complexity. I argued that Chinese logographic script, though it looks daunting to the uninitiated, is actually a fairly simple system of writing. Japanese script, on the other hand, is described by Richard Sproat (2000: 132) as "surely the most complex modern writing system". Few knowledgeable people would dissent from that verdict, and I wonder whether Sproat needed the word "modern": it is not easy to identify ancient scripts which rival Japanese writing in complexity. Perhaps Cuneiform as adapted to write Akkadian would qualify.

One reason for the astonishing complexity of Japanese script has to do with differences between Japanese and Chinese spoken languages. But there is another factor. Japanese culture, during much of the period in which the script was developed, was shaped by an aristocratic class many members of which lacked political power or indeed any serious employment, so that their only role in life was as definers and producers of civilized cultural norms (one might perhaps draw a parallel with *Ancien Régime* France). As a natural consequence, many aspects of Japanese culture, including its writing, were greatly elaborated – made exquisite and intellectually rich rather than straightforwardly functional. (This contrasts with the case of China, which for most of its history was a rather down-to-earth, workaday civilization, and where the script, for instance, was shaped in the historical period largely by civil servants who had plenty to keep them busy.) To quote Roy Miller (1967: 99–100):

> The tiny segment of the population that was at all concerned with reading and writing had in fact little if anything else to do with their time, and so quite naturally it delighted in any device that would make the process as time-consuming as possible. ... They and their culture were not interested in evolving an easy system, or one that could be written quickly or read simply and unambiguously. Such values and goals were totally absent from ancient Japanese society ...

Japanese society has changed many of its goals and values since. Correspondingly, the version of the script used in the 21c is considerably simplified by comparison with the full panoply of eccentricities it once possessed. But although many complexities have been stripped away, many remain. One reason why Japanese script deserves its place in this book is as an illustration of just how cumbersome a script can be and still serve in practice. For, remember, this script is not nowadays the private plaything of an idle élite. Japan has a very high literacy rate, and no inefficiencies in its script have hindered Japan from becoming, economically and technologically, one of the leading nations of the world.

* * *

While Chinese is an "isolating" language in which each morpheme or word is an invariant syllable, Japanese has a rich system of derivational and inflexional morphology, with associated morphophonemic alternations. So, for instance, from the root /mot-/ "hold" we find, among others, the following words formed:

motsu	"hold" (plain)
motʃimasu	"hold" (polite)
motanai	"not hold" (plain)
motʃimasen	"not hold" (polite)
motta	"held" (plain)
motʃimaʃita	"held" (polite)
motanakatta	"did not hold" (plain)
motō	"be about to hold" (plain)
motʃimaʃō	"be about to hold" (polite)
motʃi	"holding" (noun)
motte	"(is) holding"

etc.

(One of the factors relevant for verb inflexion in Japanese is the social status of the addressee.)

Japanese words, even if they consist of a single uninflected morpheme, can be several syllables long, e.g. /taʃika/ "certain". But syllable-structure is even simpler than in Chinese: to a close approximation, syllables are limited to a single consonant (or no consonant) followed by a simple vowel; only one consonant, /n/, can follow the vowel of a syllable.

The Japanese first began to write their own language in the +7c. To get an idea of the problems of writing down Japanese in Chinese script, Miller invites us to imagine that we had no writing system of our own and wanted to use Chinese script to write English. Let us suppose, he says, that we wish to write down: "The bear killed the man".

Chinese, as it happens, has no word for *the*. The definite article is not a very important word in English, so we give up on this and press on to the word *bear*. "Bear" translates into Chinese as /ʃyŋ²/, written 熊 – so we write this graph. "Kill" is Chinese /ʂa¹/, written 殺; but Chinese has no inflexion comparable to *-ed* in English. We might indicate that 殺 is to be taken as "gone past" by adding, say, 去 /tʃʰy⁴/ "go". Alternatively, since the English suffix is pronounced /d/, we might write some graph for a Chinese morpheme having a similar sound – perhaps 的 /tə/, which is a grammatical suffix in Chinese, though in Chinese it forms the genitive of a noun. Now we come to *the* again. Rather than just leaving it out as before, this time we may be emboldened by our success just now in "spelling" *-ed* and decide analogously to write *the* with the graph for a Chinese morpheme sounding something like /ðə/. The sound pattern of Chinese will not allow it to be very similar: perhaps we choose 色 /sɤ⁴/ "colour". Finally, *man*: here we will probably write 人, the graph for /ɽən²/ "man" in the "human being" sense. On the other hand, if in context we take the English word *man* to refer specifically to a male, in contrast to *woman*, Chinese has no one word for this. Chinese uses the phrase 男人 /nan²-ɽən²/, literally "male person", so we might write those two graphs to stand for the single short English word.

Japanese writing uses Chinese script in all these ways. The term for a Chinese graph used to represent a Japanese word whose meaning is the same or similar to the Chinese word written by that graph is *kun*; one says that the graph has a "*kun* reading". Thus, Japanese /hito/ "man" is written 人 (see above); Japanese /jama/ "mountain" is written 山, the graph for Chinese /ʂan¹/ "hill". Of course, since Chinese and Japanese were two unrelated languages, one would not normally expect to be able to find a perfect synonym in Chinese for a given Japanese word – often scribes had to make do with a near-equivalent, and I shall deliberately draw attention to this aspect of the *kun* system by giving the pairs of Chinese and Japanese words slightly different English glosses, where appropriate.

In early Japanese writing there would occur, interspersed with graphs intended to be given *kun* readings, other cases where graphs were used for their phonetic value, as in the hypothetical case of 色 /sɤ^{4}/ "colour" to stand for English *the*. Thus, the Japanese genitive particle /no/ was written 乃, Chinese /nai^{3}/ "your"; the Japanese topic-marking suffix /wa/ was written 波, Ch. /po^{1}/ "wave". At the period when this sort of writing was practised, rather more than a thousand years ago, these pairs of words resembled one another phonetically more than they do now; nevertheless, the equivalences often seem to have been quite inexact. (To keep things simple, I cite Japanese and Chinese forms in their present-day pronunciation.)

This second kind of writing is called *man'yōgana*, literally "phonetic writing (*kana*) of the Myriad-Leaf type", because the most famous document exemplifying it is the *Man'yōshū* or "Myriad-Leaf Collection", a late +8c anthology of poetry. Since each Chinese graph stood for a syllable, and Japanese words were of the CVCVCV... type, in *man'yōgana* a graph would stand for a CV pairing (ignoring any final consonant in the Chinese syllable). Thus one Japanese word would be represented in *man'yōgana* by a minimum of one but in most cases more than one Chinese graph.

The principle of *man'yōgana* writing may have been devised in response to the problem of Japanese grammar-words which had no obvious equivalents in the very different grammar of Chinese. But once the principle was established, an ordinary lexical word was often written in *man'yōgana* rather than with a *kun*. For instance, the first *Man'yōshū* poem spells the word /fukuʃi/ "trowel" as 布久思, Ch. /pu^{4}-tʃiou^{3}-sɯ^{1}/, "cloth-long.time-thought". To quote Miller (1967: 98) again:

> The method of writing a given word in any particular instance would depend on scribal preference, the amount of empty space available for inscribing a given text [because *man'yōgana* used more graphs per Japanese word than *kun* writing], or other aesthetic factors, and there is ample evidence that the early Japanese scribes took considerable pleasure in the possibilities for elegant graphic variation which the script afforded them.

At this period, a page of Japanese writing would consist of Chinese graphs of which some were intended to be given *kun* readings and others read as *man'yōgana*, with no indication of which was which. Faced with, for instance, a token of 波, Ch. /po^{1}/ "wave", the Japanese reader simply had to work out from context that Japanese /nami/ "wave" did not make sense and the graph must therefore be intended as the topic marker /wa/ (or vice versa). If the topic marker /wa/ were always written with 波 rather than with any of the other graphs whose Chinese pronunciations were roughly similar, then it might have been fairly easy to take 波 automatically as topic-marker except on the rare occasions where "wave" was appropriate. But the many homophones in Chinese and the different sound patterns of the two languages (together with the attitudes sketched in the above quotation) meant that the system was much less predictable than this.

Sometimes the scribes left readers to fill in for themselves items that were relatively unimportant or hard to write with Chinese graphs, as suggested for the first *the* in our hypothetical transcription of "The bear killed the man". Thus, in the first line of poem 255 of the *Man'yōshū*, which runs /tōzuma no koko ni araneba/, "because of my distant love's not being here", the genitive particle /no/ is omitted and the reader has to fill it in from his knowledge of the language – though in the next line the same Japanese word is written with the *kun* 之, a Chinese genitive particle pronounced /tʂɯ^1/, and we have already seen that on other occasions it was written with a *man'yōgana* graph. It may be that /no/ was omitted in the line quoted because Chinese would not include a genitive marker in a comparable construction; or this may have been a random decision by the scribe.

* * *

So far the discussion has proceeded as if the spoken Japanese language remained independent of Chinese, so the only issue facing Japanese writers was how to use Chinese script to write a quite un-Chinese language. But Japanese, like Korean, borrowed Chinese vocabulary on a massive scale. Chinese plays something like the same role vis-à-vis Japanese as Greek, Latin, and Norman French between them play vis-à-vis English: many words came into Japanese from Chinese along with the cultural institutions to which they refer, as English acquired words like *plaintiff, chase, dinner* when the Conquest introduced Norman law, amusements, eating habits, and the like into England, but also when the Japanese needed to coin new terms subsequently they automatically resorted to Chinese roots as we turn to the roots of Latin and Greek. Commonly a modern technical term will involve the same combination of morphemes in Japanese as in modern Chinese. (Often, the term was first coined by Japanese using Chinese roots, and later borrowed back into Chinese.)

Quite naturally, any word based on Chinese continued to be written with its Chinese graph. This implies that a given graph may be read as a native Japanese ("NJ") form, or alternatively as a Sino-Japanese ("SJ") loan. Readings of the latter kind are called *on* as opposed to *kun*.

Take, for instance, the well-known word /kimono/, "clothing". This is a compound formed from the NJ roots /ki-/ "wear" and /mono/ "thing, stuff". The compound is written with two graphs: 着物. The first corresponds to a rather vague Chinese word /tʃau^{2}/, meaning "to place, put, cause" – the Japanese have used it to represent NJ /ki-/, thinking of "wear" as "put on", evidently. The second graph corresponds to Ch. /u^{4}/ "thing, creature". But both Chinese morphemes also exist as loans in Japanese. The first has the SJ pronunciation /tʃaku/ and occurs for example in the compound 着手 /tʃakuʃu/ literally "put-hand", meaning "to start" (put one's hand to the wheel, as it were) – /ʃu/ likewise being the SJ version of Ch. /ʂou^{3}/ "hand". Similarly, Ch. /u^{4}/ "thing, creature" exists in the SJ guise /butsu/ for instance in the compound 動物 /dōbutsu/ "animal", where /dō/ is the SJ version of Ch. 動 /tuŋ^{4}/ "move" – an animal is a "moving thing". One says that the graph 物 has the *kun* reading /ki-/ and the *on* reading /tʃaku/; 物 has the *kun* reading /mono/ and the *on* reading /butsu/. Likewise, the graph 手 "hand" has a *kun* reading as NJ /te/ "hand", and 動 has a *kun* reading as NJ /ugok-/ "move, run". Notice that nothing in the script tells one to read 着物 as (*kun*) /kimono/ rather than as (*on*) */tʃakubutsu/, or to read 着手 as (*on*) /tʃakuʃu/ rather than as (*kun*) */kite/. The reader just has to know which alternative is right, by virtue of his knowledge of Japanese vocabulary. This sort of problem is non-existent when Chinese script is used to read Chinese, because each graph (with marginal exceptions) then has just one reading.

Because the sound patterns of Japanese and Chinese are very different, SJ morphemes are usually pronounced rather differently from their Chinese originals, whether the comparison is made with Chinese at the period of borrowing (so-called "Middle Chinese") or with modern Chinese. Cf. Chinese /u^{4}/ versus SJ /butsu/, for instance: in Middle Chinese the word was /mwot/ – subsequent Chinese sound changes have removed initial and final consonants, while in Japanese a second vowel was added because/t/ cannot be syllable-final in that language (and then a Japanese sound change converted /tu/ to /tsu/). Some new sounds were introduced into Japanese, for instance a consonant /r/ as an approximation to Chinese /l/, and SJ has preserved some distinctions which Mandarin has since lost. But in many more cases, SJ has eliminated Chinese phonetic contrasts. (All tone distinctions dropped, for instance, since Japanese is not a tone language, and various diphthongs and triphthongs of Chinese were replaced by pure vowels in Japanese.) Remember that Chinese is already a language in which a large number of morphemes are shared out between a small number of distinct syllables. When the effect of Japanizing the pronunciation is added, the result is a truly colossal degree of homophony in the SJ vocabulary.[1]

To illustrate, Figure 42 shows a sample of the different Chinese morphemes which all exist in the (modern, living) Japanese language with the SJ pronunciation /kan/. Each morpheme in this list has a distinct pronunciation even in the phonologically impoverished modern Mandarin variety of Chinese. Each morpheme listed naturally has several Chinese homophones, most of which also exist in Japanese as /kan/, and this list by no means exhausts the range of phonologically distinct Chinese syllables which emerge in Sino-Japanese as /kan/.

With Chinese, although there are very many homophones among morphemes taken singly, two-morpheme compounds are commonly unambiguous; if syllables *XY* form a set expression, usually only one of the various syllables pronounced *X* and one of those pronounced *Y* will fit together as

	Chinese pronunciation	*meaning*	*Japanese pronunciation*
甘	kan^{1}	sweet	kan
感	kan^{3}	be affected	
刊	k^{h}an^{1}	print	
慣	kuan^{4}	be accustomed to	
觀	kuan^{1}	view	
勘	k^{h}an^{4}	investigate	
緩	xuan^{3}	slow	
管	kuan^{3}	tube	
鐶	xuan^{2}	a ring	
歡	xuan^{1}	enjoy	
巻	tʃyan^{4}	a volume	
韓	xan^{2}	Korean	
漢	xan^{4}	Chinese	
etc. etc.			

Figure 42

a recognized compound. With Sino-Japanese even that is not true. To give one example: the disyllable /kankō/ is ambiguous as between all of the SJ compound words listed in Figure 43 (among others).

Some homophones in Figure 43 will doubtless be distinguished from context. But there are other cases where context could hardly help. For instance, /kagaku/ can be either 科學 "science" (Chinese /k^{h}ɤ^{1} ʃye^{2}/) or 化學 "chemistry" (Chinese /xua^{4} ʃye^{2}/). If the Chinese language had developed this degree of homophony in the course of its evolution, it might have taken measures of one sort or another to solve the problem (as did happen when single-morpheme words in Old Chinese were replaced by two-morpheme compounds in the modern language). But Japanese is, as it were, at the mercy of Chinese – from the point of view of Japanese society, Chinese is the authoritative source both of non-native morphemes and, to a large extent, of the approved ways of compounding them. If the result of adapting this stock of roots to Japanese habits of pronunciation is a vocabulary which is extremely ambiguous in its spoken form, that is just bad luck for the Japanese.

There are isolated parallels in English. It is unfortunate for us that the Romans used words for "mouth" and "ear", *ōris* and *auris*, which (though they sounded quite different in Latin) have fallen together in the confusing pair of English homophones *oral* and *aural*. Life might be simpler for us

<table>
<tr><th></th><th>Chinese pronunciation</th><th>meaning</th><th>Japanese pronunciation</th></tr>
<tr><td>甘汞</td><td>kan^{1}-kuŋ^{3}</td><td>mercurous chloride</td><td rowspan="8">kankō</td></tr>
<tr><td>感光</td><td>kan^{3}-kuaŋ^{1}</td><td>expose (photographically)</td></tr>
<tr><td>刊行</td><td>k^{h}an^{1}-ʃiŋ^{2}</td><td>publication</td></tr>
<tr><td>慣行</td><td>kuan^{4}-ʃiŋ^{2}</td><td>habitual</td></tr>
<tr><td>觀光</td><td>kuan^{1}-kuaŋ^{1}</td><td>sightseeing</td></tr>
<tr><td>勘考</td><td>k^{h}an^{4}-k^{h}au^{3}</td><td>consider</td></tr>
<tr><td>緩行</td><td>xuan^{3}-ʃiŋ^{2}</td><td>run slow</td></tr>
<tr><td colspan="3">etc.</td></tr>
</table>

Figure 43

if we decided to use, say, *gaur-* rather than *aur-* as the root for "ear" in technical vocabulary. But we treat Latin as a given, so that we are not willing to distort it and instead accept the awkward consequences of using the genuine roots. In English the *aural/oral* pair is a one-off; in Japanese the situation is multiplied thousands of times over. In consequence, the logographic nature of Chinese script is even more important for the Japanese than for the Chinese.

* * *

So far we have seen that many different Chinese syllables may correspond to the same SJ pronunciation. But the situation is more complicated than that. Chinese pronunciation changed over the centuries, and Chinese vocabulary was borrowed into Japanese in a series of separate waves. In each wave of borrowings, the Japanese pronunciation of a given morpheme would imitate the then-current Chinese pronunciation. Therefore there are different "layers" of *on*-readings for Chinese graphs. In other words a single graph, having just one pronunciation in any given dialect of Chinese, will often have more than one *on*-reading (as well as one or possibly more *kun* readings) in Japanese.

The point may be illustrated by analogy. Suppose that Latin had been written with a logographic script; then, say, the adjective *masculus* might have been written ♂. *Masculus* evolved by various sound changes into French *mâle*. We have both versions of the root in English, the Latin version in e.g. *masculine*, *emasculate*, and the French version in *male*. So, if we had borrowed a logographic rather than phonographic script from the Romans, we would be writing both the *mascul-* of *masculine* and the word *male* as ♂; and we might use this graph also for the native Germanic morpheme *groom* in *bridegroom*. Then:

> ♂ = /mæskjəl/ would be "Roman *on*"
> ♂ = /meil/ would be "Norman *on*"
> ♂ = /grum/ would be "*kun*".

The English reader would have to learn that < ♂-ine >, for example, is read with Roman *on*, and that < ♂ > as an independent word is usually read with Norman *on* but is given its *kun* value when it occurs as a noun in the context of weddings.

Japanese has three layers of *on*: in chronological order they are called *go'on*, *kan'on*, and *tōsō'on*. (*Go*, *Kan*, and *Tōsō* are Chinese proper names, akin to "Roman" and "Norman" in my analogy.)

Kan'on is the "default" layer: most SJ compounds use *kan'on* pronunciations, and conventionally any recent coinage will use the *kan'on* versions of Chinese roots. *Go'on* pronunciations occur in words that were borrowed particularly early, before the +7c; since the first important cultural export from China to Japan was Buddhism, most *go'on* words were originally Buddhist terms. Conversely, *tōsō'on* readings (which are the rarest) occur in a group of words that entered Japan much later than the main borrowing wave, in the 14c, and many of these words are terms used by late-emerging Buddhist sects such as Zen.

That might sound as though complications arising from different layers of *on* are of little practical significance nowadays other than for people specially interested in Buddhism. But words which have entered a language do not remain neatly penned up in the thematic containers in which they were imported. Many Latin-derived English words came into the language in connexion with Christian theology, for instance *substance* originally denoted what is common to the three persons of the Trinity. But a 21c English speaker who described foam-rubber as a spongy substance would be startled to be told he was engaging in theological discourse. The situation is similar in Japanese. For instance, 無 "without" is *kan'on* /bu/, as in e.g. 無事 literally "without business", SJ /budʒi/ "peace, quiet", and 限 "limit" is *kan'on* /kan/; but it happens that 無限 "without limit, infinite" is pronounced as *go'on* /mugen/ rather than *kan'on* */bukan/, because this compound entered Japanese as part of the technical Buddhist term "infinite compassion". Nowadays, however, /mugen/ is simply the ordinary mathematical term for "infinite", and a caterpillar tractor is a "*mugen*-track vehicle". A Japanese reading the graphs 無限 has to know that they are to be pronounced /mugen/ rather than */bukan/; nothing in the script indicates this.[2]

In many cases it is not clear whether the *go'on* v. *kan'on* distinction ever had anything to do with Buddhism. Thus it happens that 定 "fix" is *kan'on* /tei/ in 定價 /teika/ "fixed price" but *go'on* /dʒō/ in 定連 /dʒōren/ "regular customer"; 說 "discourse" is *kan'on* /zei/ in 遊說 /jūzei/ "campaign speech" but *go'on* /setsu/ in 社說 /ʃasetsu/ "editorial"; and so on.

A few graphs have *on* readings of all three layers. Thus 行, standing for a Chinese morpheme with a broad range of meanings covering "move", "practise", hence "a practice", "a commercial firm", in Japanese has the *kun* reading /ik-/, the ordinary NJ root for "to go", but it also has the following *on* readings:

- *go'on* /gjō/ in e.g. 修行 (literally "cultivate-practice"): /ʃugjō/ "training". This word is read in *go'on* because it originally referred to ascetic Buddhist training disciplines, but nowadays it is just the ordinary word for "training".
- *kan'on* /kō/ in e.g. 銀行 (literally "silver-firm"): /ginkō/ "a bank".
- *tōsō'on* /an/ in e.g. 行脚 (literally "go-foot"): /angja/, originally a Buddhist pilgrimage but nowadays just "a walking tour".

All three pronunciations derive by different routes from the same Middle Chinese syllable /hæŋ/.

The system of alternative readings for graphs, apart from being complicated in itself, throws another difficulty in the path of literacy acquisition, because it greatly reduces the mnemonic value of the phonetic elements of compound graphs. *Kun* readings of Chinese graphs offer another refutation of the suggestion by scholars such as John DeFrancis (p. 184 above) that all writing is essentially phonographic: it may be true for Chinese that phonetic elements give hints at graph pronunciations, though the hints are patchy, but graphs are chosen for native Japanese roots by reference to meaning rather than sound, so their Chinese phonetic elements tell one nothing at all about their Japanese *kun* pronunciation. Yet, when a Japanese child learns to read and write, the earliest pronunciation he encounters for a graph will tend to be its *kun* reading, because most of the commonest Japanese words belong to the native stock. And even among *on* readings, the process of Japanizing Chinese sounds, together with the fact of borrowing from different stages of Chinese, disturb the already shaky similarities among the original Chinese pronunciations of graphs sharing a common phonetic element. The signific elements of compound graphs are probably about as useful to Japanese as they are to Chinese; but significs are drawn from a small class while phonetic elements are very diverse, so most of the "information" (in the mathematical sense) is concentrated in the phonetic elements of compound graphs.

* * *

Thus far we have considered only the Japanese use of Chinese graphs in their original form. It is time now to look at the process by which the Japanese developed categories of written symbols of their own, distinct from Chinese graphs.

The early *man'yōgana* system of spelling out NJ words with Chinese graphs standing for their phonetic values, as an alternative to the *kun* system, in due course evolved in two respects.

First, the particular graphs used for *man'yōgana* were standardized. In the early days one used any graph whose Chinese pronunciation was roughly suitable. Scribes prided themselves on varying their *man'yōgana*, and even on using complex and rare rather than simple graphs when either would do. Later, a tendency arose always to use one graph or just a small range of alternatives for a given Japanese syllable. Secondly, the forms of graphs used for *man'yōgana* were greatly simplified, which served two purposes: it made them quicker to write (which was useful in view of the fact that the system required several graphs per word), but – more important – it created a clear visual distinction between symbols used purely for phonographic values ("*kana*") and graphs in their original form used with *kun* or *on* values.

What happened ultimately was that two sets of syllabic signs evolved, comparable to our minuscules and capitals (though, while all our minuscule/capital pairs derive from common ancestral forms, in some cases the sign for a given syllable in the two Japanese syllabaries derive from two different Chinese graphs). The two syllabaries are called *hiragana* ("plain *kana*"), which consist of simplified cursive outlines of whole Chinese graphs, and *katakana* ("partial *kana*") which consist of carefully written small distinctive elements of the original graphs. Chinese graphs in their full form are called *kanji*, by contrast with either type of *kana*. By the late 19c the two syllabaries had been standardized so that each contains one and only one distinct symbol for each syllable represented (49 symbols in all, in each syllabary). In handwriting people still sometimes use non-standard alternative versions of some *kana*, but such symbols are never now printed. Figure 44 shows the derivation of a few of the symbols in the two syllabaries.

For much of the period over which these *kana* systems have been used, they were slightly "incomplete"; notably, they did not mark voicing in obstruent consonants – /b d g z/ were not distinguished from /h t k s/. (Modern Japanese /h/ derives from an earlier */p/.) This was natural, since in native Japanese most voiced obstruents were merely conditioned variants of their voiceless counterparts, though the occurrence of voicing was not entirely predictable. (Voice *was* fully distinctive in SJ words, but these were always written in *kanji*.) In recent centuries, though, a diacritic has consistently been used to mark voice in obstruents (and another to distinguish modern /p/ from /h/); the two syllabaries are now fully "complete" as representations of the segmental phonology of a slightly premodern version of spoken Japanese. (They ignore the pitch accent which is marginally distinctive in Japanese, and my transcriptions likewise omit this.) Devices have even been added to allow *kana* to represent sounds and sound-sequences (such as /v/, /ti/) which are never found in Japanese but do occur in words borrowed from English.

	Katakana		Man'yōgana			Hiragana
i	イ	←	伊 i "he"	以 i "by"	→	い
ro	ロ	←	呂 Ro (a place-name)		→	ろ
ha	ハ	←	八 hatʃi "eight"	波 ha "wave"	→	は
tʃi	チ	←	千 tʃi "thousand"	知 tʃi "know"	→	ち
nu	ヌ	←	奴 nu "slave"		→	ぬ
wo	ヲ	←	乎 wo (question particle)	遠 won "far"	→	を

Figure 44

In modern Japanese writing, *kanji* in their various *kun* and *on* readings are used for the lexical morphemes (proper and common nouns, verb roots, etc.) of the NJ and SJ vocabularies. *Hiragana* are used to spell grammatical words akin to English *of*, *the*, and the inflexions of inflected words. *Katakana* are used for words borrowed from foreign languages (i.e. not from Chinese), for foreign names, and sometimes as a replacement for *hiragana* in very formal documents, or as an equivalent to our italics. The names *Tchaikovsky* and *Pretoria*, for instance, are written in Japanese as the following *katakana* sequences:[3]

チャイコフスキー < tʃi-*ja*-i-ko-fu-su-ki-: >
プレトリア < pu-re-to-ri-a >

(The use of *katakana* to spell foreign words is one of the few respects – but an important one – in which Japanese writing is more efficient than Chinese.) Either kind of *kana* may also be used to spell out the kinds of word that would normally be written in *kanji*, but where the relevant *kanji* are rare and have been given up.

Hiragana spellings are often slightly archaic; Japanese script, like many others, has preserved a phonographic system which has not always fully kept pace with historical sound changes. Thus the direct-object suffix /o/ is written < wo > rather than < o >, though the sound-sequence /wo/ never occurs in present-day Japanese; separate symbols are used for < di > and < zi > although these syllables have now merged as /dʒi/; and so on. Until recently *hiragana* spellings were much more archaic than they are now; recent *hiragana* usage is very much more phonetically "rational" than English spelling.

Hiragana used to spell out inflexions are called *okurigana*, "escorting *kana*". Broadly they begin where the root part of an inflected word ends. However, since each *kana* symbol stands for a CV combination, if the last phoneme of the root is a consonant it must be included in the *okurigana*; a *kana* for a simple vowel can represent only a vowel that has no consonant before it. Thus the NJ root /ajum-/ "to step" is written with the *kun* 步 (Ch. /pu^4/, "a pace"), but forms such as /ajumu/ "steps", /ajumanai/ "does not step", and so forth are written:

> 歩む STEP-mu *not* *歩う STEP-u
> 歩まない STEP-ma-na-i *not* *歩あない STEP-a-na-i

This point is an advantage to the reader; by giving the last consonant of the correct reading of the root, the *okurigana* may eliminate other potential readings. The graph 步 is ambiguous between two NJ values – it can also represent the near-synonym /aruk-/ "go on foot". Only the *okurigana* differentiate between the written forms of pairs such as /aruku/ "goes on foot" and /ajumu/ "steps":

> 歩く STEP/GO.ON.FOOT -ku versus 歩む STEP/GO.ON.FOOT -mu

(The same *kanji* also has two *on* readings, /ho/ and /bu/, but these cannot occur in inflected forms and are therefore irrelevant to the point under discussion.) Cases like this, where the first consonant of the *okurigana* is the sole clue to disambiguation, are not too frequent, but the information must often be helpful as one clue among others to enable readers to arrive at the correct reading of a *kanji*.

Like Chinese, Japanese has traditionally been written in vertical columns beginning from the top right, and (unlike in China) this has never been formally given up. However, horizontal writing has the same advantage for the Japanese as for the Chinese in terms of facilitating inclusion of Western words and phrases. Technical material, and most schoolbooks, are now printed horizontally; general-interest books such as novels, more commonly vertically. The trend is clearly away from vertical towards horizontal writing, partly because the latter is the default setting for Japanese word-processor programs – they can be switched to vertical writing, but people tend not to alter the default.

As an illustration of the various aspects of modern Japanese script, Figure 45 shows the written form of the sentence /itsumo doitsugo no hon o jonde iru jō desu/, "He always seems to be reading German books". (A word-by-word rendering might be "Always a-matter-of-be-reading-book-of-German exists" – the subject "he" is understood, and, because Japanese word-order rules are often the converse of English, the items I have linked with hyphens occur in the reverse order in the Japanese sentence.)

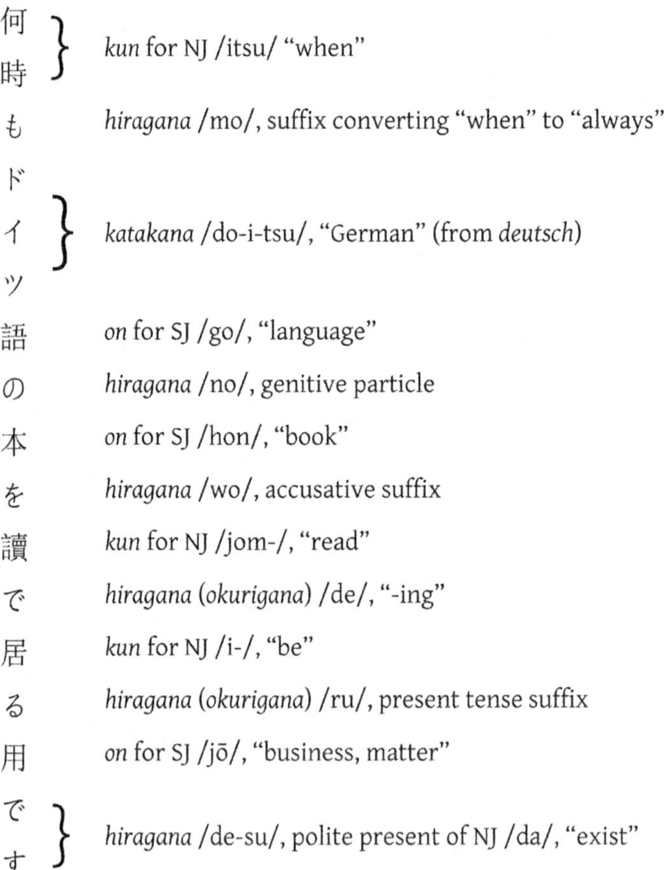

何時 } kun for NJ /itsu/ "when"
も hiragana /mo/, suffix converting "when" to "always"
ドイツ } katakana /do-i-tsu/, "German" (from deutsch)
語 on for SJ /go/, "language"
の hiragana /no/, genitive particle
本 on for SJ /hon/, "book"
を hiragana /wo/, accusative suffix
讀 kun for NJ /jom-/, "read"
で hiragana (okurigana) /de/, "-ing"
居 kun for NJ /i-/, "be"
る hiragana (okurigana) /ru/, present tense suffix
用 on for SJ /jō/, "business, matter"
です } hiragana /de-su/, polite present of NJ /da/, "exist"

Figure 45

Although Japanese as an inflecting language has a clear concept of multi-morpheme words (unlike Chinese), its orthography has no formal method of marking word boundaries. Graphs of the various categories are simply written one below another (one after another in horizontal script), spaced equally. But in this respect the reader is better placed than in the Chinese case, because the alternation of *kanji* with *kana* goes some way to showing the grouping of graphs into words. Broadly speaking, Japanese roots never have prefixes, only suffixes, so a transition from *hiragana* to *kanji* must represent a word boundary.

Note the following points about individual elements in Figure 45. Chinese, unlike Japanese and English, has no one word for "when" but expresses the concept as "what time"; so the simple NJ root /itsu/ is written with two *kanji*. In the first of the three *katakana* graphs, the double tick is the voicing diacritic which converts < to > to < do >. We have already seen that the *hiragana* spelling < wo > for the object suffix is archaic – but it is convenient to have a distinctive graphic shape for this very common grammatical unit. In the word /jonde/, the voicing of /d/ is automatic after the nasal consonant of the root, but since the modern *kana* system has been equipped with a means of indicating voicing it is used even where it is predictable. (Also in that word, the /m/ of the root becomes /n/ automatically before the alveolar suffix, but since the root is written logographically this variation is ignored.)

Three of the forms written with *kanji* in Figure 45 – /itsu/ "when", the verb root /i-/ "be", and the noun /jō/ "matter" – might alternatively be written in *hiragana*. They are all so common that they are perceived as falling on the borderline between lexical and grammatical elements. We shall see that the propensity of writers to use *kanji* or *kana* has varied at different times.

* * *

The complications in the script which I have discussed so far are essentially difficulties for reader rather than for writer. They involve alternative ways of translating a given graph into a morpheme of the language. For a Japanese, who knows his language as a repertory of possibilities, the problems posed by these alternatives will often be less great than my discussion may have suggested. In the first place he will commonly know that a particular morpheme-compound is a frequent word of the language, while a compound corresponding to alternative values of the same graphs does not exist. And the general structure of the language supplies useful clues. For instance, SJ words do not inflect, so *on* readings for a graph can be discarded immediately if it is followed by *okurigana* (though the converse does not hold – a word without *okurigana* may be either SJ or NJ). A single *kanji* standing as a word in isolation is more likely to require a *kun* than an *on* reading, since SJ morphemes occur mainly in two-root compounds, though this is only a tendency rather than an absolute rule.

However, parallel to the problems facing the reader there are also analogous problems facing the writer, who often has to make choices between alternative graphs which can each represent the same linguistic form.

In one sense, of course, this is already obvious. If one thinks of the writer's task as being to convert words considered as sequences of phonemes into written marks, we have seen that many Japanese syllables or short syllable-sequences will correspond to numerous different SJ and/or NJ homophones, each of which will have its own written representation. But that would be an artificial and limited way of conceiving the activity of writing, in any language. A writer is aware of the identity at all linguistic levels of the units he is recording; he knows their meanings as well as their sounds. So far I have given no reason to suppose that a Japanese who knows which meaningful forms of his language he wants to write will be faced with right-or-wrong choices between alternative possibilities. But that is so, for reasons having to do with lack of semantic isomorphism between Japanese and Chinese.

Take for instance the NJ verb root /kae-/. This word is polysemous, analogously to its rough English equivalent "turn" (consider the different senses that word has in "turn back", "turn the page", "turn round", "turn into a handsome Prince"). But in the semantic field covered by Japanese /kae-/, Chinese happens to have a number of more precise words. Accordingly, different shades of meaning of /kae-/ are written with different *kanji*. Taking the simple inflected form /kaeru/, Figure 46 shows some of the possibilities (there are others), with alphabetic transliteration in place of *kana* in order not to burden the Western reader unnecessarily.

1	/kaeru/ = "return home":	歸-ru	(Ch. /kuei^1/)
2	/kaeru/ = "come again, revert":	返-ru	(Ch. /fan^3/)
3	/kaeru/ = "change, vary" (transitive):	變-e-ru	(Ch. /pien^4/)
		代-e-ru	(Ch. /tai^4/)
4	/kaeru/ = "exchange, substitute":	換-e-ru	(Ch. /xuan^4/)
		替-e-ru	(Ch. /t^{h}i^4/)

etc.

Figure 46

In Chinese there are small meaning-differences between /tai^{4}/ "substitute", /xuan^{4}/ "exchange", and /t^{h}i^{4}/ "act on behalf of", but it seems that the range of meaning of Japanese /kae-/ overlaps only with the common semantic ground between these Chinese words, or perhaps that these particular semantic distinctions were originally felt by Japanese writers to be too small to maintain. The semantic distinctions between these three words as a group and Chinese /kuei^{1}/, /fan^{3}/, and /pien^{4}/, on the other hand, are systematically observed in written Japanese even though they are not reflected in spoken (native) Japanese. (Furthermore, although three of the *kanji* are interchangeable with respect to their *kun* reading /kae-/, each of them also has at least one *on* reading and these are of course distinct, non-equivalent SJ morphemes.)

The case of /kaeru/ in fact includes a special (not uncommon) complication. Although all the four Japanese words quoted are identical in pronunciation and involve the same NJ root, they are not morphologically identical: 3 and 4 include a transitivity infix /-e-/ (note that the English glosses are transitive for these cases but intransitive for 1 and 2). It happens that by the rules of Japanese phonology /kae-e-/ becomes /ka-e-/, so that with this particular root the infix makes no net difference to the pronunciation. However, the /-e-/ of 3 and 4 is this derivational infix, and is accordingly represented in the *okurigana*, while the /-e-/ of 1 and 2 is part of the root /kae-/ and is therefore covered by the *kanji*.

Not only may a given *kanji* have a range of different *on* readings because of the different waves of borrowing from Chinese, and a given NJ root have a range of different *kanji* writings because of the lack of semantic isomorphism between the two languages; this lack of semantic isomorphism also has the consequence that a single *kanji* may have a range of several different NJ, *kun* values (creating further problems for the reader).

Take, for instance, the graph 上 (Ch. /ʂaŋ^{4}/ "on, top", /ʂaŋ^{3}/ "rise" – these are etymologically the same morpheme, the tone difference is one of the rare presumed relics of earlier Chinese inflexion mentioned in note 6, p. 191). This graph has the *on* readings /dʒō/ "first, excellent" and /ʃō/ "upper part, government"; but it also has the *kun* readings shown in Figure 47.

(In the last pair of words in Figure 47 the NJ root is the same, and *okurigana* are being used to indicate derivational morphology in a slightly different way from the /kaeru/ case. The transitive verb /ageru/ is morphologically /aga-/ + transitivity-marker /-e-/ + inflexion /-ru/, with the final vowel of the root /aga-/ having dropped before /-e-/; /ageru/ is thus

上	ue	"on"
上	kami	"top"
上-ru	noboru	"rise"
上-ga-ru	agaru	"go up"
上-ge-ru	ageru	"raise"

Figure 47

naturally spelled with *okurigana* /-ge-ru/. Although the /-ga-/ of /agaru/ is wholly within the root, it is included in the *okurigana* for that word in order to differentiate it positively from its transitive counterpart. The complete rules for using *okurigana* are far too complicated to go into here; Pye (1971) quoted an authoritative statement as occupying 64 pages of a book published by the Ministry of Education.)

Of the words in Figure 47, /ue/ and /kami/ can be written only as 上; and context alone will show whether this graph is to be read as /ue/ or as /kami/, since neither word inflects. But /noboru/ can alternatively be written 登-ru (Ch. /təŋ^1/ "ascend") or 昇-ru (Ch. /ʂəŋ^1/ "arise"); while /agaru/ can alternatively be written 揚-ga-ru (Ch. /jaŋ^2/ "lift, display") or 舉-ga-ru (Ch. /tʃy^3/ "pick up") (and /ageru/ can have either of these latter writings with the appropriate change of *okurigana*). When these NJ roots are used as independent words, the context of the sentence will determine which of the alternative *kanji* is appropriate – and compounds involving these roots will use whichever *kanji* fits the meaning of the compound – *in terms of the original Chinese senses of the* kanji. So NJ /ageʃio/ "rising tide" is written 上-ge-潮 (the latter graph being *kun* for /ʃio/ "tide") rather than *揚-ge-潮, because one does not lift the tide up with one's hands; conversely, NJ /agemono/ "fried food" (literally, "lifted stuff") is written 揚-ge-物 (the latter graph, as we have already seen, being *kun* for /mono/ "thing"), not *上-ge-物, because East Asian frying involves tumbling the pieces of food in the wok with a spatula, and they will not jump up of their own accord.

In other words, to write Japanese correctly it is not enough to know the range of correct transcriptions for the various forms of the spoken Japanese language; one also needs to know the semantic distinctions which obtained between those graphs in another language, Chinese, from which they were borrowed, although these semantic distinctions are irrelevant to spoken Japanese.

It is true that a Japanese might not see things that way. The axiom of Western linguistics according to which a language is primarily a system of spoken forms, and writing is a subsidiary medium serving to render spoken language visible, is very difficult for an East Asian to accept. To speakers of languages as full of homophones as Chinese and Japanese, it seems obvious that speech is a highly imperfect, vague and ambiguous reflection of written language. So a Japanese would probably deny that *kanji* provide alternative ways of writing the same word. He would perceive, for example, "/aga/ = 上", "/aga/ = 揚", and "/aga/ = 舉" as three different words that sound the same and have closely related meanings. But historically, at least, he would be wrong.

* * *

We have seen that, for the leaders of Japanese society during much of its history, script complexity was to some extent a positive virtue rather than a pure negative. Perhaps that was not always so, but in any case, before the mid-19c the country was so insulated from the outside world that Japanese had little awareness that things could be different. Following the opening-up to the West which occurred in 1853, many Japanese began to see their script as problematic. One extreme response was by Viscount Mori Arinori, a senior diplomat and later Minister of Education, who proposed in 1874 that not just the script but the Japanese language as a whole should be abandoned, in favour of speaking and writing English.

Needless to say, that did not happen. But a number of smaller-scale measures have been adopted in order to reduce the complications of Japanese script.

One device which long predates 1853 but came into much more widespread use after that date was the addition of tiny *kana* graphs to the right of (or, with horizontal writing, above) *kanji* to resolve which of alternative readings was intended in context – such kana are called *furigana*, "nudging kana". Figure 48 displays a page from a novel printed in 1908; in this case every *kanji* word or phrase, even very common ones, is supplemented with *furigana*. Often, *furigana* were reserved for more obscure *kanji*; but after the Second World War, as education levels rose, even that use of *furigana* seemed to decline, so that for a while it looked as if they were destined to be used only in books for children. However, continuing use of *furigana* in documents for adults was officially endorsed in 1981. In recent times *furigana* have sometimes come to be used in a new way: rather than indicating the Japanese pronunciation of *kanji*, they spell out an English translation to help the reader identify the intended meaning (on current uses of *furigana* see e.g. Schreiber 2013).

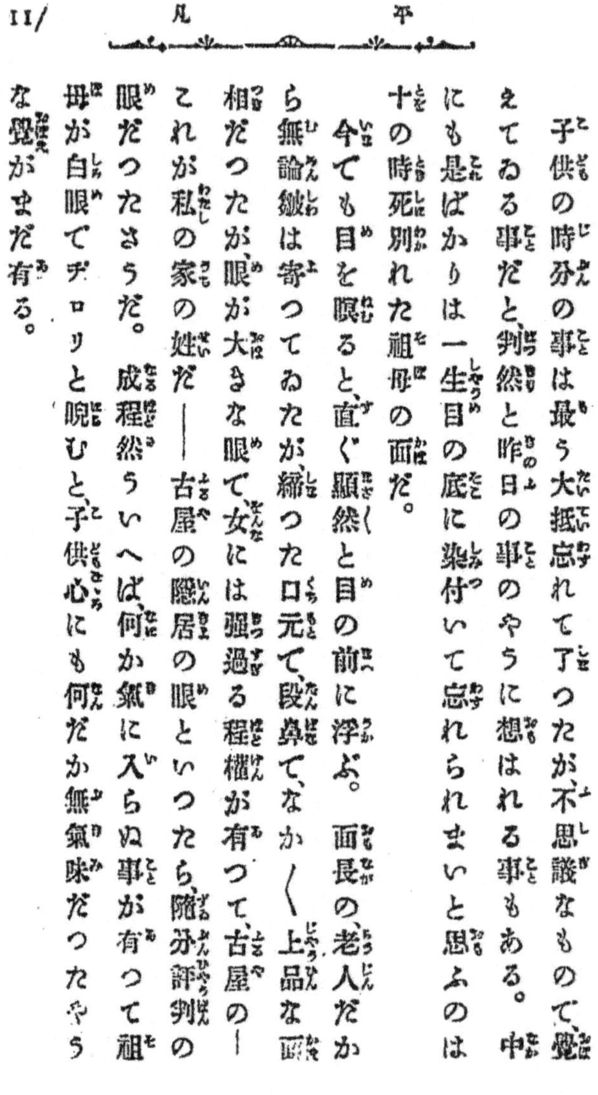

11/ 平凡

子供の時分の事は最う大抵忘れて了つたが、不思議なもので、覺えてゐる事だと、判然と昨日の事のやうに想はれる事もある。中にも是ばかりは一生目の底に染付いて忘れられまいと思ふのは十の時死別れた祖母の面だ。

今でも目を眠ると、直ぐ顯然と目の前に浮ぶ。面長の、老人だから無論皺は寄つてゐたが、縮つた口元で、段鼻で、なか〳〵上品な面相だつたが、眼が大きな眼で、女には强過る程權が有つて、古屋の—これが私の家の姓だ—古屋の隱居の眼といつたら、隨分評判の眼だつたさうだ。成程然ういへば、何か氣に入らぬ事が有つて祖母が白眼でヂロリと睨むと、子供心にも何だか無氣味だつたやうな覺がまだ有る。

Figure 48

As in the case of China, the Japanese too have simplified some of their graphs in terms of number of strokes (the Japanese did this earlier than the Chinese, and a given graph has often been simplified in different ways in the two countries). I suggested in Chapter 10 that this sort of orthographic reform offers little real advantage, and the Japanese case seems particularly futile, since the changes in shape are often quite slight – more akin to differences between two roman typefaces than between two alphabets.

The most important reform measure was the promulgation in 1946 of a limited list of only 1850 *kanji* with their approved *kun* and *on* readings, with a view to discouraging the continued use of other *kanji*, and of unusual readings of the approved *kanji*. If it had proved possible to make this cutback stick, it would have been a large simplification. A prewar Japanese newspaper printing works stocked about seven to eight thousand *kanji*, and the average educated reader was reckoned to be familiar with about five thousand of them. Newspapers in particular do aim to limit themselves to the approved list; if they need to print a lexical morpheme whose *kanji* is not on the list, either they add a *katakana* transliteration in brackets, or even give only *kana* instead of the *kanji*. But virtually all publications other than newspapers and official documents have always gone beyond the approved list of *kanji* to some extent, and short supplementary lists have periodically been issued of "rehabilitated" *kanji* that were missing from the 1946 list. Even publications which try to limit themselves to the approved *kanji* have to go beyond them for proper names, because many Japanese personal and place names use *kanji* not on the approved lists. (It is unthinkable that a Japanese should not be able to write his name in *kanji*.) In practice, it seems that the approved list and its supplements function largely as a well-defined goal for Japanese schooling.

It is often said that the policy of reducing the number of *kanji* was influenced by the postwar American occupying authorities, but this seems not to be true. Possibly more relevant was the fact that, during the Second World War, various accidents were caused by army recruits lacking enough education to read some of the *kanji* appearing in weapons manuals – cf. Seeley 1995. And pressure came from the newspaper publishing industry, for whom stocking a full range of *kanji* was an economic burden.

The most significant new factor influencing Japanese script has been the introduction of word-processing technology. Contrary to what Western readers might perhaps imagine, this has had a powerful effect of increasing the use of *kanji* at the expense of phonographic writing. There are two reasons for that. In the first place, if someone writing by hand was unsure of the precise shape of an unusual and complicated *kanji*, the line of least resistance was to write the word in *kana* instead; but the computer remembers each *kanji* shape perfectly, so the writer only needs to recognize it offered on-screen rather than to pull every graphic detail out of his memory. Also, stocking a large range of "sorts" was expensive in the days of letterpress printing, but with modern information technology it makes little difference whether an electronic dictionary lists 1850 or many thousands of graphs, so the dictionaries available to Japanese word-processing programs typically include a comprehensive range of *kanji*.

Thus, all in all, although modern times have seen a modest containment of the tangled luxuriance of Japanese orthography, it is implausible that this could be taken much further in the future. And certainly, while the spoken Japanese language remains essentially what it is now, moving to a phonographic script would be utterly impractical.

* * *

Finally, in case any readers feel inclined to challenge my view that Japanese script is outstandingly difficult, I might briefly draw attention to a factor which could equally well have been discussed in Chapter 9.

Throughout this book so far I have been tacitly assuming that the ability to identify the individual graphs in a piece of writing in a given script can be taken for granted, and that what is interesting is the relationship between graphs and language. Even for alphabetic scripts this assumption is sometimes unwarranted; we all know people whose handwriting is barely legible. Nevertheless, before printing was invented clarity and regularity of letter formation was an ideal that Western scribes aimed at even if they did not always achieve it. The "best" models of writing were the monumental capitals of inscriptions on classical buildings. And now that printing is commonplace, messy handwriting matters little in practice because handwritten documents play a minor role in our lives.

For China and Japan, on the other hand, that tacit assumption is seriously misleading. Calligraphy is a major (perhaps the leading) art form, and the aesthetic standards applicable to writing do not value regularity; on the contrary, good writing is "alive" and spontaneous – and therefore irregular. (On the aesthetics of Chinese writing see Chiang 1973.) Printing is a useful technology but, precisely because of its mechanical regularity, has no aesthetic value (there is no parallel in East Asia to the interest some Westerners have in fine typography). Lettering produced for display, say on a painted signboard, which in Europe will commonly imitate monumental capitals, is in East Asia more likely to simulate freehand brush-and-ink work.

Traditionally, to write neatly to an educated man could actually be seen as insulting, since it suggested that he was thought incapable of reading cursive forms. Normal handwriting (what the Chinese call *xíng shū*, "running style") is some way removed from the neatness of print, fusing what are printed as separate dots and strokes into continuous, smooth motions of the brush (or, now, pen); but it is not too hard to "see" the printed shapes below the surface forms of *xíng shū*. The most admired calligraphy, though – not merely for artistic purposes but for everyday use – is so-called *cǎo shū*, "grass style", which simplifies so radically that graphs involving a dozen or two dozen strokes in their regular printed forms may be reduced to a few hasty hints, and it is difficult even to separate the graphs one from another visually. Figure 49, for instance, shows a page from a Japanese copybook published in the 18c or early 19c as a model for official correspondence. (The degree of cursiveness it represents is far from extreme, and it is in no way obsolete.)

The ability to read grass-style handwriting is a study in itself, one which is mastered by very few Western Orientalists. Yet only provided a Japanese can identify the specific graphs that are lurking behind the visual jumble

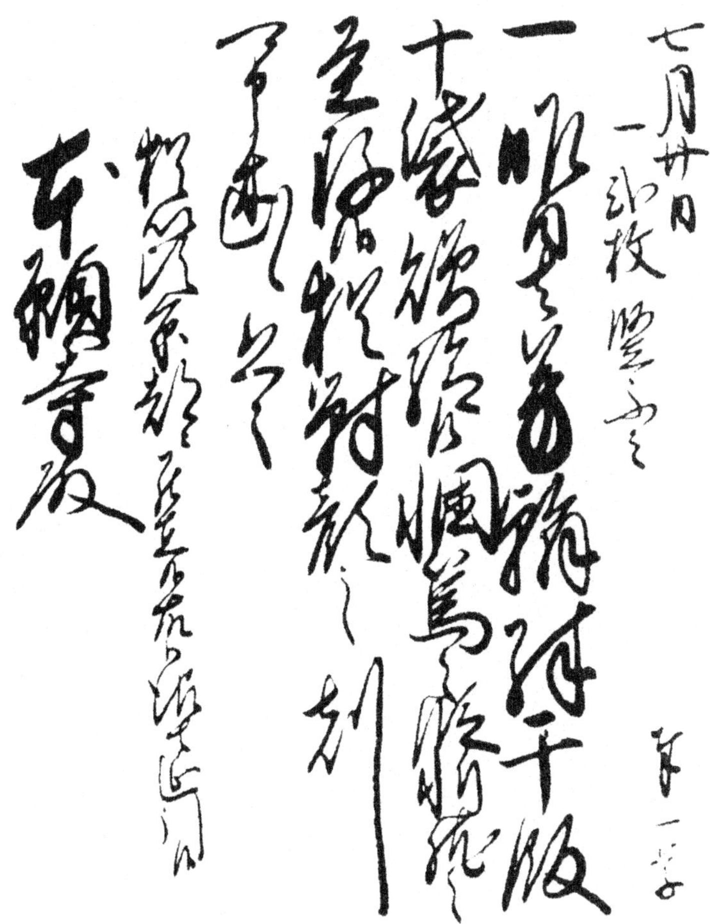

Figure 49

of a page such as Figure 49 will he be in a position to begin the complex process of decipherment described in this chapter.

Notes

1. According to Hannas (1997: 184), the 4775 Sino-Japanese morphemes listed in one standard dictionary have just 319 distinct Japanese pronunciations between them.
2. One cannot even rely on both elements of a compound word representing the same "layer". Usually they do, but there are plenty of words like English *television* (which mixes Greek with Latin) or *supergrass* (Latin + native Germanic).
3. In native Japanese the phoneme /tʃ/ occurs only before /i/, therefore there are no single *kana* symbols for /tʃV/ where V is any other vowel. Instead such a syllable is written with a full-size <tʃi> followed by <jV> in a smaller size (indicated here by italics). The mark transliterated with a colon makes the preceding vowel long. In the word for *Pretoria*, the small circle with the first symbol changes its value from /fu/ to /pu/.

12 Writing systems and information technology

If, in the English-speaking world, one raises the topic of interactions between written language and information technology, most people's immediate response is about the abbreviated spellings used by youngsters in text messages and the like, and the possibility that these may spread into general written usage. Every now and then one encounters a newspaper report about some group of schoolchildren who are indignant because their written work has been marked down for spellings such as < c u l8er > for *see you later*, and who complain that the teachers are dinosaurs out of step with the realities of 21c life. Commentators who identify with the teachers, on the other hand, express horror at the prospect of orthographic anarchy being loosed on the language. Michael Russell of the Queen's English Society commented about text messaging that "The English language is being beaten up, civilisation is in danger of crumbling" (quoted in Doward 2004).

All this strikes me as something of a non-issue – Crispin Thurlow (e.g. Thurlow and Bell 2009) categorizes it as a "moral panic" cooked up by the media. In speech, young people have always been well able to learn to use one set of habits when chatting with their friends and equals, and rather different patterns in more public and formal speech situations, where the audiences include non-members of their particular circle. The need to do this in writing too is a new thing: before the advent of information technology, almost all written communication was by its nature relatively formal. Relaxed chat with intimates was necessarily spoken, because there was no medium enabling it to be done easily in writing. But, now technology has created that medium, it is hard to see why people should be less able to adapt to varying conventions for different social circumstances in written communication than they are in speech. Perhaps some youngsters will be slow to adapt, just as some go off to job interviews wearing torn jeans; but either they learn more prudent ways, or they tend not to end up in influential social roles as adults.

This is not to say that "textisms" or "bloggisms" will never affect the general written language. Perhaps, if enough people use them, < soz > for *sorry* or < IMHO > for *in my humble opinion* may be destined in due course for acceptance in more formal writing. And if that happens, some of them might in turn influence the spoken language – perhaps we shall live to hear responsible, middle-aged citizens saying /ɪmhəu/. Languages receive influences from just about every aspect of human life, so it would be strange if information technology played no part in their future development. But that does not justify the kind of moral panic that seems to underlie some of the comments one encounters. If written English were indeed to descend into orthographic anarchy, that would be regrettable for making communication less clear and efficient; however, the fault would not lie with technology, but with the schoolteaching profession and related social institutions. Even before the new technology arrived, we acquired the ability to spell and punctuate properly only because society made clear to us, particularly through the school system, that these were desirable skills to master. Computers do not hinder society from continuing to get this message across, provided it still wishes to do so.

Consequently that range of issues will not be explored further here. Much more interesting, from the linguistic point of view, is the way that information technology has evolved in order to serve established written-language conventions better. In its infancy it served them very poorly indeed.

* * *

That may come as a surprise to some readers. In the 21c, when most people in the developed world have a computer sitting on their desk, word processing may well be the largest single category of computer use. A high proportion of all the electronic files being created and exchanged are documents of one sort or another, whether a hasty e-mail, a letter destined to be printed out, or a lengthy student dissertation or an author's book manuscript.

But this is still a relatively new situation. Only around the turn of the millennium did it become common for the average man in the street to possess a home computer. For many decades after the technology was first invented in the 1940s, computers were used exclusively by people who were to some extent technical specialists, and mainly for purposes that had little to do with language. When I first worked with computers, in the 1960s, the ability of the machines to represent written English (or any other human language) was very limited. Computers did not normally deal with extended passages of prose: they were designed to carry out scientific and engineering calculations, and for business operations such as processing payrolls or stock control. The longest alphabetic sequences normally dealt with were only individual names, say of employees or products, or things like brief captions for statistical charts.

One consequence was that character sets were small. I had the good fortune to be a graduate student at one of the most distinguished universities of the USA, so the computing equipment I worked with was advanced for the time – but it could not represent lower-case letters. Anything alphabetic appeared in all capitals. As for the accented letters of European languages, forget it. In an English-speaking country they were not relevant, and when computers were marketed in other countries they used other character sets. Internally within computing machinery, everything is numbers, so a computer sold in Spain, say, would assign the number which in the USA stood for the "at" sign, @ (not then used by Spaniards) instead to the Spanish letter Ñ. No confusion could arise, because computers were stand-alone machines. There was no Internet. (Computers were not networked at all. A computer was not something that sat on an individual office desk, it filled a large room, and if you wanted to use your institution's computer you went to the building which housed it.)

There was a good reason for the austerity of those early character sets. Computer memory was very expensive, and larger character sets use more memory. I have said that everything within a computer is represented as numbers, and these are not the familiar decimal numbers where successive places stand for units, tens, hundreds, etc., but binary numbers, which use only the digits zero and one, and where places stand for units, twos, fours, eights, and so on. The computer that I worked with in the mid-1960s used a six-bit character set, meaning that each character took up six binary memory elements. Six bits provide codes for the binary numbers 000000 to 111111, corresponding to decimal numbers 0 to 63, so the largest possible size of character set was 64. After distinct codes have been assigned to 26 capital letters, ten digits, space, and a few essential punctuation marks and symbols such as the dollar and percent signs, a six-bit codespace is full. Separate representation of lower-case letters would have required different architecture for the computer hardware, allowing at least seven bits per character (or more realistically, since seven is not a computer-friendly number, eight bits). Consequently the overall memory requirement for the machine would have increased by a third. While memory was a serious economic constraint, it was not worth accepting that cost just in order to be able to represent `JOHN SMITH` as `John Smith`. And of course there was no possibility of distinguishing italics from roman or boldface from plain, either of which would have doubled the character set size, let alone of offering a variety of typefaces or type sizes.

Memory was beginning to grow cheaper, and more powerful machines with eight-bit character sets were already in the pipeline. Eight bits allow a total of 256 distinct codes, so that it is easy to include separate capital and lower-case letters and a fuller range of punctuation and special symbols. The well-known American Standard Code for Information Interchange (ASCII) character set had, in fact, been defined as a standard in 1963, though it was not widely used until later.[1] But another problem was that, because computers were not networked, there was no pressure for different manufacturers to use the same coding scheme, and they didn't. The market was dominated by mainframes produced by IBM; in the late 1960s they introduced a new range for which they invented a character set called EBCDIC, and the new machine range was such a commercial success that EBCDIC became a *de facto* rival to ASCII as a standard. (IBM mainframes still use EBCDIC today, though nowadays few users need to be aware of the internal character-coding system; fifty years ago, computer users had to work more closely with a machine's internal data representation.) ASCII and EBCDIC both provide about ninety printable characters (together with various "control codes" such as "carriage return"), but they use different numbers for the same character: thus, capital A is decimal 65 in ASCII but 193 in EBCDIC.

What is more, although both ASCII and EBCDIC obviously provide for the core range of capital and lower-case letters, digits, and basic punctuation, there are differences with respect to which less-common special symbols are included. For instance, EBCDIC does not include square brackets (which are not exclusively technical symbols in English: they are quite often used in ordinary prose, e.g. to indicate omitted words). Conversely, EBCDIC but not ASCII has the cent sign, ¢ – an issue of no significance in a British context but which might be quite important for American computer users. Both of these coding schemes, like 20c typewriters, use straight symbols ' and " to represent apostrophes and quotation marks, with no distinction between opening and closing variants, which is why attractively printed documents sometimes betray slapdash word processing by using these symbols today.

As the A of "ASCII" indicates, this system was originally intended to be a standard for the USA alone. It was envisaged that parallel "French SCII", "German SCII", and similar standards would be developed for other countries. In practice, though, ASCII came to be seen as an international standard. Other Western European languages were handled either by reassigning less-used "special symbol" codes to accented European letters, or by representing those letters with the extra code numbers available in an eight- rather than seven-bit system; but different manufacturers went their separate ways in these extensions. If one looked beyond Western Europe, the Iron Curtain meant that few people forty or fifty years ago were concerned with enabling computers to deal with the special letters of Central European languages, such as the č š ň ř ž ů of Czech or the ą ę ł ś ć ż of Polish. Still less did they seek to handle non-Roman scripts.

For users of those Continental languages whose alphabets were covered, it was obviously an advantage to be able to spell as they would normally – but there were costs as well as benefits. Software developers were exchanging files internationally long before the man in the street had any idea of such a thing. The Wikipedia article on "ASCII" (downloaded 9 December 2013) comments on the plight of German or Swedish computer programmers who had to read and write an instruction such as

```
{ a[i] = '\n'; }
```

(which is a very ordinary, easily readable example of the C language, meaning "set element *i* of string *a* to the newline character") in a form such as

```
ä aÄiÜ = 'Ön'; ü
```

– to such a person, having national characters available might seem a mixed blessing.

Those of us who were already working with computers became used to the fact that, if one moved a file of written prose from one computing environment to another, any characters other than the core alphabetic letters and digits and the most basic punctuation marks were very likely to mutate into different characters – or just vanish – when the file was displayed or printed out. It was safest to avoid them. In consequence, for quite a long period around the 1980s, it was apparent to everyone that most written language in future was going to be mediated by electronic technology, but it looked as though the cost of that was going to be a severe degradation of orthographic detail. To get an impression of the nature of computerized prose at that period, one might examine a few of the books made available by the Project Gutenberg public service (www.gutenberg.org). Project Gutenberg is a valuable enterprise whose mission is to make out-of-copyright literature freely available online. But because it got under way as early as 1971, its offerings suffer from these kinds of typographical limitation. If one reads one of its book files, all the content is there, but the experience of reading is impoverished relative to reading traditional printed pages. And if that is so for English-language material, bear in mind that (because the technology was developed mainly in the USA) English is the language to which it was *best* adapted.

At that period, word processing was a technology of the future (Microsoft Word first became a commercial success from 1990 onwards). And even when Word and other word-processing systems did arrive, although they were well able to handle variables such as typeface, type size, italics, and so forth, their early versions suffered from the same problems about characters changing identity between computing environments as arose with plain text files.[2]

* * *

The factor which has transformed that situation is *Unicode.*

Unicode is an ambitious, but largely successful, attempt to provide a reliable, detailed, and unambiguous electronic representation for documents in any language of the world. It grew out of discussions in the late 1980s, and since the 1990s has been steered by a consortium of information-technology companies and some national government departments. Version 1 of Unicode was published in 1991.[3] Unicode is a work in progress, in the sense that it continues to expand and refine its coverage of obscure scripts and script-like systems, but already in that first version it was capable of handling the overwhelming majority of written language actually used in practice within information technology. By now, all major software systems base their representations of written language on Unicode; Internet protocols require it, for instance. That does not mean that, to count as Unicode-conformant, a software system must be capable of displaying every character included in the standard. A word-processing system marketed in the English-speaking world might not be able to display Asian scripts, for instance. But whatever script(s) it does cover must be encoded using the Unicode codes, and if a file includes valid Unicode codes which the system cannot display, it must not ignore them, but should show some symbol (perhaps a hollow square, or a white question mark on a black diamond) meaning "undisplayable character".

Unicode is essentially a sixteen-bit coding system. Developments in the technology mean that, nowadays, economizing computer memory is no longer an important consideration. Sixteen binary digits give a space of over 65,000 distinct numbers (to be precise, $2^{16} = 65{,}536$), enough to assign a different codepoint (i.e. code number) to each graph of every script (or so it was initially supposed – but see below).

Here I must digress briefly to explain how these codepoints are identified. Sequences of sixteen ones and zeros are obviously impractical for human beings to read. So a given codepoint is normally shown in *hexadecimal notation.* The sixteen binary digits are divided into four groups of four; each group will then consist of some number between 0000 (decimal zero) and 1111 (decimal fifteen), and these numbers are written using digits 0 to 9 with their normal values and A to F representing ten to fifteen. So, for instance, the Unicode codepoint 010D represents the number "thirteen (i.e. D) units, plus no sixteens, plus one 16^2, plus no 16^3's", which corresponds to decimal 269. As it happens, this is the code for the Czech letter č.

Within the total Unicode codespace, each script is allotted a non-overlapping stretch of codepoints. The Roman alphabet, with every variety of accented letters, phonetic symbols, and so forth, occupies the low numbers up to 036F (which is decimal 879). Then the remainder of the 03** range is devoted to the Greek alphabet; the Cyrillic alphabet stretches over the 04** range; and so on. Often some particular group of users will wish to encode symbols important to them which are not included in the Unicode standard – a firm's logo, for instance; a large tract of code space is reserved for private use, meaning that groups of users can agree among themselves to use these codepoints as they wish and this will never conflict with future expansions of the system. Chinese needs a large chunk of codespace, but Unicode easily accommodates it: Chinese occupies the ranges from 4*** to 9*** (with gaps), i.e. it uses three-eighths of the entire sixteen-bit codespace.

However, Unicode is far more than just a very long list of the world's written symbols. The system has to incorporate not only the identities of the various graphs but also information about how they are used in the scripts to which they belong. Reading about the various kinds of information recorded in the system is an education in the diverse issues which have to be taken care of when text in various languages is processed mechanically.

Thus, each graph is associated with a set of properties. One range of properties relate to directionality. Roman letters have the property left-to-right, Hebrew letters have the property right-to-left. It might seem unnecessary to record this information at the level of individual graphs: surely, a document as a whole will be written in one direction or the other? Actually that is not so. If a number, say < 123 >, occurs in the middle of a Hebrew document, for instance, the number will appear in the familiar left-to-right direction – Israelis do not write one hundred and twenty-three as < 321 > – although everything around the number will be right-to-left. Or what if an English document quotes some Hebrew wording? In an example like

A common greeting is שלום! (meaning "peace!")

the Unicode representation of the wording will be a series of numbers held in a single logical sequence, so that the first item following < is > will be the code for ש, representing the /ʃ/ of the Hebrew word /ʃālōm/, "peace". But a device which renders that Unicode sequence in visible form, on a screen or on paper, needs to know that ש must appear as the rightmost rather than leftmost graph in the Hebrew word. What is more, "L-to-R" and "R-to-L" are not the only possible directional properties for graphs. The exclamation mark is directionally neutral, and the system includes machinery to specify that, in this case, the exclamation mark with the Hebrew word counts as part of the R-to-L sequence (and hence occurs as the leftmost graph of that sequence), rather than as part of the L-to-R sequence which follows the Hebrew word, and to which the exclamation mark is adjacent in logical order. And the brackets round the phrase < meaning "peace!" > have another property again: brackets are *bidirectional mirrored* graphs, meaning that the Unicode code standing for "opening bracket" should appear in the form "(" when (as here) it is within an L-to-R sequence, but the same code should be rendered as ")" within an R-to-L sequence (and vice versa for the "closing bracket" code).

Another important pair of graph properties are upper and lower case, for scripts such as ours which make that distinction. But even in such scripts, capital and lower-case letters do not always pair off one-for-one, as they do in English. For instance, German has a lower-case letter ß, representing a sibilant which is voiceless, like double < ss >, but which lengthens a preceding vowel, like single < s > (there are contrasts such as < Muße > /mūsə/ "leisure" versus < Muse > /mūzə/ "Muse" versus < Musselin > /mŭsəlin/ "muslin"). However, there is no capital ß; the system has to know that the upper-case equivalent of that single letter is double < SS > – "leisure" in all-capitals is written < MUSSE >.

Furthermore, it turns out that two "case" properties are not enough. Consider Serbo-Croat. This is essentially one language, which is written in Cyrillic script in Serbia and in Roman script in Croatia. Some Cyrillic letters are represented in Croatia by what we would see as pairs of Roman letters, e.g one Serbian letter corresponds in Croat to < lj >. Because these pairs equate to single letters in the other alphabet, they are regarded in Croat as single digraphs, somewhat comparable to æ, œ in English, with their own place in Croat alphabetic order (a surname Ljubić will be listed after Lovrić, not before). Hence they are given their own Unicode code-points. Thus < lj > has the lower-case property, and the corresponding upper-case graph is < LJ >; but there also has to be a "title-case" property for < Lj >, which is the form taken by the digraph in a context, such as a proper name or a book title, where initials only are capitalized.

Accented letters can be encoded as single units, if the letter/diacritic combination is a standard one: we have seen that č has the code 010D. But for the sake of flexibility the system also allows them to be encoded as combinations of basic letter and separate diacritic code, and for this there have to be rules not only about the ordering of letter and diacritic (the basic letter comes first, so č encoded as a composite is 0063 for < c > followed by 030C for the haček mark) but also about the relative ordering of diacritics, for languages which put multiple accents on a single letter. (The rule there is that diacritic codes are given in order of increasing distance from the basic letter, so for instance Vietnamese ắ, representing a short [a] on the third tone, is encoded as < a > + short mark + acute mark.)

The Version 5 manual illustrates some of the kinds of complications which arise via the Sanskrit word *pūrti*, "completion", written in its native Devanagari script. As a logical sequence of characters, *pūrti* is composed of six elements:

1 pa
2 ū
3 ra
4 V̸̆
5 ta
6 i

– remember (p. 95) that vowel symbols, together with the vowel-cancelling sign shown here as V̸̆, all override the inherent /a/ vowel in a graph such as < pa > or < ra >. The correct Devanagari rendering of this sequence is shown in Figure 50. To achieve this rendering, the system needs to know that item 2 is ligatured to the foot of item 1; that because the /r/ of *pūrti* forms part of a consonant cluster, items 3 and 4 are not shown in their normal, separate shapes but are jointly represented as a small hook ligatured to the top of item 5; and that item 6 appears to the left of 5 although pronounced after it, since Devanagari uses left v. right placement to represent short v. long [i].

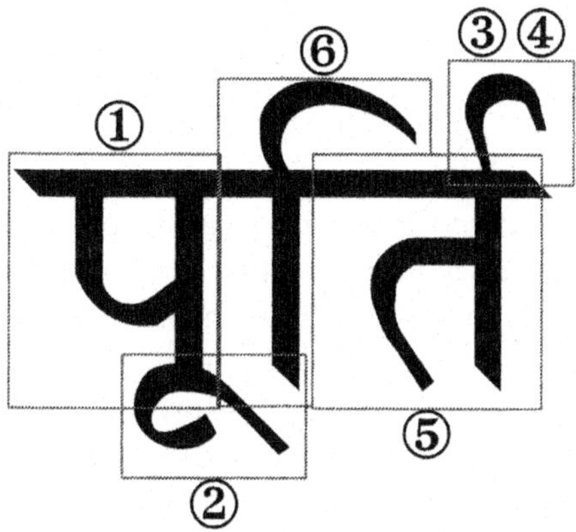

Figure 50

By the time Version 5 of Unicode was published in 2006, upwards of fifty character properties were defined, and it was anticipated that this figure will increase as the coverage of the system becomes more complete. The Version 5 manual is almost 1500 large-format pages long.

* * *

A particularly interesting Unicode issue, from the linguistic point of view, concerns decisions about which distinctions between units of writing justify giving the units separate codes.

Parallel to the familiar situation in phonology, where the phones of a language are classified as varying realizations of a smaller number of phonemes, we saw on pp. 15–16 that we can draw a distinction, in the study of a script, between *graphs* and *graphemes*. The letter Y, say, may be printed in a serifed or a sans-serif face (e.g. Y or Y), or if handwritten it may look quite different again (e.g. *Y*), but all of these visually distinct graphs count in Roman script as *allographs* of a single grapheme – the differences among them might be called cosmetic rather than meaningful, each variant stands for the "same letter".

In earlier chapters of this book I have not been particularly careful about this terminology. I have tended to use the short word "graph" where, strictly, I ought to have written "grapheme". To users of a given script it is normally obvious enough which distinctions between visual forms are significant and which are mere matters of handwriting or printing styles, so it is not worth spending much time discussing the grapheme/allograph concept. In the case of phonology it is different: an English-speaker will typically need some phonetic training to hear the difference between the English [l] and [l^{ɯ}] sounds and to understand the nature of the difference, and there will sometimes be real questions about how the phones of a language should be grouped into phonemes.

For Unicode, though, the conceptual distinction between graph and grapheme is all-important. The Unicode terminology is *glyph* versus *character*: an individual codepoint is assigned to a single "character", but that character may be rendered as any of a large variety of "glyphs". However, while phonemic analysis is always relative to a particular language, so that sounds which are allophones of one phoneme in language *A* may realize distinct phonemes in language *B*, Unicode on the other hand is a single system embracing all scripts, hence it is forced to make decisions about glyph equivalence independently of particular scripts. From a linguistic point of view this is a rather paradoxical requirement.

It is usually straightforward enough to separate out meaningful differences between letters from variations of typeface, or contrasts such as plain versus italics or boldface, and to say that Unicode recognizes the former but leaves the latter to be handled by other aspects of document-processing software. Plenty of codepoints are reserved for user-defined control codes, so that if wished it is quite easy to embed instructions such as "begin italics", "end italics" within Unicode character-sequences – though more commonly matters like that would be handled at a higher level, with Unicode sequences embedded within information about how characters are to be rendered rather than vice versa. Either way, the important point is that Unicode does not itself provide separate codes for italic and roman letterforms, nor does it define any code as meaning something like "begin italics".

The problems arise when graphs that "count as the same" in one script "count as different" in another. Consider, for instance, the different possible forms of the letter a. In ordinary prose written in English or other languages using the Roman alphabet, the form < ɑ > is merely a variant of the commoner printed form < a >, so these are allographs of one grapheme. However, another kind of script which Unicode has from the beginning aimed to cover is the International Phonetic Association alphabet, and as we know, in IPA transcriptions < ɑ > and < a > mean different things – the former stands for a back vowel and the latter for a front vowel. (On p. 14 I mentioned that I was avoiding that usage in this book, because it can be confusing – but, confusing or not, that is how the internationally agreed phonetic alphabet is defined.) So, for the IPA, these two symbols are not allographs but contrasting graphemes. In this case, the Unicode solution is to assign a distinctive code for < ɑ > when used as an IPA symbol, but the identical graph will be encoded the same as < a > when it occurs in a passage of English prose.[4]

Or consider the Unicode treatment of the sign for the pound sterling. Currency symbols, like alphabetic letters, are subject to a certain amount of typographic variation. The standard example, in manuals for successive versions of Unicode, of non-distinctive glyph variants is variation between one or two vertical lines in the dollar sign: $ $. Semantically these symbols are equivalent, so they are treated as allographs of a single character with a single codepoint. However, in the case of the pound sign the double-barred version, ₤, is treated as a separate character from the single-barred sign £, and the two versions are given separate codes. The single-barred sign is identified simply as "pound sign"; the double-barred ₤ is identified as the symbol for the Italian or Turkish lira.

To a British reader this looks quite irrational, since the graphs £ and ₤ are as interchangeable for the pound sterling as single- and double-vertical signs are for the American dollar. In present-day typography the single-barred sign is certainly more fashionable, but the double-barred variant is also seen, and not long ago it was the norm. (The double-barred £ was the version used on five-pound notes until their design was changed in 1990.)

However, it may be that this pair of symbols which are interchangeable in the eyes of British readers and writers are (or were) distinctively different for Italians or Turks. Perhaps, for them, < £ > meant specifically "lira" as opposed to < £ > for the British pound. (The issue is now academic: since Version 1 of Unicode, Italy has abandoned the lira for the euro, and in 2012 Turkey adopted a new symbol for its lira, which has been duly assigned yet another codepoint to itself in the latest Unicode version.) This situation, where distinct graphs are equivalent for one script community but contrast for another community, has no parallel in the phonemic analysis of spoken language, which is done on a language-by-language basis.

* * *

I should say that I do not know whether Turks or Italians did use < £ > and < £ > contrastively, and there is an alternative possible explanation for the anomaly: it could simply be a mistake. The team responsible for Unicode consult very widely, but they are not infallible, and it is possible that in some particular case they might take similar but non-identical graphs to stand for different things when in fact they do not. (There is wording in the Version 5 manual which could mean that with hindsight this applies to the alternative pound signs.)

Since new, updated versions of the Unicode continue to be produced (Version 7.0 was announced as the manuscript of this book was being completed), one might think that errors could easily be corrected after they are recognized. However, that would conflict with another principle of the system, which again demonstrates a contrast with linguists' phonemic analysis. The latter is a kind of scientific theorizing, and it is routine to find that a scientific theory contains a mistake and to abandon it in favour of a better theory – that is how science progresses. Unicode, though, is not a scientific theory of writing, but a practical tool, used by now to encode vast quantities of documentation in electronic form. In consequence, it has to have a rule that any assignment of a codepoint to a character, once promulgated, can never subsequently be withdrawn. Without that rule, the danger would arise that legacy documentation which was correctly encoded originally might later become in part ambiguous or meaningless. So, no matter how certainly some character assignment might later be seen as a mistake, that mistake cannot be undone. The use of some individual codepoint can be "deprecated", which more or less means "We wish we had not made that decision and we advise you not to use this codepoint in encoding new material", but the character/codepoint pairing remains a valid element of the system.

Another Unicode principle which has a clear rationale, but which leads to conflict with linguistic analyses of scripts, is that where a standard for electronic encoding of a particular script already exists at the time when Unicode sets about covering that script, the script analysis implied by the existing standard will be respected. Consider, for instance, the word-final variants of various Hebrew letters, such as ך as opposed to כ for < k >. These graph-pairs are very clear examples of allographs of single graphemes, quite comparable to the two allophones of the English /l/ phoneme. But all existing standards for encoding Hebrew, when the first version of Unicode was compiled, gave these distinct letterforms separate codes, so they are given separate Unicode codepoints. In Arabic script, on the other hand, where many letters have different shapes depending on position within a word (cf. p. 132), a single Unicode codepoint stands for all the allographs of a letter. Linguistically, the contrasting treatments of these two closely related scripts would seem indefensible, but scientific linguistic analysis is only one of the considerations which Unicode aims to take into account, and sometimes different considerations conflict.

In consequence, as the system explicitly acknowledges, "The Unicode Standard is the product of many compromises", and "one can expect a certain number of anomalies in character properties" (Unicode Consortium 2006: 129). Realistically it could not be otherwise, and it is inevitable that users who care about the details of some particular script will often find minor points in the Unicode treatment of that script which they would prefer to have been done differently. But that is not a criticism. Where desiderata genuinely conflict, compromises have to be made. What one can hope for is that they should be made in a thought-out fashion, giving due weight to countervailing considerations, rather than the first solution that comes to mind being seized on without noticing that in some respects its consequences are seriously adverse. To quote Version 5 again, "In designing a new encoding scheme for complex scripts ... tradeoffs must be evaluated and decisions made explicitly, rather than unconsciously" (Unicode Consortium 2006: 12). Unicode achieves this about as well as it could be achieved, in my judgement.

* * *

One reason why new versions of Unicode continue to be produced, more than twenty years after the first, is that as the system has evolved its ambitions have widened.

In 1991, Version 1 claimed to exclude "rare" or "obsolete" graphs. All scripts covered were those of living languages, even if some of them (e.g. the script used for the language of Laos) were little known in the Western world.

In fact it was not true that Version 1 contained no obsolete graphs. The Cyrillic tract of codespace, for instance, included many historic letters that were used in writing Russian in the past but have been obsolete at least since the 1917 Russian Revolution. One example would be the letter Ѳ, called *fita*, which derived from Greek theta and was used in words borrowed from Greek into Russian. Because Russian has no /θ/ sound, that Greek sound was replaced in Russian by the sound /f/. Fyodor Dostoevsky's Christian name, for instance, was the Russian version of *Theodore* – in Modern Greek pronunciation, /θeoðoros/ – and in the 19c *Fyodor* was spelled with Ѳ as a Russian letter. (Compare the way that we write *chiropodist* with < ch > in English, because it derives from a Greek word beginning with a chi, though in English we say it with an ordinary /k/ sound.) There was no distinction in Russian pronunciation between Ѳ and Ф – the latter being the ordinary Russian < f >, derived as a letter shape from Greek phi – so, since the Revolution, Dostoevsky's name has been spelled with Ф, and *fita* is no longer used.

However, while Version 1 did include quite a lot of individual obsolete graphs, it did not cover scripts which had been used only for dead languages or were otherwise obsolete as entire systems.

By 2006, though, Unicode aimed to cover past as well as present-day scripts comprehensively: "As the universal character encoding scheme, the Unicode Standard ... responds to scholarly needs. To preserve world cultural heritage, important archaic scripts are encoded as consensus about the encoding is developed" (Unicode Consortium 2006: 3). The graphs of Linear B (Chapter 4), for instance, have been obsolete for millennia, and are relevant today only to a small community of rarefied scholars, but they each have their place in Version 5.[5]

Even the concept of what should count as "writing" has broadened considerably. Thus, in 1991, a notation system had to be essentially one-dimensional (reflecting the linear time sequence of speech) to be considered for inclusion. For instance, electrical circuit diagrams use conventional symbols (for "earth", "resistor", and so on) which are quite like writing, but the diagrams are two-dimensional and hence were excluded. Circuit diagrams still are excluded from Version 5; but another type of notation which Version 1 omitted for similar reasons is musical scores (which combine the dimension of note pitch with that of time), yet Version 5 does provide codes for the individual note symbols such as minims and quavers. Version 1 omitted Braille (the system of raised dots which makes writing available to blind people through the sense of touch) because it was regarded as akin to a mere difference of typeface: the graph < D > is *D* in italics, 𝔇 in black-letter, and ⠙ in Braille. In Version 5, Braille has its own tract of codespace.

* * *

One consequence of these enlargements is that 65,000-odd codepoints are, after all, not enough to accommodate everything that Unicode now includes. Adding the partly logographic Cuneiform script alone, for instance, mopped up more than a thousand codepoints. By 2006, a little over 99,000 codepoints had been assigned to graphs.

Since 99,000 is far more than 2^{16}, achieving this in a sixteen-bit code sounds like getting a quart into a pint pot. But an ingenious solution was devised to do that. Two tracts, each containing about a thousand codepoints, had not yet been assigned. By using pairs drawn respectively from the first and second of these tracts to stand for single graphs, it became possible to create about a million additional codes without introducing any ambiguity.[6] (Numbers from these special tracts have Unicode meanings only taken in pairs; all other numbers are meaningful only taken singly.)

A total codespace of about 1.1 million elements surely will be far more than enough to cover every possible script or script-like notation, unless we should eventually discover literate races on worlds orbiting other stars. Unicode will continue to evolve, in order to cover further obscure dead scripts and to provide solutions for various problems which are too technical to discuss here, but it is unlikely to be replaced or to change in its core principles. The problem of representing written documents electronically, it is safe to say, has now been definitively solved.

Notes

1. Technically the original, unextended ASCII is a seven-bit scheme.
2. Within the computing profession there had long been systems such as troff and LaTeX which gave users complete control over both appearance and character content of text output, but those systems were designed for expert use, and would have had little appeal to laymen even if they had access to them.
3. References in this chapter to "Version 1" and "Version 5" of Unicode are to the publications listed in the references section as Unicode Consortium (1991) and (2006), respectively.

4. The Unicode standard states that its term "character" should not be regarded as a synonym of "grapheme", precisely because of problems like this.
5. Linear A, on the other hand, is not included, because there is not yet a scholarly consensus about how its graphs group into graphemes.
6. These approximate figures ("about a thousand", "about a million") correspond to precise round numbers in hexadecimal arithmetic, but I believe many readers will prefer me to stick to familiar decimal numbers.

13 English spelling

How should we characterize our own English writing system?

The obvious comparisons are with other European alphabetic orthographies, and notoriously, in those terms it falls far short of the ideal. English, and French to a lesser extent, are remarkable among European languages for the extent to which their spelling-systems depart from the principle of one-to-one correspondence between the phoneme sequence that occurs in a spoken utterance and the sequence of letters which appear in its written equivalent.

There is a "received view" about this which is shared, tacitly at least, by many English-speakers, and runs roughly as follows. Once, at some remote historical period, English had a "phonemic" orthography in which words were spelled as they were pronounced (here and below, by "phonemic" I mean that pronunciation can be predicted straightforwardly from spelling and vice versa – I am not laying special stress on the distinction between phonemes and allophones). But pronunciation changed over the centuries, while spelling was conservative. Thus, the orthography we use today is, in essence, a phonemic script for a spoken language that vanished long ago – while, in relation to the modern spoken language, our spelling is just chaotic. And this is a thoroughly bad thing. It may be one of the bad things that must be endured because they cannot be cured; but, if it were possible by the wave of a wand to equip every adult English-speaker with competence in a new, phonemic orthography, and to replace the millions of documents in our libraries, filing-cabinets, and computers by copies written in the new system, then this would confer a great boon on future generations. The only loss would be aesthetic: many people feel that our traditional spelling has a beauty which does something to offset its lack of rationality, and which would be lost in a system which spelled *conquer* as < konker >, or *passionate* as < pashunut >.

Spelling reform was a live issue at various times in the late 19c and early 20c. The reason why the science of phonetics that developed then was a mainly British enterprise, at a time when other aspects of scientific language-study were centred on Germany, had to do with the fact that the early phoneticians were largely motivated by a desire to reform spelling

(German orthography was near-phonemic as it stood). The 1877 book *Handbook of Phonetics* by Henry Sweet (the inspiration for Henry Higgins in Bernard Shaw's play *Pygmalion*, who in turn became the Rex Harrison character in the musical *My Fair Lady*) had the subtitle *Including a Popular Exposition of the Principles of Spelling Reform*. Daniel Jones (e.g. 1932) developed the theory of the "phoneme" as the unit for which an ideal orthography would provide a grapheme. Many detailed proposals for a revised English orthography were put forward, and the idea was sometimes discussed approvingly in the British Parliament. The leading proposals were surveyed by Haas (1969).

In the 21c it seems fair to say that spelling reform has ceased to be a live issue in the English-speaking world. The last occasion I know of when it received support from any government was in Australia in the 1970s, when for a while under Gough Whitlam's administration the Ministry of Helth was officially spelled without an "a", as a symbolic first step towards a reformed orthography. (The following, Liberal government reverted to traditional spelling.) Since that period, the advent of automatic spell-checking software has reduced the perceived need for reform. There is still an English Spelling Society, flying the flag for spelling simplification (www.spellingsociety.org), but without notable success in attracting converts.

Although the pressure for reform may have dissolved, what I described as the "received view" of English spelling still seems to be a consensus. People who would object to any revival of spelling reform as a practical policy would probably nevertheless concede that a phonemic spelling would be more efficient if universally adopted, but they would perhaps argue that efficiency is not everything, or point out the practical difficulties that would stand in the way of a changeover.

However, the received view is very questionable. It contains a number of separate components, some factual (e.g. concerning the history of spelling) and others evaluative (concerning the virtues of the phonemic principle); there is some truth in each component, but each is also at least partly false. English spelling is not simply a phonemic script overtaken by innovations in English speech: the ways in which it deviates from the phonemic principle have little to do with historical sound change, and they are not just randomly chaotic. If we were minded to do so, there would be little real difficulty in adopting a reformed spelling. But, even if such a change could be put into effect costlessly, it is not clear that society would on balance benefit from it, and it might stand to lose.

In what follows I shall argue for each of these points. The only component of the received view which I shall not challenge is the aesthetic one, on which I have no special contribution to offer. I, too, find our current orthography more attractive than proposed alternatives. It may be that the very familiarity of the standard spelling system is part of what makes it pleasing, but to say that is not to dissolve the pleasure.

* * *

In the first place, I do not believe that serious objective difficulties stand in the way of spelling reform. People often cite the massive bulk of existing documents which would require to be transliterated into the new spelling, but nothing of the kind would be necessary. Except for some small minority groups such as lawyers and humanities scholars, people rarely consult papers or books which were printed more than ten years or so earlier – people often read literary classics, but almost always in modern editions. When a book was reprinted it would be transliterated into the new script as a matter of course, and computerized transliteration software would make that a trivial task. Those people who for professional reasons need to read old documents – and doubtless many cultivated members of the general public – would develop a passive familiarity with the old script, something that is far less burdensome than the active ability to produce the correct traditional spellings. There would be plenty of reference works in which puzzling old spellings could be checked.

There is also the problem of training the population. But, if society in general wanted this problem to be solved, it easily could be. The set of individuals who would crucially need to be thoroughly competent in the new system are the primary-school teachers. If we decided to reform our spelling then knowledge of the new orthography would become an important part of teacher training. Surely it will not be suggested that potential schoolteachers brought up on old spelling would be incapable of mastering a new system? After all, the point of reformed spelling is to be easy.

Once a generation of children had grown up with the new spelling, it would matter little whether or not the bulk of their elders fell into line. Printers' English spellings were standardized by about 1650, but private spelling did not follow suit until well after Dr Johnson's dictionary appeared in 1755 (Scragg 1974: 82). Some newspapers, magazines, websites, and book publishers would shift to the new standard rapidly and others choose to stick to the old, on straightforward commercial considerations of what their particular customer base preferred. Thirty years after the changeover, the old spelling would linger only in a few self-consciously quaint periodicals.

The reason why all this seems to me unlikely to happen has to do with subjective rather than objective factors. Because there has been no change at all within living memory in our rather complex orthography, people imagine that it is unchangeable and dismiss those who urge the desirability of reform as cranks. People do not appreciate that English orthography, the least phonemic in Europe, is unusual in not having undergone reform in recent times. German, for instance, adopted a standard orthography which was pretty close to perfectly phonemic in 1901, yet in 1995 it was reformed again (the latest reform proved highly controversial; see S. Johnson 2005; Sampson 2005b). Paradoxically it seems to be broadly true that those European nations with the most phonemic scripts are the most inclined to reform them (though even French orthography, which is not very phonemic, was tweaked in minor ways by a government-appointed council in 1990). If your script is close to phonemic, then you see its graphemes as devices for representing sounds and you perceive the respects in which they fail to do so as striking and curable imperfections. An Englishman, on the other hand, does not see his spelling as a system deviating in limited respects from a phonemic ideal.

The tradition, common to English-speaking countries, of minimizing the role of the state in cultural matters means that spelling reform here would be more dependent than in some Continental countries on popular demand; governments could facilitate, but they could hardly impose reform. And since the English-speaking world no longer has a single cultural hub, such demand would have to grow in separate publics (there would not be much to be said in favour of one English-speaking nation switching to a radically novel orthography if others were unwilling to do the same). It seems to me that this kind of demand is not likely to grow, because the great majority of influential English-speakers who entertain the notion of spelling reform as a serious possibility are opposed to it. They find the idea unattractive aesthetically, and unless they have small children they see little to be gained by it. They themselves have mastered traditional orthography (otherwise they would not be influential). People may consciously or unconsciously resent the idea of spelling reform as a threat to the authority possessed by those who are masters of the traditional system – even poor spellers can share this attitude.

* * *

Turning to history: English possessed a standard national written form, based on the speech of Wessex, by the 11c, before the Norman Conquest – it was the only colloquial European language to do so at that period, since elsewhere Latin was used for all official purposes. This written language embodied a fixed set of spelling conventions which added up to an approximately (though not perfectly) phonemic orthography. However, the fact that English spelling later lost this character was not caused by developments internal to the spoken language.[1] Many sound changes did occur in later centuries, but they could have been accommodated by only minor changes in the spelling system, such as were already occurring in the 11c. Rather, the unphonemic nature of modern English spelling was caused by external influences, particularly political developments stemming from the Conquest, which introduced rival spelling conventions that competed with the native conventions and with each other. If the Normans had not prevailed in 1066, present-day English spelling would probably have been as phonemic as that of German.

The immediate consequence of the Conquest was that for more than three centuries, until the early 15c, English ceased to be a language used for official purposes, which inevitably led to breakdown in the standardization of its written form. (Also, the feudal system introduced by the Normans imposed greater regional separatism on the English-speaking population, which likewise militated against standard national orthographic norms.) The languages of public life were French and Latin. At the time of the Conquest French had not yet acquired fully consistent spelling conventions, but the partially regular conventions that had emerged were quite different from those of English. Since scribes, even if themselves English-speakers, now spent much of their time writing French, they naturally imported French spelling conventions into writing English – hence, for example, the modern use of < c > rather than < s > in a word like *ice*. Some of the French conventions took over completely: all the English words which had been spelled with < cw > came to be written with < qu >, for instance. In other cases the native orthography survived in one word while the French convention became usual in another: hence, for instance, the fact that the same Middle English (and Modern English) vowel is written < ee > in *deed*, *heel* but, following a French convention, < ie > in *fiend*, *thief*.

Many French words were borrowed into English after the Conquest, and these were naturally spelled the French way. But here an extra complication arose because of the influence of Latin orthography. Educated Englishmen before the Conquest had known Latin, but they could easily keep it separate from their own language – English did not descend from Latin, and English scribes even wrote the two languages in different styles of lettering (as Germans did while they used *Fraktur*; cf. Figure 19, p. 105). French, on the other hand, was a Romance (i.e. Latin-descended) language, so there was a tension between phonemic spelling of French pronunciations and spelling which reflected their Latin etymologies. For instance, *povre* "poor" was re-spelled *pauvre* because it derived from Latin *pauper*.

Independently of changes in spoken French, French spelling became less phonemic as the etymological principle won wider acceptance in the Middle Ages (and this principle has been supported by the French state, through the Académie Française, since the 17c; Cohen 1958: 425). Thus, the Latin /h/ which had dropped out of spoken French was reintroduced in writing, but inconsistently: hence our spellings *honour*, *hour* versus *ability* (while in modern French the etymological, non-phonemic spelling has become fully consistent in this case: *honneur*, *heure*, *habilité*).

In mediaeval England, then, a given word could commonly be spelled in many ways, each justifiable in terms of one of the accepted conventions. Furthermore, this diversity had positive advantages for some of those professionally concerned with writing. Copyists were paid by the inch, so etymologizing spellings which included redundant letters swelled their income. When printing was introduced in the late 15c, the possibility of varying the length of words was the simplest means of justifying lines of type. And printing brought further disturbances to spelling habits. It transferred control of public orthography away from the disciplined worlds of religious house and chancery to the anarchic environments of small business, reducing the possibility of maintaining national norms. Furthermore, Caxton brought printing to England after living for thirty years in the Low Countries; he knew little of current English orthographic conventions, and his compositors were foreigners. The first books printed in England were heavily influenced by the spelling conventions of Dutch; spellings such as the < gh > of *ghost* reflect this influence today.

In contrast to the case in France, in England there was only one period when writers deliberately moved away from the phonemic principle: during the tide of enthusiasm for Classical learning which reached its peak in the early 16c it became common to write words derived from Classical languages with nonphonemic spellings reflecting their etymology. But Scragg (note 1) suggests that this fashion had a disproportionate impact on modern spelling, because it occurred shortly before printers began in the late 16c to accept the convention of a single fixed spelling for each word. Thus, for example, *det* or *dette* (from Latin *debitum*) became *debt*, *samon* (from *salmōnem*) became *salmon*, *septre* (from *scēptrum*) became *sceptre*. Many such examples are concealed from us now by the fact that the spelling-changes led to changes in pronunciation. Spellings such as *absolve*, *captive*, *corpse* were originally archaizing, Latinate ways of writing words which mediaeval Englishmen spoke and wrote as *assoil*, *caitiff*, *corse*; but the new spellings were taken up in speech rather as, in our own time, /weskɩts/ are becoming /weistkəuts/ and /fɔrɩdz/, /fohedz/.

By about 1650 English spellings were fixed: it was accepted that there was a "correct" way to spell any word (with a few exceptions such as *gaol/jail*), and since then there have been only trivial changes in spelling. But it was essentially a matter of chance in the case of any particular word which of the alternative spellings available for it became standard: thus *pity* was standardized with one *t* and *ditty* with two, though both words had previously been spelled either way. Sometimes a spelling was adopted that had no justification either in pronunciation or in etymology: *foreign* derived from Old French *forain*, Latin *forānum*, and was given its modern spelling in the 16c apparently in the mistaken belief that it was related to *reign*, from Latin *rēgnum*.

* * *

The fact that modern English spellings have resulted from such a variety of causes, rather than from simple conservative refusal to alter a once-phonemic script in face of changes in the spoken language, may well reinforce our impression that current orthography is chaotic. Certainly there was nothing systematic about the manner in which our orthography evolved. Nevertheless, some have claimed that the end-result is more rational than the processes which brought it into being.

One analysis along these lines was due to Keith Albrow (1972). Albrow argued that English spelling displays fairly regular phoneme/grapheme correspondences, but these correspondences form not one but a range of alternative systems which come into play in different types of morpheme.

For instance, one linguistic contrast crucial for English orthography is between lexical and grammatical morphemes. A lexical morpheme must contain at least three letters, while a grammatical morpheme will where possible have fewer: hence *see*, *bee*, versus *me*, *be*, or the unique use (other than in proper names or dialect words) of < gg > for final /g/ in *egg* (contrast *leg*, *dreg*), and the unusual use of single < f > for final /f/ in *if* (contrast *stiff*, *cliff*). The vowel /ɪ/ is spelled < i > in a lexical morpheme but, commonly, < e > in a grammatical morpheme: hence /ɪd/ is spelled differently in *solid* versus *wanted*. These contrasting spelling rules mean that English orthography indicates not only the sounds of words but their status as lexical or grammatical forms. There is some evidence that fluent readers make use of such cues in order to take in the general structure of a piece of prose at a brief glance (Smith 1980: 127–8).

Thus far, Albrow's account seems broadly accurate and enlightening (though it is not unproblematic; e.g. Albrow overlooks the word *ox*, which seems to be an exception to his "three-letter rule" – though see Carney 1994: 133). It is less easy to follow him, however, when he goes on to divide the lexical roots into two classes using different phoneme/grapheme correspondences. For instance, Albrow suggests that one-letter vowel symbols (< a >, < e >, < i > etc., as opposed to < ai >, < ee >, < ou > etc.), when preceding single consonants in polysyllables, stand for long vowels in "system 1" but for short vowels in "system 2": for instance < a > stands for /ei/ in *maker* but for /a/ in *avid* (my examples). This only reduces orthographic confusion if we are given some independent criterion for deciding which system a given root belongs to: Albrow points out that by and large system 1 roots belong to the native Germanic vocabulary, while system 2 roots are French or Classical loans. (*Make* is a Germanic word, *avid* is from Latin *avidus*, greedy.) He suggests that the contrast between two classes of root, though having a historical cause, lives on as a synchronic fact of modern English: the two root-classes display different patterns of derivation, with system 2 roots taking a wide range of of suffixes such as *-ic*, *-ical*, *-ous*, *-ity*, *-orious*, etc. etc., while system 1 roots are limited to a smaller range such as *-er*, *-ly*, *-ship*. It could be true that native speakers of English develop a feeling for what type of derivational affixes are appropriate for a given root: if so, they would have the information they need to choose between Albrow's two orthographic systems.

This idea is interesting. But it is hard to see how native speakers could succeed in classifying words. They might see that *avid* must be "system 2" because of *avidity*, but *panel* also has /a/ rather than /ei/, and it is true that it derives from Old French (and ultimately from Latin *pannellus*, a small cloth), but it takes no derivational suffixes which might reveal that origin. Or consider *ribald* and *ribbon*: historically both derive from French, but both are the kind of informal, homely terms which in English are commonly native Germanic roots (and again neither takes any derivational suffixes), so why does one need a double *b* to stop it being pronounced /raibən/ while the other has a system 2 spelling? In my judgement Albrow's account has too many holes to be accepted as a well-founded theory of English orthography (cf. various passages in Carney 1994, e.g. p. 98).

* * *

Another line that some have taken in order to argue that there is method in the apparent madness of English spelling relates to the concept of deep versus surface linguistic analysis. We saw in Chapter 8 that a phonographic orthography may evolve from recording surface phonetics to recording underlying phonology, not as a result of mere inertia in the face of language change but as an active development; and I pointed out that the generative phonology school have claimed that English spelling is a near-perfect representation of the underlying phonological shapes of words stored in speakers' minds, though quite inaccurate as a representation of the forms actually uttered after the operation of various phonological rules.

For *The Sound Pattern of English* (Chomsky and Halle 1968: 49), it is a "fundamental principle of orthography ... that phonetic variation is not indicated where it is predictable ... an optimal orthography would have one representation for each lexical entry". Spanish (commonly seen as having an admirably phonemic spelling system) contains a rule whereby | e | in roots such as | ped- | "ask" becomes /i/ in stressed positions, giving surface contrasts such as /pe'dir/ "to ask", /pe'dimos/ "we ask", versus /'pido/ "I ask", /'pide/ "he asks". The alternation is predictable; but Spanish spelling reflects it, writing the latter two words as *pido, pide*. For the generative phonologists, this has to be seen as a flaw in Spanish orthography, which "ought" to use the spellings **pedo*, **pede*. The fact that Spaniards spell phonetically makes their orthography useful for "an actor reading lines in a language with which he is unfamiliar", but not for "readers who know the language" (*ibid.*).

The generative phonologists' theory cannot be right as it stands. Many considerations refute it. In the first place it seems implausible that ordinary users of spoken English could construct the morphophonemic rules and "underlying representations" attributed to them in *The Sound Pattern of English*, because these depend on perceiving linguistic relationships that are even subtler than those required by Albrow's approach. In many cases these relationships are obscure even to knowledgeable adults, let alone to average children during the years of language acquisition. Noam Chomsky's wife Carol published an article (C. Chomsky 1970) discussing her experience of teaching children to spell guided by the generative-phonological axiom that deep spelling is natural and that schoolteachers merely confuse children by drawing their attention to irrelevant surface pronunciations (cf. N. Chomsky 1970). She included a revealing anecdote about how she suggested to one "seventh-grade" (about 12 years old) pupil that she consider the word *signature* in deciding how to spell *sign*, to which the child replied "so what's one got to do with the other?" Yet the semantic relationship between *sign* and *signature* is relatively obvious compared to many other relationships on which generative phonologists' rules depend. In practice speakers often fail to notice relationships between words which are etymologically cognate, and sometimes they take such relationships to exist where they do not – in the same article, Carol Chomsky herself mistakenly took *prodigal*, from Latin *prōdig-us* "wasteful", to share a root with *prodigious*, from Latin *prōdigi-um* "a portent". The various attempts that have been made to investigate the psychological reality of generative-phonological analyses empirically have yielded rather uniformly negative results. And English orthography often fails to conform to the predictions of the theory. Many of its deviations from the phonemic principle have no connexion with morphophonemic alternations. *The Sound Pattern of English* justifies the < gh > of *right, righteous* by arguing from synchronic evidence that the root must be underlying | rixt |; but there is no comparable evidence for an underlying | x | in *night* or *light*.[2] No current morphophonemic alternations explain any of the cases where initial /n/ is spelled < kn > or < gn >, as in *knee, know, gnash*. The generative phonologists' account of English orthography was very influential for many years, but I conclude (with Rayner *et al.* 2012: 44) that it cannot be taken seriously.

* * *

Nevertheless, at its heart is a nugget of truth. There does seem to be a historical trend, which was very obvious in the Korean case but is visible also in English orthography, away from reflecting surface phonetic detail towards reflecting the meaningful structure of discourse. Assigning a constant written shape to morphemes, even if the language has morphophonemic rules which cause features of their pronunciation to vary in different environments, is one way in which an orthography can focus on displaying meaningful elements rather than on semantically non-significant properties of the flow of speech.

Another area in which this kind of development is very clear is the early history of European punctuation, the standard account of which is by M.B. Parkes (1992). Punctuation developed only gradually after alphabetic writing was long-established, and according to Parkes it was not until the +6c that authors began to include punctuation in the texts they offered to the public; earlier, punctuation marks were items that readers might choose to insert to guide themselves in reading a document aloud – silent reading was a late innovation. When the hierarchy of comma, semicolon, colon, and full stop emerged, people often took these to represent increasing lengths of physical silence. Sophisticated commentators probably never held such a simplistic view, but everyone understood punctuation marks as essentially guides to pronunciation. Only much later did punctuation become what it is today, a guide to the logical structure of a text, which will often bear no particular relationship to features of speech even if a passage is read aloud (which in any case is no longer a common way to use a written document). The colon in English, for instance, shows that the preceding wording issues a kind of IOU which the following wording will redeem, whereas the semicolon simply co-ordinates successive clauses. The roles are different, but there are no particular phonetic patterns correlated with the respective marks.

Parkes (1992: 69) compares two copies of the same passage in a book by the Venerable Bede, produced in the 8c and 11c respectively. The wording is unchanged, but the punctuation is very different. The earlier copy uses punctuation merely to identify "some of the grammatical and semantic elements which should present themselves to the ear", whereas in the later copy punctuation "is no longer merely a guide to the oral performance of the written word but ... contributes directly to the reader's comprehension of the message". It is easy to surmise that, when literacy is a new thing for a society, its users will be naturally inclined to stick close to the concrete reality of speech-sounds, while later when many people take reading and writing for granted and the written medium is established as a communication channel independent of speech, it will seem more important for writers to give readers cues to the logic of a text, irrespective of what it might sound like if it happened to be read aloud.

To an extent, an orthography which spells out deep rather than surface phonology can be regarded as another example of this same trend, because it provides fixed shapes for morphemes, which are meaningful units, rather than for speech-sounds, which often vary with no semantic significance. If English spelling were phonemic, only the < m > and < t > would be common to the written morpheme *metre* as a noun and as the stem of the adjective *metric*. In a *Sound Pattern of English* analysis, both forms of the morpheme derive from a common deep phonological representation, and traditional English orthography reflects that by writing the forms identically as *metr-* (except for the closing *-e* in the noun). The net consequence of the "irrationality" of English spelling is to give the morphemes of English, on average, a rather clearer and more constant visual identity than they would have in a regularized orthography. In that respect we can see English spelling as having moved some way away from the phonographic towards the logographic principle – though it certainly remains closer to pure phonography and further from pure logography than Chinese or Japanese writing. There are exceptions, where a single root has alternating spellings in different derived forms: e.g. *spEAk* versus *spEEch*, *palaCe* versus *palaTial*, *joKe* versus *joCular*, *colliDe* versus *colliSion* (some of these contrasts in spelling represent alternations in surface pronunciation, but the alternations are regular, so a systematic use of "deep phonography" in order to achieve constant spellings for morphemes would not include these spelling differences). But cases like these are fairly few. It does seem fair to say that as a general rule the spelling of

English lexical items tends to ignore variation between allomorphs (cf. Perfetti 2003; Verhoeven and Perfetti 2003).

* * *

However, one cannot press this idea too far. Although many cases where our spelling deviates from the phonemic principle can be explained in terms of regular morphophonemic alternations which derive varying surface forms from common underlying representations (this applies particularly to vowel alternations, including the *metre/metric* case, that were historically created by the operation over the 15c to 17c period of the Great Vowel Shift), there are very many other cases where the "deep phonology" concept is quite irrelevant, such as the examples *night* and *knee* already mentioned. What these unphonemic spellings do do is to make the meaningful morpheme units look more distinctive than they would be in a phonemic spelling system. Whether or not the spelling of *right* can be explained in terms of phonological rules, the fact that its homophones *rite*, *write*, and *wright* are also graphically distinct has nothing to do with "deep phonology" – historically it is a consequence of long-ago losses of previous phonological distinctions, but in the English of the present day it gives words of different meanings different visual appearances.

I do not mean to suggest that the most significant effect of irregular English spelling is to distinguish between homophones (and certainly not that the aim of avoiding homophones was a major influence on the way the spelling system evolved). Many irregularly spelled words have unique pronunciations, such as *bright*, *debt*, *psalm* (and there are homophone pairs, such as *seal* the animal and *seal* as signet, which are not distinguished in spelling). Unlike Chinese and Japanese, spoken English is not so beset with homophones that keeping them visually distinct would be a crucial desideratum for an orthography. What irregular spellings tend to do is to increase the *general visual distinctiveness* of words, whether they are homophones or not. The word /det/ is unambiguous in speech, but the fact that it is spelled *debt* makes it look more different from *bet*, *net*, *den*, etc. than it would if spelled phonemically. In general the "graphemic grammar" of written English provides a greater variety of possible letter-sequences than the phonological grammar provides possible phoneme-sequences for English words. True, not all deviations from the phonemic principle in our traditional orthography increase distinctiveness. For instance, the word *tough* would be more visually distinctive, as well as more phonemic, if it were spelled **tugh*. Diversity of spellings for a given sound makes for visual distinctiveness, whereas diversity of sounds corresponding in different words to a given grapheme or grapheme-combination is irrelevant, and both types of deviation from the phonemic principle occur in English orthography. Nevertheless, it seems fair to say that the former category of deviation is a good deal more widespread than the latter. My final point in this chapter will be that there may be real advantages in the greater distinctiveness of English spellings, relative to a hypothetical phonemic orthography.

* * *

That is not to deny that our spelling has disadvantages, particularly for learners. Enthusiasts for spelling reform urge that, if reforms were adopted, children would no longer have to waste dreary hours at the schoolroom desk rote-learning senseless orthographic fossils, when they could make better use of the time acquiring more worthwhile and interesting knowledge or skills. Adult illiteracy might be reduced or eliminated.

We saw on p. 198 that it is problematic to call a phonographic script "easier" than a more logographic script. However, it may well be that children would learn to read faster with a more phonemic orthography (though this gain cannot be quantified, and rests ultimately on faith – remember the PISA tests quoted on p. 196). At one time it was believed by some educators that children could learn an irregular orthography like ours successfully via what was called the "look-and-say" method, which treated English words as unanalysed logographs; but (although the point is still resisted in some corners of the schoolteaching profession) by now the weight of empirical evidence offers "no way of getting round the conclusion that systematic phonics instruction is the most effective approach for helping children become better readers" (Rayner *et al.* 2012: 340, citing research surveyed by Rayner *et al.* 2001). If children learn to read English better via phonics, then it is reasonable to infer that a reformed orthography more closely adapted to that teaching technique would make learning more successful still.

Adult illiteracy may be a side issue, because what adult illiterates in a modern society lack may often be motivation rather than ability. Academics for whom literacy is the alpha and omega of life, and agents of states who wish their citizens to respond promptly and efficiently to written instructions, are too ready to assume that all of humanity shares their own priorities, so that only intellectual difficulties can explain failure to learn to read. But we know that there is little correlation between early reading success and IQ (Rayner *et al.* 2012: 320). As David Barton and Mary Hamilton observe in their study of literacy in an English provincial town, adult illiterates

> ... are not empty people living in barren homes waiting to be saved and filled up by literacy [but] ordinary people leading ordinary lives. Usually ... they have networks of support and know where they can turn to for support. Alternatively, since these networks are effective, problems do not arise or are not recognised. (Barton and Hamilton 2012: 161)

A 1980s survey of literacy and numeracy among British adults (ALBSU 1983) found that more than 70 per cent of those with literacy problems denied that these caused any difficulties in their everyday lives.

Even if a phonemic script would benefit children learning to read and write, though, it would not follow that spelling reform is desirable, since the learners' interests are not the only interests to be considered. There are also the interests of competent users to take into account.

By now there is quite a lot of evidence (e.g. Perea and Rosa 2000) that for words to be "orthographic neighbours" of other high-frequency words – that is, to be spelled near-identically, irrespective of pronunciation – has an inhibitory effect on reading, at least on the performance of skilled readers. Putting it simply, people read more efficiently if words are spelled distinctively. More or less the reverse is true in early-years schooling (e.g. Duñabeitia and Vidal-Abarca 2008). The psycholinguistic data are richer and more nuanced than can be discussed here, but in broad terms it seems that beginning readers are helped to guess the identity of a word if they can make partial analogies with the spellings of other words they know, while once one has mastered the skill of reading, that kind of analogy is irrelevant: one wants to see a word and recognize it quickly, and that works best if the word looks distinctive – as a sequence of letters, rather than as a physical outline (cf. p. 131).

Zhao *et al.* (2012) find a similar effect with children acquiring literacy in the very different Chinese system. Young children identify Chinese graphs faster and more accurately if they share phonetic elements with many other known graphs, but for older children that is a negative factor, with the crossover falling at about eleven years of age.

People's views on English spelling are heavily influenced by witnessing the struggles young children go through to master it, which are visible and obvious. The processes occurring within a skilled reader are invisible and not available to introspection, but they seem to be different in kind. As Rayner *et al.* put it (2012: 88), "even a perfect understanding of the skilled reader may say little about the beginning reader" – and, one might add, vice versa. There may be a conflict of interest between beginning readers and skilled readers, in the sense that the former might be better served if our orthography were phonemic, while the latter are better served by an orthography with a diverse variety of spellings, which implies a non-phonemic orthography.

If so, then both groups no doubt deserve some consideration of their interests, and there is no saying where the ideal balance would lie between them. But we can say which direction that balance has been moving in over history. In earlier centuries, only a proportion of the population learned to read, and those often in adulthood; life expectancy was lower, and written communication was less central to life than it is in modern Britain. Now, almost everyone learns to read in childhood. That investment of time and effort is rewarded by, on average, a much longer and more intensive period of skilled reading than would once have been the case. This must imply that the ideal balance has shifted towards a more distinctive, and hence less phonemic, orthography.

There is also some evidence, though perhaps less clear-cut (there is less research on the writing than the reading process, though on the former see Treiman and Kessler 2014), for a similar conflict of interests between the reading and writing roles.[3] Psycholinguists such as Bryant and Bradley (1980) have demonstrated that these processes are less closely linked than was once supposed. Not only are English-speaking children frequently unable to spell correctly words which they can read correctly, which is no surprise, but also they can often spell correctly words which they cannot read, which is more unexpected. And there is a difference in the kinds of words with which these types of failure commonly occur. Examples of words which are read but not spelled correctly are *school, light, train, egg* – words whose spelling is relatively unpredictable on the basis of pronunciation (we saw on p. 255 that the double *gg* of *egg* is unique). Examples of words spelled but not read correctly are *bun, mat, leg, pat* – words which are phonographically regular, but are short and offer little that is visually distinctive in terms of unusual letters or letter-combinations. Uta Frith has argued that, not just for young children but more generally, "the ideal orthography for spelling is incompatible with the ideal orthography for reading" (Frith and Frith 1980: 295), with the phonemic principle being more useful to a person in his role as writer than as reader. This has been disputed, but if it were true it would again imply a changing historical balance of advantage. The invention of printing must have caused the average number of occasions on which a given text is read to grow massively over the half-millennium since Gutenberg, while each text is still written only once. (The recent advent of the Web will have exaggerated this difference even further.) There are texts, such as ephemeral personal letters and e-mails, which receive only one reading, but nowadays they exist side by side with masses of texts such as newspapers, web pages, advertising material, and so forth, which may receive millions of readings each – cases like those scarcely existed two or three centuries ago.

That implies that the balance of advantage has been tending to move towards the reader and away from the writer: extra trouble in writing a single text can now be massively repaid by increased efficiency of very many acts of reading the text. If the psycholinguists mentioned above were correct, this should again mean that the ideal orthography will now be more logographic, less phonographic than before.

Thus it may be no bad thing that modern English spelling is so much less regular than its forerunner of a millennium ago. Rather than representing an anti-social conservatism on the part of the literary élite, this could well amount to a desirable (though, certainly, unplanned) response to the changing balance of social forces.

Notes

1. The standard history of English spelling is Scragg (1974), on which I draw heavily in this chapter.
2. The fact that *delight, delicious* follow the pattern of *expedite, expeditious* in their pronunciation, rather than that of *right, righteous,* seems to imply that by the very arguments of *Sound Pattern, delight* does *not* contain an underlying | x |. The truth is that *delight* is spelled as it is because in the 16c someone mistakenly thought it was related to the word *light*, which in turn has been spelled with < gh > ever since the period when it contained the sound /x/ in its pronunciation.
3. By "writing" I simply refer to recording words on paper, not the specialized sense of published authorship.

14 Conclusion

The aim of this book was to survey the ways in which spoken languages have been reduced to written form, and that has now been done. The book did not set out to propound some abstract universal theory of writing systems; the topic does not lend itself to that.

Nevertheless, a number of general themes have recurred. To round the book off, I shall summarize these briefly.

First, scripts are diverse. Some have suggested that superficial differences among the world's writing systems mask an underlying "oneness", or that all scripts can be seen as attempts, with varying degrees of success, to evolve towards European-style alphabetic writing. To my mind this is misleading. A logographic script really is a different kind of thing from an alphabetic script, and syllabic scripts are different again. Agreed, in practice no script is a pure type. But the fact that there are traces of phonography in the predominantly logographic Chinese script, or that some European scripts (notably including English) contain logographic aspects, does not contradict the point that scripts come in different types.

Second, spoken languages too are diverse, and sometimes scripts differ because different kinds of writing suit different kinds of language. Logographic writing works well for Chinese, where morphemes are clearly separate in the spoken language. It would be much harder to adapt to a "synthetic" language such as the European classical languages, where it is difficult to decide just what morphemes an inflected word includes. Syllabic writing is a natural approach for a language whose syllables are mainly of the CV type, but the Linear B example shows that it is not easy to make it work for a language with a more complicated phonological structure. Vowel-less writing works for Semitic languages, but would work less well for European languages.

This second point should not be pressed too far. I do not suggest that differences between script types are always explainable in terms of differences between the spoken languages they record. The fact that letter shapes in the hands of Semitic scribes became so cursive that different letters became almost or wholly identical, while distinctions between those same letters were always maintained in Europe, has nothing (so far as I can see) to do with properties of the respective spoken languages. Many properties of scripts result from external historical causes unrelated to language structure. Nevertheless, spoken languages are not all cut to a common pattern, and differences between them are one reason, among others, for differences among scripts.

Finally, contrary to what is often supposed, the history of writing systems does not support the assumption that the ideal script for a language is one that records speech sounds with perfect fidelity. Phonetically accurate scripts are often associated with newly literate societies. The historical development tends to be from "shallow" towards "deeper" orthographies, as the spread of literacy promotes greater awareness of language structure, and language-users who come to take writing for granted are more focused on the meaningful elements underlying an inscription than on the surface noises which express those meanings. In some cases, shifts from shallow to deeper spelling may be merely a by-product of orthography failing to reflect language changes, but the Korean example shows that sometimes there is more to it than that.

And, as one implication, English spelling may suit English-speaking societies better than is often supposed.

References

Place of publication is not shown for publishers with a London office or whose name includes the place (e.g. Edinburgh University Press). Items shown as available online can be found by Googling; URLs are not given here if they would be unreasonably cumbersome for the reader to type.

Abend, L. 2009. The font war: IKEA fans fume over Verdana. *Time* 28 August 2009.

Abercrombie, D. 1967. *Elements of General Phonetics*. Edinburgh University Press.

Alberge, D. 1998. Scholars find fresh clues to origin of writing. *The Times* 14 September 1998.

Albrow, K.H. 1972. *The English Writing System: notes towards a description*. Longman for the Schools Council.

ALBSU. 1983. *Literacy and Numeracy: evidence from the National Child Development Survey*. Adult Literacy and Basic Skills Unit.

Allen, W.S. 1965. *Vox Latina*. Cambridge University Press.

Allen, W.S. 1968. *Vox Graeca*. Cambridge University Press.

Amiet, P. 1966. Il y a 5000 ans les élamites inventaient l'écriture. *Archeologia* 12.16–23.

Ashby, J., L.D. Sanders, and J. Kingston. 2009. Skilled readers begin processing subphonemic features by 80 ms during visual word recognition: evidence from ERPs. *Biological Psycholinguistics* 80.84–94.

Assitt, W. 2009. The academic evidence base for typeface readability. Online at typeface.blogspot.co.uk/2009/08/academic-base.html (accessed 16 August 2013).

Bagley, R.W. 2004. Anyang writing and the origin of the Chinese writing system. In Houston 2004.

Baines, J. 2004. The earliest Egyptian writing: development, context, purpose. In Houston 2004.

Barr, J. 1976. Reading a script without vowels. In Haas 1976b.

Barton, D. and M. Hamilton. 2012. *Local Literacies: reading and writing in one community*. Routledge Linguistics Classics (Abingdon).

BAS Staff. 2012. Who really invented the alphabet – illiterate miners or educated sophisticates? (by Biblical Archaeology Society staff). Online (accessed 15 March 2014).

Baxter, W.H. and L. Sagart. 2014. *Old Chinese: a new reconstruction*. Oxford University Press.

Bazell, C.E. 1956. The grapheme. *Litera* 3.43–6. Reprinted in Hamp *et al.* 1966.

Beech, J.R. and K.A. Mayall. 2005. The word shape hypothesis re-examined: evidence for an external feature advantage in visual word recognition. *Journal of Research in Reading* 28.302–19.

Bloomfield, L. 1926. A set of postulates for the science of language. *Language* 2.153–64. Reprinted in Joos 1957.
Boltz, W.G. 1994. *The Origin and Early Development of the Chinese Writing System.* American Oriental Society (New Haven, CT).
Boltz, W.G. 1999. Language and writing. In M. Loewe and E.L. Shaughnessy (eds), *The Cambridge History of Ancient China: from the origins of civilization to 221 BC.* Cambridge University Press.
Bonfante, L. 1990. Etruscan. In Hooker 1990.
Boone, E.H. and W.D. Mignolo (eds). 1994. *Writing Without Words: alternative literacies in Mesoamerica and the Andes.* Duke University Press (Durham, NC).
Breasted, J.H. 1926. *The Conquest of Civilization.* Harper and Brothers.
Bright, W. 1996. The Devanagari script. In Daniels and Bright 1996.
Bryant, P.E. and L. Bradley. 1980. Why children sometimes write words which they do not read. In U. Frith (ed.), *Cognitive Processes in Spelling.* Academic Press.
Burns, A. 1981. Athenian literacy in the fifth century BC. *Journal of the History of Ideas* 42.371–87.
Cahill, M. 2014. Non-linguistic factors in orthographies. In Cahill and Rice 2014.
Cahill, M. and K. Rice (eds). 2014. *Developing Orthographies for Unwritten Languages.* SIL International (Dallas, TX).
Carney, E. 1994. *A Survey of English Spelling.* Routledge.
Chadwick, J. 1958. *The Decipherment of Linear B.* Cambridge University Press.
Chadwick, J. 1976. *The Mycenaean World.* Cambridge University Press.
Chadwick, J. 1987. *Linear B and Related Scripts.* British Museum Press. Reprinted in Hooker 1990.
Changizi, M.A., Qiong Zhang, Hao Ye, and S. Shimojo. 2006. The structures of letters and symbols throughout human history are selected to match those found in objects in natural scenes. *American Naturalist* 167(5).E117–39.
Chen Zhiqun. 2009. *Compound Ideograph: a contested category in studies of the Chinese writing system.* PhD thesis, Monash University (Melbourne).
Chiang Yee. 1973. *Chinese Calligraphy* (3rd edn). Harvard University Press (Cambridge, MA).
Chomsky, C. 1970. Reading, writing, and phonology. *Harvard Educational Review* 40.287–310.
Chomsky, N. 1970. Phonology and reading. In H. Levin and J.P. Williams (eds), *Basic Studies on Reading.* Basic Books (New York).
Chomsky, N. and M. Halle. 1968. *The Sound Pattern of English.* Harper & Row.
Chou En-lai. 1958. Current tasks of reforming the written language. In (no editor identified) *Reform of the Chinese Written Language.* Foreign Languages Press (Peking).
Civil, M. 1973. The Sumerian writing system: some problems. *Orientalia* 42.21–34.
Civil, M. and R.D. Biggs. 1966. Notes sur des textes sumériens archaïques. *Revue d'assyriologie et d'archéologie orientale* 60.1–16.
Coe, M.D. 1992. *Breaking the Maya Code.* Thames and Hudson.
Cohen, M. 1958. *La Grande invention de l'écriture et son évolution,* Text volume. Klincksieck (Paris).
Cubberley, P. 1996. The Slavic alphabets. In Daniels and Bright 1996.

Daniels, P.T. and W. Bright (eds). 1996. *The World's Writing Systems*. Oxford University Press.

Darnell, J.C., F.W. Dobbs-Allsopp, M.J. Lundberg, P.K. McCarter, and B. Zuckerman. 2005. Two early alphabetic inscriptions from the Wadi el-Ḥôl: new evidence for the origin of the alphabet from the Western Desert of Egypt. *The Annual of the American Schools of Oriental Research* 59.63–124.

Davies, W.V. 1990. Egyptian Hieroglyphs. In Hooker 1990.

DeFrancis, J. 1984. *The Chinese Language: fact and fantasy*. University of Hawai'i Press (Honolulu).

DeFrancis, J. 1989. *Visible Speech: the diverse oneness of writing systems*. University of Hawai'i Press (Honolulu).

Derrida, J. 1976. *Of Grammatology*. English translation of 1967 French original, published by Johns Hopkins University Press (Baltimore, MD).

Deutscher, G. 2005. *The Unfolding of Language*. Heinemann.

Diemand-Yauman, C., D.M. Oppenheimer, and E.B. Vaughan. 2011. Fortune favors the bold (and the italicized): effects of disfluency on educational outcomes. *Cognition* 118.111–15.

Diringer, D. 1968. *The Alphabet*, vol. 1. Hutchinson.

Doward, J. 2004. British Gas converts its workers to the joys of text. *The Observer* 7 March 2004. Online at www.theguardian.com/uk/2004/mar/07/mobilephones.jamiedoward (accessed 14 July 2014).

Downing, J. and C.K. Leong. 1982. *Psychology of Reading*. Collier-Macmillan.

Driver, G.R. 1954. *Semitic Writing, from pictograph to alphabet* (2nd edn). Oxford University Press.

Duñabeitia, J.A. and E. Vidal-Abarca. 2008. Children like dense neighborhoods: orthographic neighborhood density effects in novel readers. *Spanish Journal of Psychology* 11.26–35.

Economist. 2013. The fight over the Doves. *The Economist* 21 December 2013.

Economist. 2014. Catching the eagle. *The Economist* 2 May 2014. Online at www.economist.com/node/21590331/print (accessed 23 May 2014).

Edzard, D.O. 1968. *Sumerische Rechtsurkunden des III. Jahrtausends aus der Zeit vor der III. Dynastie von Ur*. (*Bayerische Akademie der Wissenschaften, Philosophisch-historische Klasse, Abhandlungen*, new series, vol. 67.) Verlag der Bayerischen Akademie der Wissenschaften (Munich).

Eisenstein, E.L. 1979. *The Printing Press as an Agent of Change* (2 vols). Cambridge University Press.

Engbert, R., A. Nuthmann, E.M. Richter, and R. Kliegl. 2005. SWIFT: a dynamical model of saccade generation during reading. *Psychological Review* 112.777–813.

Finkelberg, M. 2005. *Greeks and Pre-Greeks: Aegean prehistory and Greek heroic tradition*. Cambridge University Press.

Fox, M. 2013. *The Riddle of the Labyrinth: the quest to crack an ancient code*. Ecco (New York).

Frith, U. and C. Frith. 1980. Relationships between reading and spelling. In J.F. Kavanagh and R.L. Venezky (eds), *Orthography, Reading, and Dyslexia*. University Park Press (Baltimore, MD).

Gelb, I.J. 1952. *A Study of Writing*. University of Chicago Press.

Geschwind, N. 1973. Letter to the Editor. *Science* 173.190.

Goldenberg, G. 2013. *Semitic Languages: features, structures, relations, processes.* Oxford University Press.

Goldsmith, J. and B. Laks. 2012. Generative phonology: its origins, its principles, and its successors. To be in Linda Waugh *et al.* (eds), *The Cambridge History of Linguistics*; online at hum.uchicago.edu/~jagoldsm/Papers/GenerativePhonology.pdf (accessed 4 February 2014).

Goldwasser, O. 2010. How the alphabet was born from hieroglyphs. *Biblical Archaeology Review* 36(2), March/April 2010. Online, accessed 15 March 2014.

Goodman, K.S. 1967. Reading: a psycholinguistic guessing game. *Journal of the Reading Specialist* 6.126–35. Reprinted in H. Singer and R.B. Ruddell (eds), *Theoretical Models and Processes of Reading*, International Reading Association (Newark, DE), 1976.

Goody, J. 1977. *The Domestication of the Savage Mind.* Cambridge University Press.

Goody, J. and I. Watt. 1963. The consequences of literacy. *Comparative Studies in Society and History* 5.304–45. Reprinted in P.P. Giglioli (ed.), *Language and Social Context*, Penguin (Harmondsworth), 1972.

Graham, A.C. 1959. "Being" in Western philosophy compared with *shih/fei* and *yu/wu* in Chinese philosophy. *Asia Major* 7.79–112.

Gray, W.S. 1956. *The Teaching of Reading and Writing.* UNESCO (Paris).

Green, M.W. 1981. The construction and implementation of the Cuneiform writing system. *Visible Language* 15.345–72.

Guernsey, J. 2006. *Ritual and Power in Stone: the performance of rulership in Mesoamerican Izapan Style art.* University of Texas Press (Austin, TX).

Ha, M. 2008. Linguistics scholar seeks to globalize Korean alphabet. *Korea Times* 15 October 2008. Online at www.koreatimes.co.kr/www/news/special/2009/07/178_32754.html (accessed 1 February 2014).

Haas, W. (ed.). 1969. *Alphabets for English.* Manchester University Press.

Haas, W. 1976a. Writing: the basic options. In Haas 1976b.

Haas, W. (ed.). 1976b. *Writing Without Letters.* Manchester University Press.

Hall-Lew, L.A. 2002. *English loanwords in Mandarin Chinese.* BA thesis, University of Arizona. Online at www.lel.ed.ac.uk/~lhlew/Undergraduate%20Thesis.pdf (accessed 7 March 2014).

Halle, M. 1959. *The Sound Pattern of Russian: a linguistic and acoustical investigation.* Mouton (The Hague).

Halliday, M.A.K. 1967. *Intonation and Grammar in British English.* Mouton (The Hague).

Hamp, E.P., F.W. Householder, and R. Austerlitz (eds). 1966. *Readings in Linguistics II.* University of Chicago Press.

Hannas, W.C. 1997. *Asia's Orthographic Dilemma.* University of Hawai'i Press (Honolulu).

Hannas, W.C. 2003. *The Writing on the Wall: how Asian orthography curbs creativity.* University of Pittsburgh Press (Philadelphia, PA).

Havelock, E.A. 1977. The preliteracy of the Greeks. *New Literary History* 8.369–91.

Havelock, E.A. 1986. *The Muse Learns to Write: reflections on orality and literacy from antiquity to the present.* Yale University Press (New Haven, CT).

Hooker, J.T. (ed.) 1990. *Reading the Past: ancient writing from Cuneiform to the alphabet.* British Museum Press.

Householder, F.W. 1969. Review of Langacker, *Language and its Structure*. *Language* 45.886–97.

Houston, S.D. (ed.) 2004. *The First Writing: script invention as history and process*. Cambridge University Press.

Jakobson, R., C.G.M. Fant, and M. Halle. 1961. *Preliminaries to Speech Analysis: the distinctive features and their correlates*. MIT Press (Cambridge, MA).

Jasim, S.A. and J. Oates. 1986. Early tokens and tablets in Mesopotamia: new information from Tell Abada and Tell Brak. *World Archaeology* 17.348–62.

Jeffery, L.H. 1990. *The Local Scripts of Archaic Greece: a study of the origin of the Greek alphabet and its development from the eighth to the fifth centuries BC* (revised edn). Clarendon Press (Oxford).

Jensen, H. 1970. *Sign, Symbol and Script* (3rd edn). Allen & Unwin.

Johnson, A.F. 1966. *Type Design* (3rd edn). André Deutsch.

Johnson, S. 2005. *Spelling Trouble? Language, ideology and the reform of German orthography*. Multilingual Matters (Clevedon, Som.).

Jones, D. 1932. The theory of phonemes, and its importance in practical linguistics. In *Proceedings of the* [*First*] *International Congress of Phonetic Sciences*. Reprinted in Hamp *et al.* 1966.

Joos, M. (ed.) 1957. *Readings in Linguistics*. American Council of Learned Societies (New York).

Karlgren, B. 1957. *Grammata Serica Recensa*. Museum of Far Eastern Antiquities (Stockholm).

Kettunen, H. and C. Helmke. 2011. *Introduction to Maya Hieroglyphs*. University of Copenhagen. Online at www.wayeb.org/download/resources/wh2011english .pdf (accessed 20 October 2013).

Kim, C.-W. 1965. On the autonomy of the tensity feature in stop classification. *Word* 21.339–59.

Kim, C.-W. 1968. The vowel system of Korean. *Language* 44.516–27.

King, R.D. 1967. Functional load and sound change. *Language* 43.831–52.

Knowlson, J. 1975. *Universal Language Schemes in England and France 1600–1800*. University of Toronto Press.

Kramer, S.N. 1963. *The Sumerians*. University of Chicago Press.

Kuo, W.F. 1978. A preliminary study of reading disabilities in the Republic of China. *Collected Papers of National Taiwan Normal University, Graduate School of Education* 20.57–78.

Labov, W. 1994. *Principles of Linguistic Change, 1: internal factors*. Blackwell (Oxford).

Lambdin, T.O. 1971. *Introduction to Biblical Hebrew*. Darton, Longman, & Todd.

Laubrock, J., R. Kliegl, and R. Engbert. 2006. SWIFT explorations of age differences in eye movements during reading. *Neuroscience and Biobehavioral Reviews* 30. 872–84.

Le Brun, A. and F. Vallat. 1978. L'Origine de l'écriture à Suse. *Cahiers de la délégation archéologique française en Iran* 8.11–59.

Ledyard, G.K. 1966. *The Korean Language Reform of 1446: the origin, background, and early history of the Korean alphabet*. PhD thesis, University of California, Berkeley.

Lee Ki-moon. 1977a. *Geschichte der koreanischen Sprache*. Dr Ludwig Reichert Verlag (Wiesbaden).

Lee Ki-moon. 1977b. *Research on the History of Korean Phonology* (2nd edn; in Korean). Pagoda Publishers (Seoul).

Lee Ki-moon. 1981. Ju Si-gyeong: a reconsideration of his linguistic theories (in Korean). *Eohak Yeon-gu* 17.155–65.

Lee Ki-moon and S.R. Ramsey. 2011. *A History of the Korean Language*. Cambridge University Press.

Lieberman, S.J. 1980. Of clay pebbles, hollow clay balls, and writing: a Sumerian view. *American Journal of Archaeology* 84.339–58.

Lu Chih-wei. 1960. The status of the word in Chinese linguistics. In P. Ratchnevsky (ed.), *Beiträge zum Problem des Wortes im Chinesischen*. Akademie-Verlag (Berlin).

Lupton, E. 2003. The science of typography. Online at elupton.com/2009/10/science-of-typography (accessed 1 March 2014).

Lynam, E.W. 1924. *The Irish Character in Print 1571–1923*. Oxford University Press.

McGuinne, D. 1992. *Irish Type Design: a history of printing types in the Irish character*. Irish Academic Press (Blackrock, Co. Dublin).

McKittrick, R. 1983. *The Frankish Kingdoms Under the Carolingians, 751–987*. Longman.

Mahmoud, Y. 1979. On the reform of the Arabic writing system. *The Linguistic Reporter* September, p. 4.

Mair, V.H. 1990. Old Sinitic **m^{y}ag*, Old Persian *maguš*, and English "magician". *Early China* 15.27–47.

Makita, K. 1968. The rarity of reading disability in Japanese children. *American Journal of Orthopsychiatry* 38.599–614.

Man, J. 2009. *Alpha Beta: how our alphabet shaped the modern world*. Bantam Books.

Marrou, H.-I. 1965. *Histoire de l'éducation dans l'antiquité* (6th edn). Editions du Seuil (Paris).

Martin, S.E. 1951. Korean phonemics. *Language* 27.519–33. Reprinted in Joos 1957.

Martin, S.E. 1968. Korean standardization: problems, observations, and suggestions. *Ural-Altaische Jahrbücher* 40.85–114.

Martinet, A. 1955. *Economie des changements phonétiques*. Francke (Bern).

Mattingly, I.G. 1972. Reading, the linguistic process, and linguistic awareness. In J.F. Kavanagh and I.G. Mattingly (eds), *Language by Ear and by Eye*. MIT Press (Cambridge, MA).

Michalowski, P. 1993. Tokenism. (Review of Schmandt-Besserat 1992.) *American Anthropologist* 95.996–9.

Millard, A.R. 1986. The infancy of the alphabet. *World Archaeology* 17.390–8.

Miller, R.A. 1967. *The Japanese Language*. University of Chicago Press.

Minkoff, H. 1975. Graphemics and diachrony: some evidence from Hebrew cursive. *Afroasiatic Linguistics* 1.193–208.

Missiou, A. 2011. *Literacy and Democracy in Fifth-Century Athens*. Cambridge University Press.

Mitchell, D.C. 2013. *How can we sing the Lord's song?* Deciphering the Masoretic cantillation. In A. Rosen and S. Gillingham (eds), *Jewish and Christian Approaches to the Psalms: conflict and convergence*. Oxford University Press.

Morison, S. 1972. *Politics and Script*. Clarendon Press (Oxford).

Morison, S. 1973. *A Tally of Types*. Cambridge University Press.

Mosley, J. 1993. With twenty-five soldiers of lead he has conquered the world. In

A.G. von Olenhusen (ed.), *Wege und Abwege: Beiträge zur europäischen Geistesgeschichte der Neuzeit (Festschrift für Ellic Howe)* (2nd edn). Hochschulverlag (Freiburg im Breisgau). Available online, accessed 17 March 2014.

Mouton, A., I. Rutherford, and I. Yakubovich (eds). 2013. *Luwian Identities: culture, language and religion between Anatolia and the Aegean*. Brill (Leiden).

Na Jeong-ju. 2013. Indonesia's Cia-Cia tribe learning "Hangeul" again. *Korea Times* 3 January 2013. Online at www.koreatimes.co.kr/www/news/nation/2013/01/116_128258.html (accessed 13 October 2013).

Needham, J. 1954–. *Science and Civilisation in China* (many volumes). Cambridge University Press.

O'Connor, M. 1996. Epigraphic Semitic scripts. In Daniels and Bright 1996.

Paap, K., S.L. Newsome, and R.W. Noel. 1984. Word shape's in poor shape for the race to the lexicon. *Journal of Experimental Psychology: Human Perception and Performance* 10.413–28.

Page, R.I. 1987. *Runes*. British Museum Press.

Page, R.I. 1995. *Runes and Runic Inscriptions: collected essays on Anglo-Saxon and Viking runes*. Boydell Press (Woodbridge, Suffolk).

Palmer, L.R. 1963. *The Interpretation of Mycenaean Greek Texts*. Clarendon Press (Oxford).

Paradis, M., H. Hagiwara, and N. Hildebrandt. 1985. *Neurolinguistic Aspects of the Japanese Writing System*. Academic Press.

Park Si-soo. 2009. Indonesian tribe picks Hangeul as writing system. *Korea Times* 6 August 2009. Online at www.koreatimes.co.kr/www/news/nation/2009/08/117_49729.html (accessed 10 February 2014).

Parkes, M.B. 1992. *Pause and Effect: an introduction to the history of punctuation in the West*. Scolar Press (Aldershot).

Perea, M. and E. Rosa. 2000. The effects of orthographic neighborhood in reading and laboratory word identification tasks: a review. *Psicológica* 21.327–40.

Perfetti, C.A. 2003. The universal grammar of reading. *Scientific Studies of Reading* 7.3–24.

Pinker, S. 1995. *The Language Instinct: the new science of language and mind*. Penguin.

Pitt, K. 2000. Family literacy: a pedagogy for the future? In D. Barton, M. Hamilton, and R. Ivanič (eds), *Situated Literacies: reading and writing in context*. Routledge.

Poebel, A. 1923. *Grundzüge der sumerischen Grammatik*. Privately printed (Rostock).

Pollatsek, A., S. Bolozky, A.D. Well, and K. Rayner. 1981. Asymmetries in the perceptual span for Israeli readers. *Brain and Language* 14.174–80.

Pollatsek, A., Li Hai Tan, and K. Rayner. 2000. The role of phonological codes in integrating information across saccadic eye movements in Chinese character identification. *Journal of Experimental Psychology: Human Perception and Performance* 26.607–33.

Poole, A. 2008. Which are more legible: serif or sans serif typefaces? Online at alexpoole.info/blog/which-are-more-legible-serif-or-sans-serif-typefaces (accessed 16 August 2013).

Postgate, N., Tao Wang, and T. Williamson. 1995. The evidence for early writing: utilitarian or ceremonial? *Antiquity* 69.459–80.

Powell, B.B. 1991. *Homer and the Origin of the Greek Alphabet*. Cambridge University Press.

Powell, M.A. 1981. Three problems in the history of Cuneiform writing: origins, direction of script, literacy. *Visible Language* 15.419–40.

Pulleyblank, E.G. 1991. The ganzhi as phonograms and their application to the calendar. *Early China* 16.39–80.

Pye, M. 1971. *The Study of Kanji*. Hokuseido Press (Tokyo).

Rayner, K., B.R. Foorman, C.A. Perfetti, D. Pesetsky, and M.S. Seidenberg. 2001. How psychological science informs the teaching of reading. *Psychological Science in the Public Interest* 2.31–74.

Rayner, K., A. Pollatsek, J. Ashby, and C. Clifton. 2012. *Psychology of Reading* (2nd edn). Psychology Press (Hove).

Reischauer, E.O. 1960. Traditional Korea: a variant of the Chinese cultural pattern. Chapter 10 of E.O. Reischauer and J.K. Fairbank, *East Asia: the Great Tradition*. Houghton Mifflin (Boston, MA).

Rice, K. and M. Cahill. 2014. Introduction. In Cahill and Rice 2014.

Robinson, A. 2002. *The Man Who Deciphered Linear B: the story of Michael Ventris*. Thames & Hudson.

Rosén, H.B. 1977. *Contemporary Hebrew*. Mouton (The Hague).

Salomon, R.G. 1996. Brahmi and Kharoshthi. In Daniels and Bright 1996.

Sampson, G.R. 1994. Chinese script and the diversity of writing systems. *Linguistics* 32.117–32.

Sampson, G.R. 2005a. *The "Language Instinct" Debate* (2nd edn). Continuum.

Sampson, G.R. 2005b. Review of S. Johnson 2005. *Linguist List* 16.1737; online at linguistlist.org/issues/16/16-1737.html (accessed 10 October 2014).

Sampson, G.R. 2013. A counterexample to homophony avoidance. *Diachronica* 30. 579–91.

Sampson, G.R. 2015. A Chinese phonological enigma. Forthcoming in *Journal of Chinese Linguistics*.

Sampson, G.R. and A. Babarczy. 2014. *Grammar Without Grammaticality: growth and limits of grammatical precision*. Walter de Gruyter (Berlin).

Sampson, G.R. and Chen Zhiqun. 2013. The reality of compound ideographs. *Journal of Chinese Linguistics* 41.255–72.

Sass, B. 2005. *The Alphabet at the Turn of the Millennium*. (Journal of the Institute of Archaeology of Tel Aviv University Occasional Publications, 4.) Emery and Claire Yass Publications in Archaeology (Tel Aviv).

de Saussure, F. 1966. *Course in General Linguistics*. (Translation by Wade Baskin of *Cours de linguistique générale*, ed. by Charles Bally and Albert Sechehaye, 1915.) McGraw-Hill.

Schmandt-Besserat, D. 1992. *Before Writing* (2 vols.). University of Texas Press (Austin, TX).

Schmandt-Besserat, D. 1996. *How Writing Came About*. University of Texas Press (Austin, TX).

Schmandt-Besserat, D. 1999. Artifacts and civilization. In R.A. Wilson and F.C. Keil (eds), *The MIT Encyclopedia of the Cognitive Sciences*. MIT Press (Cambridge, MA).

Schreiber, M. 2013. *Furigana*: read the fine print, decode the hidden meanings. *Japan Times* 14 July 2013. Available online.

Schuessler, A. 2007. *ABC Etymological Dictionary of Old Chinese*. University of Hawai'i Press (Honolulu).

Schwarzwald, O.R. 2001. *Modern Hebrew*. Lincom Europa (Munich).

Scragg, D.G. 1974. *A History of English Spelling*. Manchester University Press.

Scribner, S. and M. Cole. 1981. *The Psychology of Literacy*. Harvard University Press (Cambridge, MA).

Seeley, C. 1995. The 20th century Japanese writing system: reform and change. *Journal of the Simplified Spelling Society* 19.27–9. Available online.

Shannon, C.E. and W. Weaver. 1949. *The Mathematical Theory of Communication*. University of Illinois Press (Urbana, IL).

Share, D.L. and K.E. Stanovich. 1995. Cognitive processes in early reading development: accommodating individual differences into a model of acquisition. *Issues in Education: Contributions from Educational Psychology* 1.1–57. Online at keithstanovich.com/Site/Research_on_Reading_files/Share_Stanovich_IIE_1995.doc (accessed 2 July 2014).

Smith, P.T. 1980. In defence of conservatism in English orthography. *Visible Language* 14.122–36.

Snider, K. 2014. Orthography and phonological depth. In Cahill and Rice 2014.

Sommerstein, A.H. 1973. *The Sound Pattern of Ancient Greek*. Blackwell (Oxford).

Sproat, R. 2000. *A Computational Theory of Writing Systems*. Cambridge University Press.

Staunton, M.D. 2005. Trojan horses and friendly faces: Irish Gaelic typography as propaganda. *Revue LISA/LISA e-journal* 3.85–98.

Staunton, M.D. and O. Descottignies. 2010. Letters from Ankara: scriptal change in Turkey and Ireland in 1928. In C. Gillisen (ed.), *Ireland: Looking East*. Peter Lang (Brussels).

Stubbs, M. 1980. *Language and Literacy: the sociology of reading and writing*. Routledge & Kegan Paul.

Tadmor, U. 2009. Loanwords in the world's languages: findings and results. In M. Haspelmath and U. Tadmor (eds), *Loanwords in the World's Languages: a comparative handbook*. De Gruyter Mouton (Berlin).

Taylor, I. and Taylor, M.M. 1983. *The Psychology of Reading*. Academic Press.

Thurlow, C. and K. Bell. 2009. Against technologization: young people's new media discourse as creative cultural practice. *Journal of Computer-Mediated Communication* 14.1038–49.

Treiman, R. and B. Kessler. 2014. *How Children Learn to Write Words*. Oxford University Press.

Tsai, Jie-li, Chia-ying Lee, O.J.L. Tzeng, D.L. Hung, and Nai-Shing Yen. 2004. Use of phonological codes for Chinese characters: evidence from processing of parafoveal preview when reading sentences. *Brain and Language* 91.235–44.

Ullendorff, E. 1971. Is Biblical Hebrew a language? *Bulletin of the School of Oriental and African Studies* 34.241–55.

Unicode Consortium. 1991. *The Unicode Standard: worldwide character encoding, version 1.0* (2 vols). Addison-Wesley (Reading, MA).

Unicode Consortium. 2006. *The Unicode 5.0 Standard*. Addison-Wesley.

Updike, D.B. 1922. *Printing Types: their history, forms, and use* (2 vols). Harvard University Press (Cambridge, MA).

Van Jae Weon. 2002. *The Excellence of the Current Globalization of Hangul!* (in Korean). Doseo Chulpan Hanbaedal (Seoul).

Ventris, M. and J. Chadwick. 1956. *Documents in Mycenaean Greek*. Cambridge University Press.

Verhoeven, L. and C.A. Perfetti. 2003. Introduction to special issue on "The role of morphology in learning to read". *Scientific Studies of Reading* 7.209–17.

Vos, F. 1964. Papers on Korean studies in J.K. Yamagiwa (ed.), *Papers of the CIC Far Eastern Language Institute*. Committee on Far Eastern Language Instruction of the Committee on Institutional Cooperation, University of Michigan (Ann Arbor, MI).

Watts, L. and J. Nisbet. 1974. *Legibility in Children's Books: a review of research*. NFER Publishing Co. (Windsor).

Wells, J. 1982. *Accents of English*, vol. 1. Cambridge University Press.

Whitley, J. 2001. *The Archaeology of Ancient Greece*. Cambridge University Press.

Wittfogel, K.A. 1957. *Oriental Despotism: a comparative study of total power*. Yale University Press (New Haven, CT).

Xolodović, A.A. 1958. O proekte reformy korejskogo orfografii 1949 g. In *Voprosy Korejskogo i Kitajskogo Äzykoznaniä* (*Ućenye Zapiski Leningradskogo Ordena Lenina Gosudarstvennogo Universiteta imeni A.A. Ždanova*, no. 236). Leningrad University (St Petersburg).

Zachert, H. (ed.). 1980. *Hun Min Jeong Eum: die richtigen Laute zur Unterweisung des Volkes (1446)*. Otto Harrassowitz (Wiesbaden).

Zhao, J., Q.-L. Li, and H.-Y. Bi. 2012. The characteristics of Chinese orthographic neighborhood size effect for developing readers. *PLoS One* 7.e46922.

Zimansky, P. 1993. Review of Schmandt-Besserat 1992. *Journal of Field Archaeology* 20.513–17.

Index

Frequently used technical terms are indexed only for passages bearing on their definition. Entries such as "Arabic" cover both languages and scripts without distinction.

CPSIA information can be obtained at www.ICGtesting.com
Printed in the USA
BVOW08s0358220115

384420BV00002B/3/P